ORGAN & INTERPRETATION
the French *école classique*

PAOLO CRIVELLARO

ORGAN & interpretation
THE FRENCH *ÉCOLE CLASSIQUE*

blockwerk
EDITIONES

copyright © 2020 Paolo Crivellaro
BLOCKWERK EDITIONES – BE 01.E.02

All rights reserved. No part of this publication may be reproduced, stored in a retrieval system or transmitted in any form or by any means – electronic, mechanical, photocopying, and recording or otherwise – without the prior written permission of the author, except for brief passages quoted by a reviewer in a newspaper or magazine. To perform any of the above is an infringement of copyright law.

2020 / www.organ-interpretation.com

ISBN: 978-3-9821872-0-4

To Daniel

CONTENTS

Preface xi
Editorial criteria xii
Acknowledgements xiii

1) The French *école classique*
General overview 1
Harpsichord 3
Dance 4
Italian influence 7

2) Sources
The *livres d'orgue* 10
The manuscripts 12
The treatises 16
A critical reading of the sources: the "case" of de Grigny 18

3) Repertoire
Purpose of the *livres d'orgue* 23
Repertoire and liturgy 25
Elaboration of the *cantus firmus* 29

4) The *Alternatim* practice
Use of the organ 35
Alternatim in the Mass 38
Alternatim in the *Magnificat* 44
Alternatim in the hymns 48

5) The French *orgue classique*
Brief historical overview 53
Profile of the organ *classique* 62
Overview of French temperaments 70

6) Introduction to registration
The French *mélanges* 78
Adaptations for the *petits orgues* 81
Anches, Cornets, Jeux de Tierce 82
Liturgical cycles and registrations 84

7) The *Dialogue*
The concept of *Dialogue* 88
Dialogue between two soprano voices 88
Dialogue between bass and soprano voices 91
Dialogue between tenor and soprano voices 94

8) Pre-classical registrations
    Brief overview 96
    Registration table of St-Valéry-sur-Somme 97
    Registration table of Nancy 99
    The *Harmonie Universelle* by Marin Mersenne 101

9) *Plein Jeu* 108

10) *Grand Jeu* 122

11) *Fond d'orgue & Jeu doux* 135

12) *Fugue* 140

13) *Duo* 149

14) *Trio* 155

15) *Quatuor* 165

16) *Récit de dessus* 173

17) *Récit en taille* 184

18) *Basse* 193

19) *Notes inégales*
    Inégalité according to the *livres d'orgue* 201
    Inégalité according to the treatises 204
    Degree of *inégalité* 205
    Level of *inégalité* 208
    Exceptions 210

20) Tempo
    Time signatures 212
    Tempo indications 220
    Flexibility of tempo 223

21) Ornaments
    Diminution & Agrément 227
    Improvisation of ornaments 231
    Tremblement 238
    Pincé 242
    Port de Voix 244
    Coulé 248
    Doublé 250
    Arpège 251
    Georg Muffat's ornamentation *"à la Françoise"* 253

22) Fingering
- Fingering in French organ music 262
- Fingerings for scales 265
- Fingerings for chords 267
- Other fingerings 269

23) Principal composers
- General overview 275
- Eustache du Caurroy 277
- Jehan Titelouze 279
- Charles Guillet 281
- Charles Racquet 283
- François Roberday 284
- Louis Couperin 286
- Nicolas Gigault 288
- Nicolas-Antoine Lebègue 295
- Guillaume-Gabriel Nivers 299
- Lambert Chaumont 305
- André Raison 307
- Jacques Boyvin 312
- Gilles Jullien 316
- François Couperin 318
- Louis Marchand 321
- Gaspard Corrette 324
- Nicolas de Grigny 326
- Pierre du Mage 328
- Jean-Adam Guilain 330
- Louis-Nicolas Clérambault 331
- Jean-François Dandrieu 333
- François d'Agincourt 335
- Louis-Claude Daquin 336
- Michel Corrette 337
- Claude-Bénigne Balbastre 341

Illustrations 345
Bibliography 346
Musical works and editions 352
Index 353

PREFACE

The French organ school of the Baroque period is called in France *école française classique*. The term *classique* refers here to this specific repertoire and is not connected to the usual meaning of "historical classicism" used in reference to authors such as Haydn or Beethoven. For this reason, in the following chapters the French word *classique* is used and not its English translation.

The present work does not make any musicological claims but simply aims to support the practical organist who would like to have greater awareness and historical knowledge about this repertoire. The purpose of the book is to provide as much information as possible from the texts of the time, leaving them as objective stimuli and thus not offering ready-made interpretative solutions, particularly in cases of contradictions or ambiguities within the sources themselves. It is in these circumstances that the performer is invited to evaluate the different interpretative possibilities and to make his/her own choices. In addition to information extrapolated from the texts of the seventeenth and eighteenth centuries, articles or writings by modern authors are occasionally cited.

The repertoire taken into consideration ranges from the beginning of the seventeenth century (Du Caurroy and Guillet) until about the mid-eighteenth century (Dandrieu and Corrette). The writings of the second half of the eighteenth century, such as the well-known treatise *L'Art du Facteur d'Orgues* by Dom Bédos (1766/78), are mentioned only occasionally. Although the treatise of Dom Bédos summarizes and epitomizes the *ethos* of the French *école classique*, the opinions of its author often reflect a modified taste compared to composers such as Nivers, Raison, Boyvin, Couperin or Grigny.

As primary sources I obviously refer to the writings related to the organ repertoire, sometimes supplemented by information drawn from the harpsichord repertoire or from texts related to organ building.

In the chapters directly related to interpretation, e.g. registrations or notions of interpretation in general, I tried to be exhaustive in providing information from the various historical sources. By contrast, a thorough discussion of issues such as the history of the organ, temperaments, analysis and use of *plainchant* in the repertoire, etc. would go far beyond the scope of this work. Where these topics are discussed, the discussion is limited to providing a framework for the issues concerned, referring the reader to the relevant specialized literature.

Noëls have not been taken into consideration – except for occasional references – in this volume.

EDITORIAL CRITERIA

In quoting the original texts the original spelling has been retained, writing the abbreviations out in full only when necessary. Regarding spelling, accentuation, punctuation, use of upper/lower case, etc. I have remained in principle faithful to the original text, opting not to transcribe it into modern French. The changes of spelling are limited to a few exceptions, such as changing the "u" to "v" (e.g. *mouuement* = *mouvement*), the "v" to "u" (e.g. *vne* = *une*), the "f" in the double "s" (e.g. *bafse* = *basse*). Sentences beginning, sometimes in lower case in the original texts, have been normalized in upper case.

For the different musical forms as well as for technical and organ terms, it was decided to leave the text in the original language, highlighting it in italics: hence, *Livre d'orgue* instead of *Organ Book*, *Récit* rather than *Recitative*, etc..

In translating the original texts into English, I opted for a literal translation, sometimes to the detriment of a certain elegance or fluency. In cases where the translation was not clear, I tried to express the meaning of the speech. Square brackets – occasionally used in the original texts as integration or sometimes in the translations as reference to the original or for clarity – serve to make the discourse more comprehensible, especially when the text lends itself to different possible interpretations.

To define the pitch of the notes, the following terminology has been used:

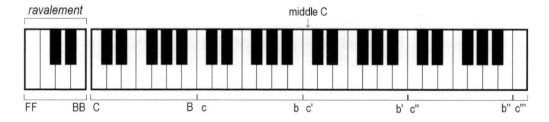

To lighten the reading and in order to achieve a cleaner layout, it was decided to put footnotes at the end of each chapter; they contain only bibliographic references and no additional information.

ACKNOWLEDGEMENTS

A "très grand merci" to Michel Bouvard, Aude Heurtematte, Olivier Latry and Christophe Mantoux for supporting me in writing this book. I have greatly benefited from their profound expertise and knowledge. I would particularly like to thank Christophe for the many hours of passionate discussion that he generously dedicated to this project and for his meticulous checking of the translations from the numerous historical citations.

I am indebted to colleagues Giancarlo Bardelli and Brett Leighton for their equally valuable suggestions and advice. I would also like to thank Marco Bonacci for his advice regarding all matters related to the liturgy.

For help with the English version, heartfelt thanks to my wife Rosemary as well as to colleagues Henry Fairs, Brett Leighton and Kimberly Marshall for their scrupulous proofreading and English corrections.

Paolo Crivellaro
Berlin / Lago Maggiore, May 2020

THE FRENCH *ÉCOLE CLASSIQUE*

GENERAL OVERVIEW

During the long regency of *Louis XIV le Grand* all fields of art experienced an extraordinary flowering. The importance of music in the society of that time was due not only to the personal interest of the Monarch but also to the high esteem in which it was held by important philosophers and men of culture such as Descartes or Mersenne: music was interpreted as an expression of the harmony of man, nature and the cosmos. To this may of course be added the political aspect of representation: the foreign visitor as well as the French nobility remained astounded and dazzled by the sumptuous *spectacles et fêtes de cour* through which *le Roi Soleil* demonstrated the greatness of France, both intellectually and economically.

This sense of *grandeur* and self-celebration is quite perceptible in the preface of one of the least known collections of organ works, le *Pieces choisies de la composition de Mr Piroye, professeur de musique, & Organiste à Paris* (1712):

Les Sciences font de la France depuis long-temps le lieu de leur sejour le plus doux & le plus honnorable; les beaux Arts qui se plaisent à les accompagner ou à les suivre, y triomphent de même sous le regne de LOUIS LE GRAND. Ils avoient établi leur plus brillant empire dans la Capitale du monde entier, & il leur a fallu toute la protection dont les honnore ce Grand Monarque, & cet accueil qu'il aime à leur continuer pour leur faire preferer Paris à Rome.[1]	The sciences have long made France the place of their sweetest and most noble sojourn; the fine arts, which are pleased to accompany or follow them, enjoy a similar triumph under the reign of LOUIS LE GRAND. They had established their most splendid empire in the Capital of the whole world, and they needed all the protection with which this Great Monarch honours them, and this reception which he likes to continue giving them so that they prefer Paris to Rome.

King *Louis XIV* rose to power in 1643, before turning five, and remained there until his death in 1715. His regency, 72 years long, corresponded to the golden age of the French baroque organ school, called by the French *école française classique*. The name *classique*, which can easily lead to confusion with the historical period known as *classicism*, finds its definition precisely in the context of the court of *Louis XIV*. In the first decades of his reign, the king – surrounded by his own architects, playwrights, artists and sculptors – intended to recreate the glories and splendours of ancient Rome, and the use of the term *classique* (from Latin *classĭcus*) aims therefore to denote a quality of the first order, something distinct and worthy of example, transcending the historical moment.[2]

The first printed music intended for the organ – although not necessarily exclusively for organ – dates back to the spring of 1531. Starting in that year, the publisher Pierre Attaingnant began printing seven collections of tablatures by anonymous authors for

Orgues Espinettes Manichordions, et telz semblables instrumentz musicaulx.	*Organs, Spinets, Clavichords (?), and similar musical instruments.*

In addition to various *Chansons, Gaillardes, Pavennes, Branles* and *Basses Dances*, there were pieces conceived for the liturgy such as *Masses, Magnificat, Te Deum*, and some *Préludes* as well. In any case, Attaignant's prints remain an isolated case and constitute today the only known repertoire for keyboard instruments that appeared in France during the entire 16th century.

The *Hymnes de l'Eglise pour toucher sur l'Orgue* of Jehan Titelouze published in 1623 traditionally mark the beginning of the French organ school. In reality, two different collections published in 1610 – i.e. 13 years before Titelouze's *Hymnes* – anticipated the compositional styles: these are the *Fantasies a III. IIII. V. et VI. parties* of Eustache du Caurroy (posthumously published) and the *Vingt-quatre Fantasies, a quatre parties* of Charles Guillet. If in the case of Du Caurroy it was music not destined for a specific instrument but which lent itself well to organ tablature, the *Fantaisies* of the Flemish Guillet (but printed by Pierre Ballard in Paris) were in fact designed to be performed on the organ, such as the author himself points out in the preface.

Guillet and Titelouze mark the beginning of the so-called pre-classical period of the organ in France, in which composers such as Charles Racquet and François Roberday were also active. Their repertoire largely adheres to the ideals of the *prima pratica* and therefore to the "purity" of counterpoint. It is in this period that the *Harmonie universelle* (1636) saw the light of day, a compendium of theoretical, practical, stylistic, organological, mathematical, acoustic and theological musical knowledge, in which ample space was devoted to the organ, its construction and design. Its author, Marin Mersenne (1588-1648) was a cleric, scholar, mathematician and philosopher whose encyclopaedic culture places him among the most important theoreticians of his time. The link between the pre-classical period and the *école classique* – the beginning of which is usually considered 1665, the year in which the first *Livre d'Orgue* of Guillaume-Gabriel Nivers was printed – can be identified in the figure of Louis Couperin (uncle of François *le Grand*). The works of Louis Couperin, written around the middle of the 17th century, progressively move away from the noble and elegant writing of Guillet or Titelouze to prefigure the language of composers such as Nivers or Lebègue. Between the mid-17th century and the first quarter of the 18th century the *école française classique* reached its maximum splendour.

One of the most singular elements that characterizes and differentiates this school from other European organ schools is the very close relationship between composition and registration. The importance of the "right sound" is the *conditio sine qua non* to enhance and fully understand this repertoire: the performance of *Pleins Jeux, Grands Jeux, Jeux de Tierce* or different types of *Récits* on non-French instruments or on instruments with different aesthetics often devalues the repertoire. Despite this instrumental specificity, some elements *extra organum* have also had a significant influence on the organ repertoire and consequently on its interpretation, namely the harpsichord, dance and Italian music.

HARPSICHORD

The harpsichord in France in the Baroque period played a role comparable to the piano in Central European culture within Romanticism. The Parisian nobility of the seventeenth and eighteenth centuries and the families of high social rank vied to acquire the best harpsichord teachers. It is therefore no coincidence that several composers took care to have the words *Maître de Clavecin* printed on the front pages of their organ works. Organists could significantly increase their income by teaching harpsichord. Moreover, every good organist had to be able to guarantee solid abilities as harpsichordist, basso continuo player or *maestro al cembalo*. It is interesting to note that some authors allowed the possibility of performing some works of their *livres d'orgue* – in particular the *Noëls* – on other instruments as well, especially the harpsichord:

- ❖ Nicolas Gigault (1682): *[…] qui peuvent estre touchez sur l'orgue et sur le clavessin, comme aussi sur le luth, les violes, violons, flûtes et autres instruments de musique*

- ❖ Nicolas Lebègue (1685): *[…] que peut joüer Sur l'Orgue et le Clavecin*
- ❖ Charles Piroye (1712): *[…] tant pour l'Orgue & le Clavecin, que pour toutes sortes d'Instrument de Musique*
- ❖ André Raison (1714): *[…] tant pour l'Orgue que pour le Clavecin*
- ❖ Michel Corrette (1753): *[…] Pour le Clavecin ou L'Orgue*
- ❖ Louis-Cl. Daquin (1757): *[…] pour l'orgue et le clavecin, Dont la plûpart peuvent s'éxécuter sur les Violons, Flutes, Hautbois, &c*

Interestigly, Michel Corrette's collection of *Noëls* pubblished in 1770 specifies in the title that it is for *Clavecin et le FortePiano*, not for organ, despite the fact that in the same frontispiece the composer describes himself as *Organiste de la Métropole de Paris, de l'Eglise Paroissiale de S.ᵗ Roch*.

DANCE

Dance played a role of fundamental importance in the France of the *Grand Siècle*. King *Louis XIII* possessed great mastery in the art of dancing, an artistic expression that was also cultivated by his son *Louis XIV*. Ability to dance was a prerequisite for the court *etiquette* and the children of the nobility began learning the art at an early age. As a matter of fact, the elegance in the attitudes and bearing acquired through dance played an important role in the daily life of the upperclass society of the time. On the frontispiece of Pierre Rameau's treatise *Le Maître a Danser* (1725) one reads:

Ouvrage très utile non seulement à la Jeunesse qui veut apprendre à bien danser, mais encore aux personnes honnêtes & polies, & qui leur donne des regles pour bien marcher, saluer & faire les reverences convenables dans toutes sortes de compagnies.[3]	*This book is very useful not only for young people who want to learn how to dance well, but also for genteel and well-educated [honnêtes] people in general, and it also offers them rules on how to walk elegantly, greet people, and make the appropriate bows and reverences according to the different type of company and situation.*

Dance was thus seen not merely as a pleasant pastime but, above and beyond, as a school of etiquette from which aristocracy and nobility, first and foremost the King, could not escape. It is therefore plausible that this *noblesse des gestes* also emerged and flourished in the organ repertoire.[4] The *Nouveau Recüeil de Dance de Bal* of the *Maître de Ballet* and choreographer Guillaume Louis Pécour, published in Paris around 1713, contains over one hundred tables that highlight the close relationship between a specific piece of music and dance steps. In the example below, we see a *Passacaille pour une femme* using the music of Jean-Baptiste Lully's *Armide*:

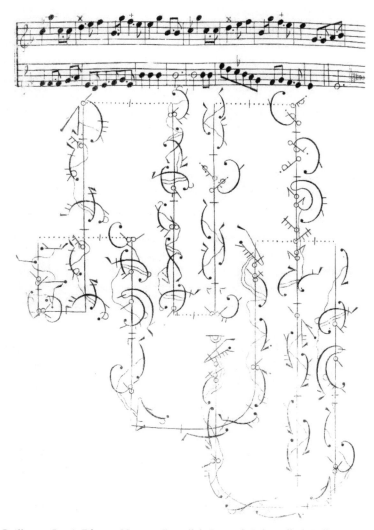

Guillaume Louis Pécour: *Nouveau Recüeil de Dance de Bal et celle de Ballet* (c. 1713)

The rhythm marked by the different dance steps significantly influenced the instrumental music of the time, in particular the different *mouvements* of harpsichord suites. *Courants, Minuets, Sarabandes* and *Gigues* are – in a broad sense – the "instrumental transcription" of dance steps. André Raison speaks of the relationship between works in the form of dance and organ repertoire in the preface to his *Livre d'Orgue* of 1688. Although the collection is primarily intended for the organ, as clearly highlighted in the title – *Livre d'Orgue Contenant Cinq*

Messes suffisantes Pour Tous les Tons de l'Eglise ou Quinze Magnificat – the reference to harpsichord dance forms is explicit:

Il faut observer le Signe de la Piece que vous touchez et considerer si il a du rapport à une Sarabande, Gigue, Gavotte, Bourrée, Canaris, Passacaille et Chacone, mouvement de Forgeron, &c. y donner le mesme Air que vous luy donneriez sur le Clavessin Excepté qu'il faut donner la cadence un peu plus lente à cause de la Sainteté du Lieu.[5]

One must observe the time signature of the piece one is playing and consider whether it is related to a Sarabande, Gigue, Gavotte, Bourrée, Canaris, Passacaglia and Chacone, tempo of Forgeron [= Blacksmith], etc., and give it the same rhythmic flow [poise] as on the harpsichord, except that one should play a little bit slower because of the holiness of the place.

The fact that Raison proceeds from the dance and the harpsichord to better illustrate the time signature of pieces for organ is significant. Ten years after Raison, Georg Muffat – strongly influenced by the style *"à la Françoise"* and in particular by Lully – voiced the same concepts in his *Florilegium Secundum* (1698):

Verùm ad perfectiùs dignoscendum verum cujusvis modulationis temperamentum [...] plurimùm juvat saltatoriæ Artis notitia, quam plerique Lullianorum callent; unde non mirum, quòd adeo exactum mensuræ incessum inveniant, & conservent.[6]

To better understand the true pace and character of each piece [...] I find knowledge of the art of dance, in which the Lullists are experts, very helpful; so it is not surprising that they always manage to find and maintain the right tempo of the bar.

In an interesting presentation on the subject published on the internet in 2016, Olivier Latry highlighted these similarities with concrete examples.[7] Some examples taken from his table are presented here, comparing compositions taken from Michel L'Affilard's treatise *Principes tres faciles pour bien apprendre la musique* (1717) and well-known works of the organ repertoire:

BOURRÉE
Lively and rhythmic dance in binary time, which requires a clear and joyful performance. Usual indications: léger, gay, vif, vite.

Michel L'Affilard: *Bourée*

Louis-Nicolas Clérambault: *Duo (Suite du 2.ᵉ ton)*

GIGUE (french)
Dance in binary time often written in 6/4. It requires a lively execution but without excess. Usual indications: gay, gaiement.

Michel L'Affilard: *Gigue*

Nicolas de Grigny: *Duo (Veni Creator)*

PASSEPIED

Tempo ranging from léger to very fast, faster then a Menuet. It consists of two sections, both repeated. The beginning is in anacrusis, unlike the Menuet that begins on the beat.

Michel L'Affilard: *Passepied*

Louis-Nicolas Clérambault: *Basse et Dessus de Trompette (1er ton)*

MENUET

Dance in three-time of elegant and noble simplicity, which the musicians beat in two unequal movements or three movements, and the dance teachers every two bars.

Michel L'Affilard: *Menuet*

François Couperin: *Trio a 2 Dessus de Chromhorne (Couvents)*

ITALIAN INFLUENCE

Another element that had some importance in France during the Baroque period was the influence of Italian music. Although the French music composed under the reign of *Louis XIV* was very different from the Italian repertoire of the same period, the influence that Italy exercised during the *Grand Siècle* and at the beginning of the 18th century was considerable. At the end of his *Dictionaire de Musique* published in 1703, Sébastien de Brossard includes a *Traité de la maniere de bien prononcer les Mots Italiens* because, as he explains in the *Avertissement*:

Jamais on n'a eu plus de goût, ny plus de passion pour la Musique Italienne, que l'on en a maintenant en France.[8]	There has never been such an interest and passion for Italian music as there is now in France.

Italian singers and instrumentalists were much appreciated at court, as was, evidently, Italian music. Among the most beloved composers whose works were often performed in France, Giacomo Carissimi and Arcangelo Corelli stand out in particular. Marc-Antoine Charpentier studied for three years under the guidance of Carissimi, while Couperin, in the preface to *Les Nations* (1726), speaks of Corelli as a composer of whom "...*j'aimerai les œuvres tant que je vivrai...*" [I will love his works as long as I live]. Couperin paid tribute to the Italian composer with his *Le Parnasse, ou L'apothéose de Corelli*. If in the organ repertoire such links are perhaps less evident, compositions like the *Duretez fantaisie* by Louis Couperin or various *Fonds d'Orgue* by other authors show a clear Italian derivation. Here below a composition (untitled) by Louis Marchand taken from the *Manuscrit de Versailles* and composed in the style of *Durezze e Ligature* or of the Frescobaldian *Toccate per l'Elevatione*:

Louis Marchand: [*Fond d'orgue?*] (*2. Livre, Manuscrit de Versailles*)

Some *Grands Dialogues* of Boyvin also betray the influence of the *Stylus phantasticus*. As David Ponsford has pointed out, in pieces like the beginning of Boyvin's *Grand dialogue du premier ton* – as well as in many *Petits pleins jeux* – the toccata-like element in the Frescobaldian style is evident:[9]

Jacques Boyvin: *Grand dialogue* (*Premier ton, Premier Livre d'Orgue*)

In this regard, it is appropriate to highlight the prominent role played by Johann Jacob Froberger in spreading the new style of the *seconda pratica* in the mid-1600s in Europe. Unlike his master Frescobaldi, Froberger traveled widely and forged ties with musicians such as Matthias Weckmann and Louis Couperin, who in turn helped to spread the new style in their respective countries. As for France, this link is evident in the *Préludes non mesurés* (see page 225) of the harpsichord repertoire. Here the metric freedom desired by Frescobaldi – *che non dee questo modo di sonare stare soggetto a battuta* [*that this way of playing must not be in strict accordance with the beat*] – finds its perfect realization. Even the notation of some passages in the late organ repertoire seems to evoke the same freedom of tempo. The middle section of Grigny's *Tierce en taille*

and the concluding bars of the *Basse de Trompette* of the same *Gloria*

seem perfect examples of the *recitar cantando* style described by Emilio de' Cavalieri in his *Rappresentatione di anima, et di corpo* (1600), a work that opens the way to the *seconda pratica*. A performance strictly *a tempo* of de Grigny's passages above would sound forced and unnatural.

With the publication of the *livres d'orgue* by Du Mage and Clérambault, the great *école française classique* wound to an end. Starting with the second quarter of the 18th century the decadent phase of the organ began: composers like d'Agincourt, Dornel, Michel Corrette, Daquin and Balbastre progressively moved away from the language of the classical period towards a new musical taste, often characterized by decidedly superficial writing compared with that of the previous authors, and not infrequently aimed at producing something with an "easy listening" character.

---

[1] Piroye 1712, Preface (without page number).
[2] Ponsford 2011, 5-6.
[3] Rameau 1725, frontispiece.
[4] Ponsford 2011, 190.
[5] Raison 1688, 30.
[6] Muffat 1698, 69.
[7] Latry 2016.
[8] Brossard 1703, 331.
[9] Ponsford 2011, 293.

SOURCES

THE *LIVRES D'ORGUE*

The situation of the sources concerning the French baroque repertoire is markedly better than that of other European countries. Most organ collections, as well as contemporary treatises, were printed at the time and, consequently, in most cases we have reliable sources. Many of the *livres d'orgue* contain prefaces, sometimes very detailed, that provide valuable information on registration, ornamentation and other aspects of performance practice: one might single out, in particular, the publications of Nivers, Lebègue, Gigault, Raison, Boyvin, Jullien, Chaumont, Gaspard and Michel Corrette. On the other hand, in books by other authors the interpretative indications are far more limited or even non-existent: this is the case of the *livres d'orgue* by François Couperin, de Grigny, Marchand, Guilain, du Mage and Clérambault.

The following list contains titles of the extant organ collections published between 1610 and the mid-eighteenth century:

Sources

1610	Charles GUILLET	*Vingt-quatre fantasies, a quatre parties*
1623	Jehan TITELOUZE	*Hymnes de l'Eglise*
1626	Jehan TITELOUZE	*Le Magnificat, ou Cantique de la Vierge*
1660	François ROBERDAY	*Fugues, et Caprices, a Quatre Partie*
1665	Guillaume-Gabriel NIVERS	*Livre d'Orgue Contenant Cent Pieces*
1667	Guillaume-Gabriel NIVERS	*2. Livre d'Orgue Contenant la Messe et les Hymnes*
1675	Guillaume-Gabriel NIVERS	*3. Livre d'Orgue Des Huit Tons de l'Eglise*
1676	Nicolas LEBÈGUE	*Les Pieces d'Orgue*
c. 1678	Nicolas LEBÈGUE	*Second Livre d'Orgue*
1682	Nicolas GIGAULT	*Livre de musique dédié à la très Ste Vierge*
1685	Nicolas LEBÈGUE	*Troisieme Livre d'Orgue*
1685	Nicolas GIGAULT	*Livre de Musique pour l'Orgue*
1688	André RAISON	*Livre d'Orgue Contenant Cinq Messes*
1690	Jacques BOYVIN	*Premier Livre d'Orgue*
1690	François COUPERIN	*Pieces d'Orgue Consistantes en deux Messes* (*)
1690	Gilles JULLIEN	*Premier Livre d'Orgue*
1695	Lambert CHAUMONT	*Pieces D'Orgue sur les 8 Tons*
1699	Nicolas de GRIGNY	*Premier Livre d'Orgue*
1700	Jacques BOYVIN	*Second Livre d'Orgue*
1703	Gaspard CORRETTE	*Messe du 8.e Ton pour l'Orgue*
1708	Pierre DU MAGE	*Ier Livre d'Orgue*
1710 ?	Louis-Nicolas CLÉRAMBAULT	*Premier Livre d'Orgue Contenant Deux Suites*
1712	Charles PIROYE	*Pieces choisies [...] tant pour l'Orgue & le Clavecin*
1714	André RAISON	*Second Livre d'Orgue*
1714	Pierre DANDRIEU	*Noels [...] mis pour L'Orgue Et pour le Claveçin*
1737	Michel CORRETTE	*Premier Livre d'Orgue*
1739	Jean-François DANDRIEU	*Premier Livre de Pièces d'Orgue* (postumo)
1740	Louis MARCHAND	*Pieces choisies pour l'Orgue. Livre Premier* (**)
1740	Michel CORRETTE	*Nouveau Livre de Noëls pour Clavecin ou l'Orgue*
1749	Claude-Bénigne BALBASTRE	*Livre Contenant des Pieces de different Genre*
1750	Michel CORRETTE	*IIe Livre de Pieces d'Orgue*
1753	Michel CORRETTE	*Nouveau Livre de Noëls*
1756	Michel CORRETTE	*IIIe Livre d'Orgue*

(*) in reality, only the first two pages were printed, the rest (the whole musical part) was manuscript
(**) posthumous re-edition of the *Livre premier* (lost) published in 1700

Some isolated organ compositions were printed in the following publications:

1636	Charles RACQUET	*12 versets de psaume en duo* based on psalm 146 are included in Mersenne's *Harmonie Universelle*
1689	Jean-Henry D'ANGLEBERT	A *Fugue grave pour l'Orgue,* four other *Fugues sur le mesme Sujet* and a *Quatuor sur le Kyrie à trois sujets tiré du plein chant* are included in the *Pieces de Clavecin* of Jean-Henry d'Anglebert

Among the printed compositions, mention should also be made of the *Fantasies a III. IIII. V. et VI. parties* of Eustache du Caurroy, published posthumously in 1610. These are polyphonic compositions without indication of the instrument, conceived *in primis* for an *ensemble* but well suited to organ performance, according to the tradition of the *intavolatura* for keyboard instruments, a very common and widespead practice at the time. The composition-style, strictly contrapuntal, is very similar to the *Fantasies* of Charles Guillet.

THE MANUSCRIPTS

Relatively few organ works have come down to us in the modern era in manuscript form. However, manuscripts are the main source for the works of some composers:

Charles RACQUET	An extensive untitled work, on the genre of the *Fantaisie* and probably composed around 1636, is contained in the personal copy of Marin Mersenne's *Harmonie Universelle*
Louis COUPERIN	Seventy autograph organ compositions are contained in Guy Oldham's private collection; some of them dated between 1650 and 1659
Étienne RICHARD	Two *Préludes* are contained in the *Manuscrit Bauyn* conserved at the *Bibliothèque Nationale de France*; Étienne Richard (c. 1621-1669) was active as an organist in several churches in Paris and from 1657 was harpsichordist and music teacher of the King

Jean-N. GEOFFROY (attributed)	The Pn Rés. 476 manuscript conserved in the *Bibliothèque Nationale de France* contains a *Livre d'orgue* attributed by Jean Bonfils to Jean-Nicolas Geoffroy (c. 1633-1694); it contains *Noëls*, works intended for liturgical purpose and transcriptions of Lully's works; according to some authors it is more likely that the collection is attributable to the circle of Nivers[10]
Louis MARCHAND	The manuscripts ML 61 (1) and ML 61 (2) conserved in the *Bibliothèque Municipale* of Versailles contain four *cahiers* which seem to correspond to the *Livres d'Orgue 2ᵉ 3ᵉ 4ᵉ* and *5ᵉ*; the *3ᵉ cahier* contains – in addition to two fragments – only the famous *Grand Dialogue composé par Mr Marchand à Paris* and bears the date *1696*
Jean-Adam GUILAIN	The only known organ works of Guilain – *4 Suites pour le Magnificat* – dated 1706 and have survived in two manuscripts, both kept at the *Staatsbibliothek* in Berlin, under the title *Pieces d'Orgue pour le Magnificat sur les huit tons differens de l'Eglise* (Mus ms 30189)
Claude BALBASTRE	*Magnificat des huit Tonts De La composition du Sieur Balbastre*. This is the manuscript of the private collection Beaudesson-Noël published in 2016 in facsimile and containing two complete collections of *Magnificat* on the eight tones (i.e. 16 cycles in total) plus an additional *Magnificat du 1er Ton*; the collection expands on the already known Balbastre printed works
François d'AGINCOURT	The only known organ compositions by François d'Agincourt were copied by Père Alexandre Guy Pingré (1711-1796) in a collection found in the *Bibliothèque S.ᵗᵉ Geneviève* in Paris (2372 ms); it consists of about 46 pieces grouped in six *Suites* ordered by tones
Louis-Antoine DORNEL	*Livre de pièces d'orgue* by Louis-Antoine Dornel (1685-1765); dated 1756, is contained in Ms. 2365 of the Bibliothèque S.ᵗᵉ Geneviève of Paris

Apart from the above cases related to compositions of certain attribution, most of the manuscripts include works by anonymous authors. Among the most important collections, the following (in approximately chronological order) can be highlighted:

Livre d'orgue de Marguerite Thiéry
Conserved in the *Bibliothèque Nationale* of Paris (Més Résés 2094) it contains 78 compositions, three of which are by Nivers and the others attributed to his school.

Livre d'Orgue de Montréal
This is a volume of over 500 pages, originally from France but found in 1978 in Montreal in Canada; the dating is estimated between 1666/1676 and 1714/1724, although the compositions contained therein were probably composed before 1690; it contains 398 pieces, only 16 of which have been identified as works by Nicolas Lebègue, while the rest remain of uncertain authorship. Written in different hands, the volume consists of 46 notebooks bound together, which probably constituted the "collection" of a parish organist, monk or nun in a convent or monastery. Most of the pieces are organized either according to cycles (in particular six masses, eleven *Magnificats*, nine other cycles without title but perhaps conceived as *Magnificats*, two *Te Deums*, etc.) or according to key.[11]

Manuscrit de Troyes
A collection of 122 works belonging to the Canon Claude Herluyson (1658-1736), presumably written towards the end of the 17th century and kept in the *Bibliothèque Municipale* of Troyes (2682 ms); several works are by well-known authors (16 by Nivers, 8 by Lebègue, 20 by Boyvin, 2 by Raison) but two-thirds of them are anonymous.

Manuscrit de Bruxelles
Three important manuscripts are conserved in the *Bibliothèque Royale Albert 1er* of Brussels; in particular, Ms. III 926 contains 134 pieces per organ, 34 of them by known authors (including 14 works by Lebègue and 10 by Nivers) and 100 anonymous, while Ms. III 1508, consisting of 178 pages, contains works by Préaux, Clérambault and anonymous; both manuscripts were probably compiled in the early 18th century.[12]

Manuscrit de Tours
The Ms. 172 conserved in the *Bibliothèque Municipale* of Tours consists of 110 pieces for organ, mostly anonymous; probably written at the beginning of the 18th century, it also contains interesting registrations.

Livre d'Orgue de Limoges
This is *Manuscript 255* conserved in the *Bibliothèque Municipale* of Limoges, the date of which is estimated between 1710 and 1725; it contains 51 pieces, 37 of which are anonymous and 14 by Raison, Jullien and Gaspard Corrette; some of the latter have been slightly modified by the copyist according to the taste of the time.[13]

Petites Pièces d'orgue de Mathieu Lanes

This is a manuscript containing 90 anonymous pieces for organ (plus some harpsichord pieces by François Couperin) housed at the *Bibliothèque du Conservatoire Municipal* in Toulouse (Res. Mus. Cons. 943); Mathieu Lanes (1660-1725) was the organist of *Saint-Étienne* Cathedral early in the 18th century.

Livre du Père Pingré

This is a collection compiled by Alexandre Guy Pingré and conserved in the *Bibliothèque S.te Geneviève* in Paris (2372 ms) where, in addition to the aforementioned 46 organ compositions by François d'Agincourt, a further 42 pieces are anonymous.

Manuscrit de Vitré (Livre I)

A collection of c. 200 compositions (*Collection P.-M. Bédard*), presumably written in the second quarter of the 18th century but also containing numerous works by 17th century composers (in particular 46 compositions by Nivers and 5 by Lebègue) and numerous works by anonymous authors.[14]

Manuscrit de Béziers

Dated 1735, the manuscript contains pieces for harpsichord and numerous organ compositions; the title page states *Messes en proses, hymnes, Magnificat pour toucher sur l'orgue. Ad majorem Dei gloriam Virginisque Mariae 1735*; following it there are short pieces composed for the *Alternatim*, then 56 compositions in the *huit tons ecclésiastiques*, and finally other works in the 3rd, 5th and 6th modes.

Manuscrits de Carpentras

Several important manuscripts are preserved in the *Bibliothèque Inguimbertine* of Carpentras, among them well-known works by Lebègue (1035: *2e and 3e Livres d'orgue*) and François Couperin (1038: the two masses); Ms. 1023 collates in seven books over 400 simple compositions for organ by the prelate Louis Archimbaud (1705-1789).

Among the manuscripts of musicological-interpretative interest, particular mention should be made of the so-called *Manuscrit de l'Arsenal*. It is a text by an anonymous author written in the late 17th century and kept at the *Bibliothèque de l'Arsenal* in Paris (F-Pa MS.3042). The title reads: "*Maniere De Toucher Lorgue Dans Toute La propeté et La Delicastesse qui est en Usage Aujourdhy a paris*". Attached to it there is a copy of the *Traité de la composition* by Nivers which was published in 1667; this connection has led some musicologists to hypothesize that the author of the manuscript could be Nivers himself.[15]

From a linguistic point of view the drafting of the text is extremely confusing and approximate (spelling mistakes, absence of punctuation, repetitions, redundancies, contradictions, etc.) and is therefore often difficult to interpret; this has led to the hypothesis that these were hastily written notes by a student during a lesson (perhaps given by Nivers?). Nevertheless – thanks to this putative didactic element – the manuscript provides very useful interpretive information of a practical nature.

Further manuscripts – all anonymous – containing useful information, particularly concerning registrations, are:

- *Meslange Des Jeux de Leglize de Bourges* (beginning of the 18th century)
- *Manuscrit de Tours* (first quarter of the 18th century)
- *Manière très facile pour apprendre la facture d'orgue par P. B. C. en Labbeÿ de Saint-Etienne de Caën* (dated 1746)

THE TREATISES

Important information can also be gained from the treatises related to the construction, planning and use of the organ:

1636	Marin MERSENNE	*Harmonie universelle, contenant la theorie et la pratique de la musique*
c. 1640	Pierre TRICHET	*Traité des instruments* (manuscript)
1702	Joseph SAUVEUR	*Application des Sons Harmoniques A la composition des Jeux d'Orgues*
1734	Christophe MOUCHEREL	*Memoire Instructif pour faire les Devis, Desseins, Plans, Marchez & Réceptions des Orgues*
1738	Louis BOLLIOUD DE MERMET	*Memoire Sur La Construction De L'orgue*
1751/72	Denis DIDEROT & Jean le Rond d'ALEMBERT	*Encyclopedie ou Dictionnaire Raisonné des Sciences, des Arts et des Métiers*
1766/78	DOM BÉDOS de CELLES	*L'Art du Facteur d'Orgues*
1775	M.D.-Joseph ENGRAMELLE	*La Tonotechnie ou l'art de noter les Cylindres*

Naturally, of no secondary importance for the organ repertoire are the treatises and compositions for harpsichord. Among them:

1670	J. Ch. De CHAMBONNIÈRES	*Les Pièces de Clavessin, Livre Premier*
1689	Jean-Henri D'ANGLEBERT	*Pieces de Clavecin*
1702	Mr de SAINT-LAMBERT	*Les Principes du Clavecin*
1716	François COUPERIN	*L'Art de Toucher le Clavecin*
1713/30	François COUPERIN	*4 livres de pièces de clavecin*
1724	Jean-Philippe RAMEAU	*Pièces de Clavecin avec une méthode pour la méchanique des doigts*
c. 1731	Louis-Antoine DORNEL	*Pièces de clavecin*
1753	Michel CORRETTE	*Le Maitre de Clavecin pour l'Accompagnement, Methode Theorique et Pratique*

Among treatises not directly connected with the organ, but which nevertheless provide valuable information, the following can be highlighted:

1668	Bénigny de BACILLY	*Remarques curieuses sur l'art de bien Chanter*
1683	Guillame-Gabriel NIVERS	*Dissertation sur le Chant Gregorien*
1696	Étienne LOULIÉ	*Elements ou Principes de Musique*
1698	Georg MUFFAT	*Florilegium Secundum*
1703	Sébastien de BROSSARD	*Dictionaire de musique*
1717	Michel L'AFFILARD	*Principes très faciles pour bien apprendre la musique*
1719	Jacques-Martin HOTTETERRE	*L'art de preluder sur la Flûte Traversière*
1726	Jean-Philippe RAMEAU	*Nouveau Systême de Musique Theorique*
1736	M. Pignolet de MONTÉCLAIR	*Principes de Musique*
1752	Jean le Rond d'ALEMBERT	*Élémens de musique, théorique et pratique, suivant les principes de Monsieur Rameau*
1760	Jean-Philippe RAMEAU	*Code de Musique Pratique, ou Méthodes Pour apprendre la Musique, même à des aveugles, pour former la voix & l'oreille, pour la position de la main avec une méchanique des doigts sur le Clavecin & l'Orgue, […].*
1768	Jean-Jacques ROUSSEAU	*Dictionnaire de Musique*

A CRITICAL READING OF THE SOURCES: THE "CASE" OF DE GRIGNY

A large part of the French organ repertoire has come down to us through original prints of the time. But this does not exclude *a priori* possible errors owing to oversights, both of the composer and typographer. The work of Nicolas de Grigny probably represents the apogee of the French organ school of the Baroque period. In 1699, two years after his appointment as *titulaire* at the Cathedral of Reims, the 27-year-old de Grigny published his *Livre d'Orgue*, a milestone of the organ repertoire that was later copied by Johann Sebastian Bach and Johann Gottfried Walther.

Paradoxically, this *Livre d'Orgue* – one of the artistic culminations of the repertoire – has been transmitted to us in a volume that, compared with others of the period, is of very poor print quality and shows clumsy work by the engraver, who left numerous inaccuracies and errors in preparation of the typographic plate. In the detailed *Contribution à la lecture et l'interprétation* published in the Fuzeau facsimile to the *Premier Livre d'Orgue* of Grigny, Jean Saint-Arroman highlights some of the typographer's "adjustments", which are not terribly elegant, and clearly visible in the original print:[16]

Et in terra pax à 5

The correct notes of the cantus firmus (tenor) at bars 8 and 9 are, respectively, g and f; the engraver first mistakenly punched a and g, and then corrected these to g and f respectively, without cancelling the error

Dialogue sur les Grands Jeux (Kyrie)

The correct note in the bass on the first beat (first ♪) of the penultimate bar – in the original in baritone clef – is an f; the engraver first wrongly marked an e (same note as the appoggiatura) and then superimposed an f, without erasing the e

A further problem is caused by the numerous errors, some obvious and others probable. There are three different types of possible errors:[17]

    type A) cases in which an error is evident
    type B) cases in which the error is probable or likely, but not certain
    type C) cases in which a given passage leaves room for doubt

Sources

type A) the error is obvious and intuitively solvable

1.ᵉʳ Kyrie en taille à 5

The G♭ on the bass line is an obvious harmonic error and it can be corrected by playing G♮

Recit de tierce en taille

The group of eight thirty-second notes is rhythmically incorrect and can be rectified by playing eight ♪

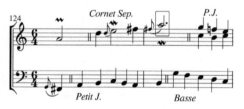

Offertoire sur les grand Jeux

The a″ in the soprano voice is certainly a mistake; by analogy to similar figures here it should be instead played as g″

Dialogue (2.ᵐᵉ Couplet Agnus Dei)

The lower pentagram is rhythmically incorrect; it can be corrected by adding an a of an eighth length

type B) the error is probable but not certain

In some cases it could in fact be an extravagance or bizarre choice intended by the composer. In most cases the alleged mistake is correctable with a modest amendment:

Recit de tierce en taille

The e′-a′-c″ chord at bar 14 is possible but unlikely; probably an e′-g′-c″ chord should be understood here

Veni creator en taille à 5

The e♭″ in the upper voice is possible though unlikely; an e♮″ should probably be understood here

19

Veni creator – Duo

The three notes of the right hand of bar 15 are very unlikely (incorrect displacement by a third); the problem can be solved by playing them a third higher

This type of error includes cases of suspicious alterations as well, i.e. cases of a "potentially missing" ♭ ♯ or ♮. The following example taken from the final bars of the *Et in terra pax à 5* is typical:

According to the original print, the third chord of bar 20 calls for a g♮' in the upper voice. It must be remembered here that at the time the alteration signs had value only for the note before which they were placed (exceptions to this rule are the immediate repetition of the altered note or the embellishments where the altered note is present several times, e.g. in trills). The absence of signs of alteration in front of this g implies that it is, therefore, a g natural. Whether de Grigny really wanted a g♮ here (in the style of a certain harmonic ambiguity typical of the *Toccate di durezze*) or intended a g♯ (missing by engraver's error or not written because implicit by the composer) remains an open question.

Equally worthy of consideration are the numerous cases of inversion of ornaments, i.e. the use of *Cadences* (trills) instead of *Pincés* (mordants) or vice versa. The basic "rule" is to use a *Pincé* when the embellished note is reached by upward stepwise movement and a *Cadence* when it is reached by descending stepwise movement. When this rule is not followed – frequently the case in the repertoire – it is legitimate to ask whether it is an oversight by the composer (and thus correct the part) or a license taken by the composer.

type C) the passage leaves room for doubt

The correction of the alleged error implies more radical intervention; the possible solutions are many and left to the interpretative choice of the performer.

The concluding section of the *Dialogue sur les grands Jeux* of the hymn *Veni Creator* would begin, according to the original print, with a rather unlikely first inversion chord in the second half of bar 71:

Assuming that the indicated chord does not correspond to the intentions of the author, there are two possible solutions:

1) the alto voice plays an f' instead of g', keeping in this way the same harmony of B♭ major as in the first half of the bar (as in N. Gorenstein's edition)
2) playing the three notes of the bass voice a third lower, i.e. as G, thus obtaining the harmony of G minor (as in the old edition by A. Guilmant)

One of the most contentious cases concerns bar 35 of the *Tierce en taille, 4ᵉ couplet* of the *Gloria*. In the original print the tenor leaps from g♯' to c'' within the harmonic context of E major, thus creating a strong tension, both harmonic and melodic:

Faithful to the original is the copy of Bach, while Walther interprets the seven notes of the passage as an error and transcribes them a degree lower:

From a harmonic point of view, as well as in reference to the sequence that develops in the following three bars, the choice of Walther and the modern edition by Nicolas Gorenstein (*Editions du Triton*) appears without doubt more logical and perhaps corresponds to de Grigny's intentions. Also the a♯' in the original version is melodically rather harsh; in the amended version – as a g♯' – it is definitely more pleasant and melodic (according to the rule above described, the sharp placed before the first g of the bar is valid only for that specific note; this explains the presence of the sign ♯ in front of the second ♪ in bar 35, a g♯' if one wants to lower the melodic line by one degree).

On the other hand, it must also be said that irregularities and certain "harmonic whims" were the essence of the *Seconda Pratica*, of the *Stylus Phantasticus*, of the *Toccate di durezze* (one might think of the *Duretez Fantaisie* of Louis Couperin), and indeed they were sought by composers to give more "flavour" to their works. Based on these assumptions, it is therefore impossible to exclude *a priori* any compositional eccentricity on the part of the author. It is interesting to note that Bach, during the copying of Grigny's *Livre d'Orgue* repeatedly intervenes by correcting those which, in his opinion, are printing errors, but leaves unchanged "*cette phrase splendide*" (Saint-Arroman).[18]

---

[10] Ponsford 2011, 14.
[11] Gallat-Morin 1988, 61-77 and 313-318.
[12] Gallat-Morin 1988, 181 and 423.
[13] Marissal 1996, 6-11.
[14] Gallat-Morin 1988, 81-88.
[15] Pruitt 1986, 238.
[16] Saint-Arroman 2001, XX-XXI.
[17] Gorenstein-Grigny, 3.
[18] Saint-Arroman 2001, XXVII.

REPERTOIRE

PURPOSE OF THE *LIVRES D'ORGUE*

A large portion of the French repertoire of the 17th and 18th centuries has come down to us through *livres d'orgue*, collections of organ compositions which, in most cases, were printed during the composers' lifetimes and enjoyed considerable diffusion.

From a quantitative point of view, the number of *livres d'orgue* is limited to one or two per author – in a few cases more – and is therefore just sufficient to cover the needs of a few liturgical cycles to be performed *alternatim*, as part of the *Ordinarium Missae* or a *Magnificat* or a hymn. Although without doubt a number of compositions have been lost – for example the *Deuxième Livre d'Orgue* by Pierre Du Mage published in 1712 – it must not be forgotten that an organist had to be, first and foremost, a capable improviser. Of interest on this subject are David Ponsford's observations in his important book *"French Organ Music in the Reign of Louis XIV"*:

> Extant organists' contracts relating to Louis Couperin (1626-1661) at St Gervais in 1653 and Nicolas-Antoine Lebègue (1631-1702) at St Merry (St Médéric) in 1676 state that they were responsible for about 400 services per year, with some major feast days requiring the organ at five or even six services (Easter Day). On such days, with each service having its own liturgy, organists could be required to play more than 100 versets. Therefore improvisation was the norm, which is the most likely reason why Jean-Philippe Rameau (1683-1764), who held various posts as organist from 1702 to 1722 or early 1723, notably at Clermont Cathedral, left behind no organ music whatsoever.[19]

These observations find indirect confirmation in compositions of Michel Corrette. In the masses of his *IIIe Livre d'Orgue* (1756), the number of *couplets* is often insufficient to cover the needs, and, for the *Kyrie* of the first Mass (*Solemnel majeur*) Corrette composed only one couplet, accompanied by the words *"encore 4 Couplets"*, implying that the remaining ones were improvised.

As regards the published works, whose high printing costs required the financial support of a patron, the motivation behind publishing a *livre d'orgue* could be manifold. First of all, there were the proceeds to be gained from the sale: the buyer could often apply to the composer directly for the purchase, as is sometimes indicated in the frontispieces. Here, as an example, is the text accompanying the three *livres d'orgue of* Nivers:

A Paris chez l'Autheur proche St Sulpice et R. Ballard seul Imp. du Roy p.^r la musique.	In Paris, directly from the author near St Sulpice and from R. Ballard, exclusive Royal printer for the music.

A *livre d'orgue* also served didactic purposes, as can easily be deduced from the title page of Raison's first book:

[...] avec des jnstructions tres utiles pour ceux qui n'ont point de M.^e et qui veulent se perfectionner Eux mèmes.[20]	[...] with very useful instructions for those who have no teacher and who want to improve [their musical skills] by themselves.

Teaching activity contributed significantly to the income of an organist, and the printing of a *livre d'orgue* was a sort of "business card" and means to promote oneself, both as musician and teacher. In some cases the author was not so much concerned with displaying his compositional prowess – as explicitly stated by Titelouze – as with gaining wider exposure:

[...] je me suis abaissé tant que j'ay peu dans la facilité, & me suis forcé de joindre plus pres les parties, afin qu'elles puissent estre touchées avec moins de difficulté.[21]	[...] I lowered myself as much as I could as regards playability and forced myself to place the voices closely together, so that they could be played with less difficulty.

The centralism exercised by Paris as economic, political, artistic and cultural capital of France was also of great importance. Many *livres d'orgue* were published there and then taken as models *en province* (= outside of Paris), as Lebègue points out:

Mon dessein dans cet Ouvrage est de donner au Public quelque connoissance de la maniere que l'on touche l'Orgue presentement à Paris.	My purpose in this work is to give the public some knowledge about how the organ is currently played in Paris.
[...] la maniere de toucher l'Orgue a present sur tous les Jeux, et particulierement ceux qui sont peu en usage dans les provinces comme la Tierce et Cromorne en Taille: les Trio a deux dessus, et autres a trois Claviers avec les Pedalles.[22]	[...] the way of playing the organ at present using all the stop combinations, especially those which are little used in the provinces like the Tierce [en Taille] and Cromorne en Taille, the Trio a deux dessus, and other three-manual Trios employing the pedal [i.e. 2 manuals plus pedal].

Even organists *en province* had to apply to the royal typographer (*Privilége du Roy*) to have their works printed, as was the case with Titelouze and Boyvin, both active in Rouen but both of whose works were printed in Paris:

TITELOUZE:	BOYVIN:
A PARIS.	A PARIS,
Par Pierre Ballard,	Chez Christophe Ballard,
Imprimeur de la Musique du Roi	seul Imprimeur du Roy pour la Musique
1626.	M.DCC.
Avec privilége du Roy.	Avec Privilege de Sa Majesté.

REPERTOIRE AND LITURGY

The greatest part of the French Baroque organ repertoire consists of *couplets* (= versets), usually short compositions to be understood as part of much larger liturgical cycles that make up the *Ordinarium Missae*, the *Magnificat* and the hymns; they were performed *alternatim* with the singing.

The small dimensions of these compositions – sometimes just a few bars – were imposed by the ecclesiastical authority, as prescribed by various *Cæremoniales*. Their brevity was sometimes regulated through the use of a bell that, commanded by a prelate in the choir stalls, signaled to the organist when to start and stop playing, as can be read in the *Cæremoniale Parisiense* (1662):

Cum in divino officio pulsantur Organa, attentè observet Organista tinnitum campanulæ, quo monetur quando inchoandum, vel finiendum, [...].[23]	When the organ is played during the divine office, the organist must pay attention to the sound of the little bell that signals when to start or finish [...].

Such practice is still attested to 40 years later in the *Cérémonial de Toul,* where it is required that the organist

[...] sera attentif au son de la clochette, quand elle l'avertira de commencer & de finir; car il est à propos qu'il y en ait une auprés de luy atachée à une petite corde, laquelle descendra dans le chœur auprés de quelque pilier, & qu'il y ait quelqu'en commis pour la sonner quand il sera nécessaire.[24]	[...] should be attentive to the sound of the little bell, that warns him when to begin & finish; for this purpose it should be placed next to the organist and attached by a little cord that descends into the choir near some pillar, and there should be someone instructed to ring it when necessary.

The only relatively long compositions are the *Offertoires,* since they have to accompany a potentially longer moment within the liturgy. They are not bound to the *alternatim* practice, and during this moment of the mass the organ had to play from the end of the *Credo* until the *Prefatio*:

Aprez le Credo, le Celebrant ayant dit Oremus, l'Orgue joüe l'Offertoire, & continuë jusques au temps de la Preface, il doit y avoir une Clochette pour faire cesser l'Organiste.[25]	After the Credo, and after that the Celebrant has said Oremus, the organ plays the Offertoire and continues until the Preface; there must be a little bell to signal to the organist when to finish.

While in other European organ schools the title of the composition designates a musical form with a more or less defined profile, such as *Ricercare, Canzona, Praeludium, Tiento, Voluntary,* etc., in France the title often indicates the intended registration. As a matter of fact, the given registration – *Plein Jeu, Grand Jeu, Fond d'Orgue, Récit de Cromorne, Tierce en taille,* etc. – corresponds to a well-defined musical plan: these connotations receive formal definition with the publication of the various *livres d'orgue* starting from the mid-17th century. In these collections precise information on both registration and performance may be found.

Regarding the purpose for which a *couplet* was destined, the repertoire can, in essence, be divided into two major groups: on the one hand, the compositions whose purpose is clearly defined by the title itself, such as masses, *Magnificats* and hymns; on the other, the "free" *couplets* whose use was at the discretion of the performer.

Nivers, Lebègue, Gigault, Raison, François Couperin, Grigny and Gaspard Corrette all composed complete organ masses, in which the various versets are specifically devoted to a precise moment of the liturgy. It is also interesting to note that the pieces by the last four mentioned (Raison, Couperin, Grigny, Corrette) always had a specific designation, be it a Mass or a hymn. The three oldest composers (Nivers, Lebègue and Gigault), in addition to composing cycles such as messes, *Magnificats,* or hymns, also left numerous pieces without specific designation. Furthermore, Raison specifies in the preface to his first *Livre d'Orgue* that the versets composed for the *Ordinarium* may also be used for a *Magnificat* if needed:

Ces 5 Messes peuvent servir aussi en Magnificat po.^r ceux qui n'ont pas besoin de Messe.[26]	These five Masses can also be used for the Magnificat [verses] in cases when a Mass is not needed.

One can find a similar prescription in Italy in the early Baroque, namely in the preface of Girolamo Frescobaldi's *Fiori Musicali* (1635):

Anchora detti versi benche siano fatti per kirie potranno servire alcuni come più piacera per altri affetti.[27]	Although these versets are made for the kyrie, they can be used for other purposes [affetti].

As a matter of fact, most of the French *livres d'orgue* consists of free *couplets* grouped by mode, the use of which is left to the performer's discretion. See for example the preface to the first *Livre d'Orgue* by Lebègue:

On pourra toucher les Versets de ce Livre aux Pseaumes & Cantiques sur tous les tons, mesme aux élevations de la Messe & aux Offertoires, & pour cela il ne faudra que prendre les pieces les plus longues, ou en joüer deux de suite d'un mesme ton.[28]	The versets of this book may be played for Psalms and Canticles in all modes, even at the Elevations of the Mass and for the Offertories; for the latter it will be sufficient to select the longest pieces, or else play two of them in the same mode, one after the other.

From about 1700 onwards, the groupings of various *couplets* by mode take the name of *Suites*. The term *Suite* should not be confused here with the traditional harpsichord *Suites* (intended as cycles of pieces such as *Allemande, Courant, Sarabande, Gigue*) as it merely identifies a group of compositions of various characters and registrations organized by mode. This concept is clear in Guilain, whose frontispiece of the collection states *Pieces d'Orgue pour le Magnificat* while the internal pieces are grouped into *Suite du Premier Ton, Suite du Second Ton,* etc. In view of the fact that pieces were primarily performed in the liturgical context, several composers underline the practical aims of the repertoire, suggesting possible changes or cuts as required. Titelouze indicates possible concluding cadences with a fermata:

Hymnes de l'Eglise (1623)

Pour la longueur des vers qui traitent les fugues, je ne pouvais les rendre plus courts, y ayant trois ou quatre fugues repetées par toutes les parties sur le sujét: mais pour s'acommoder	As far as the length of the versets containing fugue subjects is concerned, I could not make them shorter, having three or four subjects [fugues] used by all the voices: but, in order to

Organ & interpretation: the French école classique

au chœur, l'on pourra finir a quelque periode vers le milieu, dont j'en ay marqué quelques uns pour servir d'exemple.[29]

adapt them to the needs of the choir, one can finish them at some point in the middle - I have marked a few points to serve as an example.

Magnificat (1626)

On peut voir aussi que j'ay pressé les Fugues afin d'abreger les couplets; ceux qui les trouverront trop longs, pourront au lieu de la cadence mediante pratiquer la finale: il y a mesme plusieurs vers qui ont des marques pour cét effet.[30]

One can also see that I compressed the imitations [Fugues] in order to shorten the couplets; those who find them too long, may finish them with the final cadence instead of the median one; there are even several verses that have marks [coronas] for this purpose.

Jehan Titelouze: *Deposuit potentes* (*Magnificat Primi Toni*)

Lebègue indicates the possible curtailments with a small star (*Premier Livre d'Orgue*, 1676):

Ceux qui voudront abreger les pieces, ils n'auront qu'à commencer où il y aura une petite Estoille.[31]

Those who wish to shorten the pieces, need only to start where a small star is indicated.

Nicolas Lebègue: *Basse de Trompette* (1. Ton, Premier livre d'orgue)

Similarly, a quarter of a century later, Gaspard Corrette (*Premier livre d'orgue*, 1703) states:

La petite Estoille est une marque pour finir quand la piece est trop longue, elle se marque ainsi ★ .[32]

The small star is a mark indicating where to finish when the piece is too long; it is marked ★ .

Raison indicates possible conclusions with the words *fin si on veut* [end, if desired]. Similarly, Gigault specifies in the preface to his *Livre de Musique pour Orgue*:

*Je vous presente environ 180. pieces d'Orgue, l'esquelles peuvent estre touchez à 1, 2, 3 et quatre Claviers, Et que lon peut finir dans plusieurs endroits il y à des marques aux endroits, où cela peut estre fait, de sorte que d'une seule pièce on en peut faire plusieurs [...].*³³	I present you about 180 pieces for organ, which can be played on 1, 2, 3 and four manuals; and so that one can finish playing at different points, there are indications in several places of the music where this can be done - so that out of one piece one can obtain several [...].

An interesting performance indication – provided by Raison regarding *Pleins jeu* but likely to apply to other types of *couplets* – is to keep the last bar very long:

*[...] la derniere mesure soit toûjours fort longue.*³⁴	[...] the last measure is always very long.

The lengthening of the last chord has the intrinsic advantage of helping the singers prepare the intonation of the following verset. In fact, the final chord of virtually all Raison *couplets* – the exceptions are limited to very few cases – is noted in *breves* and surmounted by the fermata sign:

André Raison: *Premier Kyrie* (*Messe du Premier ton*)

ELABORATION OF THE *CANTUS FIRMUS*

In the *alternatim* practice, the organ versets take the place of some versets of *plainchant*. Consequently, some parts of the "narration" are eliminated from the Latin text or, more precisely, they are recited *sotto voce* by the celebrant. Contrary to what might be expected, the organ versets do not always present the *plainchant* line in full, which is, consequently, missing: the relationship between instrumental versets and *cantus firmus* is in fact extremely diverse. This chapter briefly analyzes the use of the *cantus firmus* in the hymns of Titelouze, Nivers and de Grigny.

In the *Hymnes* of Titelouze the relationship with the *cantus firmus* is always evident and can be presented in three different ways:

a) as *plainchant* noted in full and placed in the bass voice:

Jehan Titelouze: *Ad cænam Agni providi – Verset 1 (Hymnes de l'Eglise)*

The first verset of each of the twelve *Hymnes* of Titelouze presents the *plainchant* in the bass with the corresponding text of the first *stanza* of the hymn below. It is not known whether Titelouze was already thinking here of a "modern" registration such as a *Plein jeu* with pedal *Trompette* or whether he used *consort*-like Renaissance registrations instead. In the preface to the *Hymnes*, Titelouze, however, contemplates the possibility of "extracting" (in this context, the term *extraire* refers to the possibility of entrusting one of the voices to one or other hand) and singing one of the parts:

[…] lesquelles parties l'on pourrait, non seulement extraire, mais aussi les chanter parce qu'ils ont leurs chants distingués & leurs pauses.[35]	*[…] these parts can be not only extracted, but also sung because they have their proper texts [chants] & their rests.*

In other versets, Titelouze builds a *Canon in Diapason* (= octave) or a *Canon in Diapente* (= fifth) above the *cantus firmus* in the bass voice, as in the following example, taken from the hymn *Ave maris stella*:

Jehan Titelouze: *Ave maris stella – Verset 3 (Hymnes de l'Eglise)*

b) with the *plainchant* presented in full in the soprano or alto voice

Jehan Titelouze: *Veni Creator Spiritus – Verset 2 (Hymnes de l'Eglise)*

or even with the line of the *cantus firmus* divided among two or more voices. In the following example, the *cantus firmus* pertaining to the first phrase of the hymn *Pange lingua gloriosi* is entrusted to the soprano:

The second phrase is placed in the alto voice:

The third phrase in the tenor:

Jehan Titelouze: *Pange lingua gloriosi – Verset 3 (Hymnes de l'Eglise)*

c) rhythmically altered and integrated into the contrapuntal structure:

Jehan Titelouze: *Ad cænam Agni providi – Verset 2 (Hymnes de l'Eglise)*

All twelve hymns have at least one verset in *stile fugato*, in which the *incipit* of the *cantus firmus* – sometimes limited to just the first three or four notes – is used as a fugue subject.

Beginning with Nivers, it becomes customary to place a *Fugue sur le sujet de l'Hymne precedente* after the initial *Plein jeu*. Often the elaboration of the *cantus firmus* of such *Pleins jeux* already displays a certain decoration with respect to the original *plainchant*, through passing notes or embellishments. Here, an example taken from the hymn *Iesu nostra redemptio* of Nivers:

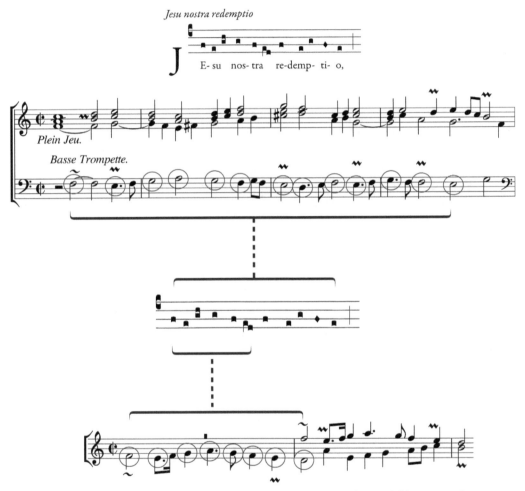

Guillaume-Gabriel Nivers: *Iesu nostra redemptio* & *Fugue graue sur le sujet de l'hymne precedente*
(2ème *Livre d'Orgue*)

Unlike the *Plein jeu*, in which the *cantus firmus* is presented in its entirety throughout the composition, in the ensuing *Fugue* only the *incipit* is elaborated: in the case presented above, the theme of the fugue corresponds to the words *Jesu nostra*.

Even the *Hymnes* by Grigny, published about thirty years later, follow and amplify the same ideas, sometimes taking the concept of *coloratura* almost to its limits. In the first verset of the *Pange lingua* the *cantus firmus* is treated in a conventional manner, i.e. entrusted as *plainchant* to the tenor voice and played in the pedal:

Nicolas de Grigny: *Pange lingua, en taille* (*Livre d'Orgue*)

In the *Fugue à 5* which follows, the *incipit* of the *cantus firmus* is presented in all voices, and in the upper four it is adorned with great imagination and mastery:

Nicolas de Grigny: *Fugue à 5* (*Livre d'Orgue*)

In the *Récit en taille* which follows, closing the cycle, the *cantus firmus* is placed in the tenor and is transformed almost beyond recognition:

Nicolas de Grigny: *Récit en taille* (*Livre d'Orgue*)

If in the hymns for organ the relationship with the *plainchant* is usually clear because the instrumental versets are based on the related *cantus firmus*, this is not always the case for the passages of the *Ordinarium* or the *Magnificat*. On the contrary, the lack of a specific *cantus firmus* allows the use of the various versets for different circumstances. The emancipation from the *plainchant* is then evident in the numerous *livres d'orgue* where the grouping of the various versets is by mode and not by thematic link to any *cantus firmus*.

---

[19] Ponsford 2011, 1-2.
[20] Raison 1688, 29.
[21] Titelouze 1626, 18.
[22] Lebègue 1676, 14.
[23] Sonnet 1662, 168.
[24] Ceremonial de Toul 1700, 102.
[25] Ceremonial de Bourges 1708, 137.
[26] Raison 1688, 30.
[27] Frescobaldi 1635, al Lettore (without page number).
[28] Lebègue 1676, 14.
[29] Titelouze 1624, 15.
[30] Titelouze 1626, 18.
[31] Lebègue 1676, 15.
[32] Corrette 1703, 124.
[33] Gigault 1685, 26.
[34] Raison 1688, 31.
[35] Titelouze 1624, 15.

THE *ALTERNATIM* PRACTICE

USE OF THE ORGAN

Numerous *Cérémonials* appeared in France during the 17th and 18th centuries providing rules for the use of music within the liturgy in different regions. As far as function and use of the organ are concerned, they take essentially as a model the *Cæremoniale episcoporum,* published in Rome in 1600. Among them are the *Cæremoniale Monasticum Romano,* printed in Paris in 1634, and, most notably, the *Cæremoniale Parisiense* by Martin Sonnet, published in 1662.

The role played by the French mystic Jean-Jacques Olier in the 17th century is very interesting.[36] In his *Explication des cérémonies de la grand'messe* (first published in 1657), in reference to the Sanctus, Olier likens the sound of the organ to the *musique du ciel*:

[...] même l'orgue, qui signifie la musique du ciel et les louanges des bien-heureux joue au Sanctus. Il chante par deux fois, Sanctus, pour représenter que cette louange est la louange du ciel, et que l'Église (ou les chapiers qui la représente) chante une fois au milieu, pour dire qu'elle se mêle, et qu'elle tâche de prendre part, et de se perdre dans les louanges du paradis.[37]	*[...] even the organ, which signifies the celestial music and songs of praise of the blessed, plays at the Sanctus. It sings twice, Sanctus, to represent that this praise is heavenly praise, while the Church (or the Canons who represent it) sings once in the middle, to say that it is joining in, seeking to be a part of it and to lose itself in the praises of paradise.*

The interventions of the organ, and of music in general, are differentiated in terms of the solemnity of their function. The organ was usually used in the most important Feast days (*Fêtes doubles de 1re et 2e classes*), on Sundays in *Ordinary Time* and at local feasts linked to the individual churches. The *Chœur polyphonique* was involved only in the most solemn celebrations. An excerpt from the *Cæremoniale Monasticum Romano* illustrates the moments entrusted to the organ during a solemn mass:

In Missa solemni pulsatur Organum ad Kyrie eleison. & Gloria excelsis, &c. alternatim. Item finitâ Epistolâ, si sit consuetudo, & ad Offertorium usque ad Præfationem: item ad Sanctus alternatim. Similiter dum elevatur SS. Sacramentum, sed graviori & dulciori sono: item ad Agnus Dei, alternatim: item ad Antiphona, quæ dicitur Communio, ac in fine Missæ.[38]	*In the solemn Mass the organ is played at the Kyrie eleison, and at the Gloria excelsis, etc. alternatim. Then after the Epistle, if it is customary to do so, and at the Offertory up to the Preface; then at the Sanctus alternatim. Similarly at the elevation of the Blessed Sacrament, but with a more solemn and meditative sound; then at the Agnus Dei, alternatim; then at the Antiphon, which is recited at the Communion, and at the end of the Mass.*

As can be seen, the use of the organ was largely *alternatim* with the *plainchant*; one of the few exceptions was the *Offertoire*, the execution of which was entrusted entirely to the organ, without vocal interventions. The old *alternatim* practice between organ and *schola*, documented from as early as the 14th century (*Codex Faenza*), was of course also employed in the Catholic Church during the baroque period in France. It implies that the various versets of any liturgical piece (*Kyrie, Gloria, Magnificat,* etc.) be distributed alternately between organ and choir. The organ replaces some of the versets that would otherwise have been sung. Its role is, therefore, not to give a musical commentary to a text previously sung by the choir, but rather to provide an instrumental verset that substitutes the sung verset. Sometimes these instrumental versets "illustrate through music" the sentiment of the text they replace, assuming a character that is at times proud, at times meditative or sorrowful. Based on this assumption it would therefore be plausible to reverse the order of the 4th and 5th versets of de Grigny's *Gloria* with respect to the original printed version, and so use the *Basse de Trompette* for the verset *Domine Deus, Rex Coelestis* and the *Tierce en taille* for *Domine Deus, Agnus Dei*: in this way the relationship between musical *affect* and adherence to the liturgical text is certainly stronger.

In most cases it is the organ that begins, thus also fulfilling the function of giving the intonation to the choir. It should be noted that the term *choir* usually meant the prelates and clerics [*les Ecclesiastiques*] who sat in the *choir stalls*. The choir, in turn, was often divided into *1ere côté du Chœur* and *2éme côté du Chœur*, i.e. *Coro Primo* and *Coro Secondo*. The *alternatim* took place then between *chorus* and organ, but sometimes between the two choirs as well.

As for the *plainchant*, it could vary considerably depending on the source that was used as reference in the various churches; in fact, the *cantus firmus* often varied among different churches, cities or religious orders. Should one wish to reconstruct the *alternatim* structure of a liturgical cycle, one should refer to the *plainchants* of the time and not to the gregorian used in modern editions (e.g. Solesmes). To this end, the most interesting sources are the writings published by Pierre Valfray in Paris in 1669 (*Les Principaux chants liturgiques*) and the *Dissertation sur le Chant Gregorien* by Nivers in 1683.[39] As proof of the differences that existed between the various sources, two versions of the *incipit* of the *Kyrie* from the *Missa Cunctipotens genitor* are shown here; on the one hand, the customary A-A-G-A model, as used by François Couperin

or, on the other, the A-G-A-A model as used by Nicolas Gigault in his *Kyrie double à 5 parties* (*Messe aux Fêtes Doubles*)

Which of the two models de Grigny referred to in his mass is unclear. It remains at the discretion of the performer whether to interpret the "missing A" in the first measure of the *Kyrie* (assuming that de Grigny wanted to use the melody A-A-G-A) as a liberty taken by the composer, or rather, as one of the many errors present in Grigny's volume:

Nicolas de Grigny: *Premier Kyrie en taille, à 5* (*Premier Livre d'Orgue*)

On the other hand, it should be noted that both de Grigny and François Couperin (the latter uses the formula A-A-G-A in the initial *Plein Jeu*) present the subject of the Fugue in the form A-G-A:

ALTERNATIM IN THE MASS

In the organ repertoire there are two types of masses.

The first type was conceived for the *Fêtes doubles*, and was based on the *Missa IV: Cunctipotens genitor Deus*. Here below is the *Incipit* most frequently used for the *Kyrie* and for the *Gloria*:

A characteristic of this type of mass is the use of different modes for each cycle (*Kyrie, Gloria, Sanctus* and *Agnus*). The masses of Nivers (*Second livre*), Lebègue (*Second livre*), Gigault, François Couperin (*Messe pour les Paroisses*) and Grigny – as well as some anonymous masses extant as manuscripts (*Ms. de Thiéry, Livre d'orgue de Montréal , Ms. de Tours,* etc.) – belong to this group.[40] The *Cæremoniale Parisiense* recommends that certain specific organ versets should be based on the corresponding *cantus firmus*:

Cantus planus igitur pulsatur in Missa ad primum & ultimum Kyrie eleison. ad Et in terra pax, &c. Suscipe deprecationem nostram. In gloria Dei Patris. Amen. [...] ad primum Sanctus ad Agnus Dei. & ad Domine Salvum fac regem.[41]	*In the Mass the plainchant should then be played in the first and last Kyrie eleison, at the Et in terra pax, etc., at the Suscipe deprecationem nostram. In gloria Dei Patris. Amen. [...] in the first Sanctus, at the Agnus Dei and at the Domine Salvum fac regem.*

An analysis of the repertoire reveals, however, that, in reality, often only the first verset obeys this rule, while the last verset, as well as those within the cycle, are very rarely based on a *cantus firmus*. In line with the *Cæremoniale Parisiense* is, for example, the *5ᵉ Couplet* of the *Kyrie* from Couperin's *Messe pour les Paroisses*.

The second type of Organ Mass, in contrast, used the same key for all pieces and was not linked to a *cantus firmus*. The absence of *cantus firmus* is explained by the fact that many religious orders had their own *plainchants*, different from those used in the *Rito Romano* or in common use in Paris: an *Ordinarium Missae* not bound to a specific *cantus firmus* is undoubtedly more versatile.[42] François Couperin's *Messe pour les Couvents*, Gaspard Corrette's *Messe du 8ᵉ ton pour l'orgue à l'usage des Dames Religieuses* and André Raison's *Messe du huictiesme ton*, all in 8th tone, belong to this category. The remaining four masses by Raison and several anonymous manuscript masses are also not linked to a *cantus firmus*.

With regard to the *plainchants* to be used for the *alternatim* in such cases, one could take as a model the *Messes en plainchant* by Henri Du Mont, *Maestro di cappella* and composer for the *Chapelle Royale*. Around 1669, Du Mont published

Cinq Messes en Plain-Chant, composées et dédiées aux révérends Pères de la Mercy, du Convent de Paris. Et propres pour toutes sortes de Religieux, & de Religieuses, de quelque Ordre qu'ils soient, qui se peuvent chanter toutes les bonnes festes de l'Année.[43]	Five Masses in plainchant, composed and dedicated to the reverend Fathers of Mercy, of the Convent of Paris. And suitable for all Monks and Nuns, whatever their Religious Order, which can be sung on all feastdays throughout the year.

The collection was widely used at the time and was reprinted several times over the following decades. It contains the *plainchants* in five different keys (*tons*) that are well suited for the *alternatim* of this second type of mass.

In particular, the *Messa du Sixiesme Ton* – sung one tone higher – suits well the *alternatim* for the organ masses of the 8th mode, such as the *Messe pour les Couvents* by François Couperin.

KYRIE

The *Kyrie* consists of the invocations *Kyrie eleison – Christe eleison – Kyrie eleison*, each repeated three times, making a total of nine versets; five of which are entrusted to the organ and four are sung:

Dans les Eglises où il y a des Orgues, l'Introït étant fini, l'Orgue jouë le premier Kyrie eleison, le Chœur chante le second, l'Orgue jouë le troisiême, & ainsi du reste.[44]	In churches with an organ, after the Introitus the organ plays the first Kyrie eleison, the choir sings the second, the organ plays the third, and so on.

The resulting structure is as follows:

Kyrie eleison	ORGAN
Kyrie eleison	choir
Kyrie eleison	ORGAN
Christe eleison	choir
Christe eleison	ORGAN
Christe eleison	choir
Kyrie eleison	ORGAN
Kyrie eleison	choir
Kyrie eleison	ORGAN

Exceptions to the above rule are sometimes found. In the *Ceremonial de Toul*, printed in the year 1700, the use of the organ is described as follows:

A la Messe, on les touche aux Kyrie cinq fois, quand on les chante dans le chœur en plain chant; quatre fois quand on les chante en musique (*); & deux fois seulement quand les Musiciens chantent les Kyrie, les Christe, & les Kyrie entieremeut tout de suite.[45]	During the Mass, it [= the organ] plays five times in the Kyrie when this is sung in plainchant in the choir; four times when it is sung by the polyphonic choir (*); and only twice when Musicians sing all the Kyries, Christes, and Kyries entirely without interruption.

(*) the term *chante en musique* should be understood as intending a *chœur polyphonique*

GLORIA

The doxology *Gloria in excelsis Deo* comprises 18 versets, nine of which are entrusted to the organ and nine sung. Unlike the other parts of the *Ordinarium*, the *Gloria* begins with the *chant* intoned by the celebrant or *Præcentor* and not with the organ:

In Missa sollemni Festorum primi & secundi ordinis, Organa cantant alternatim incipiendo Kyrie, & In terra pax hominibus, &c. postquam Celebrans præcinit Gloria in excelsis Deo.[46]	In solemn Masses of first and second class Feasts, the organ plays alternatim with the choir - it starts the [first verset of the] Kyrie, and the Et in terra pax hominibus, etc. after the celebrant has intoned the Gloria in excelsis Deo.

The resulting structure is as follows:

Gloria	Præcentor
et in terra pax	ORGAN
laudamus te	choir
benedicimus te	ORGAN
adoramus te	choir
glorificamus te	ORGAN
gratias agimus tibi	choir
Domine Deus, Rex coelestis	ORGAN
Domine fili Unigenite	choir
Domine Deus, Agnus Dei	ORGAN
qui tollis ... miserere nobis	choir
qui tollis ... deprecationem nostram	ORGAN
qui sedes	choir
Quoniam	ORGAN
tu solus Dominus	choir
tu solus altissimus	ORGAN
cum sancto Spiritu	choir
Amen	ORGAN

On the other hand, the *Ceremonial de Toul* states that the organ may not be used

[...] pendant l'élévation, ny au Gloria in excelsis, ny au graduel, ny au trait, ny aus Credo; c'est le chœur qui chante entierement toutes ces choses.[47]	[...] during the elevation, or at the Gloria in excelsis, or at the Gradual, or at the Tractus, or at the Credo; it is the choir that sings entirely these versets.

It is clear that in Toul there was a different practice to that described in most of the *Ceremonials*. In any case, the *Gloria* was omitted during Advent and Lent. Versets specifically composed for the *Gloria* are included in the organ masses of Nivers (*Deuxième Livre d'Orgue*), Raison, Gigault, François Couperin, de Grigny and Gaspard Corrette. One can assume that in cases with fewer than nine organ versets, those missing would have been improvised.[48]

SANCTUS

The distribution of the *Sanctus* is described as follows:

A la fin de la Preface l'Orgue joüe le premier Sanctus, le Chœur chante le second, l'Orgue joüe le troisième jusques à ces paroles Pleni sunt, &c. le Chœur chante Pleni sunt Cæli & Terra gloria tua, l'Orgue joüe ensuite, & ne cesse point jusqu'au Pater.[49]	At the end of the Preface, the organ plays the first Sanctus, the choir sings the second, the organ plays the third up to the words Pleni sunt etc., the choir sings Pleni sunt Cæli & Terra gloria tua, then the organ plays and continues until the Pater.

The structure of the Sanctus is:

Sanctus	ORGAN
sanctus	choir
sanctus, Dominus Deus sabaoth	ORGAN
Pleni sunt coeli	choir
Benedictus	ORGAN

Unlike *Kyrie* and *Gloria*, which usually ended with a *Grand jeu*, the *Sanctus* finished with a meditative verset (*Benedictus*). In Raison's five masses and de Grigny's Mass, the *Benedictus* is followed by an *Elévation*. But there is no *Elévation* in Couperin's *Messe pour les Paroisses*, Nivers' Mass from the second book (1667) or Gigault's second Mass (1685). On the other hand, the third verset of the *Sanctus* in Lebègue's *Deuxième Livre d'Orgue*, Couperin's *Messe pour les Couvents* as well as in Gaspard Corrette's *Messe du 8ᵉ Ton* is entitled *Elévation*. Different again is the *Sanctus* of Gigault's first Mass, which consists of only two versets: i.e. neither the *Benedictus* nor the *Elévation*. Moreover, Nivers attests to the practice of singing a motet (instead of playing the organ) for the elevation:

A la Messe pour l'Eslevation du Saint Sacrement, & à la Communion, l'on peut chanter quelquefois l'un des grands Motets du Saint Sacrement: neanmoins il n'en faut pas choisir un des plus longs à l'Eslevation, afin de ne pas faire attendre le Celebrant, quand c'est une grande Messe.⁵⁰	In the Mass, for the elevation of the Sacred Host and at the Communion, one can sometimes sing one of the great Motets of the Blessed Sacrament: however, one should not choose one of the longest for the Elevation, in order not to keep the Celebrant waiting when it is a solemn Mass.

AGNUS DEI

The *Agnus Dei* is described as follows:

L'Orgue jouë le premier Agnus Dei, le Chœur chante le second, l'Orgue jouë le troisième, & continuë jusqu'à ce qu'il soit temps de chanter l'Antienne de la Communion.⁵¹	The organ plays the first Agnus Dei, the choir sings the second, the organ plays the third, and it continues until the moment when the communion antiphon is sung.

The distribution of its three versets is very clear:

Agnus Dei ... miserere nobis	ORGAN
Agnus Dei ... miserere nobis	choir
Agnus Dei ... dona nobis pacem	ORGAN

Similarly to *Kyrie* and *Gloria*, the first verset of the *Agnus Dei* is traditionally a *Plein Jeu*, often with the *plainchant* in the tenor or bass. In contrast, the third verset differs from author to author.

ITE MISSA EST

At the end of the Mass the celebrant intones the *Ite Missa est*, followed by the *Deo Gratias*, which is played by the organ at important celebrations:

L'Orgue jouë aussi Deo gratia aprez Ite Missa est.[52]	The organ also plays Deo gratia after the Ite Missa est.

This is a short *Plein jeu* or *Petit plein jeu*, sometimes consisting of only six or seven bars. While explaining the different moments for use of the organ in the liturgy, the *Ceremonial de Toul* prescribes:

Mais pour les réponses Amen & Deo gratias, il faut un peu se presser, & ne pas traîner long tems.[53]	As for the responses Amen & Deo gratias, these should be quite brief and not drag on for too long.

In the *Messe du 8ᵉ ton* of Raison, the *Deo Gratias* is – a rather unique case – a *Tierce en taille*. Raison specifies, however, that this piece can be used as *Deo gratias ou autre piece* [*Deo gratias or another purpose*]. That the musical structure of a solemn celebration *cum organo* ended with a modest composition of a few bars may seem curious. It should be remembered that during the period of the *Ancien Régime* the verset *Domine salvum fac regem* [*Lord Save the King*] was intoned at the *Postcommunio* as an intercession for the monarch:

> *Domine salvum fac regem,*
> *Domine salvum fac regem:*
> *& exaudi nos in die qua invocaverimus te.*
> *Gloria Patri et Filio, &c.*

This could have been executed either as a *plainchant, alternatim* or motet. Many authors have composed motets on this text. The melodies in *plainchant* were also numerous and varied according to the liturgical solemnity. The following example is taken from the *Graduale Romano* published by Nivers in Paris in 1687 and was intended for a *Missa In Festis Primæ Classis*:[54]

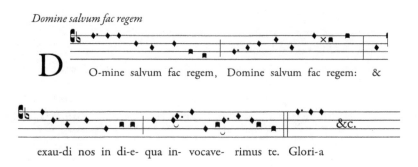

In cases when the *Liturgie des Heures* did not directly follow the Mass, the *Domine salvum fac regem* was performed at the end of the celebration. The *Cæremoniale Parisiense* (1662) states:

In Ecclesiis in quibus horæ canonicæ non cantantur in choro, Organa pulsantur ad Domine Salvum &c. de 5. tono, quod cantatur post benedictionem Missæ.[55]	In churches where the Liturgy of the Hours is not sung in choir, the organ plays the *Domine salvum [fac regem]* of the 5th mode, which is sung after the final blessing of the Mass.

From the beginning of the 19th century, France developed the tradition of performing large organ works at the end of the Mass.

ALTERNATIM IN THE *MAGNIFICAT*

While the *alternatim* structure in the *Ordinarium Missae* is clear, the situation with regard to the *Magnificat* is not quite so straightforward. The number of versets in the *Magnificat* cycles varied from author to author. Furthermore, diverse customs existed in different cities, churches and religious orders. As a result, the distribution of the versets between organ and choir could differ.

The canticle of the *Magnificat* consists of twelve versets (ten + *Gloria Patri*), each divided into two semi-verses:

1. *Magnificat * anima mea Dominum*
2. *Et exultavit spiritus meus * in Deo salutari meo*
3. *Quia respexit humilitatem ancillae suae: * ecce enim ex hoc beatam me dicent omnes generationes*
4. *Quia fecit mihi magna qui potens est: * et sanctum nomen ejus*
5. *Et misericordia ejus a progenie in progenies: * timentibus eum*
6. *Fecit potentiam in brachio suo: * dispersit superbos mente cordis sui*
7. *Deposuit potentes de sede, * et exaltavit humiles*
8. *Esurientes implevit bonis: * et divites dimisit inanes*
9. *Suscepit Israel puerum suum, * recordatus misericordiae suae*
10. *Sicut locutus est ad patres nostros, * Abraham et semini ejus in saecula*
11. *Gloria Patri, et Filio, * et Spiritui Sancto*
12. *Sicut erat in principio, et nunc, et semper, * et in saecula saeculorum. Amen.*

It was customary for the organ to play the *Magnificat* (*alternatim* with choir) on major feasts. The main organ cycles expressly dedicated to this canticle are the following:

1626	Jehan Titelouze	8 Magnificat	6 versets + an *alio modo*
1678	Nicolas Lebègue	9 Magnificat	7/8 versets
1706	Jean-Adam Guilain	4 Magnificat	7 versets
1737	Michel Corrette (*1ᵣ Livre*)	4 Magnificat	6 versets
1739	Jean-François Dandrieu	6 Magnificat	6 versets
1750	Michel Corrette (*2ᵉ Livre*)	4 Magnificat	6 versets

Further anonymous *Magnificat* cycles have come down to us as manuscripts such as those by *Thiéry, Carpentras, Tours*, and the *Livre d'orgue de Montréal*. The latter contains 11 *Magnificats* plus 9 other cycles without title, whose structure implies that they could have been conceived for the *Magnificat*. Most of them are composed of 7 versets.[56]

Recently, a manuscript by Claude Balbastre containing 17 *Magnificats* was discovered and published in facsimile (2016). The second part of the manuscript is dated 1750. Fourteen of these *Magnificats* consist of six or seven versets, while the remaining three have eight or five versets.

The eight *Magnificats* from the 1626 book *Le Magnificat, ou chant de la Vierge pour toucher sur l'orgue, suivant les huit tons de l'Église* by Titelouze each contain six versets, corresponding to the odd versets (*Magnificat, Quia respexit, Et Misericordia ejus*, etc.) as clearly indicated at the beginning of each verset. Here below, the beginning of the first two versets:

Jehan Titelouze: *Magnificat Primi Toni, Magnificat* (1626, *Magnificat*)

Jehan Titelouze: *Magnificat Primi Toni, Quia respexit* (1626, *Magnificat*)

In the eight *Magnificats* of Titelouze – which have no indication of registration – there is an additional, fourth verset (*Deposuit potentes*) *alio modo*, whose function is explained by the author:

I'ay adjouté vn Second Deposuit potentes. &c. parce qu'au Cantique Benedictus, il y a sept vers pour l'Orgue: & le Magnificat n'en ayant que six, on y fera servir celuy que l'on voudra.[57]	I have added a second Deposuit potentes etc. because in the Canticle of the Benedictus there are seven versets for the organ; as the Magnificat has only six, one can choose which [of the two] one wishes.

(*) The Canticle of the *Benedictus* is, together with the *Magnificat* and *Nunc dimittis*, one of the three great Canticles; it is placed after the hymn of the *Office of the Lauds* and requires seven organ versets for the *alternatim*

Unlike Titelouze, the cycles expressly entitled *Magnificat* by other authors, although specifying the registrations, do not state which part of the text they refer to. The division given by Titelouze

- *Magnificat* (organ)
- *Et exultavit* (choir)
- *Quia respexit* (organ)
- etc.

is the one most frequently described in French *Cérémonials*. Here are some examples:

1662 – Cæremoniale Parisiense

[...] pulsanda sunt Organa [...] Ad primum etiam versum Magnificat.[58]	[...] the organ is played [...] for the first verset of the Magnificat.

1680 – Cæremoniale Monasticum

In Monasteriis in quibus habentur Organa, convenit ea pulsari [...] incipient etiam, & alternatim prosequentur versus Hymni, & Cantici Magnificat.[59]	In the Monasteries in which there is an organ, it is to be played [...] at the beginning, and then follow alternatim for the versets of the Hymn and Canticle of the Magnificat.

1700 – Ceremonial de Toul

Tout le chœur ensemble chante alternativement avec l'orgue par v[erses] ou par strophes, les psaumes (quand on les chante en musique) les hymnes, les cantiques [...]. Les orgues commencent toûjours, à la réserve du Te Deum qui est entonné par le plus ancien du Clergé [...].[60]	The whole choir together sings alternately with the organ, by verset or stanza, psalms (when sung with the polyphonic choir), hymns, and canticles [...]. The organ always starts, except in the Te Deum, which is intoned by the eldest member of the clergy [...].

The *Cérémonial de Bourges* (1708) stipulates that the celebrant or *Præcentor* sing only the word *Magnificat* while the organ performs the entire first verset (*Magnificat anima mea Dominum*):

Le Chantre entonne Magnificat, & l'Orgue joüe le premier Verset, les deux Chœurs chantent le second, l'Orgue joüe le troisiême, ainsi du reste.[61]	The Cantor intones the Magnificat, and the organ plays the first Verset, the two choirs sing the second, the organ plays the third, and so on.

The *Cæremoniale Monasticum Romano* published in Paris in 1634 seems to indicate that the choir should begin:

Regulare est, sive in Vesperis, sive in Matutinis, sive in Missa, ut primus versus Canticorum & Hymnorum, & pariter versus ad quos genuflectendum est, cantentur à Choro in tono intelligibili, non autem ab Organo.[62]	As a rule, in the Vespers, Matins or Mass the first verset of Canticles and Hymns, and likewise for the versets in which one genuflects, is sung by the choir with intelligible tone, but not [played] by the organ.

Which means: - *Magnificat* (choir or *præcentor*)
   - *Et exultavit* (organ)
   - *Quia respexit* (choir)
   - etc.

Following these indications, the choir should sing the odd versets and the organ play the even ones, although here we also cannot exclude a procedure similar to that used in Bourges.

According to the division given by Titelouze and the other *Cérémonials* mentioned above – odd versets to the organ and even versets to the choir – and in relation to the classical structure with six versets entrusted to the organ, the *Magnificat* would end with the choir singing the *Sicut erat*. The seventh verset found in the *Magnificat* of Lebègue and Guilain, a *Petit plein jeu* and a *Plein Jeu* respectively, could replace the *Antiphon*, as indicated in the *Cérémonial de Bourges* (1708):

A la fin l'Orgue joüe l'Antienne.[63]	At the end, the Organ plays the Antiphon.

The "extra" verset found in the three Lebègue *Magnificats* of the 2e, 3e et 5e *ton* could be an *alio modo*, considering that all nine of his *Magnificats* end with a *Dialogue* (6th verset) and a *Plein Jeu* (7th verset).

Concerning the registrations of the *Magnificat*, see page 86.

ALTERNATIM IN THE HYMNS

The hymn plays an important role in the French organ repertoire of the 17th century, as evidenced by the compositions of various authors from Titelouze to Michel Corrette. The majority of the sources call for the first verset to be played by the organ:

L'Orgue joüe le premier Verset de l'Hymne, le côté du Chœur chante le second, l'Orgue joüe le troisième, l'autre côté du Chœur chante le quatrième, & ainsi alternativement; cependant lorsqu'il y a peu d'Ecclesiastiques, les deux Chœurs peuvent chanter ensemble les Versets de l'Hymne.[64]	*The organ plays the first verset of the Hymn, one side of the choir sings the second, the organ plays the third, the other side of the choir sings the fourth, and so on alternately; however, if there are few clerics [Ecclesiastiques], the two choirs can sing together the versets of the Hymn.*

The melodies of the hymns could differ significantly between regions, cities, churches and religious orders. The number of versets of the organ hymns often does not match the number of *stanzas* of the corresponding *plainchant*, making a logical structure for the *alternatim* problematic. This division is further complicated by the fact that the organ versets do not usually bear the title of the corresponding *plainchant* verset.

Very often the number of organ versets is insufficient for a regular *alternatim* structure; in such cases one can hypothesize that the "missing" versets were improvised. It should be noted that at the end of the *2. Livre d'Orgue* Nivers provides twelve short versets (two to four bars in length) as an *Amen ou Deo gratias de tous les Tons pour le petit plein Jeu*, which could also be used for the conclusion of a hymn.

The fact that in different churches and cities there were differing practices – such as alternation between choir and organ but also between two choirs – attests that the *alternatim* did not follow inflexible rules. One can take as example Nivers' preface to his *Motets à voix seule* (1689), where the author explains the division between choir and organ in the hymn *Veni Creator*:

Lorsque l'on chante avec l'Orgue le Veni Creator, on ne chante point Tu septiformis munere, &c. ny Gloria Patri Domino, &c. parce que l'Orgue seule joüe ces deux strophes-là.[65]	*When the Veni Creator is sung with the organ, neither the Tu septiformis munere etc. nor the Gloria Patri Domino etc. are sung because the organ alone plays these two versets.*

By comparing the four most important published collections of *Hymnes* – Titelouze 1623, Nivers 1667, de Grigny 1699, Michel Corrette 1756 – we also note that the number of organ versets often differs from composer to composer.

The twelve hymns of Titelouze provide three or four organ versets. The first presents the *cantus firmus* in the bass and could, in principle, be performed as a *Plein jeu avec plainchant* in the pedal. The remaining two or three versets are constructed on the model of the *Fantaisie* and do not provide information concerning registration.

Nivers provides two or three versets for his eighteen hymns. Many of them start with a *Plein jeu* with *cantus firmus* in the bass followed by a *Fugue sur le sujet de l'hymne precedente*; when present, the third verset is often a *Récit de dessus*. In some cases Nivers also gives a variant *transposée pour les voix haultes* [transposed for the high voices] or *pour les voix basses*. Many of the versets of Nivers bear precise indications of registration.

The fifteen hymns by Michel Corrette consist of one or two short versets. In the first (which usually has three voices), the *cantus firmus* is placed in the bass: it was likely intended to be performed as a *Plein jeu* with the pedal *Trompette* or a *Petit plein jeu* with the *Trompette* of the *Grand Orgue* in the left hand:

Michel Corrette: *Ave Maris Stella* (*Troisième Livre d'Orgue*)

In three cases, this verset is also the only constituent of the composition; in the other twelve, the second verset is a *Fuga* (in one case entitled *Fuga-Trio*).

The division of the five hymns by de Grigny is rather complex and needs to be discussed in detail.

The hymn *Ave Maris Stella* consists of seven *stanzas*: the inclusion of the four organ versets does not present any difficulty for a regular *alternatim*:

1. *Ave maris stella*	*En taille à 5*
2. *Sumens illud Ave*	choir
3. *Solve vincla reis*	*Fugue à 4*
4. *Monstra te esse matrem*	choir
5. *Virgo singularis*	*Duo*
6. *Vitam praesta puram*	choir
7. *Sit laus Deo Patri*	*Dialogue sur les Grands Jeux*

The hymn *Pange Lingua* consists of six *stanzas*, starting with the organ, as the *Cérémonials* recommend, and ending with the choir. It is curious that the last verset of the organ is a *Récit* - it is likely that the organ would have closed the cycle with an improvisation on the *Amen* (with a *Grand jeu*):

1. *Pange lingua gloriosi*	*En taille à 4*
2. *Nobis datus, nobis natus*	choir
3. *In supremae nocte coenae*	*Fugue à 5*
4. *Verbum caro, panem verum*	choir
5. *Tantum ergo Sacramentum*	*Récit du Chant de l'Hymne précédent*
6. *Genitori Genitoque*	choir
[8. *Amen*	*Grand jeu* improvised?]

A solis ortus cardine is a Latin poem of the 5th century that consists of 23 *stanzas*, each beginning with a consecutive letter of the alphabet, making it an *abecedarius*. In the early Middle Ages, the first seven *stanzas* – with a doxology of different origins added as an 8th *stanza* – became a widespread Christmas hymn. The four versets of de Grigny could therefore be structured as follows:

1. *A solis ortus cardine*	*A Solis Hortus en Basse*
2. *Beatus auctor saeculi*	choir
3. *Clausae parentis viscera*	*Fugue à 5*
4. *Domus pudici pectoris*	choir
5. *Enixa est puerpera*	*Trio*
6. *Feno iacere pertulit*	choir
7. *Gaudet chorus caelestium*	*Point d'Orgue sur les Grands Jeux*
[8. *Iesu, tibi sit gloria*	choir?]

The five organ versets of the *Veni Creator* are a poor fit for the seven Gregorian strophes. A regular *alternatim* structure works only if one of the middle organ versets is considered an *alio modo*, analogously to the 4th verset of Titelouze's *Magnificat*:

1. *Veni creator Spiritus*	*En taille à 5*
2. *Qui diceris Paraclitus*	choir
3. *Tu septiformis munere*	*Fugue à 5*
4. *Accende lumen sensibus*	choir
5. *Hostem repellas longius*	*Duo* or *Récit de Cromorne* (?)
6. *Per Te sciamus da Patrem*	choir
7. *Deo Patri sit gloria*	*Dialogue sur les Grands Jeux*

Another hypothesis is that the choir versets were limited to two, not three; in this case the organ would play all five versets.

The same problem arises between the six *stanzas* of the hymn *Verbum supernum prodiens* and the four versets composed by de Grigny, which, in addition, end with a *Basse de Trompette ou de Cromorne*. Here, the distribution between choir and organ can be only a matter of speculation.

In contrast, the division of four other compositions taken from the 2. *Livre d'Orgue* by Nivers, in which the author has marked each verset with the *incipit* of the corresponding *stanza* and where the number of versets corresponds exactly to the *plainchant*, is clear. They are:

- the sequence *Victimæ Paschali laudes* (4 organ versets on a total of 7 *stanzas*)
- the sequence *Veni Sancte Spiritus* (5 organ versets on a total of 10 *stanzas*)
- the sequence *Lauda Sion Salvatorem* (12 organ versets on a total of 24 *stanzas*)
- the *Te Deum laudamus* (16 organ versets on a total of 31 *stanzas*)

In the specific case of the *Victimæ Paschali laudes*, Nivers composed three versets and indicated that the last should be used both for the semi-verse *Sepulchrum Christi viventis* as well as for the semi-verse *Surrexit Christus spes mea*, but with different registrations:

Guillaume-Gabriel Nivers: *Victimæ Paschali laudes* – 3me Couplet (*Deuxième livre d'orgue*)

L'un sur le dessus de la Trompette ou de Cromhorne, lautre sur le Cornet.	One on the dessus of the Trompette or of the Cromhorne, the other on the Cornet.

As far as the *Te Deum* is concerned, it is one of the few cases in which the *præcentor* begins, singing the first semi-verse *Te Deum laudamus*, followed by the organ with the semi-verse *Te Dominum confitemur* (the two semi-verses constitute the first verset of the hymn). Thus, the organ plays the odd versets and the choir sings the even ones, as written in the *Ceremonial de Bourges*:

Le Chantre ayant entonné le Te Deum, l'Orgue continuë le premier Verset, les deux Chœurs ensemble chantent le second, & ainsi alternativement.[66]	After the Cantor has intoned the Te Deum, the organ continues the first verset, the two choirs together sing the second, and so alternately.

36 Kind communication of Michel Bouvard.
37 Olier 1657, Chapitre VII: Du Sanctus, without page number.
38 Caeremoniale Monasticum Romano 1634, 21.
39 Gilbert-Moroney 1989, 10.
40 Gallat-Morin 1988, 92-94.
41 Sonnet 1662, 171.
42 Saint-Arroman 1988/II, 208.
43 Du Mont 1669, frontispiece.
44 Ceremonial de Bourges 1708, 137.
45 Ceremonial de Toul 1700, 102.
46 Caeremoniale Monasticum 1680, 19.
47 Ceremonial de Toul 1700, 102.
48 Mielke 1996, 455.
49 Ceremonial de Bourges 1708, 137.
50 Nivers 1689, Observations, without page number.
51 Ceremonial de Bourges 1708, 137.
52 Ceremonial de Bourges 1708, 137.
53 Ceremonial de Toul 1700, 102.
54 Nivers 1687, LXXI.
55 Sonnet 1662, 170.
56 Gallat-Morin 1988, 99 and 321-327.
57 Titelouze 1626, 18.
58 Sonnet 1662, 172.
59 Caeremoniale Monasticum 1680, 19.
60 Ceremonial de Toul 1700, 102.
61 Ceremonial de Bourges 1708, 129.
62 Caeremoniale Monasticum Romano 1634, 21.
63 Ceremonial de Bourges 1708, 129.
64 Ceremonial de Bourges 1708, 128.
65 Nivers 1689, Observations, VI.
66 Ceremonial de Bourges 1708, 136.

THE FRENCH
ORGUE CLASSIQUE

BRIEF HISTORICAL OVERVIEW

French organ building throughout the 16th century was significantly influenced by organ builders from outside its own borders. In the south of the country, this influence was predominantly Italian; in the south-west, Spanish; and in the north, Flemish. It was the latter influence that most marked the nascent French *orgue classique*.

Until about mid-1500, in France, as in most parts of Europe, organs were usually built "in F": small instruments had a 3' basis, medium-small organs a 6' basis (in both cases beginning at F), and larger instruments a 12' basis (beginning at FF, i.e. in the *contra-octave*). Here are some examples:[67]

- ❖ 1529, Bordeaux *Saint-Eloi*: *hung orgue de six piés*
- ❖ 1537, Alençon *Notre-Dame*: *unes orgues […] de douze piedz*
- ❖ 1558, Bordeaux *Sant-Michel*: *le principar sera du ton de troys piedz*

Around the turn of the 16th century, the metamorphosis from a *Blockwerk* to an organ with separate stops occurred. The transition in France is documented in several sources, amongst them Baigneux 1532, Alençon 1537-40, Chartres 1542.[68]

The *Plein jeu* is the most direct result of the dismemberment of the Blockwerk. In instruments of the first half of the 16th century, one can already glimpse the future pyramid of *Plein jeu*, based on the *Montre* or *Principal* and crowned by the pair of stops *Fourniture-Cymbale*. An example of an instrument of this period is the specification of the organ of Notre-Dame in Alençon, as described in the contract and built by Gratien de Cailly and Symon le Vasseur in 1537-40:[69]

Corp d'Orgue

Principal 12
Principal 6
Principal 3
Fourniture VIII
Cymballe

} [...] sont cinq jeulz servant tous au principal du corps
[...] are five stops all used for the principal [= plenum] of the corpus

Fluste de six piedz estouppee [6' stopped = 12' real]
Fleuste de troys piedz pareillement [3' stopped = 6' real]
Doubles fleustes 3
Fleuste 1 ½
Nazard [probably 4', i.e. $2^{2/3}$ if referred to an organ in C]
Petit jeu de nazard [probably 2', i.e. $1^{1/3}$ if referred to an organ in C]
Tremblant
Rossignol

Positif

Trompette 6
Voix humaines
Jeu de herpes [Harp]

Since this was an "F-instrument", it should be pointed out that the stops of 12', 6', 3' and 1½' are in unison/octave with the note played. As keyboards could have different compasses, not unusual at the time (in the case above, *Corp d'Orgue* from FF – *Positif* from F), this means that the 12' stop of the *Corp d'Orgue* and the 6' of the *Positif* would have been in unison and correspond to the 8' of an organ "in C".

The specification clearly shows that it was, in principle, a single manual organ with the addition of a small *Positif*, both in terms of compass (from F instead of FF as in the *Corp d'Orgue*) and of number of stops. It should also be remembered that most of the instruments built before 1600 had only one manual. In the preface to the *Hymnes de l'Eglise* published in Paris in 1623, Titelouze writes:

Outre que nous luy avons encore augmenté sa perfection depuis quelques années, les faisant construire en plusieurs lieux de la France avec deux claviers separés pour les mains [...].[70]

Moreover, in recent years we have increased its perfection, having built in several places in France organs with two separate manuals for the hands [...].

In the same document Titelouze describes the compass of the pedalboard:

[...] & un clavier de pedales à l'unisson des jeux de huict pieds, contenant vingt-huict ou trente tant feintes que marches, pour y toucher la Basse-contre a part, sans la toucher de la main, la Taille sur le second clavier, la Haute-contre & le Dessus sur le troisiesme.[71]

[...] and a pedalboard in unison to the eight-foot stops, containing twenty-eight or thirty [chromatic and diatonic] pedals, in order to play the bass voice without playing it by hand, the tenor on the second manual [= second organ division after the pedal], the alto and the soprano on the third [= ditto].

One of the first instruments to present a specification that could be referred to as classic *ante litteram* is the organ (no longer existing) built by Nicolas Barbier for the church of Saint-Gervais et Saint-Protais in Gisors in 1580:[72]

Grand Orgue

Monstre 16
Jeu de 8 de plomb [of lead]
Bourdon de 4, sonnant 8 (*)
Un jeu de 4, nommé prestam
Doublette 2
Fourniture IV-VI
Cimballe III

} *Les jeux nommés ci dessus servisont pour le Plain Jeu*

The stops listed here are used for the Plein Jeu

Fluste 4
Nazard de deux tuyaux sur chacune marche (**)
Sifflet 1
Quinte fluste faicte à biberon
Jeu de cornet V
Trompette 8
Clairon 4
Régalle pour servir de [to use as] *voix humaine*
Tremblant

Positif

Jeu en bourdon 4 sonnant 8 (*)
4 de plomb [of lead]
Jeu de 2 de plomb [of lead]
Petite quinte, le corps d'estain [of tin]
Cimballe II
Jeu de crosme horne 8

Pedal

Jeu de pédalle 8' de grosse taille [large scaled], *fait de bois* [wood] *de fente*
Autre jeu de pédalles en sacquebouttes [probably a reed stop]

(*) length of 4' = sounding 8'
(**) *Nazard* with two pipes per key

In 1601, the Flemish organ builder Mathis Langhedul built a new organ at Saint-Gervais in Paris which would later become the instrument of the Couperin family. In the original construction, it had two keyboards and pedal. The specification, deduced from subsequent writings, was probably the following:[73]

Grand Orgue	Positif	
Montre 12 [from F]	Bourdon 8	GO and Pos: 45 notes, short octave
8 ouvert	Montre 4	Ped: 9 notes, short octave
Bourdon 8	Doublette	
Prestant	Fourniture III	Probably without
Flûte 4	Cymbale III	*Accouplement Grand Orgue / Positif*
Nasard	Flageolet 1	Tremblant fort
Doublette	Cromorne	
Flûte à 9 trous 2		
Flageolet 1	**Pédale**	
Fourniture (IV?)		
Cymbale III	Flûte 8	
Cornet V		
Trompette		
Clairon		

Originally, the instrument was placed in a gallery in the south transept of the church. In 1628 the organ builder Pierre Pescheur moved it to the counterfacade of the church and at the same time enlarged the specification. It is hard to say how much this instrument influenced the future organ building in France. The specification, in fact, seems to anticipate the typical organ described in 1636 by Mersenne in the *Harmonie Universelle* (see page 102), an instrument that essentially corresponds to the model that was to spread throughout France over the next 150 years. Somewhat anomalous with respect to later classical specifications is the presence of the *Flageolet 1*, a stop that was often found in pre-classical instruments, but which disappeared in the following decades and was replaced (particularly on the *Positif*) by a *Larigot 1 1/3*.

The *Trompette 8* and sometimes also *Clairon 4* were found in instruments in the 16th century, whereas 16' reeds made their appearance much later. In 1679, Lebègue did not support the proposal of the organ builder Alexandre Thierry to include a *Trompette 16* in the new organ of the *Hôtel Royal des Invalides* in Paris:

Pour la trompette de 16 p. comme ce jeu est inusité en France et fort grossier, lequel aussi ne se peut faire qu'avec une forte quantité d'etain, si on juge à propos de le supprimer et substituer à sa place une voix humaine cela ne seroit pas mal.[74]	Since the 16 foot trompette is an unusual stop in France and very unrefined, and also requires a large quantity of tin, if one considers it advantageous to suppress it and substitute it with a voix humaine, that wouldn't be bad.

Around 1620 a third keyboard appeared in France, called the *Récit*. The compass of this department is usually limited to the *dessus* (treble) and endowed with the typical solo stop, the 5-rank *Cornet*, often as the only stop on this manual. In addition, one sometimes also finds a fourth manual; the latter has the function of an *Écho* division, it is limited to the treble and is often equipped with only one stop, the *Cornet d'Écho*.

In reality, the first three-manual organ that appeared in Paris was that of Notre-Dame Cathedral. This instrument was the result of the enlargement of the previous organ (which still possessed its ancient *Blockwerk*) and had a decidedly unusual specification. The *titulaire* of this instrument was one of the most celebrated French organists of the time, Charles Racquet. The specification around 1620 was as follows:[75]

Grand Orgue	*Positif*	*Grand Orgue* (3rd man.):
Plein Jeu 16 VIII-XVIII	Montre 8	46 notes, CDE - b''
	Bourdon 8	
	Prestant	*Boucquin* (2nd man.):
Boucquin	Doublette	47 notes, CD - b''
Bourdon 16	Fourniture IV	
Bourdon 8	Cimballe III	*Positif* (1st man.):
Prestant o Flûte 4	Flûte à cheminée 4	48 notes, CD - c'''
Nasard	Nazard II [2²/³ and 2]	
Cymbale II	Flageollet 1	
Un Jeu d'Anche à 2 tuyaux par note (*)	Dessus de Cornet	
	Trompette	
	Clairon	
(*) a reed stop with 2 pipes per key (treble only?)	Vox Humaine	
	Tremblant	

In fact, the *Grand Orgue* was nothing but the old *Blockwerk*, constantly coupled to the 2nd manual (*Boucquin*). It seems that the organ had no pedalboard. A *pédalier en tirasse* was to be installed in 1646.

Returning to the aforementioned organ of Saint-Gervais: by means of alterations made between 1649 and 1659 by Pierre Thierry, the instrument was enlarged to four manuals, with the specification that Louis Couperin and (with minor alterations) his nephew François Couperin *le Grand* would have known. Based on various documents, Pierre Hardouin established what most probably was the specification of this instrument in 1685, i.e. five years before the publication of the two masses by François Couperin:[76]

Grand Orgue	Positif de dos	Écho	
Montre 16	Bourdon 8	Bourdon 8	G.O. and Pos: AACD - c'''
Bourdon 16	Montre 4	Prestant 4	Réc: c' - c'''
Montre 8	Flûte 4	Nazard	Écho: c - c'''
Bourdon 8	Nazard	Doublette	Ped: AACD - e'
Prestant	Doublette	Tierce	
Flûte 4	Tierce	Cymbale III	In the pedal, G.O. and Pos., the
Nazard	Larigot	Cromorne	C♯ sounds as AA
Quarte de Nazard	Fourniture III		
Doublette	Cymbale III		The *Écho* starts from c
Tierce	Cromorne	**Pédale**	(37 notes)
Fourniture IV		Flûte 8	
Cymbale III	*Récit* *	Flûte 4	*Tirasse Grand Orgue*
Cornet V	Cornet V	Trompette	*Tremblant fort*
Trompette			*Tremblant doux*
Clairon			
Voix humaine			* in 1714 François Thierry added a *Trompette 8* on the *Récit*

Although the stops of a French organ are usually of full compass, there are some examples of *jeux coupés*, i.e. stops divided between bass and treble; the division was usually between b and c'. Their presence may already be seen in instruments of the pre-classical period, as for example the organ built in 1602 by Isaac Huguet in Saint-Valéry-sur-Somme (see page 97). Much later, Clérambault would also speak of divided stops in his *Livre d'Orgue*:

J'ai composé ces pieces de maniere qu'on peut les joüer aussi facilement sur un cabinet d'orgue a jeux coupes que sur un grand Orgue, cest pourquoy dans la Basse de trompette, et dans les recits, les accompagnements des jeux doux ne passent pas le milieu du Clavier, non plus que les sujets du Dessus et de la Basse. Ceux qui ont de grands orgues pourront mettre les accompagnements de la main gauche à l'octave en haut s'ils les trouvent trop bas.[77]	I composed these pieces so that they could be easily performed both on a positive organ [cabinet d'orgue] with divided stops as well as on a large instrument; for this reason, in the Basse de Trompette and in the Récits the accompaniment of the Jeux doux does not cross the middle of the keyboard, nor do the subjects in the soprano or the bass. Those who possess large organs can play the accompaniment of the left hand an octave higher, if they find it too low.

The following are specifications of some important French organs from the 18th century whose original structure has been substantially preserved:

ST. MICHEL EN THIÉRACHE
Jean Boizard 1714

G.O. CD - c'''
Pos. CD - c'''
Réc. c' - c'''
Echo c' - c'''
Ped. CD - c'

Grand Orgue
Bourdon 16
Montre 8
Bourdon 8
Prestant 4
Flûte 4
Quinte 3
Doublette 2
Quarte de nasard 2
Tierce 1 3/5
Fourniture IV
Cymbale III
Grand Cornet V
Trompette 8
Voix humaine 8
Clairon 4

Positif
Bourdon 8
Flûte allemande 8
Montre 4
Nasard 3
Doublette 2
Tierce 1 3/5
Larigot 1 1/3
Fourniture III
Cymbale II
Cromhorne 8

2 tremblants
Acc. Pos/G.O.
Tirasse G.O.

Récit
Cornet V

Écho
Cornet V

Pédale
Flûte 8
Flûte 4
Trompette 8
Clairon 4

HOUDAN
Louis-Alexandre Clicquot 1739

G.O. CD - c'''
Pos. CD - c'''
Réc. c' - c'''
Ped. CD - c'

Grand Orgue
Montre 8
Bourdon 8
Prestant 4
Nazard 2 2/3
Doublette 2
Quarte de Nasard 2
Tierce 1 3/5
Cornet V
Fourniture IV
Trompette 8
Voix humaine 8
Clairon 4

Positif
Bourdon 8
Flûte 4
Nazard 2 2/3
Doublette 2
Tierce 1 3/5
Plein Jeu V
Cromhorne 8

2 tremblants
Acc. Pos/GO

Récit
Cornet V
Trompette 8

Pédale
Without its own stops, permanently coupled to the Grand Orgue

SARLAT
Jean-François Lépine 1752

Grand Orgue	Positif	Récit
Bourdon 16	Montre 8	Cornet V
Bourdon 8	Bourdon 8	Trompette 8
Montre 8	Prestant 4	
Grand Nazard 5 1/3	Nazard 2 2/3	
Prestant 4	Doublette 2	*Écho*
Grosse tierce 3 1/5	Tierce 1 3/5	Cornet V
Nazard 2 2/3	Larigot 1 1/3	
Doublette 2	Plein-Jeu VI	
Quarte 2	Trompette 8	*Pédale*
Tierce 1 3/5	Cromorne 8	Flûte 8
Fourniture V		Flûte 4
Cymbale IV		Nazard 2 2/3
Cornet V		Quarte 2
Trompette 8	Acc. Pos/G.O.	Tierce 1 3/5
Clairon 4	2 tremblants	Trompette 12
Voix humaine 8		Clairon 6

I. Pos.   AACD - d'''
II. G.O. AACD - d'''
III. Réc. g - d'''
IV. Echo f - d'''
Ped. { reeds: FFGG - d'
       fonds: AACD-d'

AA of GO and POS is placed on the C♯

ST. MAXIMIN
Jean-Esprit Isnard 1774

Grand Orgue	Positif	Raissonance
Montre 16	Montre 8	Flûte 16
Bourdon 16	Bourdon 8	Flûte 8
Montre 8	Flûte 8	Flûte 4
Bourdon 8	Prestant 4	Bombarde 16
Gros Nasard 5 1/3	Nazard 2 2/3	1ᵉ Trompette 8
Prestant 4	Doublette 2	2ᵉ Trompette 8
Grosse Tierce 3 1/5	Quarte de Nazard 2	Clairon 4
Grosse Fourniture II	Tierce 1 3/5	
Petite Fourniture IV	Larigot 1 1/3	Dessus de Flûte 8
Cymbale IV	Fourniture III	Dessus de Tromp. 8*
Cornet V	Cymbale III	Dessus de Cornet V
Trompette 8	Cornet V	
Dessus de Tromp. 8*	Trompette 8	*Récit*
Voix Humaine 8	Cromorne 8	Cornet V
Clairon 4	Clairon 4	Trompette 8
		Hautbois 8'
*The two *Dessus de Trompette* are *en chamade*		Acc. Pos/GO
		Acc. Raissonance/GO

I. Pos.   CD - d'''
II. G.O. CD - d'''
III. Rais. CD - d'''
IV. Réc. g - d'''
Ped.   C - g'

The pedal does not have its own stops but is permanently coupled to the 3rd manual (*Raissonance*); this division has the double function of *Pédale* and *Clavier de Bombarde*

SOUVIGNY
Fr.-Henri Clicquot 1783

Grand Orgue	Positif	Récit
Montre 8	Bourdon 8	Bourdon 8
Bourdon 8	Dessus de Flûte 8 (*)	Cornet IV
Prestant 4	Prestant 4	Hautbois 8
Nazard 2 $^{2/3}$	Nazard 2 $^{2/3}$	
Doublette 2	Doublette 2	
Quarte 2	Tierce 1$^{3/5}$	
Tierce 1$^{3/5}$	Plein-Jeu V	**Pédale**
Plein-Jeu VI	Cromorne 8	Flûte 8
Cornet V	Trompette 8	Flûte 4
Trompette 8		Trompette 12
Clairon 4	2 tremblants	Clairon 6
Voix humaine 8	Acc. Pos/G.O.	

I. Pos. CD - d'''
II. G.O. CD - d'''
III. Réc. c' - d'''
Ped. FFGG - a

(*) beginning from c°

POITIERS
Fr.-Henri Clicquot 1791

Grand Orgue	Positif	Récit
Montre 16	Montre 8	Flûte
Montre 8	Bourdon 8	Cornet V
Bourdon 16	Dessus de flûte	Trompette
Bourdon 8	Prestant 4	Hautbois
Second Huit Pds	Nazard 2 $^{2/3}$	
Prestant 4	Doublette 2	**Écho**
Grande Tierce 3 $^{1/5}$	Tierce 1 $^{3/5}$	Bourdon
Nazard 2 $^{2/3}$	Dessus de Cornet V	Flûte
Doublette 2	Plein-Jeu VII	Trompette
Quarte de Nazard 2	Trompette 8	
Tierce 1 $^{3/5}$	Clairon 4	**Pédale**
Dessus de Cornet V	Cromorne 8	Flûte 16 (bouchée)
Fourniture V		Flûte 8
Cymbale IV		Flûte 4
1re Trompette		Bombarde
2e Trompette		Trompette
1er Clairon		Clairon
2e Clairon		
Voix Humaine 8		

I. Pos. C - e'''
II. G.O. C - e'''
III. Réc. g - e'''
IV. Echo g - e'''
Ped. { reeds: AA - c'
fonds: C - c'

PROFILE OF THE ORGAN *CLASSIQUE*

The French classical organ usually has two 4-octave manuals for *Grand Orgue* and *Positif*; larger instruments can have a *dessus* (treble) keyboard as a *Récit* and/or *Écho*. In the four-manual organs, the 3rd manual corresponds to the *Récit* and the 4th manual to the *Écho*. In three-manual organs, the 3rd manual can be either a *Récit* or an *Écho*. Besides the keyboards, there is usually a pedalboard *à la française*, typically equipped with two, three or four stops. If, in Paris or other major cities it was not unusual to find instruments with three or four keyboards plus pedal, in most provincial parishes or convents, organs were usually limited to one or two manuals – often with divided stops in order to extend their possibilities – and the pedal only *en tirasse* (without its own stops) or entirely absent.

Two features of French organ keyboards of this period have direct consequences for interpretation: lightness of touch and diminished key width. Thanks to the former, it is easy to perform the numerous ornaments that characterize the French repertoire. The reduced key width allows ease of performance of passages in the repertoire where the span of a tenth is required. Titelouze speaks of this characteristic in the preface to the *Hymnes de l'Église*:

[…] *pour toucher deux parties de chasque main, j'ay employé en quelques lieux la dixiesme par ce qu'il y a peu d'Organistes qui ne la prennent* […].[78]

[…] in order to play two voices in each hand I have used the tenth in some places, because there are few organists who can't span it […].

The main characteristics of the various organ departments (divisions) are outlined below.

GRAND ORGUE

❖ the dimensions of an organ are defined by the *Montre* of the *Grand Orgue*, which can be 16' (= large organ), 8' (= medium-sized organ) or 4' (= small organ)

❖ the Principal chorus is almost invariably made up of *Montre 8, Prestant 4, Doublette 2, Fourniture* and *Cimbale*; in larger instruments there is also a *Montre 16* or a second *Fourniture*

❖ the Flute family normally includes *Grand Bourdon 16, Petit Bourdon 8, Flûte 4, Nazard* $2^{2/3}$, *Tierce* $1^{3/5}$ and a 5-rank *Cornet*, this latter limited to the *dessus* (c'-c'''); in larger instruments a *Quarte de Nazard 2* and the *Grosse tierce* $3^{1/5}$ can be found; more rarely, and in a rather late period, the *Gros Nasard* (or *Grande Quinte*) $5^{1/3}$ as well; on older instruments there is also a *Flageolet 1*; during the 18th century the *Flûte 4* gradually disappeared

❖ the reed family is almost always represented by *Trompette 8, Clairon 4* and *Voix Humaine 8*; in larger instruments a *2e Trompette 8* can be found; during the 18th century

the *Bombarde 16* gradually appeared; in Saint-Gervais this stop is placed on a specific keyboard (*3ᵉ Clavier - Bombarde*) constantly coupled to the *Grand Orgue*
- the compass is 48 notes (CD - c′′′), four octaves, usually without C♯

POSITIF

- the *Positif* is nearly always placed behind the player's back (*Positif de dos*) and corresponds to the first keyboard; its specification reflects in a smaller way that of the *Grand Orgue* and its compass is the same
- the *Principal* stops are usually *Montre 4*, *Doublette 2* and *Fourniture*; in larger instruments a *Montre 8* can be found (in which case the 4′ is called *Prestant*) and a *Cymbale* as well; in some cases the two stops *Fourniture* and *Cymbale* are united in a single stop called *Plein Jeu*
- the usual *Flute* stops are *Bourdon 8*, *Flûte 4*, *Nazard* $2^{2/3}$, *Tierce* $1^{3/5}$ and *Larigot* $1^{1/3}$; only rarely is there also a *Quarte de Nazard 2* or – even more rarely, in later and very large instruments – a *Cornet* (treble only); during the 18th century the *Flûte 4* gradually disappeared
- the characteristic reed of the *Positif* is the *Cromorne 8*; in larger instruments one also finds a *Trompette 8* and – rarely – a *Voix Humaine 8* (this latter was quite common in 18th century instruments in Normandy)
- the *Positif* can be coupled to the *Grand Orgue* by shove coupler

RÉCIT

- where present, it corresponds to the third manual of the organ; the compass is usually limited to the treble (*dessus*), i.e. c′-c′′′; more rarely it begins at f° or g°
- often it consists only of a 5-rank *Cornet* (*Cornet séparé*)
- as a further stop there could be a *Trompette 8*, more rarely a *Hautbois 8* or a *Bourdon 8* (in the latter case, quite often *Bourdon 8* and *Cornet IV*)

ÉCHO

- this is played from the fourth manual, or – on organs of three manuals without *Récit* – from the third manual; the compass is limited to the treble but we not infrequently find *Échos* with 37 notes (compass c-c′′′) or beginning from either f or g (30 to 32 notes)
- similarly to the *Récit*, it usually consists only of a *Cornet* (*d'Écho*) whose five ranks may be grouped into a single stop or separated
- there are examples of quite large *Écho* departments; the 1688 contract for the Cathedral of Auch included on the *Écho* a *Jeu de Tierce*, a *Plein jeu* (*Fourniture III* and *Cymbale III*) as well as a *Voix Humaine*

PÉDALE

In earlier instruments, especially of small size, the pedal was permanently coupled to the manual. Even during the 18th century, it was not uncommon to find instruments without pedal stops, particularly in the south of France. Nor were examples of organs without pedalboard uncommon.

In the contracts stipulated with the parish of Stenay sur la Meuze in 1719 and with the abbey Notre-Dame of Mouzon in 1725, the organ builder Christophe Moucherel specified that these instruments had a *pedal separé*, i.e. were equipped with their own stops and not merely coupled to the *Grand Orgue*.[79] In the classical period the typical pedal specification consisted of *Flûte 8* and *Trompette 8*. In larger instruments one could find a *Flûte 4* and a *Clairon 4* as well. As opposed to the German tradition, the pedal was not based on 16' pitch. The *Flûte* was always 8', so, when the pedal functioned as the bass voice, this was at 8' pitch (unless the pedal was coupled to the *Grand Orgue* and the latter had a 16' stop). During the 18th century, 16' stops

Example of pedalboard *à la française*

gradually began to appear on the pedal. In the 1734 project for the Metropolitan Church of Albi, the aforementioned organ builder Christophe Moucherel proposed the following stops for the pedal (compass AACD - d'):

I. La montre de seize pieds	I. The montre of 16´
II. Un huit pieds ouvert	II. An open 8' [Flûte]
III. Une trompette de grosse taille	III. A wide-scaled trumpet
IV. Un clairon de grosse taille[80]	IV. A wide-scaled clairon

In reality, there are some isolated examples of 16th century organs which had a pedal department of deep bass sonority (16' or even 32', as in the example below), but this feature did not take root in the classical period. In the contract drawn up in 1542 for the reconstruction of the organ of Chartres we read that the instrument had to have

[...] ung plain jeu de seize pieds remply d'une double, de huit tuyaulx en bas de trente-deux pieds en pédalle, le clavier commencant en fa,	[...] a plein-jeu on a sixteen foot base enriched with a double [? - perhaps the contre-octave in the pedal], eight bass pipes of thirty-two foot in

ut; et seront les huict plus gros tuyaulx desdite orgues qui se joueront en pédalle […].⁸¹	the pedal, the keyboard beginning in F; and the eight largest pipes of this organ which will be played on the pedal [...].

From the text one can deduce that the pedal began at FF and that it had eight pipes on a 24' basis (possibly: FF GG AA BB♭ BB C D E).

From the mid-17th century on, the pedal could perform two main tasks: as tenor (with the *Trompette 8*) playing the *cantus firmus* in the *Pleins jeux*, or as bass (with the *Flûte 8*) in *Trios à trois claviers*, in the *Récits en taille*, in the *Fugues à 5* as well as in *Quatuors* or in the compositions with *obbligato* pedal. There are, however, cases of *cantus firmi* in the bass, which might well be performed with the *Trompette* (in some cases doubling the bass voice on the manual in order to avoid inelegant voice crossings).

The use of the pedal *ad libitum* is also documented: in the last verset of the *Gloria* in the *Messe du Deuxiesme Ton* by Raison there is written *"pedalle si on veut"* [*pedal if desired*]:

André Raison: *Dialogue* (*Messe du Deuziesme Ton*)

The organ builder Jean de Joyeuse implied that the pedal *ad libitum* could be used in the *Grands jeux* as well, pieces in which the use of the pedal is rarely explicitly indicated:

[...] la dite pédalle [de trompette] sera fort esclatant, affin d'estre entendue distinctement avec le plain jeu lorsqu'on jouera des plain chants et grands jeux.⁸²	[...] the cited trompette on the pedal will be very sonorous [esclatant], in order to be heard distinctly with the plein jeu when performing the plainchants and grands jeux.

The pedal of some instruments was equipped with *ravalement*, i.e. a downward extension beyond the C, similar to the *contr'ottava* of Italian Renaissance organs. The *ravalement* concerned only the reeds but not the *Flûtes*, which started in the usual manner from C. This extension could have been either a *petit ravalement* or a *grand ravalement*. In the first case the reeds went down to AA, although it was most common to place the AA on the C♯ of the pedalboard. The *grand ravalement* was instead a real *contr'ottava* going down to the FF (without FF♯) or GG. The possibility of playing the pedal line one octave lower – especially when the pedal has the *plainchant* – is of great help when the pedal compass at the top is limited. This practice is testified by Gigault (1682):

Si la Basse va trop haut pour les étenduës de quelques susd. Instrumens, l'on pourra mettre une Octave plus bas.[83]	*If the bass line goes too high for the compass of any of the aforementioned instruments, it can be played an octave lower.*

A direct example of this practice is found in the first *couplet* of the *Sanctus* in Couperin's *Messe pour les Paroisses* where – in an interesting case of double pedal – the composer indicates in the score "*Pedalle une octave plus bas*":

François Couperin: *Plein chant du premier Sanctus en Canon (Messe pour les Paroisses)*

The two lines are therefore to be played in the following compass:

In organs without *grand ravalement*, such as Couperin's organ in *Saint-Gervais*, the last note of the lower voice must, out of necessity, be played an octave higher. In fact, the *grand ravalement* to FF was quite rare at the end of the 17th century; its construction is documented in the organ built between 1699 and 1703 by Robert Clicquot for the Saint-Quentin basilica.[84] Examples of *grand ravalement* to FF can be found today in the Jean-François Lépine organ of Sarlat (1752) and in the Fr.-Henri Cliquot organ of Souvigny (1783).

As for the top of the pedal compass, there are already sources from the pre-classical period exhibiting a large extension. In the preface to the *Hymnes de l'Eglise* (1623) Titelouze mentions twenty-eight or thirty notes:

Un clavier de pedales à l'unisson des jeux de huict pieds, contenant vingt-huict ou trente tant feintes que marches, […].[85]	*A keyboard of pedals in unison with the eight-foot registers, containing twenty-eight or thirty [chromatic and diatonic] pedals, […].*

Couperin's organ in *Saint-Gervais* in 1685 extended to e', while at the bottom end it started from AA. Taking into consideration repertoire with *pedale obbligato*, one notes that a large compass was often requested by the composers themselves:

- Lebègue, Raison and Grigny require a d'
- Jullien (*Prelude a cinq partie, 5e Ton*) and Couperin (*8e Couplet* del *Gloria, Messe pour le Paroisses*) require an e'
- Marchand (*Plein Jeu a 6*), Du Mage (*Tierce en taille*) and Gigault (*Qui tollis à 5 parties*) go as far as f'

In his *Grand prélude avec les pedalles de trompette meslées*, Boyvin requires not only f' but AA as well:

Jacques Boyvin: *Grand prelude avec les pedalles de trompette meslées (5me ton, Premier Livre d'Orgue)*

An interesting example of double pedal is found in the following work by Gigault where, starting from bar 9, the composer asks to double the bass voice in the pedal an octave lower:

Nicolas Gigault: *Qui tollis a 5. parties (Livre de Musique pour l'Orgue)*

TIRASSE

The presence of the *tirasse*, i.e. the *Grand Orgue* coupled to the pedal, is documented in the mid-17th century on instruments of important composers:

- 1659, Paris Saint-Gervais (organ of Louis and François Couperin)[86]
- 1689, Rouen: Cathédrale (organ of Jacques Boyvin)[87]
- 1696, Reims: Cathédrale (organ of Nicolas de Grigny)[88]

There are also several Parisian organs which possessed a *tirasse* in the second half of the 17th century: Saint-Germain-des-Prés (1665), Saint-Roch (1668), les Cordeliers (1669), and Saint-Séverin (1670).[89] The use of the *tirasse* is also prescribed in some repertoire. The *Trio du 5e Ton* contained in the *Premier Livre d'Orgue* of Jacques Boyvin bears the title *Trio pour la pedalle ou tire-clavier*, leaving the performer the choice of playing the bass part with the pedal *Flûte* or with the *tirasse* to the *Grand Orgue*. In the *Dialogue du 2nd Ton* contained in Boyvin's *Premier Livre d'Orgue*, the author also explicitly calls for the *Tyrasse* instead of the *Flûte* to play the pedal part:

Jacques Boyvin: *Dialogue de recits de cromhorne et de cornet (Second ton, Premier Livre d'Orgue)*

The fact that Boyvin sometimes uses *tirasse* instead of the pedal *Flûte* would make it possible to play the bass voice with the left hand instead of on the pedal (when the left hand is free). This is the case in the following *Trio à 3 Claviers*: although not explicitly specified by the composer, it is plausible to consider the use of the *tirasse* here instead of the pedal *Flûte* for the bass line. In this case the performance of the first bar would definitely be easier:[90]

Jacques Boyvin: *Trio a 3 Claviers (Sixiesme ton, Premier Livre d'Orgue)*

TREMBLANT

French classical organs are characterized by two different types of tremulant, the *tremblant fort* and the *tremblant doux*.

The *tremblant fort* is placed on the main wind channel and, when engaged, releases the wind outside; for this reason, it is also called *à vent perdu* and the tremulating effect is decidedly strong, hence the term *fort*. It is prescribed in particular for the *Grands jeux*.

The *tremblant doux*, by contrast, is placed inside the wind channel, producing a softer tremulant. It is prescribed for the *Concert de Flûtes*, for different *Trio* registrations and especially for the *Voix humaine*. The use of the *tremblant doux* (or *lent*) together with the *Voix humaine* is also often cited in organ contracts, such as in *St-Merry* (*Saint-Médéric*) in Paris (1669):

Plus il faut faire un bon tremblant lent pour jouer les voix humaines.[91]	In addition, a good tremblant lent must be constructed to be used with the voix humaines.

In 1636, i.e. in the pre-classical period before the appearance of numerous *livres d'orgue* which frequently prescribed its use, Mersenne wrote:

Mais plusieurs reiettent ce tremblement comme un bruit desagreable [...].[92]	But some reject this tremblement as an unpleasant noise [...].

About 130 years later Dom Bédos harshly criticized the *tremblant*, effectively accepting it only with the *Voix humaine*:

Il faut bien remarquer que c'est le seul cas [= avec la Voix Humaine] où les Organistes, qui ont le plus de goût pour l'harmonie, se servent du Tremblant-doux, même lorsqu'il est bon; ce qui est assez rare. Il affoiblit nécessairement le vent; par conséquent il change & détériore l'harmonie & l'accord de l'Orgue.[93]	It should be noted that this is the only case [with the Voix Humaine] when organists, those who can most appreciate a beautiful harmonious sound, use the Tremblant-doux, even when it is good, which is very rare. Its use causes the wind to drop; consequently, it alters and worsens the harmony [= voicing] and the tuning of the organ.

And the paragraph continues, pointing out that

Il y a de grands Organistes qui ont nommé le Tremblant-doux "le perturbateur de Jeux de l'Orgue".[94]	There are great organists who have named the Tremblant-doux "the perturber of the organ stops".

Dom Bédos abhorred the use of the *Tremblant* in the *Grand jeu* (see page 126).

OVERVIEW OF FRENCH TEMPERAMENTS

From about mid-16th century onwards, the system generally used for organ tuning throughout Europe was the so-called *meantone* – most commonly in its 1/4 comma version. The basis of this system is to reduce 11 fifths by 1/4 syntonic comma in order to obtain 8 pure major thirds; as a result, the last fifth, called the *wolf*, is extremely wide and makes the remaining four major chords impracticable. The beauty of the pure thirds of this tuning system, emphasized far more by an instrument of sustained tone like the organ than the harpsichord, is the reason for the longevity of *meantone* temperament, which continued in some European regions well into the 19th century.

During the 17th century, however, composers increasingly felt the need to go beyond the harmonic framework of *meantone*, so well suited to the ecclesiastical modes, i.e. to overcome the limits of keys of two flats and three sharps. Marin Mersenne was well aware of such constrictions. In *Harmonie Universelle* (1636) he first explained from a mathematical point of view "pure" *meantone* tuning (1/4 comma) and then added:

[...] il est aysé de conclure que le Clavier de treize marches sur l'Octave ne peut avoir toutes les Consonances iustes [...].[95]	[...] it is easy to conclude that a keyboard of thirteen notes per octave [12 + 1] cannot have all the right consonances [...].

The expedient which allows us to go beyond the harmonic limits of *meantone* and, at the same time, retain pure thirds, is the construction of enharmonic keyboards, i.e. keyboards equipped with *subsemitons* (split keys), usually for the D♯/E♭ and G♯/A♭ pairs. In the *Propositions XXII & XXIII* (*Livre Sixiesme des Orgues*) Mersenne explained at lenght the *Clavier parfait*, describing keyboards of 17, 19, 27 and 32 notes per octave. While the last two types were mainly of an academic-scientific nature, Mersenne implied the practical use of *subsemitonia* with 19 notes per octave:

[...] ie veux icy adiouster un Clavier avec les marches necessaires pour faire toutes les Consonances dans leur iustesse, car encore que les dix-neuf marches de son Octave soient, ce semble, plus difficiles à toucher que les treize des autres Claviers, neanmoins la perfection de l'harmonie, & la facilité qu'il y a à accorder les Orgues qui usent de ce quatriesme Clavier, recompense abondamment la difficulté du toucher, que les Organistes pourront surmonter dans l'espace de huit iours, ou dans fort peu de temps.[96]	[...] here I want to add a manual with the keys necessary to make all the consonances correct; but if nineteen keys per octave [18+1] are, apparently, more difficult to play than the thirteen [12+1] of the other [type of] keyboard, nevertheless the perfection of harmony and the ease of tuning the organs that use this fourth [type of] keyboard abundantly compensate for the difficulty of playing, which organists will be able to overcome in the space of eight days, or in a very short time.

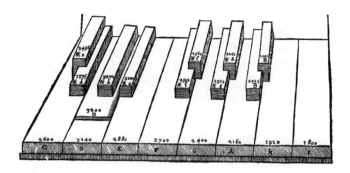

Marin Mersenne: *Clavier Harmonique, Parfait de 19. marches sur l'Octave, commençant par C sol ut.*

Despite Mersenne's *peroratio* and in contrast to other European regions, notably Italy, the construction of organs with *split keys* did not take root in France: perhaps the only known example is the organ built by Crespin Carlier in 1632 for *Saint-Nicolas-des-Champs* in Paris (where Nicolas Gigault was organist from 1652 onwards), an instrument equipped with D♯/E♭ and G♯/A♭ for the three top octaves. In 1732, exactly one hundred years after its construction, Louis-Alexandre Clicquot eliminated the split keys in the course of modifications to the instrument.[97]

During the 17th and 18th centuries numerous writings concerning the tuning of keyboard instruments appeared in France. In many cases the authors were neither professional musicians nor builders of musical instruments but mathematicians, theorists, philosophers or scholars of the time (such as Mersenne, D'Alembert, Rousseau) who often treated the topic in the manner of an academic dissertation rather than in practical terms. In addition, it should be noted that the correct interpretation and understanding of these sources is often highly problematic: to describe the tuning processes, use was frequently made of rather imprecise terms such as *forte* [*sharpening the pitch*], *foible* [*flattening the pitch*], *un poinct* [*a pinch*] or *un peu plus justes* [*a little purer*]; at times – and this not always clearly – these terms refer to a note, at others to an interval, thus encourageing false interpretations. After his extensive discussion of enharmonic keyboards – which by *raison d'être* probably implies *meantone* tuning – Mersenne explains in *Proposition XXIX* of *Harmonie Universelle*

[...] *la maniere & la methode d'accorder les Orgues tant iustes que temperées.*[98]	[...] *the manner and method of tuning organs both just and tempered.*

Here as well as in later writings (*Harmonicorum Books XII*, published posthumously in 1649) Mersenne illustrated possible modifications of meantone tuning. The principle described consists in modifying the three distant fifths in order to slightly narrow the *wolf*-fifth, whereas the initial nine fifths are tuned as in *meantone*, i.e. narrowed by a 1/4 comma. In this way the most often used tonalities benefit from pure thirds and, at the same time, the D♯ – the most used note "extraneous" to the *meantone* at the time – is considerably softened and to some extent usable. In the table below, where the starting note is F, Mersenne indicates with the sign ° the *Quintes foibles* [*narrowed fifths*]; the dashes -- placed under the two fifths in the lower stave (*Accord des Feintes*, i.e. tuning of the chromatic keys) show the *Intervalles iustes* [*pure intervals*]. Mersenne does not give any indication for the remaining *wolf*-fifth, i.e. the G♯-E♭ interval:

Marin Mersenne: *Proposition XXIX* (*Harmonie Universelle*)

The result is a *modified meantone* that causes only a moderate harmonic deviation from the "pure" meantone, but which partly preserves its beauty.

One vehement advocate of *meantone* was Jean Denis in his *Traité de l'accord de l'espinette* of 1643. Denis defended the ancient tuning system against equal temperament, which in those years was promulgated by some authors in Paris, calling it *fort mauvais et fort rude à l'oreille* [*very bad and very rough to the ear*].[99]

Although the tuning instructions provided by Denis are rather vague, they still seem to refer to 1/4 comma meantone and not to a modified meantone. In the same text, Denis also explains how important it is for organists to be able to perform transpositions in the correct tonalities – the reference is obviously to the practice of *alternatim* – reconciling the choir's needs with the harmonic limits of meantone, so as to avoid the extremely unpleasant chords that would be produced.

At the end of the century, in 1695, Lambert Chaumont still described the usual 1/4 comma meantone tuning and a variant of it, in a similar vein to Mersenne half a century earlier. In his *Methode d'accorder le Clavessin*, Chaumont indicated that nine fifths (from F to G♯) should be tuned *foibles* [*flat*] while for two fifths B♭-F and E♭-B♭ one could choose either *foibles* [*flat*] or *fortes* [*sharp*]: in the first case a "pure" *meantone* is obtained, in the second a modified *meantone*. In both cases, a more or less pronounced *wolf*-fifth persists between G♯-E♭. In the *Demonstration* Chaumont indicates the different intervals with the following abbreviations:

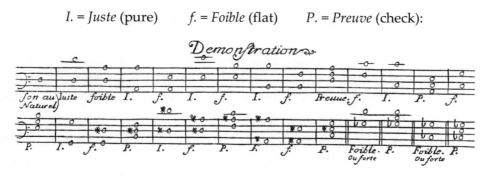

Lambert Chaumont: *Methode d'accorder le Clavessin* (*Pieces D'Orgues sur les 8 Tons*)

The writings published in the following century remained wedded to the principle of tuning the initial fifths meantone (narrowed by a 1/4 comma), but reducing them in number, which led to a gradual distancing from *meantone* tuning: in the *Nouveau Système de Musique Theorique* of 1726, Rameau requires seven fifths, while the remaining five must be tuned *"un peu plus justes"*:

[...] Lorsqu'on est arrivé au milieu de la Partition, on rend les Quintes un peu plus justes, et cela de plus en plus jusqu'à la derniere [...].[100]	[...] Half way through the tuning process, one can make the [still to be tuned] fifths a little more just, adjusting them more and more up to the last one [...].

It is clear that this vagueness of indication opens the possibility of different interpretations and, thus, different results. What makes Rameau's temperament interesting is the possibility of starting the tuning from two different points: from C, favouring in this case the tonalities with sharps, or from B♭ favouring those with flats:

Pour que les Intervales conservent toute la justesse possible dans les Modulations les plus usitées, il faut commencer la Partition par Si B-mol et ne rendre pour lors les Quin-tes un peu plus justes, que depuis Si à Fa♯.[101]	In order for the intervals to retain all the correctness possible in the most commonly used modulations, one must begin tuning from the B flat and begin making the fifths a little purer starting from the fifth B-F♯.

In both cases, the possibilities of going beyond *meantone* tuning are very limited.

In the mid-18th century, the term *Tempérament Ordinaire* began to spead throughout France. This was not a specific temperament, but rather the tuning system (or more precisely the tuning systems) most used at the time; for this very reason it was therefore defined *Ordinaire*, i.e. common, ordinary. The mathematician, philosopher and co-author of the famous *Encyclopédie* Jean le Ronde d'Alembert was the first to use the term *Tempérament Ordinaire* in 1752 (*Elémens de musique théorique et pratique suivant les princes de M. Rameau*). As stated by the author himself, d'Alembert based his concepts on those of Rameau, although partly modifying the mode of tuning. After the first 4 fifths were narrowed by a 1/4 comma, in order to obtain the third pure C-E, d'Alembert indicated that 4 fifths should be very slightly narrowed and 4 fifths very slightly sharpened (or more precisely: 3 fifths slightly sharp and one fifth pure or almost pure):

[…] partant ensuite de ce mi, on accorde les quintes si, fa♯, ut♯, sol♯, mais en les affoiblissant moins que les premieres, de maniere que sol♯ fasse à peu près la tierce majeure juste avec mi. Quand on est arrivé au sol♯ on s'arrête; on reprend le premier ut, on accorde sa quinte fa en descendant, puis la quinte si♭, et cetera et on renforce un peu toutes ces quintes jusqu'à ce qu'on soit arrivé au ré♭ [recte: mi♭], qui doit faire en descendant la quinte juste, ou à très-peu près, avec le sol♯ déjà accordé.[102]	*[…] starting therefore from this e, one tunes the fifths B, F♯, C♯, G♯, but lowering them less than the first [four], so that the G♯ gives almost a pure [juste] major third with the e. When you arrive at the G♯ you stop; you start then from the initial c, and tune the descendant fifth f, then the fifth B♭, etc., and reinforce all these fifths until you reach the D♭ [recte: E♭], which must give a pure or almost pure fifth in descending to the already tuned G♯.*

Identical or very close to the temperament described by d'Alembert – depending on how one likes to interpret the text – is the procedure described by Jean-Jacques Rousseau in the *Tempérament* chapter of his *Dictionnaire de Musique* published in 1765. The temperaments of d'Alembert and Rousseau – which along with that of Rameau were those most used at the time and therefore known as *Ordinaires* – are essentially very similar: we approach a system that tends to be "circulating" (i.e. a system in which all tonalities should be usable) but where, in fact, the distant tonalities are extremely harsh.

One could consider as rather anachronistic the position of Michel Corrette in 1753 with the four temperaments described in his *Le Maitre du Clavecin pour l'Accompagnement, Methode Theorique et Pratique*. The first is nothing but modified *meantone* giving rise to a rather wide *wolf*-fifth:

Cette Partition consiste à temperer 11. quintes, huite qu'on diminue de chacune un quart de Comma la neuvieme 5.te un peu plus juste et la 10. et 11.e quinte encore plus forte que les autres […].[103]	*This tuning system consists in tempering 11 fifths, eight of which are flattened by a quarter of a comma, the ninth is a little more just and the 10th and 11th slightly sharper than the others […].*

The second temperament cited by Corrette is the *"Partition de Keller Auteur Anglois"* [*tuning of the English author Keller*], a *meantone* tuning with thirds that are not perfectly pure, which Corrette dismisses haughtily:

Tout ce qu'on peut remarquer dans cet Auteur laconique c'est que la Partition Temperée s'apprend plutôt par la pratique que par les plus grands discours.[104]	All one can say of this laconic author is that tempered tuning is learned more by practice than by long discourses.

The third system – a modified *meantone* tuning similar to Mersenne and Chaumont – is described succinctly as

Partition dont se servoit le S.^r [Antoine] Vincent fameux Facteur d'Orgue à Rouen en 1712.[105]	Tuning used by Monsieur [Antoine] Vincent, the famous organ-builder, in Rouen in 1712.

The fourth system referred to – *Dissertation sur une nouvelle Partition* – is equal temperament, which Corrette attacks bitterly:

[…] les 3.^{ces} sont trop fortes cequi rend ce nouveau Temperam.^t dur à l'oreille sur tout à l'Orgue ou les sons sont soutenus. […]	[…] the thirds are too sharp, and this makes this new temperament hard sounding to the ear, especially on the organ where the sounds are sustained. […]
Tous les praticiens tant à Paris que dans les pays etrangers suivent l'ancienne partition, […]	All [music] practicians both in Paris and in foreign countries follow the ancient tuning, […]
il faut que nous suivions toujours nos anciens qui ont eu l'oreille aussi juste que nous; […]	we should always follow our ancestors who had ears as just as ours; […]
le temperam.^t ne peut pas etre egale partout autrem.^t toutes les consonances seroient desagreables et les dissonances encore plus.[106]	the tuning cannot be equal everywhere otherwise all consonances would be unpleasant and dissonances even more so.

The conclusions that can be drawn are the following:

❖ most composers active until the mid-18th century (i.e. up to Du Mage, Guilain and Clérambault) essentially played meantone or modified meantone organs

❖ the point of departure for most tuning systems used in France at the time was to maintain as many pure thirds as possible (by narrowing the corresponding fifths by 1/4 syntonic comma) for the most commonly used tonalities, to the detriment of the lesser used tonalities

❖ in the oldest sources (Mersenne) the fifths narrowed by a 1/4 comma were nine (i.e. a high number of pure thirds but at the same time an almost non-*circulating* system); in the later sources the number of pure thirds decreased, benefitting the more distant tonalities

- ❖ even the most "advanced" temperaments can only with great difficulty be defined as *circulating*, because the distant tonalities are often extremely harsh and at the borderline of usability
- ❖ equal temperament – known and used for other instruments – was rejected, in particular because of the continuous sounding of the organ, which highlights far more than other instruments the imperfection of the equal thirds

Analyzing the repertoire from Titelouze (1623) to the *livres d'orgue* of the mid-18th century, the tonalities employed in the vast majority of cases conform to ecclesiastical modes and therefore to the traditional keys. Very rarely are there modulations to more audacious tonalities; the latter are reserved for the harpsichord repertoire, i.e. an instrument which can be retuned in a short time and so adapted to the harmonic needs of the piece to be performed. The compositions of pre-classical authors such as Titelouze and Roberday can be performed on a meantone instrument without difficulty: the notes extraneous to this system – in fact only the D♯ – are very rare.

Forty-nine of the seventy pieces for organ by Louis Couperin remain within the framework of the three sharps and two flats. The presence of some D♯s in the remaining twenty-one pieces – in many cases just a single note within an entire composition – may give rise to some perplexity if performed on a meantone instrument; it must however be emphasized that in many cases these are passing notes or of short duration. Even most of the compositions by Nivers remain within the limits of meantone tuning: the few exceptions are to be found in transposed pieces, where some D♯s are present. In this regard it is interesting to read what Nivers himself says in the text at the conclusion of his *Motets à voix seule, accompagnée de la basse continue* (1689), where, in order to

[…] éviter les fausses Tierces qui se rencontrent dans les Tons transposez […]	*[…] avoid the false thirds encountered in the transposed tones […]*

he suggests that

[…] il vaut mieux dans ces rencontres espineuses lascher cette mauvaise Tierce, & se contenter de la Quinte & de l'Octave […].[107]	*[…] it is better in these thorny passages to leave out this bad third, and to be content with the fifth and the octave […].*

Beginning with Jaques Boyvin and François Couperin, the quantity of notes extraneous to meantone intensifies, although limited to D♯ and A♭. These two notes are also abundantly present in Grigny's *Livre d'Orgue* and not infrequently last a *minim* (half note) or longer. Strictly composed within the meantone frame, on the contrary, is the *Livre d'Orgue* by Du Mage.

The most common extraneous notes to meantone are thus the D♯ and, to a lesser extent, the A♭ which, according to the modification of the meantone used, can be (almost) acceptable. It must also be said that in many cases these are just passing notes or placed within the chord in such a way that they do not offend the ear. The extent to which the organ repertoire might nevertheless be "damaged" by an inadequate tuning system shifts the focus of the question, i.e. how much of the written repertoire was, in fact, to be used by an organist in his "routine activity". In view of the number of *couplets* that an organist at the time was required to perform (see page 24) it is clear that the written repertoire represented only an infinitesimal part of what was played: organists were *in primis* expected to improvise their versets for the *alternatim*, which therefore allowed adaptation of the extemporaneous piece to the characteristics of the instrument and, accordingly, also its tuning profile.

---

[67] Douglass 1995, 146 and 151 and 158.
[68] Douglass 1995, 57 and 151-154.
[69] Douglass 1995, 151-152.
[70] Titelouze 1624, 14.
[71] Titelouze 1624, 14.
[72] Douglass 1995, 59.
[73] Hardouin 1996, 8.
[74] Douglass 1995, 90.
[75] Hardouin 1973, 11.
[76] Hardouin 1996, 12.
[77] Clérambault c. 1710, 139.
[78] Titelouze 1624, 15.
[79] Moucherel 1734, 144.
[80] Moucherel 1734, 146.
[81] Douglass 1995, 153.
[82] Douglass 1995, 101.
[83] Gigault 1682, 21.
[84] Saint-Arroman 2001, XVII.
[85] Titelouze 1624, 14.
[86] Hardouin 1996, 10.
[87] Gorenstein-Boyvin, 10.
[88] Gorenstein-Boyvin, 10.
[89] Gorenstein-Boyvin, 9.
[90] Gorenstein-Boyvin, 33.
[91] Douglass 1995, 99.
[92] Mersenne 1636, 88.
[93] Dom Bédos 1766-1778, 206.
[94] Dom Bédos 1766-1778, 206.
[95] Mersenne 1636, 66.
[96] Mersenne 1636, 67f.
[97] http://organ-au-logis.pagesperso-orange.fr/Pages/Abecedaire/StNicolas.html (accessed 7.12.2018).
[98] Mersenne 1636, 79.
[99] Denis 1643, 12.
[100] Rameau 1726, 108.
[101] Rameau 1726, 110.
[102] D'Alembert 1752, 48.
[103] Corrette 1753, 84.
[104] Corrette 1753, 86.
[105] Corrette 1753, 86.
[106] Corrette 1753, 87.
[107] Nivers 1689, 169.

INTRODUCTION TO REGISTRATION

THE FRENCH *MÉLANGES*

Probably in no other school is the sound – and, hence, the choice of registrations – of such paramount importance as in that of the French baroque era, where a modification of the required timbre risks undermining the musical result.

Most of the registrations of the pre-classical period are not linked to specific musical forms: the descriptions of the various *mélanges* (stop combinations) found in sources of the first half of the 17th century are, for the most part, unrelated to specific works. This allows the performer a certain freedom, especially with genres such as the *Fantaisie, Fugue,* and versets conceived for the *alternatim* (normally constructed in the manner of a *Fantaisie*), which were the most common musical forms for the organ at this time. It is worth mentioning that only six of the seventy known organ compositions by Louis Couperin (mostly *Fugues* and *Fantaisies*) provide information concerning the desired registration.

From 1665, the year of publication of the first *Livre d'Orgue* by Nivers, registrations were closely linked to a specific musical texture such as *Récit*, *Duo*, *Trio*, etc. Therefore, the performer was at liberty to choose registrations in the pre-classical period, whereas, in the period that followed, registrations were prescribed by the composer, as Lebègue emphasizes:

Ie souhaiterois fort que tous ceux qui me feront l'honneur de toucher ces pieces voulussent les joüer selon mon intention, c'est à dire avec le meslange des Ieux & avec le mouvement propre pour chaque piece.[108]	*I very much hope that all those who will do me the honour of playing these pieces will wish to perform them according to my intentions, that is to say with the registrations and the appropriate ductus for each piece.*

Boyvin, too, stressed the importance of selecting the right sound:

Un des plus beaux agrémens de l'Orgue c'est de sçavoir bien marier les jeux.[109]	*One of the most beautiful charms [agrémens] of the organ is to know how to couple the stops well together.*

In reality, prescribed registrations were less mandatory than one might think. In the *3. Livre d'Orgue Des Huit Tons de l'Eglise*, Nivers presented 16 *Récits de dessus* and as many *Basses*, both without precise registration indications, and in line with what was expressed in the preface to his first *Livre d'Orgue*:[110]

Les Recitz, Diminutions, Basses, Cornets, Echos, Grāds Jeux &tc, ainsy qu'ils sont marquéz aux pieces particulieres: neantmoins on les peut tous changer et toucher sur d'autres Jeux a discretion et selon la disposition de l'Orgue.[111]	*Récits, Diminutions, Basses, Cornets, Echos, Grands Jeux etc., as they are indicated on the pieces; but they can nonetheless all be changed and played with other stops at the player's discretion and according to the organ specification.*

Even Raison seemed quite liberal as regards his registration proposals:

J'ay beaucoup varié les Jeux et les Claviers, yl ne faut pas que cela vous embarasse d'autant que toutes mes Pieces ne sont pas fixées aux Jeux qui sont marquez.	*I have greatly varied the [choice of] stops and manuals, but this should not be a problem for you because in none of my pieces are the indicated registrations binding.*
Ainsi ce qui se joüe a une Basse de Trompette peut se toucher sur vn Cromorne ou Clairon ou le jeu de Tierce, ce qui se joüe en recit de Cornet se peut toucher sur la Tierce. le Recit	*What is played as Basse de Trompette can be played with a Cromorne or Clairon or Jeu de Tierce; what is played as Récit de Cornet can be played with a [Jeu de] Tierce; the Récit de*

de Cromorne peut aussi se toucher sur une voix humaine, ou la Trompette sans fond ainsi du reste selon la disposition de l'Orgue.	Cromorne can also be played with a Voix humaine, or with the Trompette without adding flue stops; and so on, according to the organ specification.
Les Claviers se pratiquent de mème. Ce qui se touche au grand Clavier se peut toucher sur le petit excepté qu'il le faut toucher plus gayement. Ainsi du petit au grand ou il faut observer le contraire. Le Recit de Cromorne avec le Cornet Separé, ou l'Eco se peut toucher seul sur un mème Clavier.[112]	The use of the manuals is similar. What is played on the grand Clavier can also be played on the petit [Clavier] except that it should be played more lightly. And passing from the petit to the grand [orgue], the contrary applies. The Récit de Cromorne with the Cornet Separé, or the Eco can be played on a single manual.

One point in common shared by all authors of the period is that the registrations, however differentiated, were based almost exclusively on *mélanges* (combinations) of two or more stops; the use of a single stop is to be considered an exception.

When consulting the sources, one should be aware of some conventions. In writings of the period, when an author spoke of *Huit pieds ouvert*, he referred to the *Montre* (or *Prestant*); whereas a *Huit pieds ouvert* on the pedal called for the *Flûte* (in its construction, a *grosse flûte*).

In the older texts – particularly in the pre-classical period – the nomenclature used to describe the pitch of stopped-pipes referred to the pipe length but not the actual pitch it produced: thus, when Mersenne speaks of *Bourdon quattre pieds* he meant a *Bourdon 8*, whose longest pipe length was, in fact, 4 feet. The term *Petit Bourdon* refers to the *Bourdon 8* on the *Grand Orgue*, as opposed to the *Grand Bourdon 16'*.

The term *Grosse tierce* is sometimes misleading. In the instruments of the pre-classical period two *Tierces* of $1^{3/5}$ could be found on the *Grand Orgue*: one narrow-scaled and the other wide-scaled, the latter often called *Grosse tierce*. Furthermore, the term *Grosse tierce* (or *Gros Jeu de Tierce*) sometimes simply identified the *Jeu de Tierce* of the *Grand Orgue* in contrast to the *Jeu de Tierce du Positif*.

The *Tierce* of $3^{1/5}$ makes its appearance in the second half of the 17th century: it was included by Étienne Énocq in the organ of the *Jacobins* in 1660 (where d'Anglebert became organist) and by Pierre Cauchois in the new organ of Bourges Cathedral in 1663. It was often called *Double Tierce*, but was sometimes also referred to as *Grosse tierce*.

One can usually infer from the context and a careful reading of the text whether by the term *Grosse tierce* the author was referring to the $1^{3/5}$ or the *Tierce* $3^{1/5}$. It should be pointed out that there were relatively few instruments with a *Tierce* $3^{1/5}$.

ADAPTATION FOR *PETITS ORGUES*

Although the ideal of the Parisian organ was an instrument possessing four manuals plus pedal, and three-manual organs were, likewise, quite common, in the provinces, convents and smaller churches the reality was that it was common to find instruments with just one or two keyboards. For this reason, several prefaces to *livres d'orgue* provide advice on how to adapt compositions to smaller organs, including this text by Gigault (1685):

[…] les pieces marquez à deux, trois, et quatre chœurs pouront estre touchez sur un, ou sur deux claviers, les notes pour un Escho marquez pour le premier clavier pouront estre repetez sur les autres, […].[113]

[...] the pieces indicated for two, three and four keyboards [chœurs] can be played on one or two manuals, the notes for an echo marked for the first manual can be repeated on the others, [...].

Or Jacques Boyvin (1690):

Ceux qui n'ont que deux Claviers ne laisseront pas que de se servir fort bien des Dialogues de Recits, quoy qu'ils se touchent ordinairement sur trois Claviers ils prendront au Grand Corps l'accompagnement sur le fond ordinaire & toucheront tout de suitte sans changer de Clavier sur le Cromhorne ou sur la petite tierce, & quand au trio ou les deux parties se joignent cela se touche sur le même jeu & la basse avec la tyrasse ou la pedalle de flûte.

Those who have only two keyboards can very well perform Dialogues de Recits, which are usually performed on three manuals, by playing on the Grand Corps the accompaniment with the usual fonds and playing [the solo] without changing the manual on either the Cromhorne or petite tierce; and when in the trio the two parts combine, one can play them on the same stop, and play the bass with the tyrasse or the flûte on the pedal.

Ceux qui n'ont qu'un Orgue a un Clavier feront de même parceque les jeux de mutations, comme la tierce, le nazard, les jeux d'hanches comme la trompette la voix humaine, & autres y sont coupez. Ils se serviront aussi sur un seul Clavier de toutes sortes de Dialogues […].[114]

Those who only have a single manual organ will do the same, because the mutation stops such as the tierce and nazard, and reeds like the trompette, voix humaine and others, are divided [between bass and treble]. Hence, they will be able to use just one manual for all types of Dialogues [...].

In reference to the *Quatuor*, Jullien (1690) wrote:

On sait asséz qu'on peut encores joüer le quatuor En bien d'autres manieres Sur les grands et petits Orgues; mais, comme les jeux ne sont pas toujours d'une Egale bonté, ce la fait que Messieurs les organistes y adjoustent on diminuent Comme bon leur semble.[115]

It is well known that one can play the quatuor in many different ways, on large and small organs; but, as the stops are not always of the same quality, it is necessary that Messieurs the organists add or subtract [stops] as they like.

Raison had a special word of advice for organists who were not especially adept at pedal playing (a common occurrence in the provinces, where organs often had no pedal department) suggesting that the pedal part could be played by a second person on the *Grand Orgue* (in the citation below with a *Jeu doux*):

Le Trio à 3 Claviers, et le Cromorne ou Tierce en Taille se peuvent exercer avec un amy qui toucheroit le jeu doux de la main droite au grand Orgue a la place de la pedalle de flutte, laquelle je n'ay gueres chargé pour faciliter les Pieces le plus qu'il m'a esté possible.[116]	The Trio à 3 Claviers and the Cromorne or Tierce en Taille can be practised with a friend who plays the jeu doux of the right hand on the grand Orgue instead of (the organist playing) the pedal flute, which I scarcely require in order to make the pieces as easy as I could.

ANCHES, CORNETS, JEUX DE TIERCE

Reeds, cornets and *Jeux de tierce* are undoubtedly the sounds that most characterise the French baroque organ and also those which were used most frequently in the various organ works. Reed stops were almost always used together with some *Fonds*, typically *Bourdon 8* or *Bourdon 8* and *Prestant 4*. Nivers, as well as later authors, pointed out that the reeds were not to be used alone, except for the *Cromorne*:

Avec les Jeux d'hanches on ne met ordinairement que le Bourdon: mesme le Cromhorne se peut bien joüer seul: neantmoins avec la Trompette on met le Bourdon et le Prestant, et le Clairon si l'on veut, quelque fois aussy le Cornet.[117]	With the reed stops, usually only the Bourdon is used, although the Cromhorne can be played well by itself; nevertheless, with the Trompette, one adds the Bourdon and the Prestant, and if desired the Clairon as well; sometimes also the Cornet.

Reeds played a fundamental role, both in the different types of *Récit* (*de dessus, de basse, en taille*) as well as in *Fugues*, and especially in the *Grands jeux*. The diverse *mélanges* of reed stops were used with great frequency. The pedal reeds, in particular, needed to be clearly distinct within the whole *Plein jeu*, as the organ builder Jean de Joyeuse recalled in the contract for the enlargement of the organ in Béziers in 1679:

Plus sera fait à neuf un jeu de pédalle de trompette sonnant huict pieds, les corps d'estin de grosse taille […] ce jeu servant beaucoup pour fortifier de beaucoup les plains jeux et pour battre un plain chant en basses, un plain chant en taille, et pour battre les responds.[118]	In addition, a new trompette stop will be built in the pedal, an eight foot stop with the body of tin and of wide scale […] this stop will greatly help to strengthen the plains jeux and also to play a plainchant in the bass, a plainchant in the tenor, and for playing the responses.

Referring to the reconstruction of the organ of Perpignan Cathedral in 1688, the same organ builder, de Joyeuse, stated:

Plus sera fait un jeu de pedalle de trompette de grosse taille [...] le dit jeu sera fort eclatant pour estre entendu distinctement lorsqu'on joüera les plain jeux, quand mesme les deux claviers seront tirés l'un sur l'autre [...].[119]	*Furthermore, a wide-scale trompette will be built for the pedal [...] this stop will be very sonorous [eclatant] in order to be heard distinctly when one plays the plein jeux, even when the two manuals are coupled [...].*

The various *Tierce*-registrations were also very popular in France. The differences between the diverse *Cornets* and the *Jeux de Tierce* should be pointed out here.

The *Cornet* is a wide-scale 5-rank stop, with sounding pitches of 8 (stopped or chimney flute), 4, $2^{2/3}$, 2, and $1^{3/5}$, that has well-defined roles according to the manual on which it is situated. Its compass is limited to the dessus, usually c'-c'''. The *Cornet* of the *Grand Orgue* is placed on its own raised chest (with respect to the main chest) – hence the name *Cornet separé* (mounted cornet) – and is characterized by its very strong and penetrating voicing; its function is to balance the reeds in the *Grand jeu*, which are notoriously weak in the treble. The *Cornet* of the 3rd manual (*Récit*) is the typical *solo-Cornet* used in the *Récits de dessus* and, depending on the composer, in *Duos, Trios, Quatuors, Fugues à 5* and *Dialogues sur le Grands Jeux* as well. The indication *Cornet separé* often found in the course of such pieces refers to the *Cornet* of the *Récit*. It is placed behind the case pipes in an elevated position so that its sound is very prominent. The *Cornet* placed on the 4th manual (*Écho*), as the term itself clearly states, has only an echo function; it is used in the *Dialogues en Echo* and in the *(Grands) Dialogues sur les Grands jeux*.

The *Jeu de Tierce* can be formed both on the *Grand Orgue* and on the *Positif* and embraces the entire manual compass. It is composed of *Bourdon 8, Prestant/Montre 4, Nasard* and *Tierce*. Some authors prescribe the *Quarte de Nazard* as well or sometimes the *Doublette*. It is the *mélange* normally used for *Duos, Trios* and sometimes *Fugues* and *Quatuors*. Nivers' words on the subject:

Le Jeu de Tierce, que l'on appelle aussy le gros Jeu de diminutions, se compose du Prestant du Bourdon de la Tierce et de la Quinte: on y adioute la Doublette quand on veut, et le huitpied aussy, mesme le seizepied s'il y en a.[120]	*The Jeu de Tierce, also called gros Jeu de diminutions, consists of the Prestant, Bourdon, Tierce and Quinte: adding the Doublette, if one wants, and also the eight-foot [Montre], or even the sixteen-foot, if there is one.*

Probably the request for a 16' in the text of Nivers refers to the *Duos* and the *Basses de Tierce* (*Jeu de diminutions*) where a registration on 16' basis is (or could be) intended for the left hand.

"Harsh" registrations for the low range of the organ (*basse*), composed of quint and tierce mutation stops, were very popular in France. These are the registrations normally prescribed for the left hand of *Duos* and *Trios* but also for some *Fugues* by Louis Couperin, as in the following example:

Louis Couperin: *Fugue qu'il fault jouer d'un mouvement fort lent sur la tierce du Grand Clavier avec le tremblant lent*

This type of sonority was prevalent for a long time. It was still recommended in the second half of the 18th century by Dom Bédos, who prescribed it in eight of his registrations for the *Trio à trois Claviers*:

[...] la basse sur les fonds de la Pédale, ou encore mieux sur le Jeu de Tierce, s'il y en a à la Pédale.[121]	[...] the bass voice on the fonds of the pedal, or even better on the Jeu de Tierce, if there is one on the pedal.

In this regard, mention should also be made of the pedal specification of the organ built by Jean-François Lépine in 1752 in Sarlat, in which the usual *Flûtes 8 et 4*, *Trompette* and *Clairon* are flanked by the decidedly less common pedal stops *Nasard* 2 2/3, *Quarte* 2 and *Tierce* 1 3/5.

LITURGICAL CYCLES AND REGISTRATIONS

The "timbrale structure" of the various organ cycles (i.e. registration of the individual *couplets* that form a a liturgical cycle) was not strictly standardized. Nonetheless, there are some common traits in the cycles of different composers:

- ❖ the first verset is always a *Plein jeu*, sometimes with sections in *Petit plein jeu*
- ❖ the second verset of *Kyrie* and *Gloria* is often a *Fugue*, while, in the *Magnificats* it is more often a *Duo*
- ❖ the last verset of *Kyrie, Gloria* and *Magnificat* is usually a *Grand jeu* but it can often also be a *Plein jeu* or *Petit plein jeu*
- ❖ the Deo gratias is almost invariably a *Plein Jeu* or *Petit plein jeu*

The practice that the *Grand jeu* closes a liturgical cycle is confirmed by numerous authors, amongst them Raison, François Couperin and de Grigny. Nevertheless, the number of cycles ending with a *Plein jeu* is not negligible. According to Nicole Gravet this practice is alluded to in the *Règlement* written for the church of Troyes (probably the *Cathédrale Saint-Pierre et Saint-Paul*) in 1630, in which it was prescribed that the first and last verset of *Kyrie* be played with the *Plein jeu*.[122] In fact, the last versets of the *Kyrie* of Couperin's *Messe pour les Paroisses* and of Lebègue's Mass (*2ᵈ Livre*) as well as of the Gigault's three *Kyries* all call for a *Plein jeu*. The nine *Magnificats* by Lebègue and the four by Guilain conclude with a *Plein jeu* and a *Petit plein jeu* respectively.

In addition, several organ *Suites* end with a *Plein jeu*: numerous examples may be found in the *Livres d'Orgue* of Nivers, Lebègue, Boyvin and Jullien. The eight *Suites* by Chaumont conclude the "organ section" with a *Plein jeu*, after which there are one or two harpsichord-like pieces (*Allemande, Gigue* or *Chaconne*) which conclude the *Suite*. It should be noted that in most of the cycles of Nivers (1665) and Lebègue (1676) – as well as in the four *Magnificats* by Guilain – a *Grand jeu* is used as the penultimate verset and a *Plein jeu* (or *Petit plein jeu*) as the last one. Most of the *Magnificats* (manuscripts) contained in the *Livre d'Orgue de Montréal* also consist of seven versets and end with a *Dialogue* or with the pairing *Dialogue/Plein jeu*.[123]

In relation to the choices of registration for the *Magnificat*, it should be mentioned that the 6th verset *Gloria Patri* (which is also the last verset in the case of Corrette and Dandrieu) is a *Grand jeu*, while the 7th verset (reiteration of the antiphon), when present, is a *Plein jeu* or *Petit plein jeu*.

For the remaining versets there are no fixed criteria, although each composer had his own preferences: the 2nd verset (*Quia respexit*) was often a *Duo* while the 4th verset (*Deposuit potentes*) was often a *Basse de Trompette*.

In the chapter *De Organista & Organis*, the *Cæremoniale Parisiense* prescribes in which moments

[...] *pulsanda sunt Organa ad modulos, graviter, suaviter, dulciter & modulate.*[124]	[...] the organ should be played in a grave, soft, gentle and melodic/harmonious way.

Here the precise moments of the mass are listed (such as the versets *Suscipe deprecationem nostram* and *Tu solus altissimus* from the *Gloria*) and it is stated that the main hours of the office that should be played "with particular devotion". It can easily be inferred that, in such cases, the registration would be in accord with the prescriptions provided by the same *Cæremoniale*, in order to give the verset in question the requisite character.

The following table provides a summary of the registrations concerning the main *Magnificat* collections published between 1678 (Lebègue) and 1750 (Michel Corrette):

Lebègue 1678

	1st verset	2nd verset	3rd verset	4th verset	5th verset	6th verset	7th verset
1r ton	prélude	duo	réc. crom.	basse tromp.	trio	dialogue	plein jeu
4e ton	prélude	duo	trio	cornet	basse tromp.	dialogue	plein jeu
6e ton	prélude	duo	récit	trio	dessus tierce	dialogue	prélude
6e trasp.	prélude	duo	cornet	basse tromp.	récit crom.	dialogue	plein jeu
7e ton	prélude	dessus tromp.	trio	duo	cornet	dialogue	plein jeu
8e ton	prélude	duo	basse tromp.	récit crom.	cornet	dialogue	plein jeu

Guilain 1706

	1st verset	2nd verset	3rd verset	4th verset	5th verset	6th verset	7th verset
1r ton	plein jeu	trio	duo	basse tromp.	récit	dialogue	petit p.j.
2e ton	prélude	tierce taille	duo	basse tromp.	trio de flûtes	dialogue	petit p.j.
3e ton	plein jeu	quatuor	dialogue v.h.	basse tromp.	duo	grand jeu	petit p.j.
4e ton	prélude	crom. taille	duo	basse tromp.	trio	dialogue	petit p.j.

M. Corrette 1737

	1st verset	2nd verset	3rd verset	4th verset	5th verset	6th verset	7th verset
1r ton	plein jeu	duo	tierce taille	basse de crom.	trio	grand jeu	
2e ton	plein jeu	duo	trio	basse tromp.	musettes	grand jeu	
3e et 4e	plein jeu	récit nazard	duo	flûtes	crom. taille	fuga doppia	
8e ton	plein jeu	duo	trio	basse tromp.	musettes	grand jeu	

Dandrieu 1739

	1st verset	2nd verset	3rd verset	4th verset	5th verset	6th verset	7th verset
1r ton	plein jeu	duo	trio	basse tromp.	flûtes	dialogue	
2e ton	plein jeu	duo	trio	bas/des. trom.	flûtes	dialogue	
3e ton	plein jeu	duo	trio	basse crom.	récit nazard	dialogue	
4e ton	plein jeu	duo	trio	basse tromp.	flûtes	dialogue	
5e ton	plein jeu	duo	trio	bas/des. trom.	récit	dialogue	
6e ton	plein jeu	duo	trio	bas/des. trom.	flûtes	dialogue	

M. Corrette 1750

	1st verset	2nd verset	3rd verset	4th verset	5th verset	6th verset	7th verset
5e ton	plein jeu	duo	basse tromp.	musette	tambourin	grand jeu	
6e ton	plein jeu	duo	basse tromp.	récit de tierce	trio	g.j. / fuga	
7e ton	plein jeu	duo	basse tromp.	trio	flûtes	grand jeu	
8e ton	plein jeu	duo	tierce taille	récit de trom.	musette	g.j. / fuga	

In addition to these, there are three further *Magnificats* of the 2.*e*, 3.*e* and 5.*e ton* by Lebègue, each consisting of eight versets:

	1st v.	2nd v.	3rd v.	4th v.	5th v.	6th v.	7th v.	8th v.
2e ton	prélude	duo	basse tromp.	récit	trio	cornet	dialogue	plein jeu
3e ton	prélude	fugue	duo	trio	dial. v.h.	récit	dialogue	plein jeu
5e ton	prélude	récit	cornet	duo	basse tromp.	trio	dialogue	plein jeu

[108] Lebègue 1676, 14.
[109] Boyven 1690, 55.
[110] Saint-Arroman 1994, 7.
[111] Nivers 1665, 177.
[112] Raison 1688, 31.
[113] Gigault 1685, 26.
[114] Boyvin 1690, 55-56.
[115] Jullien 1690, 51.
[116] Raison 1688, 31.
[117] Nivers 1665, 177.
[118] Douglass 1995, 100.
[119] Douglass 1995, 103.
[120] Nivers 1665, 177.
[121] Dom Bédos 1766-1778, 205.
[122] Gravet 1996, 16.
[123] Gallat-Morin 1988, 99 and 321-327.
[124] Sonnet 1662, 172.

THE *DIALOGUE*

THE CONCEPT OF *DIALOGUE*

The *Dialogue* is widely used in the French repertoire of the period. The form of *Dialogue* most often encountered is that which uses the same registrations between *Grand Orgue* and *Positif*. The most common of them are the dialogue between (*Grand*) *Plein jeu* and *Petit plein jeu*, and the *Dialogue sur le Grands jeux*. These are discussed in the chapters *"Plein jeu"* (p. 108) and *"Grand jeu"* (p. 122). Less common types of dialogue are *Flûtes* (Guilain) or *Dialogues de Flûtes* (de Grigny). In addition to the juxtaposition of sounds between *Grand Orgue* and *Positif* there are other models of *Dialogue* as illustrated below.

DIALOGUE BETWEEN TWO SOPRANO VOICES

An extension of the *Récit*-form is the *Dialogue de Récit*. In this case the *dessus* line is divided between two keyboards (typically *Positif* and *Récit*) in order to make two contrasting sounds "converse". The structure of these pieces is usually as follows:

- short opening on the *Jeux doux* of the *Grand Orgue*
- *dessus*-dialogue between *Positif* and *Récit* (right hand) with accompaniment on the *Grand Orgue* (left hand)
- continuation of the two solos on *Positif* and *Récit* (with both hands) while the pedal performs the bass line, like a *Trio à trois claviers*

This type is found in the works of various composers. Here is an example from the hymn *Verbum supernum* (*3ᵉ couplet*) of de Grigny:

Nicolas de Grigny: *Récit en Dialogue* (*Verbum supernum*)

Boyvin writes in the preface to his *Premier Livre d'Orgue*:

On a aussi decouvert des meslanges depuis peu qui parroissent fort beaux & les quels jusqu'icy n'avoient pas esté en usage.[125]	There have also recently been discovered combinations of stops that seem very beautiful and have never been used before.

One of these new registrations might well be the use of the rather uncommon *petite Trompette* of the *Récit*, a stop to be found in the organ of the Cathedral of Rouen where Boyvin was organist from 1674. The *Dialogue de récits de cromhorne et de cornet, ou bien de petite Trompette, et de petite tierce* by Boyvin allows the possibility of two different registrations: the first, and more traditional, implies the use of the *Cromhorne* in the *Positif* in dialogue with the *Cornet* of the *Récit*; the second, by contrast, utilizes the *petite Trompette* on the *Récit* against the *petite Tierce* in the *Positif*:

Jacques Boyvin: *Dialogue de recits […]* (*Second ton, Premier Livre d'Orgue*)

The use of the *Trompette de Récit* is also indicated in one of Boyvin's *Quatuor* registrations.

Closely related to the *Récit en Dialogue* is the *Récit en Écho*. Here the dialogue takes place between a solo voice usually played on the *Récit* and its *Écho* on the 4th manual.

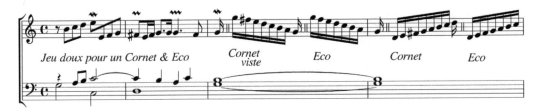

André Raison: *Cornet & Eco* (Gloria, *Messe du Huictiesme ton*)

Nicolas Lebègue (1676) provides registrations as well as performance suggestions in relation to this:

L'Echo hardiment & vistement, L'Accompagnement sur le Bourdon & la Montre du Positif. Le Cornet, le petit Bourdon, & le Prestant à la Grand' Orgue, ou le Cornet seul s'il est assez fort: Les repetitions sur le Cornet d'Echo,	The Echo boldly and quickly: the accompaniment on the Bourdon and Montre [4'] of the Positif. The Cornet, the petit Bourdon [8'], and the Prestant of the Grand Orgue or the Cornet only [= Récit?] if it is strong enough; the echoes on the Cornet d'Echo,
ou bien l'Accompagnement sur le Huit pieds seul de la grand'Orgue. La Seconde repetition sur la Fluste seule du Positif.[126]	or else the accompaniment on the eight-foot stop alone of the Grand Orgue and the second repetition [echo] on the flute alone [i.e. 4'] of the Positif.

Such *Récits en Écho* were cultivated by the French organists in a rather marginal way. The use of the *Écho* occurs rather more often in the *Grands Dialogues sur les Grands jeux* where a short musical motif is usually presented in succession on three different keyboards, typically *Positif-Récit-Écho*.

DIALOGUE BETWEEN BASS AND SOPRANO VOICES

A further form of *Dialogue* is represented by those pieces where the dialogue takes place on the same stop but in different tessituras of the manual, most commonly between soprano and bass. The *Dialogues de Voix humaine* are constructed after this model, and usually conclude with all voices played on the *Voix humaine*. Here is an example taken from Jacques Boyvin's *Premier Livre d'Orgue*:

Jacques Boyvin: *Dialogue de Voix Humaine* (Second ton, *Premier Livre d'Orgue*)

The *Dialogues de Voix humaine* are to be performed slowly. Here is an explicit example from the *Benedictus de 1er Ton* by Raison:

André Raison: *Benedictus* (*Messe du Premier ton*)

Regardless of the type of *Dialogue*, the *Voix humaine* (as a stop) is always played at a slow pace, as stated by Nivers in his *Livre d'Orgue* of 1665:

Le Mouvem.ᵗ des [...] Basses et Recitz de Voix humaine [...] est fort lent.[127]	The movement of [...] Basses and Récits de Voix humaine [...] is very slow.

The *Dialogues* between *Basse et Dessus de Trompette* are structured in a similar way, although they require a well-differentiated performance. The following *Kyrie*-verset of Raison – in fact a sort of fusion between *Basse de Trompette* and *Dialogue* – can be considered as being among the first examples of this form:

André Raison: *Second Kyrie (Messe du Sixiemse ton)*

A well-known example of *Dialogue* between *basse et dessus* is the 4ᵗʰ *Couplet* from the *Gloria* of the *Messe pour les Paroisses* by François Couperin. The required registration for the *solo* is not far from a *Grand Jeu*: *Dialogue sur les Trompettes, Clairon et Tierces du G.C. [Grand Clavier] et le Bourdon avec le Larigot du Positif.* While the beginning and the end of this piece are constructed in the manner of a *Basse de Trompette*, the middle section (bars 29-72) resembles a *Dialogue*:

François Couperin: *Dialogue - 4ᵉ couplet du Gloria* (*Messe pour les Paroisses*)

It should be noted that the combination *Bourdon 8 et Larigot* is one of the few *mélanges creux* ("gap registrations") that have survived from the Renaissance and the pre-classical period. Along with Michel Corrette and François Couperin, Dandrieu and Nivers explicitly prescribe it:

Avec le flageollet ou Larigot on ne met que le Bourdon.[128]	With the flageollet or the Larigot one should use only the Bourdon.

A few decades later, Dom Bédos suggested a similar registration for a *Basse de Trompette*, relating it to the concept of *Dialogue de basse & dessus*:

Pour toucher une Basse de Trompette. On mettra au grand Orgue le Prestant, les Trompettes & les Clairons, s'il y en a plusieurs; & au Positif, les deux 8 pieds, la Doublette & le Larigot. Si l'on veut faire un dialogue de dessus & de basse, on se servira du Cornet de Récit pour les dessus.[129]	To play a Basse de Trompette. One should draw the Prestant, and the Trompettes and Clairons on the Grand Orgue, if there are more than one; on the Positif the two 8 foot stops, the Doublette and Larigot. If one wants to play a Dialogue between soprano and bass, one should use the Cornet de Récit for the treble.

A brilliant registration of *Basse et Dessus de Trompette* is also found in the *Manuscrit de Bourges*, written around late 17th/early 18th century:

Petit bourdon, nazard et quart de nazard, doublet, doublet-tierce (*), tierce, flageollet, trompette, tremblant à vent perdu. Au positif bourdon, nazard, larigot. Il faut commencer une fugue preste et droite sur le positif, puis quand la quatrième partie est entrée, il fault entrer sur les jeux de la grande orgue de la basse et puis du dessus alternativement, faire des imitations du dessus à la basse, des conflicts des deux mains sur les dicts jeux d'en hault; cela est assez plaisant.[130]	Petit bourdon [8'], Nazard, Quart de Nazard, Doublet, Doublet-Tierce (*), Tierce, Flageolet, Trompette, Tremblant à vent perdu. On the Positif: Bourdon, Nazard, Larigot. One should start a fugue "fast and brightly" on the Positif, and after the entry of the fourth voice one should pass to the Grand Orgue with the bass [voice], and then, alternating with the soprano voice, create imitations between soprano and bass, "duels" between the two hands on the aforesaid stops of the Grand Orgue; this is very pleasant.

(*) this could be an erroneous repetition of text

The *Dialogue* between *Basse et Dessus* can also take place with two different registrations. In this case, the most recurrent constellation is *Trompette* vs. *Cornet*, as in the following example by Jullien, in 6/8 (although noted as 8/6 in the score) and characterized by a very rapid dialogue:

Gilles Jullien: *Basse de trompette* (4ᵉ *Ton, Premier livre d'orgue*)

DIALOGUE BETWEEN TENOR AND SOPRANO VOICES

Less common is the *Dialogue* between tenor and soprano voices. An interesting example of this genre is the following piece taken from the *Suite du 6ᵐᵉ ton* by Boyvin which begins as a *Cromhorne en taille*, then proceeds with an alternating section of *Récit de dessus* and *Récit en taille*

and finishes as a *Trio à 3 Claviers:*

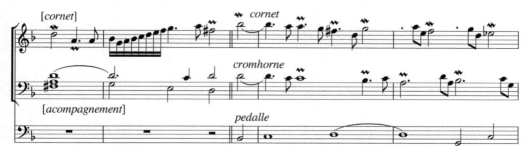

J. Boyvin: *Dialogue de cromhorne en taille et de cornet separé, ou sur tout le chromhorne* (6me ton, Premier livre d'Orgue)

A further development of the principle of *Dialogue* between tenor and soprano is found in de Grigny's *Dialogue à 2 Tailles de Cromorne et 2 dessus de Cornet pour la Communion,* in which the author envisages two voices for each of the dialogue sections. The requisite registration is the same as that used by de Grigny in his *Fugues à 5,* i.e. *Cornet separé* for the right hand (*Récit*), *Cromorne* for the left (*Positif*) and *Flûte* in the pedal:

N. de Grigny: *Dialogue à 2 Tailles de Cromorne et 2 dessus de Cornet pour la Communion* (*Livre d'Orgue*)

---

[125] Boyvin 1690, 55.
[126] Lebègue 1676, 14.
[127] Nivers 1665, 177.
[128] Nivers 1665, 177.
[129] Dom Bédos 1766-1778, 206.
[130] Manuscrit de Bourges, 88.

PRE-CLASSICAL REGISTRATIONS

BRIEF OVERVIEW

The birth of the French baroque organ school (*école française classique*) is conventionally dated to 1665, the year of publication the *Livre d'Orgue Contenant Cent Pieces de tous les Tons de l'Eglise* by Guillaume-Gabriel Nivers. From this date onwards, the *livres d'orgue* and their information on registrations became increasingly numerous, but, above all, a stylistic identity and coherence were formed, which would last for over a century.

The registrations discussed in this chapter, however, go back to the first half of the 17th century and pertain to composers defined today as pre-classical and whose manuscripts or published works are dated before 1665. Among them are Charles Guillet, Jehan Titelouze, Charles Racquet, François Roberday and Louis Couperin.

The "standardization" of registrations, a peculiarity of the French baroque, had not yet been implemented. Inventiveness and personal taste characterize the timbral preferences, leaving the choice of registration

[...] a la fantaisie de l'organiste comme il trouvera bon	*[...] up to the organist's imagination and what he finds most appropriate*

as noted by the anonymous writer of the registration table of Nancy (see page 100).

In this chapter, the following writings are taken into account: the registration table of Saint-Valéry-sur-Somme (1602), the registration table of Nancy (c. 1622) and two *Propositions* from the treatise *Harmonie Universelle* by Marin Mersenne (1636).

REGISTRATION TABLE OF SAINT–VALÉRY-SUR-SOMME

In 1602 Isaac Huguet renovated and enlarged the organ of *St. Martin* in Saint-Valéry-sur-Somme (Hauts de France). It was a 6' organ (no longer extant), with a single keyboard and stops divided between *basse* and *dessus*.

Together with the instrument's reconstruction contract, a registration table is also preserved.[131] The precise specification is not reported in the document, but can be deduced – with careful approximation – from the registration table. A possible specification might be as follows:

	left column		right column
I	.......?.......	VII	*grosse flustes*
II	*trois pieds*	VIII	*trois pieds*
III	*grosse flustes*	IX	*nasard*
IIII	*nasard*	X	*cornet a boucquin*
V	*ung pied et demy*	XI	*ung pied et demy*
VI	*cimballe*	XII	*cimballe*

In light of the lack of information, some comments are necessary. Stop I was not mentioned in the registration table and could perhaps have been an accessory (*Tramblant, Rossignol, Tambour*) or a pedal stop. In the case of stop III (*Grosse flustes*), it cannot be ruled out that it was a stop for the whole manual (i.e. not divided). In this case, stop number VII could possibly have been a *Montre*. Finally, it cannot be ruled out that the two *cimballes* (VI and XII) were actually two whole stops (like *Fourniture* and *Cimbale*).

As we are dealing with a 6' organ (the keyboard beginning from F), it is important that the given pitches (in feet) are correctly interpreted:

- ❖ the 6' *grosse flustes* [*Flûte*] corresponds to an 8' (on a C compass organ)
- ❖ the *trois pieds* corresponds to the *Prestant*, i.e. to a 4' (as above)
- ❖ the *ung pied et demy* corresponds to a *Doublette*, i.e. to a 2' (as above)
- ❖ it is not specified whether the *nasard* is 2' or 1', i.e. $2^{2/3}$ or $1^{1/3}$ (as above)

Ce sont les jeux pour faire sonner les orgues

				Equivalent registrations in reference to an organ in C (8′)
III	*Grosse flustes avecq tramblant*	VII	⇨	8′ + Tremblant
II	*Trois piedz*	VIII	⇨	4′
II III IIII	*Gros nazard*	VII VIII IX	⇨	8′ 4′ Nazard
III	*Grosse Cimballe avecq le tramblant*	VII XII	⇨	8′ Cimbale sop. + Tremblant
II III	*Aultre jeu*	VII VIII	⇨	8′ 4′
IIII	*Fluste d'allemant avecq le tramblant*	IX	⇨	Nazard solo + Tremblant
III	*Fluste avecq le tabourin et le rossignol*	VII	⇨	8′ + Drum + *rossignol*
II III	*Petit nazard*	VIII IX	⇨	8′ 4′ Nazard treble (*)
III V	*Aultre bon jeu avecq le tramblant*	VII XI	⇨	8′ 2′ + Tremblant
II III	*Grosse fluste et cornet*	VII VIII X	⇨	8′ 4′ Cornet treble
III	*Larigot*	IX	⇨	8′ Nazard treble (*)
II VI	*Petite cimballe avec le tramblant*	VIII	⇨	4′ Cimbale + Tremblant (**)
II III V	*Aultre bon jeu*	VII VIII XI	⇨	8′ 4′ 2′
III	*Fifre et Tambour*	XI	⇨	8′ + 2′ sopr. [*piffero*] + *Tambour*
II V	*Voix enfances avecq le tramblant*	VIII XI	⇨	4′ 2′ Tremblant
III VI	*Moienne Cimballe avecq le Tambour*	VII	⇨	8′ Cimbale + *Tambour* (**)
III VI	*Grosse flustes et petites flustes*	VIII XI	⇨	? (***)
II III IIII V	*Cornet avecq pedalles et tramblant*	VII VIII X XII	⇨	? (***)
II III V VI	*Plain jeu*	VII VIII XI XII	⇨	8′ 4′ 2′ Cimbale

(*) here stop VII is probably missing, or the *grosse flustes* (III) is to be understood as a stop for the whole manual

(**) here stop XII is probably missing, or the *cimballe* (VI) is to be understood as a stop for the whole manual

(***) the two registrations here are probably incorrect

REGISTRATION TABLE OF NANCY

This is an undated document, probably written on the occasion of, or after the rebuilding of the organ of *Saint-Epvre* in Nancy, undertaken by the organ builder Nicolas Hocquet in 1622.

Although a second manual was added as part of this work, the specification highlights the single-manual origin of the instrument: on the *Grand Orgue* there are essentially only stops which make up the *Plein jeu*, while flutes and reeds are found on the *Positif*.

The document lists first the specification and then the registration table:[132]

Premierement	*Pour le Positif*
1 La Monstre de huict pieds	Bourdon de 4 pieds [respondant à 8]
2 Le Bourdon de 4 pieds respondant ausd. 8 pieds	Fluttes de 2 pieds respondant a 4
3 L'octave de 4 pieds	Un sifflet respondant a 2 pieds
4 Doublette (ou superoctave) de deux pieds	Un jeu de nazard
5 Un Cesquialtera a deux tuyaux par marche le plus gros a trois pieds et l'autre deux [pieds,] le reste tout en diminuant	Trompettes de 8 pieds et clairons de 4 pieds
6 Une fourniture a 4 tyaux par marche,	*Le cornet qui est en façon de positif qui est celuy qui fait face embas Il y a six tuyaux par marche le tout faisant 144 tuyaux*
7 Une Cymbale a 3 thuyaux et à 4.	

Concerning stop number 5, we cannot be sure whether the writer of the table really intended the given pitches ($2^{2/3'}$ and 2') rather than a classic Sesqualtera ($2^{2/3'}$ and $1^{3/5'}$).

Regarding the information on the 6-rank *Cornet* placed below the *Positif* stops, it should be added that in the contract for the extension of the organ – dated March 21, 1622 – one can read: *ung cornet lequel saplicquera apres la chere de l'orgue en forme de positif*. According to the registration table, this stop seems to relate to the *Grand Orgue* (registration No. 12, see below) and not to the *Positif*.

It should also be noted that the writer of the document, perhaps the organ builder himself, in listing the stopped registers, indicated – as was the custom in the period – the real length of the pipe and not the sound produced; this means that the *Bourdons de 4 pieds* of the *Grand Orgue* and *Positif* are to be understood as 8' stops while the *Fluttes de 2 pieds* on the *Positif* is actually a 4'.

Below is the registration table:

La manière ou Méthode pour jouer lesdits jeux

schematic translation:

Premierement La Monstre de 8 pieds, le bourdon de 4 pieds, respondant a 8 pieds, L'octave de 4 pieds, doublette de 2 pieds, Fourniture et Cymbale pour le plein-jeu

plein-jeu = M8' B8' 4' 2' Four. Cym.

   Et la trompette lorsque l'on voudra

plein-jeu + in case, also with Tromp. (?)

   De mesme que le Cesquialtera.

plein-jeu + Sesq.

2) La Monstre et le Bourdon seuls — M8' B8'

3) La Monstre et l'octave — M8' 4'

4) La Monstre, le bourdon et Cesquialtera — M8' B8' Sesq.

5) La Monstre, Bourdon, octave, Superoctave et Cesquialtera — M8' B8' 4' 2' Sesq.

6) Monstre toute seule — M8'

7) La Monstre et Doublette avec le Rossignol — M8' 2' + Rossignol

8) La monstre et Cesquialtera avec le Rossignol — M8' Sesq. + Rossignol

9) La Bourdon avec l'octave — B8' 4'

10) Bourdon et fourniture avec Cesquialtera — B8' Four. Sesq.

11) Monstre, Bourdon et Cymbal — M8' B8' Cym.

12) Monstre Bourdon, et Cornetz — M8' B8' Cornet

Pour le jeu du positif

1) Bourdons fluttes, sifflets et Nazard — B8' F4' F2' Naz. ($2^{2/3'}$ or $1^{1/3'}$?)

2) Bourdon et fluttes — B8' F4'

3) Bourdon nazard et fluttes — B8' F4' Naz.

4) Bourdons et siflets — B8' F2'

5) Bourdons fluttes et Trompettes — B8' F4' Tr8'

6) Bourdons fluttes et clairons — B8' F4' Cl4'

7) Bourdons et clairons — B8' Cl4'

8) Flutes et clairons — F4' Cl4'

Tous lesdits jeux du positif se pourront jouer séparément avec tous les autres jeuz cy devant, a la fantaisie de l'organiste comme il trouvera bon.

All the positif stops can be played separately with all the others indicated above, according to the organist's imagination and what he finds most appropriate.

Concerning the registration placed at the beginning, immediately after the *Plein jeu* description, it is very unlikely here that a *Plein jeu* together with a *Trompette* is intended. Nor was it a *Plein jeu* with *Trompette* on the pedal: the *Trompette* is placed on the *Positif*, and therefore not playable on the pedal since no *tirasse Positif* existed (and in the document there is no mention of a pedal in any case). On the contrary, it is possible to hypothesize that a type of *couplet* was intended here that requires the *Plein jeu* in the right hand and the *Trompette* in the left hand (in the organ in Nancy, the *Trompette* was on the *Positif*), as requested several times by Nivers in his *2. Livre d'Orgue*. Here is an example:

Guillaume-Gabriel Nivers: *L'Himne des Martyrs, Vierges, et non Vierges. Deus tuorum militum* (2. Livre d'Orgue)

THE *HARMONIE UNIVERSELLE* BY MARIN MERSENNE

In the sixth book of the *Harmonie Universelle*, Marin Mersenne examines the question of registration in two different chapters, namely in *Proposition III* and *Proposition XXXI*. Although Mersenne was not an organist and some of his registrations may sometimes appear extravagant or unclear, many of the *Ieux composez* treated in *Proposition III* – if one makes the necessary corrections – anticipate the registrations of the following decades.

In general, it may be said that Mersenne's registrations are transitional, but, at the same time, that they already reveal the aesthetic ideal of the French *orgue classique*. It is also important to note that Mersenne mentions Charles Racquet as a mentor for the registrations:

Mais parce que chaque jeu composé se varie en plusieurs manieres, j'ay mis les plus usitez vis à vis de chaque jeu composé [recte: jeu simple], suivant la maniere dont use Monsieur Raquette Organiste de nostre Dame de Paris, qui est l'un des plus habiles de France.[133]

But since each registration [jeu composé] can be varied in different ways, I have put the most commonly used ones next to each jeu composé [recte: jeu simple], following the mode used by Monsieur Raquette Organist of Notre Dame de Paris, who is the one of the most expert organists in France.

It is notable that, at the time Racquet played an organ in Notre-Dame which was a composite of various preceding historical periods, including an old *Blockwerk*, and had a somewhat unusual specification (see page 57), quite far away from the "standard instrument" described in *Harmonie Universelle*.

PROPOSITION III[134]

First, a description of the individual stops (*Ieux simples*) is given. Each stop is marked with a letter which is then used for the various *Ieux composez*:

Ieux simples.

A *Monstre de 16 pieds, d'estain fin.*
B *Bourdon de huict pieds bouché, ou de 16 pieds ouvert, de bois.*
C *Huit pieds ouvert moitié bois, moitié estain.*
D *Bourdon de 4 pieds bouché, de bois.*
E *Le Prestant ou le 4 pieds ouvert, d'estain.*
F *Doublette, les pieds de plomb, & le corps d'estain.*
G *Fourniture, de mesme matiere; elle recommence d'Octave en Octave, & a 5, 6, 7, 8, ou 9 tuyaux sur chaque marche, & est d'un pied ouvert.*
H *Cymbale, de mesme, & a 3 pouces d'estain.*
I *Flageollet d'un pied & demy.*
K *Tierce, de mesme.*
L *Nazart à cheminée, ou en fuseau.*
M *Fluste de deux pieds bouché d'estain à cheminée.*
N *Fluste douce, ou à neuf trous d'un pied.*
O *Flageollet d'un pied.*
P *Cornet à cinq tuyaux d'un pied.*
Q *Trompette d'estain de huit pieds.*
R *Cleron d'estain de quatre pieds.*
S *Voix humaine, d'estain.*
T *Cromorne d'estain, de quatre pieds.*
V *Pedale d'anche, d'estain, de huict pieds.*
X *Pedale de Fluste de bois, de huict pieds.*

For each type of *mélange* described in the table below, Mersenne suggests one to four different stop combinations:

Ieux composéz.

Plain ieu:	A, B, C, D, E, F, G et K.			
Ieu musical:	C, D, E.	D, E.		
Doublette:	D, F.			
Gros Bourdon:	B, E.	B, C, E.		
Gros Cornet:	D, K, L.	B, I.	B, E, K.	
Cymbale:	D, H.	H, L, M.		
Nazard:	D, L, M, N.	D, L.	D, L, N.	L, M, N.
Flageollet:	D, O.	D, L, O.		
Cornet:	D, E, L, P.	D, E, P.		
Trompette & Cleron:	D, E, G.	E, G.	D, E, G, R.	
Cleron:	B, R.	L, M, R.	D, R.	
Voix humaine:	D, E, S.	D, S.	D, L, R, S.	D, L, S.
Cromorne:	D, E, T.	D, L, T.	D, L, N, T.	
Pedale de Fluste:	D, M, X.	D, L, X.		
Pedale d'Anche:	C, D, E, T, V.	C, D, E, M, B.		

Here, as in the previous texts, the author indicates the actual length of the pipe and not the sounding pitch, i.e. letter B = 16', D = 8', M = 4', T = 8'. The *Fluste* indicated at letter N is probably a *Quarte de Nazard* 2'.

Some of the registrations are worthy of mention. In particular, the several so-called "gap registrations", i.e. combinations formed by a *fond* (foundation stop) and one or more mutation stops:

- *Bourdon 16 + Flageollet 1 ½* ⇨ *Gros Cornet*: stops B, I
- *Bourdon 8 + Cymbale* ⇨ *Cymbale*: stops D, H
- *Bourdon 8 + Flageollet 1* ⇨ *Flageollet*: stops D, O
- *Bourdon 8 + Nazart + Flageollet 1* ⇨ *Flageollet*: stops D, L, O

The following registrations, based on a 4', containing the *Nazard* (probably $2^{2/3}$ and not the *Petit Nazard* $1^{1/3}$) are also rather peculiar:

- *Fluste 4 + Nazart + Cymbale* ⇨ *Cymbale*: stops H, L, M
- *Fluste 4 + Nazart + Fluste douce* ⇨ *Nazard*: stops L, M, N
- *Fluste 4 + Nazart + Cleron* ⇨ *Cleron*: stops L, M, R

For a long time – from the 16th to 18th century – the term *Nazard* could have different meanings, in France, as well as in Spain and the Flanders: sometimes it was used (as it is currently) to indicate the *Nazard* stop, i.e. the wide-scaled fifth (which, in turn, can be $5^{1/3}$, $2^{2/3}$ or $1^{1/3}$) but often it could define combinations of several stops, as in the various *Nazard* registrations suggested by Mersenne.[135] Not infrequently there are also 2-rank *Nazards*, corresponding to $2^{2/3'}$ and 2'.

Both *Cornet* registrations given by Mersenne double the *fonds* 8' and 4' (therefore, in addition to the 5-rank *Cornet*, the *Bourdon 8* and *Prestant 4* are also drawn as well). This implies that both hands play on the same manual (left hand: accompaniment in the bass – right hand: *solo* in the treble).

As far as the *Plein jeu* on the *Grand Orgue* is concerned, Mersenne described it four times, from which several discrepancies emerge: twice the stop *Tierce* is included and twice the *Cymbale* is missing.

In *Proposition III*, the description of the *Plain ieu* includes the stops corresponding to the letters A, B, C, D, E, F, G and K, where the letter K corresponds to the *Tierce*; it may have been an error of the author, who may have wanted to indicate (in its place or in addition?) the letter H, corresponding to the *Cymbale*. In *Proposition XXXI*, the *Bourdon 16* and even the *Montre 8* are missing (clearly forgotten in the stop list). It should be noted that in the *Petit plein jeu* (i.e. on the *Positif*) in *Proposition XXXI* Mersenne did not include the *Tierce*. Regarding the use of the *Tierce* in the *Plein jeu*, see page 110.

One should regard the combinations under *Trompette & Cleron*, where, in all three cases, the *Fourniture* (letter G) is indicated instead of the *Trompette* (letter Q) as clearly erroneous. Likewise, in the second registration of *Pedale d'Anche* the letter B (*Bourdon 16*) should be replaced by the letter V (*Pedale d'anche*).

The indications for the pedal (*Pedale de Fluste* and *Pedale d'Anche*) requiring manual stops (via the *tirasse*?) are ambiguous. The second registration of *Pedale d'Anche* is also incorrect, since no pedal stops are indicated.

PROPOSITION XXXI[136]

In *Proposition XXXI*, Mersenne also marked each individual stop with a letter and then suggested its use in the various *mélanges*. In Mersenne's text, the names of the individual stops are followed by a technical description (length of the pipe, pipe material, etc.) which is omitted here, with the exception of a few special cases cited below.

The first table concerns the *Grand Orgue*. It should be noted that in the original, certainly by mistake, the *Huit pieds ouvert* (*Montre 8*) is missing. One should therefore question in which registrations, besides the *Plein jeu*, the *Montre 8* might have been used, or – most likely hypothesise – whether Mersenne intended by letter A the *Montre 8* instead of *Montre 16*.

Table des simples Ieux des grands Orgues

A	Montre 16	N	Grosse Cymbale 2 f.
B	Bourdon 16	O	Cymbale 5 f.
C	Bourdon 8	P	Cornet 5 f.
D	Prestant 4	Q	Larigot 1 1/3
E	Doublette 2	R	Trompette 8
F	Flajollet 1	S	Cleron 4
G	Nazard 5 1/3	T	Cromhorne 8
H	Nazard à l'Octave du precedent 2 2/3	V	Voix Humaine 8
I	Fleute d'Allemand 4	X	La Pedale a huict pieds bouchez
L	Tierce 1 3/5	Y	La Trompette de Pedale 8
M	Fourniture 3 f.	Z	La Fleute en Pedale est de quatre pieds bouchez

Ieux composez des precedens

I. *Le plain jeu A, C, D, E, M, N, O.*
II. *Autre excellent avec, ou sans le Tremblant C, D, E, H, L, R.*
III. *Le Nazard B, C, D, G.*
IV. *Autre Nazard C, D, E, H.*
V. *C, D, E, F, H, avec le tremblant.*
VI. *A, C, jeu fort harmonieux.*
VII. *B, C, I, jeu fort doux avec le tremblant, c'est la fleute d'Allemand.*
VIII. *La Trompette A, C, D, R.*
IX. *Le Cornet B, C, D, E, P.*
X. *Le Cromhorne B, C, D, T.*
XI. *Le Cleron B, C, D, H, S, sans ou avec le tremblant.*
XII. *Ieu fort aigu A, D, C, E, L.*
XIII. *Le Flajolet B, C, F.*
XIV. *Autre B, C, F, H, avec le tremblant.*
XV. *Autre B, C, D, F, H, T, avec le tremblant.*
XVI. *Le Larigot B, C, Q, avec, ou sans le tremblant.*
XVII. *Autre bien fort A, C, D, E.*
XVIII. *Autre B, C, O, avec le tremblant.*
XIX. *La Voix Humaine B, C, D, V.*
XX. *La Trompette & le Cleron A, C, D, E, R, S.*
XXI. *Ieu fort melodieux B, C, avec le tremblant.*
XXII. *Ieu aigu A, D, F.*
XXIII. *Nazard tres-fort B, C, D, E, H, Q*
XXIV. *Cornet entier sur le Clavier B, C, D, E, H, L, Q.*

Regarding the description of some individual stops, Mersenne specified:

[F] *Le Flajollet est d'un pied ouvert, & est à la Vingt-neufiesme de la Montre [de 16'], il se doit iouër tout seul naturellement avec le 4 pieds bouchéz.*

[F] The Flajollet is a 1-foot open stop and it sounds at the twenty-ninth of the Montre [of 16'?]; it must be played alone with the 4' stopped [= 8'].

[P] *Le Cornet commence au milieu du clavier en C sol [...] si l'on y cōprend le Bourdon & le Prestant, dont il est accōpagné, il a sept tuyaux.*

[P] The Cornet starts at the middle of the keyboard on c'; if Bourdon and Prestant are included in the accompaniment, then there will be a total of 7 pipes. (*)

[Q] *Le Larigot est d'un pied cinq pouces ouverts, & commence en G re sol.*

[Q] The Larigot is an open stop of one foot five inches starting from $g°$.

(*) this implied that accompaniment and *solo* were performed on the same manual: accompaniment in the *bass* and *solo* in the *treble*

The indication of stopped pipes (*bouchez*) in relation to letters X and Z is likely to be an error, since the pedal *Flûtes* 8' and 4' in the French organ tradition are usually open.

Compared to the more traditional *Ieux composez* of *Proposition III*, it should be noted that many of the combinations shown here are certainly atypical. Below are some examples, based on 16':

- XIII. Bourdon 16, Bourdon 8, Flajollet 1
- XIV. Bourdon 16, Bourdon 8, Nazard 2 2/3, Flajollet 1, tremblant
- XV. Bourdon 16, Bourdon 8, Nazard 2 2/3, Flajollet 1, Cromhorne 8, tremblant
- XVI. Bourdon 16, Bourdon 8, Larigot 1 1/3 with or without *tremblant*
- XVIII. Bourdon 16, Bourdon 8, Cymbale 2 f. with *tremblant*

The stop *Flajollet 1* is used in several combinations – five to be precise – in contrast to what was specified above by the author himself in the description of this stop, i.e.

[...] il se doit iouër tout seul naturellement avec le 4 pieds bouchéz.	[...] it must be played alone with the 4' stopped [= 8'].

Finally, in contrast to *Proposition III*, the *Plein jeu* described here has neither *Montre 8* (which does not figure in the stop table, and is therefore clearly a mistake) nor *Bourdon 16* nor *Tierce*. Whether the absence of the *Tierce* in *Proposition XXXI* was an oversight (as presumably is the case with *Bourdon 16*) or was itended, is uncertain.

Similarly to the *Grand Orgue*, a list of individual stops (*Ieux simples*) and their possible combinations (*Ieux meslez*) is given for the *Positif*:

Ieux simples du Positif

A	Montre 8		G	Fourniture 3 f.
B	Bourdon 8		H	Petite Cymbale 2 f.
C	Prestant 4		I	Tiercette 4/5
D	Doublette 2		L	Nazard 2 2/3
E	Flajolet 1		M	Petit Cromhorne 4 [recte 8' ?]
F	Fleute d'Allemand 2 [recte 4' ?]		N	Petit Nazard 1 1/3

NB: each *jeu simple* is accompanied in the original table by a description, which is omitted here

Ieux meslez, ou composez pour le Positif

1. *Le plain jeu A, C, D, G, H.*
2. *Le petit Cornet pour iouër à deux Claviers B, C, D, N, E, I.*
3. *La Fleute d'Allemand B, F, avec le tremblant.*
4. *Ieu harmonieux A, C, F.*
5. *Autre fort A, B, C, D.*
6. *Le Nazard B, C, L, sans, ou avec le tremblant.*
7. *Autre jeu excellent B, E, L, avec le tremblant.*
8. *Le Flajolet seul B, E.*
9. *Autre avec le tremblant B, F, H.*
10. *La Doublette seule B, D.*
11. *Ieu renversé, ou Nazard fort D, L, pour iouër quelque fantasie en façon du Cornet sur deux Claviers.*
12. *Nazard fort B, C, D, L, N.*
13. *Ieu fort melodieux A, B, sans ou avec le tremblant.*

The combinations given for the *Positif* are, in general, more traditional. Here too there is a certain propensity for so-called "gap registrations" as well as the frequent use of a tremulant. It is very likely that the pitch given for the stops *Fleute d'Allemand* and *Petit Cromhorne* in the *Positif* indicate the real length of the pipe and not the pitch produced, which implies that they are to be understood as *Fleute d'Allemand 4* and *Cromhorne 8*.

---

[131] see Biography: Vanmackelberg 1967.
[132] see Biography: Anonymous from Nancy.
[133] Mersenne 1636, 33.
[134] Mersenne 1636, 33-34.
[135] Douglass 1995, 50-55.
[136] Mersenne 1636, 85-88.

PLEIN JEU

The registration that typically opens classical French organ cycles, such as the masses (*Kyrie, Gloria*), *Magnificats* and various hymns, is the *Plein jeu*. The *Plein jeu* is the French equivalent to the Italian *Ripieno*, Spanish *Lleno* or the northern European *Organum Plenum*; a logical development of the *Blockwerk* at the time when separate stops were formed.

Documents concerning organs built in the first half of the 16th century (Bordeaux 1510, Chartres 1542) confirm the presence of the classic pairing of *Fourniture* and *Cymbale* as the crown of the Principal chorus, a feature that was to be maintained until the 18th century. It should also be noted that the two stops *Fourniture* and *Cymbale* – from the time of Nivers at the latest – were never drawn separately.

The term *Plein jeu* refers generically to the *Plenum*, which consists of the Principal chorus from *Montre* to *Cymbale* and includes the *Bourdons* 16' and 8'. The *Positif* and *Grand Orgue* manuals are coupled, as explicity requested in the registrations given by Jacques Boyvin and Gaspard Corrette (see below). When played on the *Grand Orgue*, the *Plein jeu* is called *Grand plein jeu*; on the *Positif, Petit plein jeu*.

Numerous historical sources describe the *Plein jeu*. Its composition is very uniform and is summarized in the following table:

Grand Orgue	**Positif**
(Montre 16)	(Montre 8)
Bourdon 16	Bourdon 8
Montre 8	Prestant 4
Bourdon 8	Doublette 2
Prestant 4	Fourniture
Doublette 2	(Cymbale)
Fourniture	
Cymbale	Accouplement Positif - Grand Orgue

The detailed *Plein jeu* registrations of the various composers are given below, beginning with Nivers:

1665 – Guillaume-Gabriel Nivers

Le Plein Jeu se compose du Prestant, du Bourdon, de la Doublette, de la Cymbale, et de la fourniture: on y adioute le huitpied, et le seizepied aussy s'il y en a; s'il n'y a point de Prestant, on y met la flutte.[137]

The Plein Jeu consists of the Prestant [4'], Bourdon [8'], Doublette, Cymbale and Fourniture; one can also add the 8 foot [Montre] and 16 foot if available; if there is no Prestant one can use the flutte [4'].

post 1678 – Anonymous

Pour un plain jeu, il faut bourdon, montre, prestant, doublette, fourniture et cimbale, on ajoute dans les grandes orgues le bourdon de huit pieds.[138]

For a Plein jeu one should draw the Bourdon, Montre, Prestant, Doublette, Fourniture and Cimbale; on larger organs, one can draw the Bourdon eight foot [recte: 16']. (*)

(*) what is meant is, in fact, the *Bourdon 16*, which is described here as an 8', according to the archaic method of indicating the length of the pipe and not the pitch produced; this hypothesis is confirmed by the words *"dans les grandes orgues"*

1688 – André Raison

Le Plein Jeu à un Orgue de 4 pieds est composé de la Montre, du Bourdon, de la Doublette, de la Cimbale et fourniture. Si au grand Orgue il y à un 8 et 16 pieds, on les y adjoute. Le petit Plein Jeu est Composé de mème qu'un Orgue de 4 pieds.[139]

The Plein Jeu of a 4' organ consists of Montre [4'], Bourdon [8'], Doublette, Cymbale and Fourniture. If on the Grand Orgue there is an 8' [Montre] and 16', they are to be added. The petit Plein Jeu has the same composition as a 4' organ.

1690 – Jacques Boyvin

Pour le plein Ieu, dans les Orgues amples ou il-y-a Positif, On tire les claviers ensemble, & on met au Positif, la montre qui est ou huit pieds,

For the Plein Jeu, on large organs which have a Positif the manuals should be coupled. On the Positif, one should draw the Montre, which is 8

ou 4 pieds. Si elle est de quatre pieds, elle sert de prestant, si elle est de huit pieds, il faut qu'il-y-ait un prestant séparé, On y met avec le bourdon, la Doublette, la fourniture, & Cymballe. Au Grand Corps on y met les mêmes jeux & l'on y adjoute le huit pieds ouvert, le bourdon de seize pieds & la montre de seize pieds s'il y en a.[140]

foot or 4 foot. If it is a 4 foot it is used as a Prestant, if it is an 8 foot, there must be a separate Prestant [4']. They should be drawn together with the Bourdon, Doublette, Fourniture and Cymballe. The same stops should be used at the Grand Orgue with the addition of the open eight-foot [Montre], the sixteen-foot Bourdon and the sixteen-foot Montre if available.

late 17th/early 18th century – Manuscrit de Bourges

Les 2 seize pieds, le 8 pieds ouvert, le bourdon de quatre pieds bouché, le prestant, la doublette, la fourniture et la cymballe.[141]

The two sixteen foot stops, the open 8 foot, the stopped four-foot bourdon [= 8'], the prestant, the doublette, the fourniture and the cymballe.

1703 – Gaspard Corrette

Pour le Plein Jeu, L'on tire les Claviers ensemble, au Grand Jeu, Bourdon de 16 pieds, Bourdon, Montre Prestant, Doublette, Fourniture et Cymballe, Au Positif, Bourdon, Montre [ou] Prestant, Doublette, Fourniture et Cymballe.[142]

For the Plein Jeu, one couples the manuals; on the Grand Jeu [= Grand Orgue], 16' Bourdon, Bourdon [8'], Montre, Prestant, Doublette, Fourniture and Cymballe; on the Positif, Bourdon, Montre [or] Prestant [4'], Doublette, Fourniture and Cymballe.

c. 1710/20 – Manuscrit de Tours

Fourniture, Bourdon, Montre, Prestant, Cimballe Pédale.[143]

Fourniture, Bourdon, Montre, Prestant, Cimballe [and] pedal.

1737 – Michel Corrette

Pour le Plein Jeu On tire le grand Clavier. Au Grand jeu Bourdon, Bourdon de 16 pieds, Montre, Prestant, Doublette, Fourniture et Cymballe. Au Positif. Bourdon, Montre, Prestant, Doublette, Fourniture et Cymballe.[144]

For the Plein Jeu one draws the Grand Orgue [= one couples the manuals]. On the Grand Jeu [= G.O.]: Bourdon [8'], 16' Bourdon, Montre, Prestant, Doublette, Fourniture and Cymballe. On the Positif: Bourdon, Montre, Prestant, Doublette, Fourniture and Cymballe.

In contrast to the above, several documents relating to the pre-classical period confirm the use of a *Tierce étroite* (narrow-scaled *Tierce*) in the *Plein jeu*. In this regard Mersenne wrote:

[…] le principal des jeux composez s'appelle le plain jeu, que l'on compose de sept or huict simples jeux, à sçavoir de la Monstre, du Bourdon de seize, & de huict pieds, du 8 pieds ouvert, du Prestant, de la Doublette, de la Fourniture, de la Cymbale & de la Tierce.[145]

[…] the most important of the jeux composez [registrations] is the plain jeu, which is made up of seven or eight single stops: namely, the Monstre, the Bourdon of sixteen and eight foot, the open 8 foot, the Prestant, Doublette, Fourniture, Cymbale & Tierce.

It should, however, be emphasized that in the different descriptions of the *Plein jeu* by Mersenne there are some discrepancies (see page 103). Nevertheless, the use of a *Tierce étroite* in the *Plein jeu* in the first half of the 17th century is corroborated by other documents. In 1628, on the occasion of the reconstruction of the organ of *Saint-Gervais* in Paris, the organbuider Pierre Pescheur replaced the *Flageolet 1* of the *Grand Orgue* with a narrow-scaled *Tierce*, stating explicitly his desire that it be added to the *Plein Jeu* ["*mettre dans le Plein-Jeu*"].[146] This stop was removed in 1685, which means that it was available to Louis Couperin during his tenure as organist between 1653 and 1661.[147] Although there are no documents confirming that Louis Couperin had used a *Tierce* in his *Pleins jeux*, it should be noted that during this period the *Saint-Gervais* organ had two *Tierces* on the Grand Orgue, both $1^{3/5'}$ (one narrow-scaled and one wide-scaled), which supports this hypothesis.[148] Furthermore, in a document dated 20 July 1632, relating to the organ of *Saint-Nicolas-de-Champs* in Paris, one can read:

Item ung jeu de Tierce dont le corps sera d'estain [...] lesd. jeux susnommez serviront pour le plain je.[149]	*Then, a Tierce [third] stop with the body made of tin [...] and these stops will be used for the plain je [plein jeu].*

Usually the opening piece of an organ cycle is entitled *Plein jeu*, but there are cases in which the title is *Prélude*. Nonetheless, its most appropriate registration remains the *Plein jeu*, as Nivers recalls:

Les Preludes et les Pleins Jeux se touchent sur le Plein Jeu.[150]	*The Preludes and Pleins Jeux should be played with [the registration of] Plein Jeu.*

Although several sources establish a close relationship between *Pleins jeux* and *Préludes*, Nicolas Gigault (1685) suggests an interesting alternative:

[...] les preludes se touche[nt] sur les plains jeux, ou sur les grands jeux d'anches avec le grand tremblant [...].[151]	*[...] the preludes are played on the plains jeux, or on the grands jeux d'anches [reeds] with the grand tremblant [...].*

Pleins jeux can be divided into two categories:

a) *Pleins jeux* with *cantus firmus*, in the tenor or bass, played in the pedal

François Couperin: *Plein chant du premier Kyrie, en Taille* (*Messe pour les Paroisses*)

b) *Pleins jeux* without *cantus firmus* which are to be played *manualiter*

François Couperin: *Plein jeu, Premier Kyrie* (*Messe pour les Couvents*)

In the first case the implied registration for the pedal is usually the *Trompette 8*, to which a *Clairon 4* can be added, where available. In addition to this, Dom Bédos also contemplated the possibility of playing the *cantus firmus* with the left hand on the *Grand Orgue* instead of in the pedal:

Pour toucher le Plain-chant gravement, on l'exécute sur les Pédales de Trompette & de Clairon, & on l'accompagne sur tout le Plein-Jeu, tant du grand Orgue que du Positif, les Claviers ensemble.

To perform the plainchant with gravity [*gravement*], it should be played on the pedal with Trompette and Clairon, accompanying it with the full Plein Jeu, both on the Grand Orgue and on the Positif, with the manuals coupled.

Si on veut le toucher à la main, & rondement comme une prose, &c, on le fera sur les Trompettes, Clairons & Prestant du grand Orgue: on l'accompagnera sur le Plein-Jeu du Positif; on pourra mettre les Claviers ensemble, si l'on veut, pour remplir davantage.[152]

If one wants to play it on the manual, and rondement [= at a moderate pace, in a simple and natural way] as prose, it should be done with the Trompettes, Clairons and Prestant of the Grand Orgue; the accompaniment will then be on the Plein Jeu of the Positif. If one wishes, one can couple the manuals to give a fuller sound [*pour remplir davantage*].

Several pieces of this kind are present in the 2. *Livre d'Orgue* by Nivers:

Guillaume-Gabriel Nivers: *1.er Couplet du Victimæ Paschali laudes* (2. *Livre d'Orgue*)

Atypical is Raison's use of the pedal *Trompette* to play a line of short notes (mainly eighth notes and not wedded to a *cantus firmus*), as in the case of the *Premier Kyrie* of the masses in the 1st and 8th modes. Here – as well as in other cases where Raison contemplated the use of a pedal – the author suggests that this voice be entrusted to another person (*3e main*). In the following example, one can play the tenor voice with the *Trompette* of the *Grand Orgue* and play the other parts with the *Petit Plein jeu* on the *Positif*. At the same time, Raison also considered the possibility of leaving out the tenor line altogether:

André Raison: *Autre Premier Kyrie* (*Messe du Premier ton*)

The use of *Pedalle de Trompette en taille* without *cantus firmus* is also envisaged by other composers, including Jullien (*Préludes* of the 3rd and 8th Tone), Marchand (*Plein Jeu du 1 ° Ton*) and Michel Corrette (*Plein Jeu avec la Pédale de Trompette pour toucher avec les deux pieds, Magnificat du 3° et 4° Ton*). Here is a *Prélude* by Jullien:

Gilles Jullien: *Prelude a 5 partie* (*3ᵉ ton, Premier livre d'orgue*)

The earliest sources document the practice of placing the *cantus firmus* in the bass voice rather than in the tenor, as Titelouze states in the *Hymnes de l'Eglise*:

| [...] pour mieux former l'intonation au chœur, l'Organiste fait tenir ordinairement le plain-chant à la Basse-contre [...].[153] | [...] in order to better give the intonation to the choir, the organist will normally put the plainchant in the bass voice [...]. |

And also – indirectly – in his description of the different organ divisions:

| [...] un clavier de pedales à l'unisson des jeux de huict pieds, contenant vingt-huict ou trente tant feintes que marches, pour y toucher la Basse-contre a part, sans la toucher de la main [...].[154] | [...] a pedal board in unison with the eight-foot stops, containing twenty-eight or thirty diatonic and chromatic notes, so as to be able to separately play the bass part without having to do it with the hands [...]. |

All opening versets of Titelouze's hymns (1623) are, in fact, composed with the *plainchant* in the bass voice:

Jehan Titelouze: *Ave maris Stella* (*Hymnes de l'Eglise*)

Although Titelouze does not provide information regarding registration, one might assume that the *cantus firmus* placed in the bass could be performed with the pedal (*Plein jeu* + pedal *Trompette?*). At the end of the 17th century, the anonymous writer of the *Manuscrit de l'Arsenal* wrote:

| Le plainchant ce joüée de plusieurs manierre savoir ala basse ala taille haute contre et odesus mais lordinaire et le plus commun est de la joüer a quatre partie avec la pedalle et en trio quand a celuy de quatre parties la pedalle suit le petit doit de la main gauche [...].[155] | The [pieces based on] plainchant can be done in several ways: by placing the cantus firmus in the bass, tenor, alto or soprano voice. The most common and ordinary way is to play in four parts with the pedal, or in three. As for the one in four parts, the pedal follows the little finger of the left hand [which plays the chant] [...]. |

From this last remark, it is clear then that it was still common practice in the late 17th century to place the *plainchant* in the bass voice. The first versets of Nivers' hymns (1667) also have the *plainchant* in the bass, although in most cases it includes passing notes or is an ornamented *cantus firmus*. On the other hand, Clérambault's indication at the beginning of the *Grand Plein jeu* which opens the *Suite du Premier Ton*, suggesting that the bass line – not linked to a *cantus firmus* – can be entrusted to the *Trompette*, is very unusual:

| On pourra joüer cette Basse sur la Pedale de Trompette si l'on veut. | One can play this bass voice with the Trompette of the pedal if one wishes. |

Louis-Nicolas Clérambault: *Grand plein jeu* (*Suite di 1er ton*)

Finally, two particular cases of *Pleins jeux* are presented here:

a) the six-voice *Plein jeu* with double pedal by Louis Marchand:

Louis Marchand: *Plein Jeu* (*1r Ton, Pièces choisies pour l'orgue*)

b) the *Grand plein jeu à 3 chœurs* by Boyvin, in which a *Plein jeu d'écho* is required; this very rare stop was present in the organ of the Cathedral of Rouen where Boyvin was *titulaire*:

Jacques Boyvin: *Grand plein jeu a 3 Chœurs* (*8e Ton, Premier Livre d'Orgue*)

Various historical sources also provide information on the manner in which *Pleins jeux* should be played. It is very important to point out that the indications (*Grand*) *Plein jeu* and *Petit plein jeu* refer not only to two registrations (for the *Grand Orgue* and *Positif* respectively) but also to two different interpretative styles: the first, *adagio* and *legato*, and the second, lively and brilliant. Explicit tempo indications are marked in the first *Couplet* of the *Agnus Dei* of the *Messe du Sixiesme ton* by Raison with the terms *Lentement* and *Viste* (fast):

André Raison: *Grand plein Jeu* (*Agnus Dei, Messe du Sixiesme ton*)

Often the change of musical notation seems to go hand in hand with a change of *affect* and tempo. In the following example by Du Mage, the rapid notation on the *Positif* (mainly ♪ and ♫) suggests a fast tempo

whereas the notation in longer notes on the *Grand Orgue* (mainly 𝅗𝅥 and 𝅘𝅥) suggests a *grave* tempo:

Pierre Du Mage: *Plein Jeu* (*Livre d'Orgue*)

A slow tempo can be inferred from pieces such as the *Premier Kyrie* of Raison's *Messe du 1er Ton*, should one choose to follow the composer's intention of playing the tenor part in the pedal (see page 113). Numerous indications provided by the composers (Lebègue, Gigault, Raison, Jullien, Clérambault, etc.) can be found in various pieces such as:

(Grand) Plein jeu:	*lentement*	**Petit Plein jeu:**	*gay*
	fort lentement		*gayement*
	gravement		*viste*

There are exceptions of course. In the following piece, Gigault requested a slow tempo (*Lantement*) for the opening section on the *Positif* (prevalent notation in ♪ and ♪),

whereas, for the section with notation in o ♩ and ♩ (on the *Grand Orgue*) he called for a tempo *"un peuplus gayement"* [*a little more gaily*]:

Nicolas Gigault: *1.er ton prelude* (*Livre de Musique pour l'Orgue*)

Also unconventional is the indication *gayement* found at the beginning of the *Prelude du 4e ton* by Jullien, which displays characteristic (slow) *Plein jeu* writing with a prevalence of ♩ and ♩ (it could be speculated that the author intended *gravement* instead of *gayement* here):

Gilles Jullien: *Prelude* (*4e ton, Premier livre d'orgue*)

Numerous indications concerning the performance of *Pleins jeux* can be found in the writings of the period and, in particular, in the prefaces of the different *livres d'orgue*:

1665 – Guillaume-Gabriel Nivers

Le Mouvem.ᵗ des Preludes, […] et Pleins Jeux, est fort lent.[156]	The pace of the Preludes […] and Pleins Jeux is very slow.

1676 – Nicolas Lebègue

Le Prelude et Plein Ieu se doit toucher gravement, et le Plein Ieu du Positif legerement.[157]	The Prelude and Plein Jeu should be played with gravity; Plein Jeu on the Positif fast [legerement].

The term *Legerement* (*Légèrement*) can mean *light* but it is frequently used as an indication for a flowing, or even fast, manner of playing. Several descriptions offered by François Couperin in his harpsichord compositions – such as *d'une legereté moderée, legereté gracieuse* or *legereté tendre* – as well as the definition given by Brossard in his *Dictionaire de Musique* (1703) would seem to confirm this:[158]

Leggiadro, ou Leggiadramente. Veut dire, gaillardement, gayement, legerement, &c.[159]	Leggiadro, or Leggiadramente. It means boldly, cheerfully, lightly, etc.

1688 – André Raison

Le Grand plein jeu se touche fort lentement. Il faut lier les Accords les uns aux autres, ne point lever un doigt [avant] q[ue] l'autre ne baisse en même temps et que la derniere mesure soit toûjours fort longue. Le petit plein jeu se touche legerement et le bien Couler.[160]	The Grand plein jeu should be played very slowly. One should play the chords in a legato manner, never lifting one finger until the other [finger] has depressed the key at the same time; and the last bar is always very long. The petit plein jeu is played quickly [legerement] and very legato [bien Couler].

It should be noted that even on the *Positif* – although the tempo is faster – Raison desired a *legato* manner of playing.

last quarter of 17th century – Manuscrit de l'Arsenal

Pour toucher le prelude dans sa derniere perfection il se doit joüer gravement et fort doucement car ces ycy ou il faut se coutter [s'écouter] joüer et goutter la douceur des âcords toutte fois il ce doit toucher hardiment on ne peut le toucher trop doucement pour veü que la messure y soit regullierement observée […].[161]	In order to play a prelude with the utmost perfection, it should be played with gravity and very slowly [fort doucement], because it is here [in the preludes] that one has to listen to oneself and savour the sweetness of the chords. At the same time, one should play boldly [hardiment], one cannot overdo the slowness [doucement], given that the beat is regular here […].

A little further on in the same text, it is stated that *Préludes* should be played in a "well-dotted" [*bien pointer*] manner, i.e. *inégal*:

Une autre remarque de la dernierre consequence pour le prelude est de le bien pointer il faut remarquer que ces ce pointement qui donne la grace le mouvement et la beaute et lagrement aux piece, sans cela les pieces sont plate sant gout ny mouvement et ne paroisse rien.[162]

Another remark of greatest importance for the prelude is that it should be played in a very dotted manner; in fact it is this dotted manner that gives grace, movement and beauty and enhancement to the piece. Without it pieces are flat, without taste or movement, and seem as nothing.

1695 – Lambert Chaumont

Le Prelude et plein Jeu au grand Orgue gravement, au positif plus legerement.[163]

The Prelude and plein Jeu on the grand Orgue with gravity, faster [plus legerement] on the positif.

Regarding the ornamentation for *Pleins jeux*, it is interesting to cite the indications contained in the *Manuscrit de l'Arsenal*, in which it is encouraged to play a *pincé* at the beginning of the piece:

Le prelude de lorgue ce doit toucher de la même manierre que lon touche le prelude du clavessin c'est a dire faire un pincement soit de la main droite soit de la main gauche ou de toutte les deux en semble selon que les partis commencement des la premiere notte en commancant et cêst une regle generalle que toutte sorte de piece doive commencer par ce pincement quoi quil ne soit point marqué.

The prelude on the organ must be played in the same way as on the harpsichord, i.e. by doing a pincement either with the right hand or the left hand or with both hands together if (several) voices start from the first note. This is a general rule that applies to all sorts of pieces, even when the pincement is not indicated.

[...] voicy comme il ce fait il doit être fait legerement vivement imperceptiblement et tres courtement [...].[164]

[...] here's how it should be played: it should be performed lightly, quickly, in an imperceptible way and it should be very short [...].

At the same time, the writer recommends avoiding other ornaments; this is certainly related to the poor clarity of ornaments in a *Plein jeu* registration (especially true in a very reverberant acoustic) as well as to a possible eccessive unsteadiness caused by an insufficient wind supply:

Il est de la Dernierre Consequence de bien prendre garde quand on touche le prelude plain jeu et dialogue [...] de ne point faire de repetitions coullement ou port de voix ces la mesme chose. Car il ny â rien de sy dezagreable dans ces jeuxs lâ et on peut dire que ceux qui le font doive appeller cêst sortes dâgremens placage bouziliage et â sommement des acords [...].[165]

It is of the utmost importance to pay attention, when playing the prelude plain jeu and dialogue [...], not to make note repetitions, or coullements or ports de voix (which are the same thing), since in these registrations there is nothing more annoying; those who do so should call these ornaments a "beating" [screwing up of the keys] or "making a mess" [knocking out] on the chords [...].

Jacques Boyvin (*Second Livre d'Orgue*, 1700) explains that the *Plein jeu* on the *Grand Orgue* should be played with a good *legato*:

[...] *sur le plein Jeu, il ne faut lever la main que le moins qu'on peut, afin d'entendre toûjours un fond d'Harmonie qui remplisse l'oreille.*[166]	[...] on the plein Jeu, the hand should be lifted as little as possible, so as one can always hear a foundation of harmony which fills the ear.

Then he explains that *cadences, pincés* and other ornaments could be performed on the *Positif*, implying that one should tend to avoid them on the *Grand Orgue*:

Sur un plein Jeu de Positif, on peut faire des vitesses, des cadences, des pincements & d'autres agréements, comme sur un Clavessin, hors qu'il faut que l'une des deux mains se tienne plus appuyée.[167]	On a plein Jeu of the Positif one can play vitesses (= fast passages), cadences (= trills), pincements and other ornaments, as on the harpsichord, but being sure to keep one of the two hands down on the keys [= so that there are no "voids of sound"].

Boyvin is echoed three years later by Gaspard Corrette (*Messe du 8.ᵉ ton*, 1703). Corrette writes that the *Petit plein jeu* should be brilliant and ornamented:

Le Plein Jeu du Positif, se doit toucher vivement bien former, et marquer les Cadences, ou Tremblements. Il faut lever les doigts dans les Vitesses et toucher presque aussi legerement que sur le Clauessin, excepté quand'il faut que l'une des deux mains porte toûjours sur le Clavier, a fin qu'il n'y ait point trop de vuide.[168]	The Plein Jeu on the Positif should be played quickly, playing the Cadences or Tremblements clearly and marking them [= emphasizing them]. In fast passages it is necessary to articulate [lever les doigts] playing with almost the same lightness as as on the harpsichord; it is important, however, that one of the two hands remains on the keys so that there is not too much void [of sound].

However, on the *Grand Orgue* he desires a "subdued" performance (*fort Modestement*), almost without *cadences* (the paragraph clearly refers to improvisation):

Mais sur le Grand Plein Jeu, Il faut toucher fort Modestement et fournir beaucoup pour veu que l'on sache fournir a propos selon les Regles de l'Acompagnement; Il ne faut guerre lever la main. On ne fait point de vitesse; et presque point de cadence specialement sur les Orgues a Double seize pieds.[169]	But the Grand Plein Jeu should be played in a very moderate way [fort modestement] and "filling in the chords", assuming that one knows the rules on how to perform a basso continuo. One should scarcely lift one's hands; one should play no fast passages, and almost no cadences (= trills), especially on double sixteen-foot organs [Montre 16' and Bourdon 16'].

While almost all the sources emphasize that the *Plein jeu* on the *Grand Orgue* (*Grand plein jeu*) should be played without excessive ornamentation, the *Pleins jeux* by de Grigny show a rich use of embellishments and note repetitions:

Nicolas de Grigny: *Pange Lingua, en taille à 4* (*Livre d'Orgue*)

It is difficult to know whether this was an idiosyncrasy on de Grigny's part or indicative of the existence of different "schools of thought" at the time, possibly in conflict with each other. This is a fact of no small importance, which certainly cannot be ignored, given that de Grigny was one of the most outstanding composers of the French *école classique*.

---

[137] Nivers 1665, 177.
[138] Gravet 1996, 75.
[139] Raison 1688, 31.
[140] Boyvin 1690, 55.
[141] Manuscrit de Bourges, 87.
[142] Corrette 1703, 122.
[143] Gravet 1996, 85.
[144] Corrette 1737, 160.
[145] Mersenne 1636, 33.
[146] Hardouin 1996, 9.
[147] Ponsford 2011, 125.
[148] Hardouin 1996, 9.
[149] Douglass 1995, 75.
[150] Nivers 1665, 177.
[151] Gigault 1685, 26.
[152] Dom Bédos 1766-1778, 206.
[153] Titelouze 1624, 15.
[154] Titelouze 1624, 14.
[155] Pruitt 1986, 248.
[156] Nivers 1665, 177.
[157] Lebègue 1676, 14.
[158] Ponsford 2011, 133.
[159] Brossard 1703, definition of term *Leggiadro*, without page number.
[160] Raison 1688, 31.
[161] Pruitt 1986, 238.
[162] Pruitt 1986, 240.
[163] Chaumont 1695, 61.
[164] Pruitt 1986, 238.
[165] Pruitt 1986, 241.
[166] Boyvin 1700, 92.
[167] Boyvin 1700, 92.
[168] Corrette 1703, 123.
[169] Corrette 1703, 123.

GRAND JEU

The second type of French *Plenum* is the *Grand jeu*, a *mélange* consisting primarily of the reeds and *Cornet*. Several authors prescribe two or three slightly different registrations for *Grands jeux* that differ substantially in terms of the presence/absence of a *Jeu de Tierce* and the use of the third and fourth manuals (this latter in the case of a *Grand Dialogue*). Despite these differences, the registration of the *Grand jeu* is actually quite uniform, as summarized below:

(Petit) Dialogue		Grand Dialogue		
Grand Orgue	**Positif**	**Grand Orgue**	**Positif**	**Récit**
Bourdon 8	Bourdon 8	Bourdon 8	Bourdon 8	Cornet separé
Prestant 4	Montre 4	Prestant 4	Montre 4	
Trompette	Cromorne	Nazard	Nazard	
Clairon and/or Cornet		Quarte/Doublette	Tierce	**Echo**
		Tierce	Cromorne	Cornet d'Echo
		Trompette		
		Clairon		
		Cornet		

Accouplement G.O. / Positif
Tremblant à vent perdu

Accouplement G.O. / Positif
Tremblant à vent perdu

Below are the *Grand jeu* registrations in detail:

1665 – Guillaume-Gabriel Nivers

Le Grand Jeu se compose du Jeu de Tierce (il faut entendre aussy toute sa suitte) avec lequel on met la Trompette le Clairon, le Cromhorne, le Cornet, et le tremblant à vent perdu s'il y en a. Et le reste a discretion dont le meslange est arbitraire.[170]

The Grand Jeu is composed of the Jeu de Tierce (meaning all its stops) to which is added the Trompette, Clairon, Cromhorne, Cornet and the tremblant à vent perdu if there is one. The rest is at one's discretion, i.e. the mélange is ad libitum.

1676 – Nicolas Lebègue

Pour le Grand Ieu, petit Bourdon, Prestant, Trompette & Cornet. Pour le Petit Ieu Bourdon, Montre & Cromhorne. Autre Grand Ieu: Petit Bourdon Prestant, Trompette & Clairon. Altro: Petit Bourdon, Prestant, Doublette, Nazard, Quarte de Nazard, grosse Tierce, Trompette, Clairon, Cornet & Tremblant à vent perdu, Petit Ieu, Montre, Bourdon, Nazard, Tierce & Cromhorne.[171]

For the Grand Ieu: petit Bourdon [8'], Prestant, Trompette and Cornet. For the Petit Ieu: Bourdon, Montre [4'] and Cromhorne. Other Grand Ieu: Petit Bourdon [8'], Prestant, Trompette and Clairon. Other: Petit Bourdon [8'], Prestant, Doublette, Nazard, Quarte de Nazard, grosse Tierce [= 1 3/5'], Trompette, Clairon, Cornet and Tremblant à vent perdu. Petit Ieu: Montre [4'], Bourdon, Nazard, Tierce and Cromhorne.

post 1678 – Anonymous

Pour un Grand jeu il faut tire le bourdon, montre... prestant, doublette, nazard, tierce, cornet, trompette... Au Grand orgue et au positif bourdon, montre, doublette nazard, tierce, cromhorne. A lésco [l'Echo] bourdon, prestant, doublette, nazard, tierce.[172]

For a Grand jeu one should draw the bourdon, montre... prestant, doublette, nazard, tierce, cornet, trompette... On the Grand orgue and the positif: bourdon, montre, doublette, nazard, tierce, cromhorne. On the Echo: bourdon, prestant, doublette, nazard, tierce.

1688 – André Raison

Le Dialogue se touche sur tous les Claviers: Au grand Orgue Le Bourdon, le 4 pieds, la Tierce, le Nazard, le Cornet, la Tromp. le Clairon et le Tremblant à Vent perdu: Au positif le Bourdon, Montre, Nazard, Tierce et Cromorne: Si il y à un Cornet separé, et un Eco: vous les tirez quand il est à 4 Claviers; si il n'y en à que 3, vo[us] touchez les repetitions sur le 3.e: Il se touche encore a 2 Claviers, pour lors on retranche les Tierces et Nazards; au grand et petit Orgue, avec le Tremblant.[173]

The Dialogue is played on all manuals. On the grand Orgue: the Bourdon, 4'-stop [= Prestant], Tierce, Nazard, Cornet, Trompette, Clairon and the Tremblant à vent perdu. On the Positif: Bourdon, Montre [4'], Nazard, Tierce and Cromorne. If there is a Cornet separé [3rd man.] and an Echo [4th man.] use them when it [the Dialogue] is [played] on 4 manuals; if it is on 3 manuals only, the repetitions should be played on the 3rd manual; it can also be played on 2 manuals, in which case the Tierces and Nazards are not drawn; on the grand and petit Orgue, with the Tremblant.

1690 – Jacques Boyvin

Pour les petits Dialogues, au Positif, le Cromhorne avec le fond comme cy dessus, au Grand Corps la trompette, Clairon, & le Cornet avec le fond; On tire les Claviers, on ne met point de tremblant.

Au Grand Dialogues la même chose comme dessus, mais on adjoutte au Grand Corps, nazar, quarte, & tierce, Cromhorne même s'il y en a. Au Positif, on y adjoûte le nazar quelques uns y mettent la tierce, il y faut le tremblant a vent perdu, On les touche a quatre Chœurs, le troisieme Chœur est le Cornet separé & le quatrieme est le Cornet d'Echo.[174]

For the petits Dialogues, on the Positif, the Cromhorne with the fonds above described [= Bourdon 8 and Prestant 4]; on the Grand Corps, the trompette, Clairon and Cornet with the fonds [= Bourdon 8 and Prestant 4]; the manuals are coupled and the tremblant is not used.

For the Grand Dialogues, the same as above but on the Grand Corps one should add nazar, quarte and tierce, also Cromhorne if there is one. On the Positif, one should add the nazar (some organists draw the tierce as well) and tremblant à vent perdu. When they are played on four manuals [Chœurs], the third one is the Cornet separé and the fourth the Cornet d'Echo.

1695 – Lambert Chaumont

Le Dialogue au grand Jeu petit Bourdon, prestant[,] Trompette, et Cornet. Ou Tromp et Clairon. Ou petit Bourd, prestant, Doublet[,] Nazard[,] 4te de Naz, grosse Tierce, Tromp, Clairon[,] Cornet et tremblant a vent Perdus[.] Pour le petit Jeu montre[,] bourdon[,] Nazard, Tierce, Et Cromh.[175]

Dialogue on the grand Jeu: petit Bourdon [8'], Prestant, Trompette and Cornet. Or Trompette and Clairon. Or Petit Bourdon, Prestant, Doublette, Nazard, 4te de Nazard, grosse Tierce [1 3/5'], Trompette, Clairon, Cornet and Tremblant à vent perdu. For the Petit Jeu: montre [4'], Bourdon, Nazard, Tierce and Cromhorne.

late 17th/early 18th century – Manuscrit de Bourges

Le petit bourdon, le prestant, la trompette et clairon et le cornet si l'on veult à la grande orgue. Au positif, la montre, le bourdon, nazard, et cromorne ou doublette.

Autre à deux cœurs a vent perdu.
Au positif montre, bourdon, nazard, doublette, cromorne. A la grande orgue petit bourdon, prestant, doublette, nazard, quart de nazard, tierce, double-tierce sy l'on veult trompette, clairon, cromorne et cornet ; jouer les dict jeux d'un air délliberé et d'allegresse et faire un troisieme coeur sur le cornet d'esco.[176]

On the grande orgue, the petit bourdon [8'], prestant, trompette and clairon, and the cornet if one wishes. On the positif, montre [4'], bourdon, nazard, and cromorne or doublette.

Other [Grand Jeu] on two choirs [cœurs] à vent perdu. On the positif: montre [4'], bourdon, nazard, doublette, cromorne. On the grand orgue: petit bourdon, prestant, doublette, nazard, quart de nazard, tierce, double-tierce [3 1/5'] if desired, trompette, clairon, cromorne and cornet; play the above stops resolutely [d'un air délliberé] and joyfully and use the cornet echo as a third chorus.

1703 – Gaspard Corrette

Dialogue a deux Chœurs, On tire les Claviers l'un sur l'autre. Au Grand Jeu, Bourdon, Prestant, Trompette, Clairon, et le Cornet, Au positif, Bourdon, Prestant ou Montre et le Cromhorne. Dialogue a trois Chœurs, On tire les Claviers l'un sur l'autre, Au Grand Jeu, Bourdon, Prestant, Trompette, Clairon, Cornet, Nazar, Quarte de Nazar et Tierce, Au Positif, Bourdon, Prestant ou Montre, Cromhorne, Tierce et Nazar, le Troisieme Chœur sur le Clavier d'Echo, et le Tremblant a Vent Perdu.[177]	In the two-choir [a deux Chœurs] Dialogue the manuals are coupled. On the Grand Jeu [= G.O.]: Bourdon, Prestant, Trompette, Clairon and Cornet. On the Positif: Bourdon, Prestant or Montre and Cromhorne. In the three-choir Dialogue the manuals are coupled. On the Grand Jeu: Bourdon, Prestant, Trompette, Clairon, Cornet, Nazar, Quarte de Nazar and Tierce. On the Positif: Bourdon, Prestant or Montre, Cromhorne, Tierce and Nazard. The third choir on the Echo [Claviers d'Echo], and the Tremblant à Vent Perdu.

c. 1710/20 – Manuscrit de Tours

Nasard, Cornet, Bourdon, Prestant, Montre, Quarte de Nasard, Trompette	Nasard, Cornet, Bourdon, Prestant, Montre, Quarte de Nasard, Trompette
ou: Les fonds, Doublette, Nasard et Tierce, Dessus et basse de Cromorne, Cornet s'il y en a et le tremblant.[178]	or: Fonds, Doublette, Nasard and Tierce, bass and treble Cromorne, Cornet if there is one, and tremblant.

1737 – Michel Corrette

Pour le Grand jeu [...] au G.j. Bourdon, Prestant, Trompette, Clairon, Grand Cornet, Tierce, Nazar, et quarte de Nazar. au Positif Bourdon, Prestant, Cromhorne, Tierce et Nazar. Le Tremblant a vent perdu. On peut suprimer les Bourdons.[179]	For the Grand jeu [...] on the G.j. [= G.O.]: Bourdon, Prestant, Trompette, Clarion, Grand Cornet, Tierce, Nazar and quarte de Nazar. On the Positif: Bourdon, Prestant, Cromhorne, Tierce and Nazar. Tremblant à vent perdu. One can omit the Bourdons.

Something that immediately catches the eye is the use – cited in practically all sources – of a *Tremblant à vent perdu* (*Tremblant fort*) in the *Grand jeu*. Such a registration may seem rather extravagant, but it must be said that the effect that this combination would have produced cannot be verified with certainty today, as practically no instruments from that period have come down to us without alterations having been made to the wind channels and relative *Tremblants* over the years.[180] It should also be said that, at the time, the charm of a "wavering" (oscillating) sound was probably very popular. A brief *excursus* to North Germany in the 17th century confirms that the use of the *Tremulant* had become so common that Matthaeus Hertel in 1666 went as far as to say

Tremulanten müßen nicht in allen stücken gebraucht werden [...].[181]	Tremulants do not have to be used in all pieces [...].

There is practically no author in France in the Baroque period who did not prescribe it. In the second half of the 18th century, Dom Bédos – notoriously opposed to the use of the *Tremblant* in the *Grand jeu* – partly justified its use:

Si les Jeux d'Anche ont une mauvaise harmonie, & qu'ils ne soient pas d'accord, c'est le cas où l'on pourra se servir du Tremblant-fort. Cette modification du vent mettra de la confusion dans l'harmonie, & pourra peut-être masquer un peu les défauts, si elle ne les augmente ; mais dans les Orgues qui sont bonnes & qui vont bien, on fera beaucoup mieux de ne point s'en servir, à l'exemple des Organistes qui ont le plus de goût, comme je l'ai déjà dit.[182]	*If the reed stops are badly voiced and out of tune [ne soient pas d'accord], in this a case where the Tremblant-fort can be used. This modification of the wind will blur the harmony, and perhaps mask the imperfections a little, if it does not increase them; but in organs which are good and work well, it would be much better not to use it, following the example of those organists who have better taste, as I have already said.*

In an era in which musical tastes had already changed, Dom Bédos did not forego an opportunity to rant against this practice:

Il y a plusieurs Organistes, qui ne touchent presque jamais le Grand Jeu, sans y faire jouer le Tremblant-fort. Il est remarquable que ce ne sont jamais les plus habiles, & qui ont le plus de goût; ceux-ci sentent trop bien que cette modification du vent barbouille & gâte la belle harmonie: les Tuyaux n'en parlent pas si bien, ni si nettement. [...]	*There are some organists who practically never use the Grand Jeu without drawing the Tremblant-fort. It is remarkable that they are never the most able nor those with the best taste; these latter are well aware that this modification of the wind blurs and ruins the harmony: the pipes do not speak well or clearly. [...]*
Le Cromorne sur-tout en est le plus mal affecté; le Tremblant défigure tout ce qu'il a d'agréable dans son harmonie; ce Jeu ne fait alors que nasarder: on fera donc très-bien de ne s'en servir presque jamais au Grand Jeu, à l'exemple des plus grands Organistes, qui naturellement doivent être le modele des autres.[183]	*The Cromorne, above all, is the worst affected thereby; the tremulant disfigures all that is pleasant in its intonation; this stop thus does nothing but "nazardize" [nasarder]. So it would be better hardly ever to use it in the Grand Jeu, following the example of the best organists, who naturally must be the model for others.*

Boyvin did not wish to have the tremulant in the *Petits Dialogues* but called for it in the *Grands Dialogues*, as highlighted in his indications (see page 124). An example of this is the *Petit dialogue en fugue sans tremblant* from Boyvin's *Suite du Sixiesme Ton* (the fact that this work is *sur le Grand jeu* and not another type of *Dialogue* is confirmed in bar 12, where the required registration on the *Grand Orgue* is the *Grand jeu*):

Jacques Boyvin: *Petit dialogue en fugue sans tremblant (Sixiesme ton, Premier Livre d'Orgue)*

Just as the *Plein jeu* typically opens a liturgical cycle, the *Grand jeu* usually closes it, although exceptions are numerous (see page 85). Among the first examples of *Grand jeu*, one might mention the five *Grands jeux* by Nivers, contained in the 1665 *Livre d'Orgue*; short, homophonic compositions without dialogue between the manuals:

Guillaume-Gabriel Nivers: *Grand Ieu (6ʳ Ton, Premier livre d'orgue)*

The four short pieces by the same composer, entitled *A 2. Coeurs* are prototypes of the *Dialogues sur le Grands jeux*:

Guillaume-Gabriel Nivers: *A 2. Coeurs (1ᵉʳ Ton, Premier livre d'orgue)*

The *Grand jeu* finds its ideal "home" in the *Dialogue* structure, as witnessed by the countless examples to be found in the repertoire. The *Dialogue* usually takes place between *Grand Orgue* and *Positif*. Not infrequently, a manner of *duo* between *Cornet separé* on the *Récit* (right hand) and *Cromorne* in the *Positif* (left hand) follows the initial *Grand jeu*. The change of manual from *Grand Orgue* to *Positif* (or *Positif/Récit*) is often characterized by a change of tempo, writing or character:

Louis-Nicolas Clérambault: *Dialogue sur les grands jeux (Suite di 1er ton)*

Of note is Clérambault's comment at the head of the aforementioned piece:

Ceux qui n'auront point de Cornet separé pourront se servir du Positif pour toucher le dessus dans les endroits qui sont a 2.	Those without a mounted Cornet [3rd manual] can use the Positif for the treble voice in the sections in 2 [voices].

The *Dialogue sur le Grands jeux* is often constructed as a dialogue between two tessituras in the manuals, usually *basse* and *dessus*:

Louis Marchand: *Grand Dialogue composé par Mr Marchand a Paris. 1696*
(*Manuscrit de Versailles*)

In the example above, the term *Récit* does not refer to the third manual but simply means *Solo*, to be performed – out of necessity, owing to the low range of the left hand – on the *Grand Orgue*.

In the case of *Grand Dialogue*, the third and fourth manuals (*Récit* and *Echo* respectively) are also used. In the following example by Gigault, the term *Cornet separé* refers to the third manual and *Echo* to the fourth:

Nicolas Gigault: *A 2. 3 et 4 Chœurs du 3e. et 4e. Ton* (*Livre de Musique pour l'Orgue*)

Not infrequently, the *Dialogue* – particularly the *Grand Dialogue* – ends with a section marked *gravement, lentement* or *fort lentement*:

Louis-Nicolas Clérambault: *Dialogue sur les grands jeux* (*Suite di 1er ton*)

The *Offertoires* are built on the same principle as the *Dialogue sur les Grands jeux*. These are the most extensive compositions of the French baroque organ repertoire, and were conceived for the moment during the Mass in which the organist potentially had the greatest opportunity to play at length. Nivers was once again one of the first to use this term with his *Offers en fugue et Dialogue* published in his *Deuxième Livre d'Orgue* (1667):[184]

Guillaume-Gabriel Nivers: *Offerte en fugue et Dialogue* (*Deuxième livre d'orgue*)

Among the most notable examples of *Offertoires* are those by François Couperin, de Grigny and Marchand (if one considers the well-known *Grand Dialogue* in C of the latter to be an *Offertoire* – as the structure of the piece would suggest). A distinctive feature of these pieces is the presence of a central section characterized by a slower pace. In Couperin's two *Offertoires* this slower tempo is the result of a modification of notation and not (or not necessarily) of a change of tempo:

François Couperin: *Offertoire sur les Grands jeux* (*Messe pour les Paroisses*)

More explicit, by contrast, is Marchand, who indicates the change of tempo in the central section by the term *Lentement*:

Louis Marchand: *Grand Dialogue composé par Mr Marchand a Paris. 1696* (*Manuscrit de Versailles*)

In the case of de Grigny's *Offertoire*, the central section is characterized by dialogues between *Cornet separé* and *Petit jeu* vs. *Grand jeu*:

Nicolas de Grigny: *Offertoire sur les Grands Jeux* (*Livre d'Orgue*)

An unusual example of *Grand jeu* is the piece that closes de Grigny's *Livre d'Orgue* entitled *Point d'Orgue sur les Grands Jeux*, which, for the entire composition, employs the pedal in the manner of the *Toccate sopra li pedali* contained in Frescobaldi's *Il Secondo Libro di Toccate* (1627-37):

Nicolas de Grigny: *Point d'Orgue sur les Grands Jeux* (*Livre d'Orgue*)

The *Offerte du 5.ᵉ Ton* that closes Raison's *Livre d'Orgue* is modelled on the *Offertoires sur les Grands Jeux*. This composition, of a commemorative and pompous character, was related to an event that took place a year before the publication of the volume, as referred to in the full title:

> *Offerte du 5.ᵉ Ton*
> *Le Vive le Roy des Parisiens*
> *A Son Entrée a l'hotel de Ville*
> *Le Trentiéme de Januier 1687.*

The first section is built on the model of the classic *Dialogue sur les Grand jeux*:

It is followed by several short sections which are diverse in character (*Trompette en taille, Trio, Echo, Duo,* etc.) sometimes with rather uncommon registrations:

After an unusual *Trio des Trompettes* and echoes on different manuals, the text *Vive le Roy* (presumably to be sung) appears together with the *Grand jeu*:

The piece ends with all voices singing the motif *Vive le Roy* (indicated on the score with the initial "V"), with a most sumptuous pomposity:

Not infrequently, the *Dialogues sur les Grands jeux* are structured in several parts, with different tempi and, consequently, different *affects*:

- six of the eight *Dialogues* in Lebègue's *Premier Livre d'Orgue* bear the indication *Gayement* at the beginning and *Gravement* at the end
- several of Boyvin's *Dialogues* (*2e Livre*) have, with slight variations, the following structure: (without indication) / *fort lentement* / *vite* / *lentement*
- Marchand's *Grand Dialogue du 5e Ton* also has a similar layout: (without indication) / *lentement* / *légèrement* / *gravement*

A corresponding differentiation in the manner of playing is also indicated by several authors. Raison specifically requests this in the preface to his *Livre d'Orgue*:

Le Dialogue à 2. 3. et 4. Claviers se touche selon le mouvem.ᵗ qu'il est marqué.[185]	Dialogues on 2, 3 and 4 manuals are played according to the ductus [mouvement] indicated.

Jacques Boyvin, who, as mentioned above, often indicates his desired character and tempo, limited himself to the following comment in his *Deuxième Livre* of 1700:

Dans les Dialogues, de la hardiesse & de l'execution.[186]	In the Dialogues, a decisive manner [hardiesse] and [propriety of] execution.

In reference to the *Dialogue a deux cœurs*, in the *Manuscrit de Bourges* one can read:

Toucher les dicts jeux de plusieurs mouvements différents, quelquefois graves, tantost gayes en pleine mesure, et puis en triples et sur tout bien annuncer et bien observer la mesure.[187]	One should play the aforementioned registrations at different paces: sometimes with gravity, sometimes gaily in binary bar signatures [en pleine mesure], and then in the ternary sections one should, above all, play precisely [bien annuncer] observing well the tactus.

Gaspard Corrette also emphasizes the importance of highlighting the variety of pace:

Le Dialogue se touche fort hardiment; on y fait entrer toutes sortes de mouvements; de la gayeté, et des langueurs.[188]	The Dialogue is played very boldly [fort hardiment]; one should include all kinds of pace [and affects]; some with gaiety, some languid.

[170] Nivers 1665, 177.
[171] Lebègue 1676, 15.
[172] Gravet 1996, 75.
[173] Raison 1688, 31.
[174] Boyvin 1690, 55-56.
[175] Chaumont 1695, 61.
[176] Manuscrit de Bourges, 89.
[177] Corrette 1703, 122.
[178] Gravet 1996, 85.
[179] Corrette 1737, 161.
[180] Ponsford 2011, 276.
[181] Schünemann 1922, 341.
[182] Dom Bédos 1766-1778, 207.
[183] Dom Bédos 1766-1778, 204.
[184] Ponsford 2011, 278.
[185] Raison 1688, 31.
[186] Boyvin 1700, 92.
[187] Manuscrit de Bourges, 89.
[188] Corrette 1703, 123.

FOND D'ORGUE & JEU DOUX

The use of the terms *Fond d'orgue* and *Jeu doux* appears to be rather versatile. A *Jeu doux* registration is found in very many cases as an accompaniment to various types of *Récit*. François Couperin and Nicolas de Grigny normally used the expression *Fond d'orgue* for their *Récits en taille* and *Jeu doux* in other cases.[189] On the other hand, there are extremely few compositions in the entire *école classique* repertoire bearing the title *Fond d'orgue*; one of them is the following by Boyvin:

Jacques Boyvin: *Fond Dorgue* (Premier Livre d'Orgue, Premier ton)

Quite apart from the title, there are very few examples of compositions calling for an entire piece to be played on the *Jeu doux* or *Fond d'orgue*. Here an *Elévation* by Raison:

André Raison: *Elevation en a mi la beccarre* (*Messe du Troisiesme ton*)

The registration written at the beginning of this work calls for

Au Grand Orgue le petit et gros bourdon avec le prestant.	On the Grand Orgue the petit [8'] and gros bourdon [16'] with the prestant.

Interesting is the suggestion made at the end of the piece for a completely different registration as a possible alternative:

Cette piece se peut toucher sur tous les grands Jeux.	This piece can be performed on all grands Jeux.

In contrast to other genres, no standard registrations exist for *Jeu doux* and *Fond d'orgue*. For the *Jeu doux*, Nivers proposed several solutions of increasing intensity:

Bourdon 8	Bourdon 8	Bourdon 8	Bourdon 8	Bourdon 8	16 pied
Flutte 4	Montre 8	Prestant 4	Prestant 4	Montre 8	Bourdon 8
			Doublette 2	Prestant 4	Montre 8
				Doublette 2	Prestant 4
					Doublette 2

Here is the description by Nivers (1665) in detail:

Le Jeu doux se compose du Bourdon et de la flutte; ou du Bourdon et du huitpied: un peu plus fort avec le Bourdon on met le Prestant: encore plus fort on y adioute la Doublette, quelquefois aussi le huitpied: mesme encore le seize pied.[190]	The Jeu doux is composed of the Bourdon [8'] and flutte [4']; or of the Bourdon and eight foot [= Montre]; for a slightly stronger sonority, the Prestant can be added to the Bourdon and for an even stronger sound one can add the Doublette, sometimes also the eight foot; and even the sixteen foot.

Chaumont (1695) left a certain freedom to the performer:

Tous ces Jeux [Cornet, Dessus et Basse de Voix Humaine, Dessus de Cromhorne]	All these stops [Cornet, Dessus and Basse de Voix Humaine, Dessus de Cromhorne] are

s'accompagnent presque de meme, par le melange du bourdon, de la montre, ou prestant flutte ou Nazard selon l'effet qu'il feront.[191]

accompanied almost in the same way by a mélange of bourdon, montre, or prestant flutte or nazard according to the effect they will produce.

Gaspard Corrette (1703) prescribed a registration for the *Fond d'orgue* comprising flue stops of 16' 8' and 4' on *Grand Orgue* and *Positif* coupled:

Fond d'Orgue, On tire les Claviers l'un sur l'autre. Au Grand Jeu, Bourdon de 16 pieds, Bourdon, Prestant, et Montre, Au Positif, Bourdon, Prestant ou Montre.[192]

Fond d'Orgue: the manuals are coupled. On the *Grand Jeu* [= G.O.]: Bourdon 16, Bourdon [8'], Prestant and Montre. On the *Positif*: Bourdon, Prestant or Montre.

Gaspard Corrette: *Fond d'Orgue-Elevation* (*Messe du 8e Ton*)

In some pieces, precise *Jeu doux* registrations are sometimes found, as in Jacques Boyvin's *Dialogue de Voix humaine* (*2. ton, Premier Livre d'Orgue*), where *Bourdon et fluste* (i.e. *Bourdon 8* and *Flûte 4*) are specified for the accompaniment.

Similar to the concept of *Fond d'orgue* is the *Concert de flûtes*, described in two pieces of the same title in Boyvin's *Second Livre d'Orgue* (1700): the *Suite du Troisième Ton*, containing a *Concert de flûtes, ou fond d'Orgue* and, in the *Suite du Septième Ton* a *Fond d'Orgue, ou Concert de flûtes*:

Jacques Boyvin: *Fond d'Orgue, ou Concert de flûtes* (*Suite du Septième Ton, Second Livre d'Orgue*)

The registration for the *Concert de flûtes* includes the *Bourdons 8* and the *Flûtes 4* of both manuals coupled, together with the *Tremblant doux*. Quite different is the case of Michel Corrette, who wanted *pour les Flûtes* a sound closer to a *Fond d'orgue*, including the *Montre 8* and excluding the 4' registers. The registrations in detail are as follows:

1690 – Jacques Boyvin

Pour le Concert de fluste on tire les claviers & on met au Grand Corps huit pieds bourdon, & fluste, au Positif bourdon & fluste & le tremblant doux.[193]

For the Concert de fluste the manuals are coupled; on the Grand Corps one draws the eight-foot bourdon and fluste; on the Positif, the bourdon and fluste and the tremblant doux.

1703 – Gaspard Corrette

Concert de Flûte, On tire les Claviers l'un sur l'autre, Au Grand Jeu, Bourdon et Flûte, Au Positif, Bourdon, Flûte et le Tremblant doux.[194]

Concert de Flûte: the manuals are coupled; on the Grand Jeu, Bourdon and Flûte; on the Positif, Bourdon, Flûte and the Tremblant doux.

c. 1710/20 – Manuscrit de Tours

Flûte: Fluste, Prestant ou le Bourdon seul... ou: Montre seule pour le petit orgue.[195]

Flûte: Fluste, Prestant or Bourdon alone... or: Montre alone for the small organ.

1737 – Michel Corrette

Pour les Flûtes [...] On tire le G. Clavier. au G.j. Bourdon et Montre. au Positif. Bourdon seul le Tremblant doux, Et les Pedalles de Flûtes.[196]

For the Flûtes [...] the manuals are coupled; on the Grand Jeu, Bourdon and Montre; on the Positif Bourdon alone and Tremblant doux; on the pedal, the Flûtes [i.e. 8'].

Despite the variety of titles – *Dialogue de Flûtes pour l'Elevation* (de Grigny), *Trio des Flûtes* (Guilain), *Concert pour le Flûtes* (G. Corrette), *Flûtes* (Clérambault), – these compositions were usually based on the principle of dialogue between *Grand Orgue* and *Positif*:

Jean-Adam Guilain: *Trio des Flûtes (Suite du Second ton, Pièces d'orgue pour le Magnificat)*

For the few pieces entitled *Fond d'orgue* and *Elévation*, as well as the *Concerts de Flûte(s)*, a calm and relaxed pace was always recommended, as clearly stated by Gaspard Corrette:

Le Fond d'Orgue se doit toucher tendrement avec beaucoup de tendresse, et d'Imitation de Voix.

The Fond d'Orgue must be played gently with much tenderness, imitating the voice.

Le Concert de Flûte et la Voix Humaine se touche lentement, et dans les mouvements les plus gays, on ne doit jamais aller vite; acause du tremblant.[197]

The Concert de Flûte and the Voix Humaine are played slowly, and even in the quickest pieces one should never go fast because of the tremulant.

The piece performed at the *Elévation* could either be sung (a motet) or played on the organ. In the latter case, the various *Cérémonials* expressly state that such pieces should be played in a slow and grave manner:

Similiter dum elevatur SS. Sacramentum, sed graviori & dulciori sono.[198]	Similarly at the elevation of the Blessed Sacrament, with a more solemn and sweet sound.

In Raison's *Elévation du 3ᵉ Ton*, the tempo specified at the beginning (see page 136) is *Lentement*; there is a subsequent change of tempo to *gayment* in the eight central bars (in 3/8) entrusted to the *Positif*, after which the initial tempo (*Lentement*) returns:

André Raison: *Elevation en a mi la beccarre* (*Messe du Troisiesme ton*)

For the various types of *Récit* (*de dessus, de basse, en taille*), which begin, almost without exception, on the *Fonds* or *Jeu doux*, the tempo is influenced by the *affect* of the work.

---

[189] Ponsford 2011, 272.
[190] Nivers 1665, 177.
[191] Chaumont 1695, 61.
[192] Corrette 1703, 122.
[193] Boyvin 1690, 55.
[194] Corrette 1703, 122.
[195] Gravet 1996, 86.
[196] Corrette 1737, 161.
[197] Corrette 1703, 123.
[198] Caeremoniale Monasticum Romano 1634, 21.

FUGUE

Similarly to composers from other geographical areas (such as Frescobaldi, Sweelinck, Scheidt, Froberger, Sancta Maria or Byrd), some of the earlier French authors used the terms *Fugue* and *Fantaisie* almost as synonyms. In Louis Couperin's *Pièces d'Orgue* the titles *Fugues* and *Fantaisies* are equally represented, without substantial differences: structure and style of is similar to the Italian *Ricercari*. Here is an example of a *Fantaisie*:

Louis Couperin: *Fantaisie* (*Pièces d'orgue*)

Even the works of Titelouze – which do not bear specific titles but are *couplets* constituting the cycles of *Hymnes* (1623) and *Magnificat* (1626) – in fact belong to the genre of *Fantaisie*; the only difference being that they are built on a *cantus firmus*. The registration for such *Fugues* or *Fantaisies* should not be confused with that of the typical *Fugues d'anches* which would become popular from the mid-17th century onwards. Almost no pre-classical composer left any indication with regard to registrations: one can only speculate as to the *mélanges* that Jehan Titelouze, Charles Racquet or Louis Couperin may have desired for their *Fantaisies* or the various *couplets*. The only exceptions appear to be six pieces (of the 70 extant) by Louis Couperin which have precise indications, e.g. *Fantaisie sur le Cromhorne* or *Fugue sur la tierce*. For the registrations of the pre-classical compositions, one can refer to the indications provided in the chapter *"Pre-classical registrations"* (see page 96).

Turning to the classical period, the term *Fugue* is often used in a rather generic way, sometimes simply to indicate a piece in imitative style. This is the case, for example, of the second *Couplet* of the *Sanctus* from the *2ᵉ Livre d'Orgue contenant la Messe et les Hymnes de l'Église* (1667) by Nivers, entitled *Fugue*, but which is actually a *Basse de Trompette*:

Guillaume-Gabriel Nivers: *Fugue* (*Sanctus, 2ᵉ Livre d'Orgue*)

In contrast to the analogous genre in Germany, the French *Fugue* of the Baroque period is characterized by its brevity and registrations based on reeds or the *Jeu de Tierce*. Registrations using mixtures were avoided, not only as a matter of taste but also owing to the scant "polyphony" of the French *Plein jeu*. The reduced dimensions, in comparison to the contemporary fugues of Bach, can be explained by the fact that the *couplet* was a constituent element of a much larger cycle (*Kyrie, Gloria, Magnificat*, etc.) and was played *alternatim* with the *plainchant*.

A characteristic of some *Fugues* – in particular when placed as *2ᵉ Couplet* after the initial *Plein jeu* – is that they were built on the same subject (*"sur le mesme suject"*) as the *cantus firmus*, especially when the latter was enunciated *en plainchant* by the pedal in the initial *Plein jeu*.

As for registration, notation and structure, there are two basic types of French *Fugue*: the *Fugue grave* and – in the words of Nivers – *"autres fugues ... plus guay"* [*other ... gayer fugues*]. The latter, defined as *Fugue de mouvement*, is called *Fugue légère* (Nivers, *2. Livre d'orgue, Te Deum*) or *Fugue gaie* (Chaumont, *Deuxième Ton*). Couperin calls the second *couplet* of the *Gloria* (of both masses) *Petitte fugue* and indicates that it be played with the *Chromhorne* on the *Positif*.

The *Fugue grave*, written in ₵ or C, is often characterized by a *stile antico* notation (o / 𝅗𝅥 / 𝅘𝅥):

Jacques Boyvin: *Fugue grave (8ᵉ Ton, Premier Livre d'Orgue)*

In the case of the *Fugue grave* of the 1st tone by Lebègue, the author also wrote the indication *Lentement* and used the sign C :

Nicolas Lebègue: *Fugue grave (1ᵉʳ Ton, Premier Livre d'Orgue)*

The notation of a *Fugue grave* does not always consist of long note values. The following composition by Raison has a typical *Fugue légère* notation, although it is specifically entitled *Fugue grave*:

André Raison: *Fugue grave sur la Trompette (Kyrie, Messe du Troisiesme ton)*

Also the *Fugue* from Clérambault's *Suite du premier ton* bears the indication *Lentement,* despite the prevailing notation in ♪ and ♫:

Louis-Nicolas Clérambault: *Fugue (Suite di 1er ton)*

The notation of a *Fugue de mouvement* (indicated in C as well as in ₵) requires a brisker tempo and is usually based on the ♩ / ♪ and sometimes the ♫:

François Couperin: *Petitte fugue sur le Chromhorne (Gloria, Messe pour les Paroisses)*

Fugues de mouvement do not necessarily have to be played on the *Positif*. One can consider the second *couplet* of the *Kyrie* of François Couperin's *Messe pour les Couvents*, which should be played on the *Grand Orgue*, as a *Fugue de mouvement*:

François Couperin: *Fugue sur la trompette (Kyrie, Messe pour les Couvents)*

The two *Fugues* used as the 2ème *Couplet* in Couperin's *Kyries*, although both were conceived for the *Grand Orgue*, have a different notation: ♩ / ♪ in the *Messe pour les Couvents* vs. ♩ / ♩ in the *Messe pour les Paroisses*:

François Couperin: *Fugue sur les jeux d'anches (Kyrie, Messe pour les Paroisses)*

Both compositions are notated in ₵:

In the absence of precise information, i.e. in the case of the very many compositions whose title is the term *Fugue* alone, it is up to the player to deduce whether it refers to a *Fugue grave* or a *Fugue de mouvement* and to perform accordingly. An example is the following *Fugue* by Louis Couperin, written for the most part in ♩ / ♪ / ♬, notated in ₵ and intended to be played on the *Grand Orgue*:

Louis Couperin: *Fugue sur la tierce du Grand Clavier* (*Pièces d'Orgue*)

The majority of descriptions of *Fugue* registrations, which can often be rather vague, refer to the *Fugue grave* type. The two most recurring modes of registration can be summarized as follows:

Grand Orgue	Positif		Grand Orgue	Positif
Bourdon 8	Bourdon 8	or	Bourdon 8	Bourdon 8
Prestant 4	(Prestant 4)		Prestant 4	Prestant 4
Trompette 8	Cromorne 8		Nasard 2 2/3	Nasard 2 2/3
(Clairon 4)			(Doublette 2?)	(Doublette 2?)
			Tierce 1 3/5	Tierce 1 3/5
possibly also with *Accouplement Positif/G.O.*			*Tremblant (doux)*	

The registrations are listed in detail below:

1665 – Guillaume-Gabriel Nivers

Les fugues graves sur le gros Jeu de Tierce avec le tremblant, ou sur la Trompette sans tremblant. Les autres fugues sur un Jeu mediocre ou sur le petit Jeu de Tierce.[199]

The fugues graves on the gros Jeu de Tierce with the tremblant, or on the Trompette without tremblant. The other fugues with a moderate registration [mediocre] or on the petit Jeu de Tierce [= Positif].

1676 – Nicolas Lebègue

Fugue Grave; Bourdon, Prestant, Trompette & Clairon de la Grand' Orgue. Aux Petites Orgues Bourdon de 4 pieds & Cromhorne.[200]

Fugue Grave: Bourdon, Prestant, Trompette and Clairon of the Grand Orgue. On the positive: 4' Bourdon [= 8'] and Cromhorne.

post 1678 – Anonymous

[...] une fugue grave sur la trompette et tierce.²⁰¹

[...] a fugue grave with the trompette and tierce [= jeu de tierce].

1685 – Nicolas Gigault

[...] les fugues graves sur la trompette, [...].²⁰²

[...] the fugues graves on the trompette, [...].

1690 – Jacques Boyvin

Les fugues graves se touchent sur la trompette accompagnée de son fond qui est le bourdon, & le prestant, avec le Cromhorne seul au Positif on tire les Claviers. Ou bien on les peut toucher sur le Positif seulement y mettant le Cromhorne avec son fond qui est le bourdon, & le 4 pieds.²⁰³

The fugues graves are played with the trompette and its fond which is bourdon and prestant, with the Cromhorne alone on the Positif and the manuals coupled. Otherwise one can play them only on the Positif with the Cromhorne and its fond, which is bourdon and the 4 foot [= Montre].

1695 – Lambert Chaumont

La fugue gaye sur un Jeu éclattant, cõe la petite tierce, Bourdon, Montre, Nazard &c

The fugue gaye with a brilliant registration [éclattant] for example petite tierce, Bourdon, Montre [4'], Nazard etc.

La Fugue grave sur le Bourdon, Prestant, et la Trompette, Clairon, et Nazard[;] aux petites orgues sur le Cromh et Bourdon de 4 pieds.²⁰⁴

The Fugue grave with Bourdon, Prestant, Trompette, Clairon and Nazard; on the Positif with Cromhorne and 4 foot Bourdon [= 8'].

late 17th/early 18th century – Manuscrit de Bourges

Petit bourdon, prestant, trompette et clairon pour jouer une fugue gravement.²⁰⁵

Petit bourdon, prestant, trompette and clairon to play a fugue with gravity [gravement].

1703 – Gaspard Corrette

Pour la Fugue, Lon tire les Claviers ensemble, au Grand Jeu, Bourdon, Prestant, Trompette. Au Positif, Bourdon, Prestant ou Montre, et le Cromhorne.²⁰⁶

For the Fugue, the manuals are coupled; on the Grand Jeu [= G.O.]: Bourdon, Prestant, Trompette; on the Positif: Bourdon, Prestant or Montre [4'], and Cromhorne.

c. 1710/20 – manuscrit de Tours

Les fonds avec le dessus et basse de Cromorne.²⁰⁷

The fonds with the Cromorne (treble and bass).

Sometimes it is the title itself of the piece that indicates the registration: *Fugue sur le Cromhorne, Fugue sur la tierce, Fugue sur la trompette, Fugue sur les jeux d'anches*, etc. Among the *Pièces d'Orgue* by Louis Couperin is the following composition entitled:

Fugue qu'il fault jouer d'un mouvement fort lent sur la tierce du Grand Clavier avec le tremblant lent.	*Fugue to be played at a very slow pace on the tierce of the Grand Clavier with the tremblant lent.*

Louis Couperin: *Fugue qu'il fault jouer d'un mouvement fort lent* (Pièces d'Orgue)

Gilles Jullien (1690) also mentions the possibility of playing the four-part *Fugue* on two manuals, following the *Quatuor* model:

Il Est pourtant Necessaire d'auertir que les fugues a quatre parties que lon joüe sur la trompette ou Cromhorne pouront se Jouer Aux Grands Orgues sur deux claviers En quatüor.[208]	One should however note that the four-part fugues played on the trompette or Cromhorne can be played, on large instruments, on two manuals in quatuor.

To this end, he also suggests some registrations (see page 169).

A rather peculiar case are the *Fugues à 5* (voices) by de Grigny. They require the two upper voices to be played on the *Cornet* of the *Récit*, the two middle voices on the *Cromorne* of the *Positif* and the bass voice with the *Flûte* on the pedal:

Nicolas de Grigny: *Fugue à 5* (Veni Creator)

In reality, already in 1690, i.e. nine years before the publication of de Grigny's *Livre d'Orgue*, Gilles Jullien took credit for this *nouvelle Invention*:

Je me suis advisé de donner a l'Orgue, qui est sans Contredit, le plus parfait des Instrumens, une nouvelle Invention d'y toücher des pieces á cinq parties, d'une façon qui napoint Encor Esté Mise au jour;	I sought to invent for the organ, which is undoubtedly the most perfect of all instruments, a new genre, i.e. pieces consisting of five voices, something that has never been done before;
*[...] la fugue renversée á Cinq du mesme [2.ᵉ] ton, se jouera avec le meslange des jeux du quatuor Marqué cy dessus [cfr. p. 1690] de differente Maniere, et la Cinquiesme partie qui Est une taille particuliere se joüera Sur les pedalles de fluste.*²⁰⁹	[...] the fugue renversée à Cinq of the same [2.ᵉ] ton is to be played with the quatuor registration indicated above [see p. 170] in a different manner, while the fifth part, placed in the tenor, will be played on the pedal with the fluste [flûte].

Unlike de Grigny, here the pedal plays the middle voice, leaving the two lower voices to be played by the left hand:

Gilles Jullien: *Fugue renversée a cinq parties* (2ⁿᵈ Ton, Premier Livre d'Orgue)

Numerically, the *Fugues graves* – i.e. those which called explicitly for a *gravement* or *lentement* pace – constitute the majority. For their performance the weightier sonority of the Grand Orgue is preferable. The title of the aforementioned *Fugue* by Louis Couperin describes both the tempo and registration:

Fugue qu'il fault jouer d'un mouvement fort lent sur la tierce du Grand Clavier avec le tremblant lent.	Fugue to be played at a very slow pace on the tierce of the Grand Clavier with the tremblant lent.

Writing about *Fugues*, Jacques Boyvin (1700) states:

*Il faut toucher les Fugues lentement.*²¹⁰	One should play the Fugues slowly.

Similarly Gaspard Corrette (1703) wrote:

*La Fugue doit etre grave avec beaucoup de propreté.*²¹¹	The Fugue must be slow and solemn [grave] and with great propriety.

On the importance of distinguishing the two types of fugues, one should recall the words of Nivers, who differentiates the *Fugue grave* from the *autres fugues*:

Le Mouvem.ᵗ des [...] fugues graves [...] est fort lent: celuy des autres fugues [...] est plus guay.[212]	The pace of the [...] fugues graves [...] is very slow; that of the other fugues [...] is gayer.

---

[199] Nivers 1665, 177.
[200] Lebègue 1676, 15.
[201] Gravet 1996, 75.
[202] Gigault 1685, 26.
[203] Boyvin 1690, 55.
[204] Chaumont 1695, 61.
[205] Manuscrit de Bourges, 87.
[206] Corrette 1703, 122.
[207] Gravet 1996, 85.
[208] Jullien 1690, 50.
[209] Jullien 1690, 51.
[210] Boyvin 1700, 92.
[211] Corrette 1703, 123.
[212] Nivers 1665, 177.

DUO

Among the earliest *Duos* in France are those of Charles Racquet and Louis Couperin, i.e. they appeared slightly later than the *Duos* of Antonio de Cabezón or the *Bicinia* of Jan Pieterszoon Sweelinck and Samuel Scheidt. Despite the delayed start, the genre established itself strongly in France from the middle of the 17th century, and it can be found in most of the *livres d'orgue* of the classical period.

Duos are to be found in both binary and ternary time. The former are usually marked ₵ or **2**, more rarely **C**. Triple metre is usually denoted by a **3** signature, which is also used, without distinction, to indicate 6/4 and 3/4. Indications such as 6/8 or 3/8 are less frequently used. The *Duos* marked in **3** often feature the rhythm ♩. ♪ ♩ (*Rythme de Canarie*):

Nicolas Lebègue: *Duo (6. Ton, Premier livre d'orgue)*

The registration for a *Duo* is rarely stated in the title. Exceptions are the two *Glorias* of François Couperin's masses, where *Duo sur les Tierces* is specified in the title. In most cases, when the title is simply *Duo*, the registrations described in the prefaces of the various *livres d'orgue* offer valuable guidance.

The registration *par excellence* of a *Duo* calls for two *Jeux de Tierces*. A peculiarity of the French repertoire of the time is the use on the *Grand Orgue* of the *Grosse tierce* (*Double Tierce*) $3^{1/5}$ on a 16' basis in the left hand. In some cases the registration in the left hand may be also enriched – particularly in 18th century repertoire – by the *Grand Quinte* (*Gros Nazard*) $5^{1/3}$ when available. For the right hand, played on the *Positif*, the *Petite tierce* $1^{3/5}$ should be used. *Grosse tierce* and *Petite tierce* are of course to be understood as *mélanges* of a number of stops, as can be clearly seen in the sources. On small organs or instruments without *Grosse tierce*, an alternative registration is recommended: *Trompette* on the *Grand Orgue* (left hand) and a *Tierce* combination for the right hand, the latter with either the *Cornet du Récit* or with the *Jeu de Tierce* on the *Positif*. The following table summarizes the different options:

left hand **Grand Orgue**	right hand **Positif**	left hand **Grand Orgue**	right hand **Récit**
Bourdon 16	Bourdon 8	Bourdon 8	Cornet 5 f.
Bourdon 8	Prestant 4	Prestant 4	
(Gros Nazard $5^{1/3}$)	Nazard $2^{2/3}$	Trompette 8	
Prestant o Flûte 4	Tierce $1^{3/5}$		or
(Grosse Tierce $3^{1/5}$)		**Grand Orgue**	**Positif**
Nazard $2^{2/3}$		Bourdon 8	Bourdon 8
Quarte/Doublette 2		Prestant 4	Prestant 4
Tierce $1^{3/5}$		Trompette 8	Nazard $2^{2/3}$
			Tierce $1^{3/5}$

Below are the detailed indications contained in the different *Livres d'orgue*:

1665 – Guillaume-Gabriel Nivers

Les Duos se touchent sur le dessus de petite Tierce et la basse de grosse Tierce: ou bien sur le Cornet et la Trompette.[213]	In the Duos the dessus is played with the petite Tierce and the bass with the grosse Tierce; or else, with the Cornet and the Trompette.

1676 – Nicolas Lebègue

Aux Grandes Orgues. Le Dessus sur la Tierce du Positif, Et la Basse sur la grosse Tierce accompagnée du Bourdon de seize pieds.	On large organs: the dessus on the Tierce of the Positif, and the bass on the grosse Tierce [G.O.] accompanied by the sixteen-foot Bourdon.

Aux mediocres et petites Orgues, sur la Tierce, ou la Trompette & le Cornet.[214]

On organs of medium and small dimensions: with the Tierce, or the Trompette and the Cornet.

post 1678 – Anonymous

Le jeu de tierce pour les duos et trios, il faut le bourdon, le prestant, doublette, le nazard et la tierce.[215]

The jeu de tierce for duos and trios, i.e. bourdon, prestant, doublette, nazard and tierce.

1688 – André Raison

Le Duo se touche sur les 2 Tierces, au positif de la main droite Le Bourdon, la Montre, la Tierce et le Nazard; Au grand Orgue de la main gauche, le Bourdon de 8 et de 16 pieds, la flutte, la Tierce, le Nazard et gros Nazard, avec la Double Tierce si ily en à une; Il se peut encore toucher sur le Cornet separé, ou le jeu de tierce du positif avec la Tromp. au grand Orgue accompagnée de son fond.[216]

The Duo is played with the two Tierces; on the positif, the right hand with Bourdon, Montre, Tierce and Nazard; on the grand Orgue, the left hand with the Bourdon of 8 and 16 foot, the flutte, Tierce, Nazard and gros Nazard, with the Double Tierce if there is one. It can also be played with the Cornet separé [Récit] or with the jeu de tierce of the positif with the Trompette of the grand Orgue accompanied by its fond [Bourdon 8 and Prestant 4].

1690 – Jacques Boyvin

Le Duo se touche sur les deux tierces, a la petite tierce on y met bourdon, prestant, nazar, & tierce, Au Grand Corps, on y met la même chose & on y adjoutte le bourdon de seize pieds & la quatre [sic] de nazar ou bien afaute de quarte on y met la Doublette.[217]

The Duo is played on the two tierces; the petite tierce [Positif], with the bourdon, prestant, nazar & tierce; on the Grand Corps [G.O.] the same thing with the addition of the sixteen-foot bourdon and the quarte de nazar or, if there is no quarte, the Doublette.

1695 – Lambert Chaumont

[...] au grand Orgue la Basse sur la grosse Tierce, Bourdon et le prestant, Nazard, 4te de Naz, Bourdon de 16 pied. Au positif: le Dessus sur la petite Tierce &c ou la Basse sur la Tromp, le dessus sur Cornet.[218]

[...] on the grand Orgue the Basse with the grosse Tierce, Bourdon and prestant, Nazard, 4te de Nazard, 16' Bourdon. On the positif: the Dessus on the petite Tierce, etc., or the Basse with the Trompette and the dessus with the Cornet.

late 17th/early 18th century – manuscrit de Bourges

Bourdon de seize pieds, petit bourdon, prestant, nazard, quart de nazard, grosse tierce [1 $^{3/5}$ ou 3 $^{1/5}$?] de la grande orgue, jouer la basse [recte: dessus] au positif, la montre, Bourdon, doublette, tierce (*).[219]

Sixteen foot Bourdon, petit bourdon, prestant, nazard, quarte de nazard, grosse tierce [1$^{3/5}$ or 3$^{1/5}$?] on the grand orgue; play the basse [recte: dessus] on the positif with the montre [4'], Bourdon, doublette, tierce (*).

(*) in the registration for the *Positif*, the *Nasard* is missing (certainly by mistake)

1703 – Gaspard Corrette

On pousse les Claviers, la Main droite sur le Positif, et la Main Gauche sur le Grand Jeu. Au Grand Jeu, Bourdon de 16 pieds, Bourdon, Prestant, Tierce, Grosse Tierce, Nazar, et Quarte de Nazar. Au Positif, Bourdon, Prestant ou Montre, Tierce, et Nazar.[220]	The manuals are not coupled. The right hand on the Positif and the left hand on the Grand Jeu. On the Grand Jeu: 16-foot Bourdon, Bourdon, Prestant, Tierce, Grosse Tierce, Nazar, and Quarte de Nazar. On the Positif: Bourdon, Prestant or Montre, Tierce, and Nazar.

c. 1710/20 – Manuscrit de Tours

Nasard, Bourdon, Montre, Tierce et Prestant, Tierce, Nasard	Nasard, Bourdon, Montre, Tierce and Prestant, Tierce, Nasard
ou: Nasard, Bourdon, Montre, Tierce, Prestant, Doublette; Basse de Cromorne pour diversifier.[221]	or: Nasard, Bourdon, Montre, Tierce, Prestant, Doublette; Basse de Cromorne, to diversify.

1737 – Michel Corrette

Pour le Duo [...] Le Dessus sur le Cornet de Recit. La Basse sur le Positif Cromhorne et Nazar seul.	For the Duo [...] The Dessus on the Cornet of the Récit. The Basse on the Positif with only Cromhorne and Nazar.
Autre Meslange pour le Duo [...] Le Dessus sur le Cornet de Recit. La Basse au Positif Bourdon, Prestant, Tierce et Nazar.	Other registration for the Duo [...] The Dessus on the Cornet of the Récit. The Basse on the Positif with Bourdon, Prestant, Tierce and Nazar.
Autre Meslange pour le Duo [...] Les Claviers tirés au G.j. Trompette Clairon. Au Positif. Cromhorne seul.[222]	Other registration for the Duo [...] The manuals are coupled; on the G.j. [= G.O.] Trompette and Clairon. On the Positif, Cromhorne alone.

The *mélanges* indicated by Michel Corrette tend to break with the earlier tradition of classical registrations.

With regard to the performance practice of *Duos*, the sources suggest a brilliant, decisive and lively manner of playing. In addition, specific indications of a fast tempo, such as *Vite*, *Gayement* or *Légèrement*, are found very frequently in the repertoire, as in the case of the following *Duo* by Du Mage (*Fort gai* = very gay):

Pierre Du Mage: *Duo* (*Livre d'Orgue*)

Below are details concerning the interpretation of *Duos* as reported in various *livres d'orgue*. Note in particular Nivers' suggestion to play *Duos* in ternary time very quickly:

1665 – Guillaume-Gabriel Nivers

Le Mouvem.^t des [...] Duos [...] est plus guay, et celuy des Duos marquez au signe trinaire, fort leger.[223]

The tempo of the [...] Duos [...] is more gai, and that of the Duos in ternary time is very fast [fort leger].

1676 – Nicolas Lebègue

Le Duo fort hardiment & legerement.[224]

The Duo very boldly and fast [legerement].

1688 – André Raison

Le Duo se joüe viste, un jeu libre et net, et le pointer quand il est en croche.[225]

The Duo is played quickly, in a free and precise manner, and with a dotted rhythm when in quavers.

1690 – Jacques Boyvin

[...] les Duo veulent du mouvement, & de la gayeté.[226]

[...] the Duos call for a quick tempo and joyful character.

1695 – Lambert Chaumont

Le Duo hardiment et legerement.[227]

The Duo boldly and fast [legerement].

1703 – Gaspard Corrette

Le Duo Vivement avec beaucoup de gayeté, et d'execution selon le mouvement.[228]

The Duo lively with much gaiety, and played boldly according to the tempo.

Even more detailed are the instructions contained in the *Manuscrit de l'Arsenal* (last quarter of 17th century):

Le Duo ce touche gayment hardiment et tres legerement et dune manierre vive plaine de feu et pour y bien reusir il faut observer a bien detacher ces doist [...].

The Duo is played gaily, boldly, very lightly [= fast], in a lively way, full of fire. To this end, one must be sure to articulate well with the fingers [...].

Il faut etremement pointer le duo car ces en cela ou est sa beauté. Cest ausy dan le Duo ausy bien que dans le recit ou toute les cadence ce zequtte [s'execute] avec plaisir.[229]

The duo must be played in an extremely dotted manner, because its beauty lies precisely in this. In both duos and récits, trills [cadences] are played with pleasure. (*)

(*) it is somewhat unclear whether the author meant by the words *"zequtte avec plaisir"* that *"trills are played with pleasure"* or *"trills are executed [= added] ad libitum"*

The text goes on to explain the correct execution of ornaments:

Le pincement se fait ausy dabor atoute les partie en commançant la premiere notte il faut etre fort ezat a faire tous les tremblemens et pincemens marquées. Il faut faire ensorte que toutte les notte sonne net et quil ny ait au qun brouillement de son il vaux mieux aller plus doucement on en est jamais blamé.[230]

A pincement should be placed at the start of each voice, commencing with the first note. Care must be taken to play all the tremblements and pincements indicated and to make sure that all the notes are clear, avoiding confusion; it is better to go slower, a choice for which one is never criticized.

An exception is Boyvin's indication concerning the *Duo du Second ton* (in ₵), where the author prescribes an *inégale* performance and a slow pace with the words *pointés lentement*:

Jacques Boyvin: *Duo (Second ton, Premier Livre d'Orgue)*

---

[213] Nivers 1665, 177.
[214] Lebègue 1676, 14.
[215] Gravet 1996, 75.
[216] Raison 1688, 31.
[217] Boyvin 1690, 55.
[218] Chaumont 1695, 61.
[219] Manuscrit de Bourges, 88.
[220] Corrette 1703, 122.
[221] Gravet 1996, 85.
[222] Corrette 1737, 160.
[223] Nivers 1665, 177.
[224] Lebègue 1676, 14.
[225] Raison 1688, 31.
[226] Boyvin 1700, 92.
[227] Chaumont 1695, 61.
[228] Corrette 1703, 123.
[229] Pruitt 1986, 247.
[230] Pruitt 1986, 248.

TRIO

In contrast to German *Trios* which are always for two manuals and pedal – taking as their model the Italian *Sonata a 2* (i.e. for two solo instruments and *basso continuo*) – French *Trios* are of two different types: the *Trio à deux dessus*, with two upper voices in the right hand and bass voice in the left hand, and the *Trio à trois claviers* for two manuals plus pedal.

The first type is the most widespread and was considered as the norm or *"ordinaire"*, as stated by Raison in his title to the *Trio* that serves as the *Benedictus* in his *Messe du Troisiesme ton*:

Trio a Trois Claviers ou a deux a L'ordinaire.   *Trio à Trois Claviers, or for two in the usual manner [à l'ordinaire].*

André Raison: *Trio a trois Claviers* (*Benedictus, Messe du Troisiesme ton*)

It should be noted that in the version *à trois claviers* (two manuals and pedal) Raison suggests the possibility of allowing the bass voice to be played by another person (*une 3e main*).

In contrast to the *Duo*, the *Trio* appeared in France quite early: it was already present in Titelouze's *Hymnes de l'Eglise* in 1623. In the *Pièces d'Orgue* by Louis Couperin, which date from the mid-17th century, there are also 14 Trios. Unlike the *Trios* of these two authors – which were based on *plainchant* – from Lebègue onwards (Nivers in his three *livres d'orgue* did not publish any *Trio*) this form became free of any tie to a *cantus firmus*.[231] Raison also wanted to expand the possibilities of the *Trio* by linking it to forms of dance and *ostinato*: this is the case with the *Trio en Gigue* (*Gloria* of the *Messe du Huictiesme ton*), *Trio en Passacaille* (*Christe* of the *Messe du Deuziesme ton*) and the *Trio en Chaconne* (*Christe* of the *Messe du Sixiesme ton*):

André Raison: *Trio en Chaconne* (*Messe du Sixiesme ton*)

The *Trios à deux dessus*, conceived as explained above to be played on two manuals and without pedal, commonly used a *Jeu de Tierce* against a reed registration (*Cromorne* or *Trompette*) or two opposing *Jeux de Tierces*. The most frequent registrations are as follows:

Basse	Dessus
G.O. Jeu de Tierce	POS. Cromorne
or	
G.O. Trompette	POS. Jeu de Tierce
or	
G.O. Jeu de Tierce	POS. Jeu de Tierce

Atypical is the registration suggested by Gigault, which requires different colours for the two *dessus* but without the use of the pedal:

[...] pour les trios à deux dessus on poura toucher le premier dessus, sur la tierce du grand orgue, le deuxieme dessus sur le cromorne du positif avec le pouce de la main droite, et la basse sur la tierce du grand orgue [...].[232]

[...] in the trios à deux dessus, one can play the first dessus with the tierce on the grand orgue, the second dessus on the cromorne of the positif with the thumb of the right hand, and the basse on the tierce of the grand orgue [...].

It is notable that many of the sources call for the use of the *Tremblant* (*doux*). Here below are the details:

1676 – Nicolas Lebègue

Le Trio a deux dessus, La Basse sur la Tierce de la Grand'Orgue, avec le petit Bourdon, le Prestant, le Nazard, la Quarte de Nazard, & le Tremblant doux, Au Positif, le Cromhorne seul, ou s'il n'est pas assez fort, y mettre le Bourdon ou la Fluste, ou la Montre.

Trio a deux dessus: the Basse with the Tierce on the Grand'Orgue with petit Bourdon, Prestant, Nazard, Quarte de Nazard & Tremblant doux; on the Positif Cromhorne alone or, if it is not loud enough, one can add Bourdon or Fluste [4'], or Montre [4'].

Autre Meslange pour le Trio a deux Dessus, La Basse sur la Trompette seule de la Grand'Orgue. Le Dessus sur la Montre, le Bourdon, le Nazard & la Tierce du Positif.

Other registration for the Trio à deux Dessus: the Basse with the Trompette alone on the Grand'Orgue; the Dessus with Montre, Bourdon, Nazard & Tierce on the Positif.

Aux Petites Orgues le tout sur la Tierce.

On small organs: all on the Tierce.

Aux Mediocres le tout sur la Trompette & le Cornet.[233]

On medium-size organs: all on the Trompette & Cornet.

post 1678 – Anonymous

Le jeu de tierce pour les duos et trios, il faut le bourdon, le prestant, doublette, le nazard et la tierce.[234]

The jeu de tierce for the duos and trios; one should use the bourdon, prestant, doublette, nazard and tierce.

1685 – Nicolas Gigault

[...] les deux dessus sur le cromorne, et la basse sur la tierce [...].[235]

[...] the two dessus on the cromorne and the basse on the tierce [...].

1688 – André Raison

Le Trio se touche sur le Cromorne sans fond de la M. droite et de la M. gauche le Bourdon, le 4 pieds et la flute, le Nazard, la Tierce et le tremblât doux:

The Trio is played with the right hand on the Cromorne without foundations; the left hand on the Bourdon, the 4 foot [= Prestant] and flute [4'], Nazard, Tierce and tremblant doux:

Organ & interpretation: the French *école classique*

On le peut toucher aussi coe. [= comme] le meslange des Duos cy dessus [see p. 151].[236]	It can also be played with the Duo registrations as described above [see page 151].

Raison also includes a registration that calls for the *Voix humaine* in the left hand against a *Jeu de Nazard* in the right hand:

On le meslange encore avec la voix humaine, au grand Orgue de la M. g. avec le Bourdon et la flute, et de la M. d. le Bourd. la flute et le Nazard, avec le Tremblant doux.[237]	Or furthermore with the voix humaine of the grand Orgue with Bourdon and flute (left hand), and the right hand with Bourdon, flute and Nazard, with the Tremblant doux.

1690 – Jacques Boyvin

Pour les trios a deux dessus, on met en haut la grosse tierce comme au Duo hormis qu'il n'y faut point de seize pieds, au Positif le Cromhorne seul on y met le tramblant doux.[238]	In the trios à deux dessus one should draw en haut the grosse tierce, as in the Duo but without the sixteen foot; on the Positif the Cromhorne alone with the tramblant doux.

Boyvin's indication *"on met en haut la grosse tierce"* does not mean that one should play the upper voices with the *Grosse tierce*: the term *"en haut"* implies rather the use of the upper manual, i.e. the *Grand Orgue*, for the left hand. This is confirmed by the continuation of the sentence where Boyvin specifies *"comme au Duo"*.[239]

1695 – Lambert Chaumont

Le Trio a 2 Dessus, au grand Orgue la basse sur la Tromp au positif le Dessus sur la Montre, Bourdon, Tierce, Nazard.	The Trio à 2 Dessus: the basse on the grand Orgue with the Trompette; on the positif the Dessus with Montre, Bourdon, Tierce and Nazard.
Ou au grand Orgue sur le petit Bourdon, prestant[,] Nazard, 4te de Naz[,] Tierce, et tremblant doux. Au positif sur le Cromh. Bourdon et Flute.[240]	Or: on the grand Orgue with the petit Bourdon, prestant, Nazard, 4te de Naz, Tierce and tremblant doux; on the positif with Cromhorne, Bourdon and Flute.

1703 – Gaspard Corrette

Le Trio a deux dessus, On pousse les Claviers, la Main droite sur le Positif, et la Main Gauche sur le Grand Jeu. Au Grand Jeu, Bourdon, Prestant, Montre, Tierce, Grosse Tierce, Nazar, et Quarte de Nazar. Au Positif, Bourdon, Prestant ou Montre, le Cromhorne, et le Tremblant Doux.[241]	For the Trio a deux dessus, the manuals should not be coupled; the right hand on the Positif and the left hand on the Grand Jeu. On the Grand Jeu [= G.O.]: Bourdon, Prestant, Montre, Tierce, Grosse Tierce, Nazar, and Quarte de Nazar. On the Positif: Bourdon Prestant or Montre, Cromhorne and the Tremblant Doux.

One can assume that, in this registration, Gaspard Corrette forgot to mention the 16' on the *Grand Orgue*, as it appears in the analogous registration of his son Michel.

In the case of Gaspard Corrette, the term *Grosse tierce* means here the *Tierce* $3^{1/5}$, since both the *Tierce* and *Grosse tierce* are required.

1737 – Michel Corrette

Pour le Trio [...] On pousse le Grand Clavier. Au G.j. [= G.O.] Bourdon, Bourdon de 16 pied, Prestant, Montre, Tierce, Grosse Tierce, Nazar et quatre de Nazar. Au Positif. Bourdon, Prestant et Cromhorne.

For the Trio [...] the manuals are not coupled. On the G.j. [= G.O.]: Bourdon, 16-foot Bourdon, Prestant, Montre, Tierce, Grosse Tierce, Nazar and quarte de Nazar. On the Positif: Bourdon, Prestant and Cromhorne.

Autre Meslange pour le Trio [...] On pousse le Grand Clavier. Au G.j. Bourdon, Prestant, Bourdon 16. pieds et Clairon. Au Positif. Bourdon, Prestant et Nazar.[242]

Other registration for the Trio [...] The manuals are not coupled. On the G.j.: Bourdon, Prestant, 16-foot Bourdon and Clairon. On the Positif: Bourdon, Prestant and Nazar.

Compared to the *Trio à 2 dessus*, always written on two staves, the *Trio à trois claviers* could also be on two, but was, more often on three staves; in the case of the latter the lower line is for the pedal:

Nicolas Lebègue: *Trio a 3 claviers* (1. Ton, Premier livre d'orgue)

Similarly to the *Trios à deux dessus*, those *à trois claviers* also use a registration with *Jeu de Tierce* or *Cornet separé* in order to contrast another based on reeds (*Cromorne, Voix humaine* or *Trompette*) together with the *fonds*. The pedal line is played with the *Flûte 8* while the most common combinations for the manuals are:

Premier Dessus	Second Dessus
POS. Cromorne	G.O. Jeu de Tierce
or	
POS. Jeu de Tierce	G.O. Voix humaine
or	
RÉC. Cornet	POS. Cromorne
or	
G.O. Trompette	POS. Jeu de Tierce

Below are the specific indications given by the various composers:

1676 – Nicolas Lebègue

Le Trio a trois Claviers; Le Premier Dessus sur le Cromhorne, le Bourdon & le Prestant du Positif, L'autre partie sur la Tierce, petit Bourdon, Prestant, Nazard, Quarte de Nazard & Tremblant doux de la Grand' Orgue & la Pedalle de Fluste.

The Trio à trois Claviers. The first Dessus with the Cromhorne, Bourdon & Prestant on the Positif; the other [upper] voice with the Tierce, petit Bourdon, Prestant, Nazard, Quarte de Nazard & Tremblant doux on the Grand'Orgue; and with the Fluste on the pedal.

Ou bien le Premier Dessus, sur la Tierce du Positif, l'autre Partie sur la voix Humaine, le petit Bourdon, le Prestant & Tremblant doux à la Grand' Orgue, et la Pedalle de Fluste

Or the first Dessus with the Tierce on the Positif, the other voice with voix Humaine, petit Bourdon, Prestant & Tremblant doux on the Grand'Orgue; and with the Fluste on the pedal

ou bien le Premier Dessus sur le Cornet, l'autre Partie sur le Cromhorne, le Bourdon, le Prestant du Positif, la Pedalle de Fluste,

or the first Dessus with the Cornet [on the Récit], the other voice with Cromhorne, Bourdon, Prestant on the Positif; the Fluste on the pedal,

ou bien le Premier Dessus sur la Trompette, le Second Dessus sur la Tierce du Positif, et la Pedalle.[243]

or the first Dessus on the Trompette, the second Dessus on the Tierce of the Positif, and the pedal [with Flûte].

1688 – André Raison

Le Trio à 3. Claviers est de même que les autres en y adjoutant aussi la Pedalle de Flute.[244]

The Trio à 3. Claviers is like the others [à deux dessus] with the addition of the Flute on the pedal.

1690 – Jacques Boyvin

Les autres trios se touchent sur le Cromhorne avec son fond, le Cornet separé, & la pedalle de flustes, ou bien avec le marche pied, ou tyrasse mettant sur le Grand Corps, bourdon, prestant, & nazar.[245]

The other trios [= à trois claviers] are played with Cromhorne and its fond, the Cornet separé [Récit] and the pedal of flustes or with the tyrasse, drawing on the Grand Corps [= Grand Orgue] bourdon, prestant & nazar.

1695 – Lambert Chaumont

Le Trio a 3 Claviers. Le premier Dessus sur le Bourdon, Prestant ou flutte, et Cromhorne. Le second dessus au grand Orgue sur le petit Bourdon, Prestant, Tierce, Nazard, et tremblant doux.

Trio à 3 Claviers. The first Dessus with Bourdon, Prestant or flutte, and Cromhorne; the second dessus on the grand Orgue with petit Bourdon, Prestant, Tierce, Nazard and tremblant doux.

Ou au 1er Dessus la Tierce. Au 2^d la voix H. Ou le 1er Dessus sur le Cornet. le 2 sur le Cromh. Ou le 1er Dessus sur la Tromp le 2 sur la Tierce.[246]

Or for the 1st Dessus the Tierce and for the 2nd the voix Humaine. Or the 1st Dessus with the Cornet and the 2nd with the Cromhorne. Or the 1st Dessus with the Trompette and the 2nd with the Tierce.

late 17th/early 18th century – Manuscrit de Bourges

Petit Bourdon, prestant et cromorne de la grande orgue. Au positif la tierce et son accompagnement, pédalle de huict pieds et de quatre pieds.[247]

Petit Bourdon [8'], prestant and cromorne of the grand orgue. On the positif the tierce and its accompanying stops [= Jeu de Tierce]; pedal with eight and four foot.

1737 – Michel Corrette

Pour Le Trio a 3 Claviers [...] Le Premier Dessus sur le Positif. Bourdon, Prestant, Tierce et Nazar. Le Second Dessus sur le Cornet de Recit. La Basse sur les Pedalles de Flûtes et le Tremblant Doux.[248]

For the Trio a 3 Claviers [...] The first Dessus on the Positif with Bourdon, Prestant, Tierce and Nazar. The second Dessus on the Cornet of the Récit. The Basse on the pedal with the Flûtes, and the Tremblant Doux.

In general, *Trios* were intended to be played at a moderate or slow tempo. Most of Jullien's *Trios* bear the indication *Gravement*:

Gilles Jullien: *Trio du 2nd ton* (*Premier livre d'orgue*)

The *Trio a 3 claviers* of the *Second Ton* by Lebègue, marked in ₵, bears the indication *gravement*:

Nicolas Lebègue: *Trio a 3 Claviers* (2. Ton, *Premier livre d'orgue*)

A slow tempo (*fort lentement*) was also prescribed by the anonymous writer of the *Manuscrit de l'Arsenal* (last quarter of 17th century). A slow tempo is implied by the instructions in most of the *Trio* registrations to use the *Trembland doux*, a device that is ill-suited to fast playing:

| Le trio ce touche hardiment mais fort lentement et on ne peut aller trop doucement [...].[249] | The trio is played boldly but very slowly; one cannot err on the side of playing too slowly [...]. |

The same manuscript also underscores the great importance of playing a *Trio* with dotted rhythms (*inégal*):

| [...] le principal du trio est de le bien pointer mais il faut que ce pointement ce face avec grand feu et grande hardiesse [...].[250] | [...] the most important thing in a trio is to play it with a well dotted rhythm, but this dotted manner must be done with fire and very boldly [...]. |

The contrasting *affect* required for *Duos* and *Trios* should also be highlighted: fast and brilliant for the former, moderate and *gracieusement* for the latter.

However, various practical considerations would seem to suggest a moderate tempo for *Trios*. The presence of numerous embellishments is certainly one such factor, as in the following example by de Grigny:

Nicolas de Grigny: *Trio (Gloria, Livre d'Orgue)*

In a *Trio à trois Claviers*, passages of short notes in the bass, as in the following example, would make it difficult to play fast, especially considering the structural characteristics of a pedalboard *à la française*:

André Raison: *Elevation Trio a 3 Claviers (Messe du Premier Ton)*

There are also considerations of a musical nature. The *Trio en passacaille* taken from Raison's *Messe du Deuziesme ton*, well known for its resemblance to Johann Sebastian Bach's Passacaglia, would seem to call for a moderate tempo, both on account of the *affect*

André Raison: *Trio en passacaille* (*Christe, Messe du Deuziesme ton*)

and owing to the expressive nature of the *Passacaille*, as stated by Brossard:

Passacaglio, veut dire, Passacaille. C'est proprement une Chacone.	*Passacaglio, i.e. Passacaille. It is properly speaking a Chacone.*
[...]	[...]
Toute la différence est que le mouvement en est ordinairement plus grave que celuy de la Chacone, le Chant plus tendre, & les expressions moins vives, c'est pour cela que les Passacailles sont presque toûjours travaillées sur des Modes mineurs.[251]	*The only difference is that its tempo is usually slower than that of the Chacone, the Chant is more tender and the expressions are less vivacious; for this reason the Passacailles are almost always written in minor tonalities.*

There are clearly also some exceptions. Gaspard Corrette advised a more flowing tempo for his *Trios*:

Le Trio demande beaucoup d'exactitude de mesure et de Legerete suivant le mouvement.[252]	*The Trio requires a lot of precision of timing and lightness [Legerete] according to the tempo.*

It is of note, however, that both *Trios* contained in his *Messe du 8.ᵉ Ton* have a very simple notation and make limited use of ornaments:

Gaspard Corrette: *Graduel - Trio* (*Messe du 8.ᵉ Ton*)

Similar are two *Trios* of Jullien, in which speed and lightness of performance are required:

Gilles Jullien: *Trio du 4ᵉ ton* (*Premier Livre d'Orgue*)

---

[231] Ponsford 2011, 255.
[232] Gigault 1685, 26.
[233] Lebègue 1676, 15.
[234] Gravet 1996, 75.
[235] Gigault 1685, 26.
[236] Raison 1688, 31.
[237] Raison 1688, 31.
[238] Boyvin 1690, 55.
[239] Gorenstein-Boyvin, 33.
[240] Chaumont 1695, 61.
[241] Corrette 1703, 122.
[242] Corrette 1737, 160.
[243] Lebègue 1676, 15.
[244] Raison 1688, 31.
[245] Boyvin 1690, 55.
[246] Chaumont 1695, 61.
[247] Manuscrit de Bourges, 88.
[248] Corrette 1737, 160.
[249] Pruitt 1986, 247.
[250] Pruitt 1986, 247.
[251] Brossard 1703, definition of term *Passacaglio*, without page number.
[252] Corrette 1703, 123.

QUATUOR

The genre of *Quatuor*, a four-voice composition in imitative style, derives from the *Fugue* or *Fantaisie*. Unlike these, however, the *Quatuor* ideally requires the four voices to be played simultaneously on different divisions of the organ. The manner of scoring a *Quatuor* differs according to the composer; Boyvin uses the customary two-stave system:

Jacques Boyvin: *Quatuor* (*Cinquieme Ton, Second Livre d'Orgue*)

Other authors such as d'Anglebert, Marchand and Guilain use the open-score system on four staves. Jean-Henri d'Anglebert's *Quatuor sur le Kyrie à trois sujets tirés du plein chant*, dated 1689, is among the first examples of this genre:[253]

Jean-Henri d'Anglebert: *Quatuor sur le Kyrie à trois sujets tirés du plein chant* (*Pieces de Clavecin*, 1689)

In the preface, d'Anglebert invites one to play this piece in such a way that each voice is on a different *Clavier*:

Cõme cette piece est plus travaillée que les autres, elle ne peut bien faire son effet que sur un grand Orgue, et même sur quatre Claviers differens, j'entens trois Claviers pour les mains et le Clavier des pedales, avec des jeux d'egale force et de differente harmonie, pour faire distinguer les entrées des parties.[254]	As this piece is more elaborate than the others, to appreciate its full effect requires a large organ, and it should be played even on four different manuals, I mean, three manuals for the hands and pedal (for the feet), with stops of equal strength and different colour, to better distinguish each part as it enters.

In fact, the same is also recommended for other *Quatuor* registrations. The example of d'Anglebert clearly calls for the use of three manuals and pedal, i.e. to play with one hand on two keyboards at the same time.

Indications to play with one hand on two keyboards simultaneously are found in two pieces by Louis Couperin, *Conditor* and *Urbs Beata Jherusalem*:

Louis Couperin: *Urbs Beata Jherusalem* (*Pièces d'Orgue*)

Urbs Beata Jherusalem en Haulte Contre avec le poulce droict ou en trio	Urbs Beata Jherusalem played in the alto voice with the right thumb, or as a trio

Lebègue gives a similar indication in the (*Dialogue de*) *Vox humaine du 3 ton*. At the end of the piece the author suggests two alternatives: either to play all voices – as usual – on the *Grand Orgue* with the *Voix humaine* or to play the soprano (1er *dessus*) on the *Grand Orgue* with the *Voix humaine*, and the alto (2me *dessus*) with the thumb on the *Jeu doux* of the *Positif*:

Nicolas Lebègue: *Vox humaine* (3e *Ton, Premier livre d'orgue*)

Also Gigault's *Fugue à 3 du 5e et 8e ton pour la voix humaine* (*Livre de Musique pour l'Orgue*, 1685) states in the subtitle

[...] avec le pouce de la main droite sur le jeu doux	[...] with the thumb of the right hand on the *jeu doux*

i.e. – in a similar manner to the previous example – to play the soprano voice on the second manual (*Grand Orgue*) with the *Voix humaine* and the alto on the first manual (*Positif*) with the *Jeu doux*.

Another, simpler possibility is to entrust the performance of one of the voices to a second person. In his *Livre d'Orgue* published in 1688, André Raison did not include any *Quatuor*, but referring to the *Trios* and the *Récits en taille* he wrote:

Le Trio à 3 Claviers, et le Cromorne ou Tierce en Taille se peuvent exercer avec un amy qui toucheroit le jeu doux de la main droit au grand Orgue a la place de la pedalle de flutte, laquelle je n'ay gueres chargé pour faciliter les Pieces le plus qu'il m'a esté possible.[255]	The *Trio à 3 Claviers* as well as the *Cromorne* or *Tierce en Taille* can be performed by having a friend play the part written for the pedal (*flutte*) on the *jeu doux* (of the *grand Orgue*, used for the right hand); I made sure not to overcomplicate this part in order to facilitate the playing as much as possible.

What Raison here means is that a second person should play the bass voice on the *Grand Orgue*: in the case of a *Récit en taille* this means playing on the same manual as the right hand (*Jeux doux*). In the case of the *Trio à 3 Claviers* the two top voices would play on the *Positif* and *Récit* while the bass, entrusted to a second person, would be played on the *Fonds* of the *Grand Orgue*. The same notion could, hence, also apply to the *Quatuor*. *Quatuors* to be performed *expressis verbis* on four different organ divisions are actually rarely documented. A late testimony attesting this practice is found in Dom Bédos' *L'Art du Facteur d'Orgues*; the author envisaged two different registration possibilities, with different manuals used as well:

Pour le Quatuor à quatre Claviers 1°. *On fera le premier dessus sur la Trompette de Récit, ou sur deux 8 pieds (s'ils y sont séparés;) le second dessus sur le petit Jeu de Tierce du grand Orgue; la troisieme partie sur le Cromorne du Positif avec le Prestant; la Basse sur la Pédale de Flûte, ou du Jeu de Tierce; ou bien,* 2°. *On fera le premier dessus sur le Cornet de Récit, le second sur la Trompette & le Prestant du grand Orgue, la troisieme partie sur le Jeu de Tierce du Positif, & la Basse sur la Pédale de Flûte.*[256]	*For the Quatuor with four manuals* 1st: the first *dessus* will be played on the *Trompette* of the *Récit*, or on two 8 foot stops (if present as separate stops), the second *dessus* on the *petit Jeu de Tierce* of the *grand Orgue*; the third part on the *Cromorne* of the *Positif* with the *Prestant*; the *Basse* with the pedal *Flûte* or with a *Jeu de Tierce*; or, 2nd: the first *dessus* will be played on the *Cornet* of the *Récit*, the second on the *Trompette* and *Prestant* of the *grand Orgue*, the third part on the *Jeu de Tierce* of the *Positif* and the *Basse* with the pedal *Flûte*.

At the same time, Dom Bédos emphasized the difficulty of performing the two examples described above:

Cette maniere de faire le Quatuor sur quatre Claviers est difficile pour l'exécution: on ne peut guere faire chanter les deux dessus, parce qu'on est obligé de les toucher de la seule main droite sur deux Claviers différents; ou selon la seconde maniere, l'on est obligé de faire les deux parties moyennes de la seule main gauche sur deux Claviers différents.[257]	This way of playing the *Quatuor* on four manuals is difficult to perform: the two upper parts cannot be played in a proper cantabile manner [*faire chanter*] because they must be played with the right hand alone on two different manuals; or referring to the second way, the two middle parts must be played with the left hand alone on two different manuals.

On account of these very difficulties, sources that provide registrations for a *Quatuor* – indeed not many – suggest simpler alternatives. Jacques Boyvin (1690) proposes three different solutions involving the use of two keyboards, two of which are with pedal and one without:

[...] on met la main gauche sur le grand Orgue auq[ue]l on met le jeu de tierce qui se compose ainsy bourdon, prestant, nazard, quarte, & tierce, la main droitte sur le Positif, ou l'on met le Cromhorne avec son fond, [...] & le tremblant doux.	[...] the left hand is played on the grand Orgue with the jeu de tierce, which consists of bourdon, prestant, nazard, quarte & tierce; the right hand on the Positif with the Cromhorne and its fond [...] and the tremblant doux.
Ou bien [...] la basse, & le dessus sur la tierce du grand Orgue avec son mélange ordinaire & les parties mediantes, qui sont la taille, & la haute-contre, sur le Cromhorne du Positif avec son fond, cette manière est plus belle & plus difficile a moins qu'on ne soit aydé d'une tyrasse ou marche pieds;	Or [...] the basse and the dessus on the tierce of the grand Orgue with its usual mélange [= Jeu de Tierce] while the middle parts, which are the tenor and the alto, on the Cromhorne of the Positif with its fond; this is the most beautiful way and the most difficult unless one has the help of a tyrasse or pedal coupler;
On peut encor toucher le Quatuor ainsi, ayant une tyrasse vous mettrés au grand Corps, bourdon, huit pieds, prestant, & nazar; Au Positif la tierce en taille, sçavoir, bourdon, prestant nazar doublette, tierce & larigot, & les deux autres parties de la main droitte sur la trompette de recit [...].[258]	The Quatuor can also be played this way: if there is a tyrasse one should draw, on the grand Corps, bourdon, eight foot, prestant & nazar; on the Positif the tierce en taille, i.e. bourdon, prestant, nazar, doublette, tierce & larigot; the other two parts of the right hand with the trompette on the récit [...].

For the latter registration, he specified that it was necessary to have

[...] un Orgue a quatre Claviers; cette manière est fort belle, mais il faut que les quatre parties chantent egalement bien, particulierement la taille qui est la tierce du Positif, ce qui pince mieux, & aproche le plus de l'Oreille, Mais il n'y a presque que ceux qui sont capables de composer ces sortes de pieces, qui puissent les executer c'est pourquoy j'en ay fort peu mis dans mon livre [...].[259]	[...] an organ with four manuals [= 3 manuals plus pedal]; this manner is very beautiful but it is important that the four parts sing equally well, in particular the tenor played with the tierce of the Positif, which is more incisive and sounds closer to the ear. But virtually the only ones capable of playing these pieces are the composers themselves; for this reason I have included very few of them in my book [...].

In the same year 1690, in the preface to the *Premier Livre d'Orgue*, Gilles Jullien mentioned, first of all, the possibility of playing normal, four-voice *Fugues* on two manuals, in the style of a *Quatuor*:

Il Est pourtant Necessaire d'avertir que les fugues a quatre parties que lon joüe sur la	It is therefore necessary to point out that four-part fugues that are [normally] played with the

trompette ou Cromhorne pouront se Jouer Aux Grands Orgues sur deux claviers En quatüor.²⁶⁰

trompette or Cromhorne can be performed, on large instruments, on two manuals, as a quatüor.

Then, referring to three pieces in the first mode, including the following *Fantesie Cromatique*

Gilles Jullien: *Fantesie Cromatique* (1ᵉʳ Ton, *Premier Livre d'Orgue*)

he suggested an interesting registration:

Le Dessus, et la basse Sur le clavier du grand Orgue, avec le bourdon, prestant, huit pieds, nazard, et quarte de Nazard, la haute contre et taille sur le Cromhorne du positif avec le bourdon, prestant, y Joignant Sj lon veut le nazard, affin de rendre le Cromhorne plus rond En harmonie, le tremblant doux pouruei qu'il batte Egallement, Sinon le tremblant a vent perdu.²⁶¹

The Dessus and the Basse on the grand Orgue with bourdon, prestant, eight-foot [= Montre], nazard and quarte de Nazard; the alto and the tenor on the positif with the Cromhorne, bourdon, prestant, adding if one wishes the nazard, in order to give the Cromhorne a more rounded sound; the tremblant doux can also be used as long as it beats regularly. Otherwise the tremblant à vent perdu.

This registration implies the use of a *tirasse* to the *Grand Orgue* to perform the bass part. Here, Jullien explicitly prohibited the use of the *Grosse Tierce*:

Je ne Comprends point dans le meslange des jeux du grand Orgue la grosse tierce, par ce que le dessus et la basse domineroient trop sur la taille et haute Contre qui se jouent Sur le Cromhorne.²⁶²

I did not include, in the registration on the grand Orgue, the grosse tierce, because the Dessus and the Basse would be too dominant compared to the tenor and alto, that are played on the Cromhorne.

The second registration is simpler, with the right hand playing the soprano and alto voices while the left hand plays the tenor and bass voices:

Le Quatuor se peut toucher d'une maniere bien plus aysee, sçavoir le dessus et haute Contre Sur le Cornet Séparé, la basse et la taille Sur le Cromhorne, bourdon, et prestant.²⁶³

The Quatuor can be played in a much easier way, i.e. the Dessus and the alto with the Cornet Séparé [Récit], Basse and tenor with the Cromhorne, bourdon and prestant [Positif].

This concept finds perfect application in the following composition by Boyvin, entitled *Fugue-quatuor*:

Jacques Boyvin: *Fugue-quatuor* (*Sixieme ton, Premier Livre d'Orgue*)

Jullien also contemplated a registration for a single-manual organ with divided stops:

[...] *pour les Orgue, ou Il ny a que un Clavier et dont les jeux Sont coupez, l'on tirera le bourdon, prestant, le dessus de tierce et nazard, et la basse de Cromhorne ou Voix humaine.*[264]	[...] *for organs endowed with a single manual and divided stops, one should draw the bourdon, prestant, the treble tierce and [treble] nazard; in the bass [low range of the manual] Cromhorne or Voix humaine.*

Instead of playing simultaneously on four different divisions of the organ, Dom Bédos also suggests two simpler alternatives:

[...] *voici un autre mélange sur lequel on pourra exécuter plus aisément le Quatuor de deux manieres, en le faisant sur trois Claviers seulement.*	[...] *here is another registration with which one can play the Quatuor more easily in two ways, using three manuals only.*
Pour le Quatuor à trois Claviers.	*For the Quatuor à trois Claviers.*
On fera les premier & second dessus sur le Cornet de Récit; la troisieme partie sur le Cromorne & le Prestant du Positif; & la Basse sur les Pédales de Flûte, ou du Jeu de Tierce.	*The first & second dessus will be played on the Cornet of the Récit; the third part on Cromorne & Prestant of the Positif; & the Basse with the pedal Flûte or with a Jeu de Tierce.*
Ou bien avec le même mélange, on touchera le premier dessus sur le Cornet de Récit; les deux moyennes parties sur les tailles du Cromorne; & la Basse sur les Pédales de Flûte ou du Jeu de Tierce; cette seconde maniere aura plus de brillant & d'harmonie, sans plus de difficulté pour l'exécution.[265]	*Or even, with the same registration, the first dessus will be played on the Cornet de Récit; the two middle parts on the Cromorne; & the Basse with the pedal Flûte or with a Jeu de Tierce; this second way will have greater brilliance & harmony, without making it more difficult to perform.*

Concerning the manner of playing a *Quatuor*, there are essentially no concrete indications to be found; only these vague words by Jacques Boyvin, who defined the *Quatuor* as

[...] *une fugue de mouvement dont les parties sont plus agissantes & plus chantantes que la fugue [...].*[266]	[...] *a fugue de mouvement where the parts are more active [agissantes] & more cantabile than in the fugue [...].*

[253] Ponsford 2011, 181.
[254] D'Anglebert 1689, 47.
[255] Raison 1688, 31.
[256] Dom Bédos 1766-1778, 205.
[257] Dom Bédos 1766-1778, 205.
[258] Boyvin 1690, 55.
[259] Boyvin 1690, 55.
[260] Jullien 1690, 50-51.
[261] Jullien 1690, 50-51.
[262] Jullien 1690, 50-51.
[263] Jullien 1690, 51.
[264] Jullien 1690, 51.
[265] Dom Bédos 1766-1778, 205-206.
[266] Boyvin 1690, 55.

RÉCIT DE DESSUS

The term *Récit* makes its first appearance in the organ repertory – at least in so far as printed music is concerned – in the first *Livre d'Orgue* by Nivers, published in 1665.[267] Among the musical genres treated therein, the term *Récit* is used primarily to indicate a *solo* and is related to the concept of *recitativo cantato*. Numerous composers state in the prefaces to their *livres d'orgue* that a *Récit* should be played in a manner that imitates singing and the *manière de chanter*. Nivers is no exception; in the chapter dedicated to ornaments and *touché* of the aforementioned volume, he wrote:

De touttes ces choses on doit consulter la methode de chanter, parce qu'en ces rencontres l'Orgue doit imiter la Voix.[268]	In all these things, one should be guided by the manner of singing, because, in this regard, the organ has to imitate the voice.

The *Récit de dessus*, i.e. a *Récit* with the *solo* in the soprano voice, is the most common. The French *orgue classique*, thanks to its many colours, is the ideal instrument to "make the various timbres sing". Curiously, the registrations suggested by the composers are relatively few in number. The following table summarizes the most frequent *mélanges* for a *Récit de dessus* suggested in the prefaces to the different *livres d'orgue*:

	Dessus on the *Positif*	
Récit de Cromorne	*Récit de Nazard*	*Récit avec Jeu de Tierce*
Cromorne 8	Bourdon 8	Bourdon 8
(Bourdon 8)	Prestant 4	Prestant 4
	Nazard $2^{2/3}$	Nazard $2^{2/3}$
		Tierce $1^{3/5}$

Dessus on the *Récit*		*Dessus* on the *Grand Orgue*
Récit de Cornet	*Récit de Trompette*	*Récit de Voix Humaine*
Cornet separé	Trompette 8	Bourdon 8
	(Bourdon 8)	Flûte 4 or Prestant 4
		Voix Humaine 8
		Tremblant doux

In some cases the author offers more than one possibility, with titles such as *Récit de Cromhorne ou de petitte tierce* (Boyvin 1690), *Dessus de Cromhorne ou de trompette* (Jullien 1690) or *Couplet en Récit de Voix humaine ou de Cromhorne* (Nivers 1667). Below is an example by Boyvin:

Jacques Boyvin: *Recit de Cromhorne ou de petitte tierce* (*Premier ton, Premier Livre d'Orgue*)

The accompaniment is played on the *Grand Orgue* if the *dessus* is on the *Positif*, with a *Jeux doux* registration adjusted such that there is a good balance between *solo* and accompaniment. Below some examples (see also page 136):

Accompaniment on the *Grand Orgue*				
Bourdon 8	or	Bourdon 8	or	Montre 8
Prestant 4		Flûte 4		

Where the *dessus* is, instead, on the *Grand Orgue*, the accompaniment will be played on the *Positif*:

Accompaniment on the *Positif*		
Bourdon 8	or	Bourdon 8
Prestant 4		Flûte 4

The most common *solo* registrations are based either on the reeds (in particular *Cromorne* or *Voix humaine*) or on *mélanges* with the *Nasard* or *Tierce* (*Cornet* or *Jeu de Tierce*). When used for a *Récit de dessus*, the *Trompette* is usually that of the *Récit* (3rd manual) – available however only on large instruments of a later period – rather than that of the *Grand Orgue*. The *Récits de Trompette* became popular during the 18th century, in parallel with the more widespread use of the *Trompette* on the 3rd manual. *Récits de Trompette* composed in the 17th century are rare; one of the few is in the *Second Livre d'Orgue* by Lebègue (1678). Of note is that in 1669 a *Trompette de Récit* was added to the organ of *St. Merry* (*St. Médéric*) in Paris, where Lebègue had been appointed organist a few years earlier:

Nicolas Lebègue: *Dessus de trompette* (*Magnificat du 7me Ton, Second Livre d'Orgue*)

The *Cornet* used for the *Récits* is usually that of the 3rd manual and not the *Cornet* of the *Grand Orgue*, which is primarily used in the *Grand Jeu*. On the other hand, the *Jeu de Tierce* can be formed on the *Positif* as well as on the *Grand Orgue*.

The registrations concerning the *Récits de dessus* are rather uniform, although there are some subtle differences:

1665 – Guillaume-Gabriel Nivers

Avec le Cornet on met un Jeu doux de la Basse.[269]	With the Cornet one should use a Jeu doux for the Basse [= accompaniment].

1676 – Nicolas Lebègue

Le Dessus de Cromhorne [...] La Basse sur le petit Bourdon & le Prestant de la grand'Orgue, ou le Huit pied tout seul, & le Cromhorne seul ou accompagné du Bourdon, ou de la Fluste au Positif.	The Dessus de Cromhorne [...] The Basse on the grand'Orgue with petit Bourdon [8'] and Prestant, or with just the eight foot [= Montre]; the Cromhorne alone or together with the Bourdon or with the Fluste [Flute 4] on the Positif.
Le Cornet [...] La Basse sur le Bourdon & la Montre au Positif.	The Cornet [...] The Basse with Bourdon & Montre [4'] on the Positif.
La Voix Humaine [...] L'accompagnement sur le Bourdon, la Fluste, ou la Montre du Positif. A la Grand' Orgue le petit Bourdon, le Prestant ou la	The Voix Humaine [...] The accompaniment on the Positif with Bourdon, Fluste or Montre. On the Grand'Orgue the petit Bourdon, Prestant or

Fluste de quatre pieds, La Voix Humaine & le Tremblant doux avec le Nasard si l'on veut.[270]

Fluste 4', the Voix Humaine & Tremblant doux, with the Nasard if one wishes.

post 1678 – Anonymous

Pour une cromhorne, il faut la basse sur le bourdon et le prestant du grand orgue, et le dessus sur le cromhorne du positif accompagné du bourdon.

In a [Récit de] cromhorne, one should play the bass [= accompaniment] on the grand orgue with bourdon and prestant, and the Dessus on the positif with cromhorne and bourdon.

Pour un dessus de trompette le jeu doux de la main gauche sur le bourdon et la montre du positif et le dessus sur la trompette seule ou accompagnée du bourdon.

For a Dessus de trompette: the left hand on the jeu doux of the positif with bourdon and montre [4'], the Dessus with the trompette alone or together with the bourdon.

Le Cornet, la basse de l'article ci-dessus et le cornet au grand orgue.[271]

For the [Récit de] Cornet: the accompaniment as above and the cornet on the grand orgue.

1688 – André Raison

Le Cornet se touche de la main droite, il à po accompagnem.ᵗ de la M. gauche le petit Bourdon et la flute ou le 4 pieds.

The Cornet [= Récit] is played with the right hand and with, as accompaniment in the left hand, the petit Bourdon [8'], and the flute [4'] or the 4 foot [Prestant].

Le Recit de Cromorne se touche de la M. d. sans fond, et de la M. g. au grand Orgue, le Bourd. et la flute.

The Recit de Cromorne is played with the right hand without fonds [on the Positif], and with the left hand on the grand Orgue with Bourdon and flute [4'].

La Voix humaine à pour accompagnem. le Bourd. et la flute ou 4 pieds avec le tremblant doux, quand elle est joüéé en Recit il faut mettre au positif le bourd. et la flute, avec le Nazard.[272]

The Voix humaine has as fonds [pour accompagnem.] the Bourdon and the flute [4'] or 4 foot [Montre] with the tremblant doux; when it is played as a Récit one should draw on the Positif the bourdon and flute [4'] with the Nazard.

1690 – Jacques Boyvin

Les Recits se touchent diversement, leur accompagnement au Grand Corps, est toujours le bourdon, & le Prestant, pour le Cromhorne, son accompagnement au Grand Corps est le huit pieds ouvert seul, On touche des recits sur la petite tierce, comme au Duo; ou bien sur le nazar sans tierce, avec le fond. Ou bien sur la trompette de recit, ou bien sur le Cromhorne seul ou bien sur le Cornet separé; [...].[273]

The récits are played in different ways. Their accompaniment on the Grand Corps [= G.O.] is always with bourdon and prestant; for the Cromhorne [as solo] the accompaniment on the Grand Corps is with the open 8-foot [Montre] alone. The récits are played with the petite tierce, as in the Duo, or also with the nazar without tierce, with the fond [= Bourdon 8 and Prestant 4]. Or else with the trompette of the récit, or else with the Cromhorne alone or else with the Cornet separé; [...].

late 17th/early 18th century – Manuscrit de Bourges

Le petit bourdon, et le prestant de la grande orgue pour les partyes. Au positif la montre, le bourdon et le cromorne en dessus [...] qu'il fault toucher fort mignardement à l'imitation d'une voix qui chante un air.[274]

The petit bourdon and prestant of the grand orgue for the accompaniment [les partyes]. On the positif the montre [4'], bourdon and cromorne as dessus [...] which must be played in a very sweet and elegant manner, imitating a voice singing an aria.

1703 – Gaspard Corrette

Le Recit de Nazar, Se touche sur le Positif, et l'acompagnement sur le Grand Jeu. Au Grand Jeu, Bourdon, et Montre de quatre pieds. Au Positif, Bourdon, Prestant ou Montre et le Nazar.

The Récit de Nazar is played on the Positif with the accompaniment on the Grand Jeu [= G.O.]. On the Grand Jeu: Bourdon and four-foot Montre. On the Positif: Bourdon, Prestant or Montre [4'] and the Nazar.

Dessus de Petite Tierce, Se touche sur le Positif, et l'acompagnement sur le Grand Jeu. Au Grand Jeu, Bourdon, et Prestant. Au Positif, Bourdon, Prestant ou Montre, Tierce, et Nazar.

The Dessus de Petite Tierce is played on the Positif and the accompaniment on the Grand Jeu. On the Grand Jeu: Bourdon and Prestant. On the Positif: Bourdon, Prestant or Montre [4'], Tierce and Nazar.

Dialogue de Voix Humaine, On ne tire point les Claviers l'un sur l'autre, Au Grand Jeu, Bourdon et Flûte, Au Positif, Bourdon, Flûte, la Voix Humaine [*], et le Tremblant doux.[275]

Dialogue de Voix Humaine. The manuals are not coupled. On the Grand Jeu: Bourdon and Flûte [4']. On the Positif: Bourdon, Flûte [4'], Voix Humaine [*] and the Tremblant doux.

(*) the *Voix humaine* is usually placed on the *Grand Orgue* – an exception to the rule are organs in Normandy, in which this stop was often placed on the *Positif*

c. 1710/20 – Manuscrit de Tours

Bourdon et Cromorne.
ou: Cromorne, Bourdon, Flute.
ou : Bourdon, Prestant et Montre et dessus de Cromorne en récit, ou de Nasard
ou de Tierce ou de Trompette seule.
ou : pour un dessus de Cornet, les fonds, le Nasard et Tierce au dessus de récit.
ou Nasard: Nasard, Quarte de Nasard, Bourdon, Prestant, Doublette.
Cornet: Prestant, Cornet, Quarte de Nasard.[276]

Bourdon and Cromorne.
Or: Cromorne, Bourdon, Flute.
Or: Bourdon, Prestant and Montre and dessus de Cromorne for the récit, or [dessus] de Nasard or [dessus] de Tierce or de Trompette alone.
Or: for a dessus de Cornet, fonds, Nasard and Tierce on the dessus de récit.
Or Nasard: Nasard, Quarte de Nasard, Bourdon, Prestant, Doublette.
Cornet: Prestant, Cornet, Quarte de Nasard.

1737 – Michel Corrette

Récit de Nazar [...] On pousse le G. Clavier. au G.j. Bourdon et Prestant ou Montre. au Positif. Bourdon, Prestant et Nazar.

Récit de Nazar [...] The manuals are not coupled. On the G.j. [= G.O.] Bourdon and Prestant or Montre. On the Positif: Bourdon, Prestant and Nazar.

Recit de Trompette [...] Le Dessus sur la petite Trompette de Recit. l'Acompagnement sur le Positif Bourdon et Flûte ou Montre.[277]	Récit de Trompette [...] The Dessus on the petite Trompette of the Récit. The accompaniment on the Positif with Bourdon and Flûte or Montre [4'].

Possible *mélanges* with the *Voix humaine* are described in several sources:

1665 – Guillaume-Gabriel Nivers

Avec la Voix humaine on peut adiouter au Bourdon la flutte et le tremblant à vent lent.[278]	With the Voix humaine one can add to the Bourdon the flutte [4'] and tremblant à vent lent.

1690 – Jacques Boyvin

Avec la Voix humaine, ou Regalle il ne faut que le bourdon, & la fluste tant en haut qu'en bas; & le tremblant doux.[279]	With the Voix humaine or Regale only the bourdon & the fluste [flûte] should be drawn, both above [en haut] and below [en bas] (*); and the tremblant doux.

(*) probably Boyvin is referring here to the manual "above" (*en haut*, i.e. *Grand Orgue*) and to the manual "below" (*en bas*, i.e. *Positif*); if the reference had been to divided stops he would have used the terms *Dessus* and *Basse*

late 17th/early 18th century – Manuscrit de Bourges

Petit bourdon, prestant, Nazard, flute de quatre pieds, Nazard, voix humaine et tremblant doux au positif. Il faut toucher les partyes sur la monstre ou la flutte, le bourdon, le nazard, la pédalle de flutte de huit pieds et faire des dialogues et des récits avec la voix humaine d'escho [...].[280]	Petit bourdon, prestant, Nazard, four-foot flute, Nazard [redundancy?], voix humaine and tremblant doux on the positif. The accompaniment [les partyes] should be played with the montre or flutte [4'], bourdon, nazard, and pedal with eight-foot flutte; and dialogues and récits with the voix humaine d'eco [...].

c. 1710/20 – Manuscrit de Tours

Voix humaine: Nasard, Bourdon, Voix humaine et Quarte (Doublette), Cromorne, Bourdon.	Voix humaine: Nasard, Bourdon, Voix humaine and Quarte (Doublette), Cromorne, Bourdon.
ou: Bourdon, Prestant, Voix humaine.[281]	Or: Bourdon, Prestant, Voix humaine.

The tempo and character of a *Récit* vary considerably according to the registration. Summarizing (and with the usual exceptions), it can be said that *Récits* with reeds, especially *Cromorne* and *Voix Humaine*, are to be played slowly and with *affetto*, while those with the *Cornet* and *Jeu de Tierce* should be played in a fast and brilliant manner. Probably a tempo somewhere between the two aforementioned should be used for a *Récit de Nasard*. The anonymous writer of the *Manuscrit de l'Arsenal* (last quarter of the 17th century) focused much attention to the qualities required to properly play a *Récit*:

[...] on peut dire sans ezagerer que lorganiste qui scait bien toucher un Recit ce qui est tres rare atrouver avec les agremens la tendresse le	[...] one can say without exaggerating that it is very rare to find an organist who knows how to play a Recit well, with the ornaments [well

feu et la manierre de se posseder en jouant en y mittant la manierre de chanter car cela ce doit faire avec une delicastesse neteté de son et un son nect et un jeu len qui ce coutte chanter [...]	played], with the tenderness, fire and mastery required to imitate, in the way of playing, the manner of singing; this singing style must be done with delicacy and precision of sound and slowly, so that one perceives the quality of the singing [...]
je ne parle pas du scavoir mais de la delicastesse.[282]	I am not talking about knowledge but about delicacy.

Then he provided practical advice on how to perform it:

Voicy dont la manierre de toucher le Recit pour y bien reusir il ce doit faire nettement vivement doucement et tres lentement et on ne peut sil faut ainsi parler aller trop doucement pour veü que la messure y soit gardée a fin davoir lieu de goutter la tendresse de larmonie et de prendre a son aise tout le têms convenable pour bien faire tous ses âgremens dans la perfection ce qui ne cepeut autrement.[283]	Here is how to play a Récit well: it must be clear, lively, sweet and very slow: one cannot err on the side of playing too slow, as long as one keeps a regular tempo, so as to savour the tenderness of the harmony and have the time and ease to be able to perform well all the ornaments, with the perfection that otherwise would not be possible.

He concluded with an in-depth explanation of the way in which to perform a *port de voix* (appoggiatura) or *coulement* – a commonly used ornament, especially in the slow-paced *Récits* – for which he strongly recommended an *over legato* performance:

Cette repetition coullement ou port de voix ce fait de cette sort Il faut que le doit qui suit la notte repetée ou coulee ouport de voix soit arivée et ait touché la notte suivante avant que le doit qui coulle etc. ait quité [...] mais ne faire que les couller et tramporter sans jamais les lever et on ne doit jamais voir remuer les dois il doive estre comme atacher tellement quil nya que le bout des dois qui agit surles touche et cela remarquee toujours en faisant ce coullement etc, ou continuellement afin que le chant soit continuellement lié ne faisant point cela cêst ce qui perd tout.[284]	This repetition, coulement or port de voix is played as follows: the finger that comes after the repeated note or coulé or port de voix must depress the next key before the finger has released the previous one [...] but always play the notes legato, and move [the fingers] without ever raising them. One should never see too much movement of the fingers; they should remain attached [to the keys] so that it is only the tip of the finger that presses the key. Always remember this when playing coullements, etc., so that the melody [le chant] is constantly legato. If this is not observed, all is in vain.

Regarding the choice of tempo for a *Récit* with reeds, it is necessary to further differentiate between the *Récit de Cromorne* and *Récit de Voix humaine*. In this regard, the words of Nivers concerning the third *couplet* of the *Veni Creator*, published in the *Deuxième Livre d'Orgue* (1667) are illuminating. For this piece, the author contemplated both possibilities, but with different tempi:

3. Couplet en Récit de Voix humaine, gravement: ou de Cromhorne, plus légèrement.

3rd Couplet as a Récit de Voix humaine, solemnly [gravement]; or de Cromhorne, quicker [plus légèrement].

Guillaume-Gabriel Nivers: 3. *Couplet du Veni Creator Spiritus* (*Deuxième Livre d'Orgue*)

Various composers stressed that the *Récit de Cromorne* or *de Voix humaine* should be played in a slow, *cantabile* manner but also *fort tendrement* (very tenderly); thus implying an *affect* characterized by a certain flexibility of tempo:

1676 – Nicolas Lebègue

Le Dessus de Cromhorne doucement & agreablement en imitant la maniere de chanter. La Voix Humaine un peu lentement en imitant aussi la maniere de chanter.[285]

The Dessus de Cromhorne sweetly & pleasantly, imitating the manner of singing. The Voix Humaine a little slowly, also imitating the manner of singing.

1688 – André Raison

Le Recit de Cromorne, ou de Tierce se touche fort tendrem.ᵗ, tenir les Cadences du Mode longues, sur tout la finalle.

The Récit de Cromorne or de Tierce is played with great tenderness; dwell long on the Cadences of the Mode, especially the final one.

La Voix hum.ᵉ se joüe tendrem.ᵗ et la bien lier.[286]

The Voix humaine is played tenderly and very legato.

1695 – Lambert Chaumont

Le Dessus et Basse de Voix Humaine lentement.

The Dessus et Basse [= Dialogue] de Voix Humaine slowly.

Le Dessus de Cromh agreablement en imitant la maniere de chanter.[287]

The Dessus de Cromhorne pleasantly, imitating the manner of singing.

late 17th/early 18th century – Manuscrit de Bourges

[…] et toucher des dicts jeux [Voix humaine] sérieusement avec mélodie et dévotion. Ils se doibvent toucher particulièrement a l'eslévation du Saint Sacrement.

[…] and playing these stops [including the Voix humaine] in a serious, melodious way and with devotion. They should be used above all for the elevation of the Blessed Sacrament.

[...] *le cromorne en dessus qu'il fault toucher fort mignardement à l'imitation d'une voix qui chante un air.*[288]

[...] the cromorne en dessus should be played very gently and elegantly, in imitation of a voice singing an aria.

1700 – Jacques Boyvin

[...] *tout les Recits [veulent] beaucoup de tendre en imitant la voix.*[289]

[...] all Récits [call for] much tenderness, in imitating the voice.

1703 – Gaspard Corrette

Le Recit tendrement et proprement et imiter la Voix le plus qu'il est possible.

The Récit tenderly and with propriety, and imitating the voice as much as possible.

Le Concert de Flûte et la Voix Humaine se touche lentement, et dans les mouvements les plus gays, on ne doit jamais aller vite; acause du tremblant.[290]

The Concert de Flûte and the Voix Humaine are played slowly, and [even] in the most cheerful movements one should never go fast, because of the tremblant.

Rather uncommon for a *Dessus de Cromhorne* is the indication *gayement*, which is placed at the entry of the *solo* voice in the following *Récit* by Lebègue:

Nicolas Lebègue: *Dessus de Cromhorne* (1er Ton, *Premier livre d'orgue*)

Brilliant and lively playing is, on the other hand, required for the *Récits de Cornet* or *de Tierce*, as evidenced in this composition by Lebègue and the following sources:

Nicolas Lebègue: *Dessus de Tierce ou Cornet* (7e Ton, *Premier Livre d'Orgue*)

1676 – Nicolas Lebègue

Le Cornet fort hardiment & gayement.[291]   The Cornet very boldly and gaily.

1688 – André Raison

Le Cornet se touche viste, le bien animer et le bien couler; et faire les Cadences du Mode longues particulierem.^t la finalle.[292]

The Cornet is played in a fast and lively manner and well legato [couler]; dwell long on the Cadences of the Mode, especially the final.

1695 – Lambert Chaumont

Le Cornet et l'Echo gayement.[293]   The Cornet and the Echo gaily.

last quarter of 17th century – Manuscrit de l'Arsenal

Il faut jouer le cornet fort viste et vivement sans pointer. et le dessus de tierce il ne le faut pas jouer si preste et on le peut pointer mais pour le dessus de nazard il le faut iouer gravement et agreablement et sur tout distinctement et mesme le cornet sans le precipiter ny le brouiller.[294]

One should play the cornet quickly and vivaciously but without dotted rhythms. The dessus de tierce should not be played so fast and one can play it with dotted rhythms; but the dessus de nazard must be played solemnly [gravement] and pleasantly, and above all distinctly; and the same for the cornet, without running ahead [precipiter] or muddling the sound [le brouiller].

There are, however, exceptions, such as in the *Dessus de tierce ou cornet* by Jullien, where, in the title itself a *Gravement* pace is indicated:

Gilles Jullien: *Dessus de tierce ou cornet grauem.^t* (4e ton, Premier Livre d'Orgue)

Interesting is the following *Récit* by Boyvin, in which the composer called for three different tempi during the piece: *Grave* at the beginning

Légèrement (= quick) in the central section

and *Lentement* at the end

Jacques Boyvin: *Récit grave de Nazar, ou de tierce, ou de cromhorne* (4ème Ton, *Second Livre d'Orgue*)

---

[267] Ponsford 2011, 212.
[268] Nivers 1665, 177.
[269] Nivers 1665, 177.
[270] Lebègue 1676, 14.
[271] Gravet 1996, 75.
[272] Raison 1688, 31.
[273] Boyvin 1690, 55.
[274] Manuscrit de Bourges, 89.
[275] Corrette 1703, 122.
[276] Gravet 1996, 85.
[277] Corrette 1737, 161.
[278] Nivers 1665, 177.
[279] Boyvin 1690, 55.
[280] Manuscrit de Bourges, 87.
[281] Gravet 1996, 85-86.
[282] Pruitt 1986, 243-244.
[283] Pruitt 1986, 243-244.
[284] Pruitt 1986, 243-244.
[285] Lebègue 1676, 14.
[286] Raison 1688, 31.
[287] Chaumont 1695, 61.
[288] Manuscrit de Bourges, 87 and 89.
[289] Boyvin 1700, 92.
[290] Corrette 1703, 123.
[291] Lebègue 1676, 14.
[292] Raison 1688, 31.
[293] Chaumont 1695, 61.
[294] Pruitt 1986, 250.

RÉCIT EN TAILLE

Although in the large corpus of *Récits* those *en dessus* are the most numerous and variegated, the *Récit en taille* (= in the tenor) remains perhaps the most characteristic musical form in French organ repertoire of the time. Lebègue writes in this regard:

Cette maniere de Verset est à mon advis la plus belle & la plus considerable de l'Orgue.[295]	In my opinion, this type of verset is the most beautiful and worthy of consideration for the organ.

Thanks to his nine *Récits en taille* published in 1676 (five for *Tierce*, two for *Cromhorne* and two for *Cromhorne ou Tierce*), it was Lebègue – the first composer to publish a *livre d'orgue* containing *Récits en taille* – who gave a great impetus to this new genre:

Nicolas Lebègue: *Tierce en Taille* (1. Ton, Premier Livre d'Orgue)

As many as 18 *Récits en taille* are included in the *Livre d'Orgue de Montréal*.

The pieces *en taille* are one of the few musical forms in the *école classique française* for which a *pedale obbligato* is provided, often – but not always – with a dedicated stave (see previous example).

The diverse sources are all very similar in relation to the registration of the *taille*, which is usually entrusted to the *Cromorne* or to the *Jeu de Tierce* of the *Positif*. There are also cases with alternative registrations, such as the following *couplet* from the *Benedictus* from Raison's *Messe du deuziesme ton*, the title of which is *Fugue pour un cromorne ou Voix humaine en Taille*:

André Raison: *Fugue pour un cromorne or Voix humaine en Taille*
(*Benedictus, Messe du Deuziesme Ton*)

As regards the registration for the accompaniment, which is played by the right hand on the *Grand Orgue*, there are many and diverse possibilities. The choice of registration should, therefore, be guided by pragmatism in order to achieve a balanced sonority with the solo on the *Positif*.

Several authors suggest the possibility of building the registration for the accompaniment on a 16' basis, with the bass part played with the *Flûte 8* in the pedal (until about the mid-18th century, French organs did not have a 16' stop in the pedal). This can occasionally create inversions of harmony (second inversion chords), which can possibly only be avoided with the use of the *tirasse* to the *Grand Orgue*, or by having a second person play the bass voice on the *Grand Orgue* (this possibility was contemplated by Raison).

In some cases the use of the *tirasse* could be debatable or considered inessential, whereas, in others, it seems quite necessary. Although the *tirasse* to the *Grand Orgue* is documented in several instruments of the time (see page 68), its use in a *Récit en taille* is not supported by any historical evidence: that its use was implicit for organists of the time is a matter of speculation and debate among organists today. The tie in the bass voice between bars 8 and 9 (from the beginning of the piece until bar 8, one plays the notes in the lower stave with the left hand, then, from bar 9 onwards, in the pedal) in Chaumont's *Tierce ou Cromhorne en Taille du 4ᵉ Ton* seems to suggest the use of the *tirasse*:

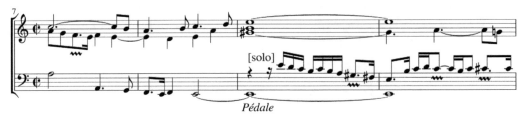

Lambert Chaumont: *Tierce ou Cromhorne en Taille du 4ᵉ Ton* (*Pièces d'Orgue*)

Boyvin's writing in several pieces *en taille*, both in the first and in the second *Livre d'Orgue*, also seems to suggest the possible use of the *tirasse* in order to preserve the continuity of the musical line in the bass voice, as in the following example taken from the *Cromhorne en taille* of the 4th mode:

Jacques Boyvin: *Cromhorne en Taille, 4ᵉ Ton* (*Second Livre d'Orgue*)

The following table summarizes the most frequently used registrations:

Tierce en taille	*Cromorne en taille*	*accompaniment*	*Pédale*
Bourdon 8	Bourdon 8	Bourdon or Montre 16	Flûte 8
Prestant 4	Prestant 4	Bourdon 8	
(Flûte 4)	(Nazard 2 2/3)	Prestant 4	
Nazard 2 2/3	Cromorne 8	or	
Doublette 2		(Montre 8)	
Tierce 1 3/5		Bourdon 8	
Larigot 1 1/3		Prestant 4	
		or	
		Bourdon 8	
		Montre 8	

Below are the indications in detail:

1676 – Nicolas Lebègue

La Tierce ou Cromhorne en Taille gravement. L'accompagnement sur le petit Bourdon, Prestant, Bourdon ou Montre de seize pieds de la Grand Orgue. La Tierce, le Bourdon, la Montre, la Fluste, la Doublette, le Nazard & Larigot du Positif, Pedalle. Ou Cromhorne, Montre, Bourdon & Nazard au Positif.

The Tierce or Cromhorne en Taille, gravement. The accompaniment with petit Bourdon [8'], Prestant, and the sixteen-foot Bourdon or Montre on the Grand Orgue. [For the solo:] The Tierce, Bourdon, Montre, Fluste, Doublette, Nazard and Larigot on the Positif. Pedal [Flûte]. Or Cromhorne, Montre, Bourdon and Nazard on the Positif.

Autre Accompagnement petit Bourdon, Prestant & Huit pieds de la Grand' Orgue, ou bien petit Bourdon & Prestant, ou bien petit Bourdon & Huit pieds selon que l'Orgue fera d'effet.[296]

Other accompaniment: petit Bourdon, Prestant [4'] and eight foot [Montre] on the Grand' Orgue, or else petit Bourdon and Prestant, otherwise petit Bourdon and eight foot according to the effect on the organ.

1688 – André Raison

Raison first of all illustrates the registration for a *Basse de Tierce*:

La Basse de Tierce se joüe au positif de la M. g. Elle est composée de la Montre, du Bourd. de la doublete, de la flute, du Nazard, de la Tierce et du Larigot si il y en à un, et de la M. d. au grand Orgue Bourd. et 4 pieds.

The Basse de Tierce is played on the positif with the left hand and consists of Montre [4'], Bourdon, doublette, flute [4'], Nazard, Tierce and Larigot if there is one; the right hand on the grand Orgue with Bourdon and 4 foot [Prestant].

Then he applies it to the case of a composition *en taille*:

Ce meslange est propre pour la Tierce en taille excepté qu'il faut adjouter au grand Orgue le Bourd. de 16 pieds avec la pedale de flute.	The above registration is appropriate for the Tierce en taille, with the difference that [for the latter] one should add to the grand Orgue the 16' Bourdon, and the pedale de flute.
Le Cromorne en Taille à le même accompagnement de la Basse en y adjoutant la Pedalle de Flute.[297]	The Cromorne en Taille has the same accompaniment as the Basse with the addition of the Pedalle de Flute.

1695 – Lambert Chaumont

La Tierce ou Cromh. en Taille [...] au grand Orgue le Dessus sur le petit Bour, Prestant, Bourdon, Ou montre de 16 pied[.] Au Positif pour la Taille le Bourdon, Montre, flutte[,] Tierce, Nazard, Doublet, et Larigot[.] Ou le Bourd, Montre[,] Nazard, Cromhorne. Pour la Basse la pedale de flutte.[298]

The Tierce or Cromhorne en Taille [...]: on the grand Orgue, the Dessus with petit Bourdon [8'], Prestant, 16-foot Bourdon or Montre; on the Positif, the Taille with Bourdon, Montre, flutte, Tierce, Nazard, Doublet and Larigot. Or Bourdon, Montre, Nazard, Cromhorne. For the Basse the pedale de flutte.

late 17th/early 18th century – Manuscrit de Bourges

Bourdon de seize pieds et le huit pieds de la grande Orgue pour faire les partyes, au positif, la montre, le bourdon, le nazard, doublette, tierce et larigot pour jouer en taille et les pédalles de huict pieds et de quatre pieds, lequel jeu le jouer doctement.[299]

Bourdon of sixteen foot and the eight foot [Montre] on the grand Orgue for the accompani-ment [les partyes]; on the positif montre, bourdon, nazard, doublette, tierce and larigot to play the taille; on the pedal the eight and four foot; this registration will render it in a learned fashion.

1703 – Gaspard Corrette

Cromhorne en Taille, Au Grand Jeu, Montre, Bourdon, et les Pedalle de Flûte, Au Positif, Bourdon, Prestant ou Montre, et le Cromhorne.

Cromhorne en Taille. On the Grand Jeu [= G.O.], Montre, Bourdon; Pedalle de Flûte; on the Positif, Bourdon, Prestant or Montre, and Cromhorne.

Tierce en Taille, Au Grand Jeu, Bourdon de 16 pieds, Montre et Prestant, et les Pedalle de Flûte. Au Positif, Bourdon, Prestant ou Montre, Nazar, Tierce, Doublette, et Larigot.[300]

Tierce en Taille. On the Grand Jeu, Bourdon of 16 foot, Montre and Prestant; Pedalle de Flûte; on the Positif, Bourdon, Prestant or Montre, Nazar, Tierce, Doublette and Larigot.

1737 – Michel Corrette

Tierce en Taille [...] On pousse le G. Clavier. au G.j. Bourdon et Prestant ou Montre. au Positif. Bourdon, Prestant, Tierce, Nazar, Doublette et Larigo. Les Pedalles de Flûtes.

Tierce en Taille [...] The manuals are not coupled. On the G.j. [= G.O.] Bourdon and Prestant or Montre. On the Positif Bourdon, Prestant, Tierce, Nazar, Doublette and Larigo. Pedalles de Flûtes.

Cromhorne en Taille [...] On pousse le G. Clavier. au G.j. Bourdon, Prestant et Bourdon de 16 pieds. au Positif. Bourdon, Prestant et Cromhorne. Et les Pedalles de Flûtes.[301]

Cromhorne en Taille [...] The manuals are not coupled. On the G.j. Bourdon, Prestant and 16-foot Bourdon. On the Positif, Bourdon, Prestant and Cromhorne. And Pedalles de Flûtes.

Nicolas de Grigny's *Cromorne en taille à 2 parties* (*3ᵉ couplet* of the *Kyrie*) represents a development of this form, in which two *solo* voices are entrusted to the tenor. In this case the style is very close to the *Fugues à 5* by the same composer; the major difference being that here the right hand has a *Fond d'orgue* registration rather than the *Cornet séparé*:

Nicolas de Grigny: *Cromorne en taille à 2 parties* (Kyrie, Livre d'Orgue)

Although the term *Récit* rarely appears in the title of compositions *en taille*, it is important to treat these pieces in the manner of the "*Récit*-form" for a correct understanding of their *affect* and interpretation. Here, as in the *Récits en dessus*, the composers' indications suggest a rather slow pace (*Gravement*), and that the music be played tenderly (*Tendrement*), with a certain flexibility of tempo so as to emphasize the many different *affetti* contained within such compositions.

In the following piece, Jullien specified *Cromhorne Gravement*:

Gilles Jullien: *Cromhorne en taille* (1ᵉʳ ton, *Premier Livre d'Orgue*)

Likewise, Lebègue for his *Cromhorne ou Tierce en taille* of the second mode prescribed *Fort lentement* (very slow). The most detailed information on how to play a *Récit en taille* is found in the *Manuscrit de l'Arsenal* (last quarter of the 17th century):

*La tierce et chromorne en taille [...] ce joüe semblable au recit de cromorne sans auqun diference car cela doit etre ausy tendre dans son chant et touché au sy proprement que le recit puis quil est veritablement un vray recit de la taille et tout les même agremens du recit sy doive faire avec la même proprete et lenteur que nous avons dit sans y rien changer quoy que dans les tierce et chromorne entaille on ne regard pas a beaucoup pres garde a la mesure comme on fait dans le recit car pour lordinaire on le laisse aller a ce laisser flatter loraille et on ne fait nul atention syl faut ainsy parler ala mesur [...].*³⁰²

The tierce or chromorne en taille [...] is played like a récit de cromorne, without any difference, since it must sing just as tenderly and be played with the same affect as the récit. In fact, it is truly a récit in the tenor, and one should perform all the same ornaments as in a récit, and with the same propriety and slowness of which we have spoken, without changing anything. All the same, in the tierce and chromorne en taille one should not be too concerned about keeping a regular beat, like in the récit, for normally one lets it flow, caressing the ear, and one doesn't pay any attention, so to speak, to the measure [...].

This flexibility of pulse is indicated *expressis verbis* by Michel Corrette in the *Tierce en taille* contained in the *Magnificat du 1ᵉʳ Ton*. At the beginning he indicates *Largo*

and further on in the piece *Presto* (bar 14), and then *Adagio* (bar 16):

Michel Corrette: *Tierce en Taille* (*Magnificat du 1er ton, Premier livre d'orgue*)

Similar indications are found in other *livres d'orgue*:

1688 – André Raison

Le Cromorne en Taille se touche fort tendrem.ᵗ	The Cromorne en Taille is played very tenderly.
La Tierce en Taille se touche rondem.ᵗ et la bien Couler.[303]	The Tierce en Taille is played rondement (*) and well legato.

(*) the term *rondement* can be translated today as: with a moderate pace, in a simple and natural way[304]

1695 – Lambert Chaumont

La Tierce ou Cromh. en Taille gravement.[305]	The Tierce or Cromhorne en Taille solemnly [gravement].

1700 – Jacques Boyvin

[...] les Tierces, Cromhorne en Taille [veulent] beaucoup de tendre en imitant la voix.[306]	[...] the Tierces, Cromhorne en Taille require great tenderness in imitating the voice.

1703 – Gaspard Corrette

Le Cromhorne en Taille tres tendrement avec imitation de la Voix.	The Cromhorne en Taille very tenderly and imitating the voice.
La Tierce en Taille veut des langueurs, des Cadences, des vitesses, et des mouvements.[307]	The Tierce en Taille requires moments of languor, Cadences, fast runs [= tiratas or similar] and regularity [= mouvements] as well.

If the *solo* part of a *Tierce en taille* could be likened to a stringed instrument (Viola da gamba), the desired *affect* in the *Cromhorne en taille* seems closer to a vocal line.[308]

Sixty years later, Dom Bédos underlines the importance of playing compositions *en taille* with elegance, imitating the vocal line and avoiding garish or vulgar virtuosic exhibition:

Le Récit qu'on joue sur les tailles dans cette maniere de toucher, doit être bien chantant & orné avec beaucoup de goût. Il y a des Organistes qui ne font que des roulades d'un bout de Clavier à l'autre, beaucoup de rapidités, de passages & de cadences, le tout sans presqu'aucun chant: ce n'est pas-là un véritable Récit; il faut essentiellement du chant pour la mélodie.[309]	*The Récit in the tenor voice should be played in such a way that it is very cantabile and ornamented with great taste. There are some organists who do nothing but roll up and down the keyboard from one end to the other, with lots of fast runs, passages and cadences, this all with nearly no cantabile [aucun chant]: this is not at all a true Récit; a cantabile manner is essential for the melody.*

---

[295] Lebègue 1676, 15.
[296] Lebègue 1676, 15.
[297] Raison 1688, 31.
[298] Chaumont 1695, 61.
[299] Manuscrit de Bourges, 87-88.
[300] Corrette 1703, 122.
[301] Corrette 1737, 161.
[302] Pruitt 1986, 250.
[303] Raison 1688, 31.
[304] Saint-Arroman 1988/I, 34 and 335.
[305] Chaumont 1695, 61.
[306] Boyvin 1700, 92.
[307] Corrette 1703, 123.
[308] Saint-Arroman 1988/I, 126.
[309] Dom Bédos 1766-1778, 205.

BASSE

It is difficult to say whether the Spanish *Tientos de mano izquierda* or *Tientos de baxon* – already known at the time of Aguilera de Heredia – were used as a model for the French *Basses*, which developed from the mid-17th century onwards. It is known that Louis Couperin was an excellent and respected viol (gamba) player, so it is possible that he might have created for the organ a musical form based on a similar idiom. Among the earliest examples of this genre are several works by Louis Couperin that bear the title *Fantaisie* but which are, in reality, *Basses* (or *Récits de basse*), such as the following piece composed *"a paris au mois de decembre 1656"*:

Louis Couperin: *Fantaisie* (*Pièces d'orgue*)

In the first two *Livres d'Orgue* by Nivers, dated 1665 and 1667, there are some compositions entitled *Diminution de la Basse* which, in contrast to the later *Basses* (*de Trompette* or *de Cromorne*), include fast runs and virtuosic passages in the *solo* voice:

Guillaume-Gabriel Nivers: *Diminution de la Basse* (*1er Ton, Premier livre d'orgue*)

Not infrequent among the compositions by Nivers or Gigault are pieces entitled *Fugues* but which are, in fact, *Basses*:

Nicolas Gigault: *Fugue à 3 du 1er pour la basse de tierce ou trompe* (*Livre de Musique pour l'Orgue*)

With Nivers, Lebègue and Raison, the form *Récit de basse* became definitively established in the French repertoire. Compared to the *Récits de dessus* and *Récits en taille*, the *Récits de basse* tend to be less *cantabile* and *tendre* (tender) but have a more brilliant, instrumental quality. Concerning the registration for a *Basse de Trompette*, apart from some marginal differences, the descriptions given by different authors are quite similar:

Grand Orgue	*Positif*
Bourdon 8	Bourdon 8
Prestant 4	Prestant 4
Trompette 8	

The registration required for the left hand in a *Basse de Cromorne* is clearly much more differentiated:

Lebègue	Raison	Boyvin	Chaumont	G. Corrette	M. Corrette
	Bourdon 8		Bourdon 8		
Montre [4]	Montre [4]	Montre [4]	Montre [4]	Montre [4]	
Nazard	Nazard	Nazard	Nazard	Nazard	Nazard
		Doublette		Doublette	
Tierce		Tierce	Tierce	Tierce	
		Larigot		Larigot	
Cromorne	Cromorne	Cromorne	Cromorne	Cromorne	Cromorne

In addition to the *Basses de Trompette* and *de Cromorne*, there are also the less common *Basses de Tierce*; in particular in the works by Nivers, Raison and Gigault. André Raison describes its registration:

La Basse de Tierce se joüe au positif de la M. g. Elle est composée de la Montre, du Bourd. de la doublete, de la flute, du Nazard, de la Tierce et du Larigot si il y en à un, et de la M. d. au grand Orgue Bourd. et 4 pieds.[310]	*The Basse de Tierce is played on the Positif with the left hand; it is composed of Montre [4'], Bourdon, doublete, flute [4'], Nazard, Tierce and Larigot if present; right hand on the Grand Orgue with Bourdon and 4 foot.*

A very peculiar registration, rarely called for but, curiously, which survived until the mid-1800s (notably in the *Grande Pièce Symphonique* by César Franck), is the combination of *Clairon 4* and *Bourdon 16*. This combination dates back to the pre-classical period: it is the first of the three registrations indicated by Mersenne under *Cleron*, namely *Bourdon 16* and *Clairon 4* (see page 102). Raison also suggested it as a *Basse de Clairon*:

Le Clairon se joüe aussi en Basse en y meslant seulem. le Bourd. de 16 pieds: au positif le Bourd. et la flute.[311]	*The Clairon is also used in the [Récit de] Basse, with only the 16 foot Bourd.; on the Positif, Bourd. and flute [4'].*

An enriched version is found in the *Manuscrit de Bourges* (late 17th/early 18th century):

Clairon: Au positif, le bourdon, la flutte, le nazard, pour faire les partyes, au grand orgue le bourdon de seize pieds, le prestant, le flageollet, la double tierce, le clairon. Il faut toucher les dicts jeux d'un air délibéré et spécialement en triple.[312]	*Clairon: On the positif, bourdon, flutte [4'] and nazard for the accompaniment [pour faire les partyes]; on the grand orgue, 16 foot bourdon, prestant, flageollet, double tierce and clairon. These stops should be played in a deliberate way [d'un air délibéré], especially in ternary time.*

Dom Bédos suggested it as one of the possible registrations for the basse voice in a *Duo*:

Cromorne avec le Prestant, & la basse sur les deux 16 pieds & le Clairon du grand Orgue.[313]	Cromorne with the Prestant, and the bass voice on the two 16 foot stops plus the Clairon of the grand Orgue.

Rather unusual are some registrations for a *Récit de basse* indicated by Nivers in his *2. Livre d'Orgue* (1667). A model that occurs repeatedly is that of a *Plein jeu* or *Petit plein jeu* used as an accompaniment to a *Basse de Trompette*. In fact, the bass here is based on the *cantus firmus* (in a similar manner to Titelouze). Although slightly ornamented, the line does not exhibit the characteristic features of a *Basse de Trompette*:

Guillaume-Gabriel Nivers: *L'Himne des Martyrs, Vierges, et non Vierges* (2ème *Livre d'Orgue*)

In one case (verset *Sit laus plena* from *Lauda Sion Salvatorem*, taken from the *2. Livre d'Orgue*) Nivers specified for the *solo* a *Dessus de Trompette* and, as an accompaniment in the left hand, a *Petit plein jeu*. Also unusual is the use of a *Plein jeu* or *Petit plein jeu* as accompaniment for a *Basse de Tierce* or *Basse de grosse Tierce*. This combination is found three times in Nivers' *2. Livre d'Orgue*:

Guillaume-Gabriel Nivers: *Victimæ Paschali laudes, Mors et Vita* (2ème *Livre d'Orgue*)

Below are the registrations of various authors for *Basse de Trompette* and *Basse de Cromorne*:

1676 – Nicolas Lebègue

La Basse de Trompette. L'Accompagnement sur le Bourdon & la Montre du Positif; A la Grand'Orgue le petit Bourdon, le Prestant avec la Trompette.	Basse de Trompette. Accompaniment on Bourdon and Montre of the Positif; [the solo voice] on the Grand'Orgue with the petit Bourdon [8'], Prestant and Trompette.

Ou bien La Basse sur le Cromhorne avec la Montre, le Nazard & la Tierce du Positif, L'Accompagnement sur le petit Bourdon & le Prestant de la Grand'Orgue.[314]

Or the bass voice on the Cromorne with Montre, Nazard and Tierce of the Positif; the accompaniment on the petit Bourdon [8'] and Prestant of the Grand'Orgue.

post 1678 – Anonymous

Pour une basse de trompette, le dessus sur le bourdon du positif et la montre, et la basse sur la trompette accompagnée du bourdon et du prestant.[315]

For a basse de trompette: the upper voices on the positif with bourdon and montre; the bass voice [on the G.O.] with trompette, bourdon and prestant.

1688 – André Raison

La Basse de Tromp. ou de Cromorne à por. accompagnem. le Bourd. et le 4 pieds de la M. g. et de la M. d. le Bourd. et 4 pieds. [...]

The Basse de Trompette or de Cromorne calls for the Bourdon and the 4 foot, both in the left hand and in the right hand. [...]

La Basse de Tierce se joüe au positif de la M. g. Elle est composée de la Montre, du Bourd. de la doublete, de la flute, du Nazard, de la Tierce et du Larigot si il y en à un, et de la M. d. au grand Orgue Bourd. et 4 pieds:

The Basse de Tierce is played on the positif with the left hand; it consists of Montre [4'], Bourd., doublete, flute [4'], Nazard, Tierce and Larigot if available; the right hand on the grand Orgue with Bourd. and 4 foot.

Ce meslange est propre pour la Tierce en taille excepté qu'il faut adjouter au grand Orgue le Bourd. de 16 pieds avec la pedale de flute.[316]

This registration is suitable for the Tierce en taille, with the difference that in the latter the 16-foot Bourd. is added on the grand Orgue, and the flute on the pedal.

1690 – Jacques Boyvin

Pour les basses on les touchent plus communement sur le Cromhorne du Positif, que sur la trompette, avec le quel on met, Prestant ou montre, nazar doublette tierce & larigot, comme a la tierce en taille, hormis le bourdon parceque le bourdon estant a l'union du Cromhorne l'allentit, et les vitesses ne paroissent pas tant[.]

The [récits de] basses are played more commonly on the Cromhorne of the Positif than on the trompette; with it one draws Prestant or montre [4'], nazar, doublette, tierce and larigot, like in the tierce en taille, but omitting the bourdon because this would slow [the speech] of the Cromhorne and the fast passages would not be as effective.

S'il on veut toucher les basses sur la trompette il faut y mettre avec le prestant, & le nazard, quelques uns au lieu de nazar y mettent le bourdon, mais le bourdon allentit. On touche aussi les basses de trompette avec le tremblant a vent perdu [...]

If one wants to play the [récits de] basses on the trompette, then one should add the prestant and nazard; some, instead of the nazar, use the bourdon but the bourdon slows [the speech of the Trompette]. Basses de trompette are also played with the tremblant à vent perdu [...]

& au Positif, on y met pour accompagnement le bourdon, & le larigot.[317]

and on the Positif, for accompaniment, bourdon and larigot.

1695 – Lambert Chaumont

La Basse de Tromp et de Cromh. [...] au grand Orgue le petit Bourdon et Prestant. Au positif la montre et le Bourd. Mais Avec la basse de Cromh. il faut tirer la montre, la Tierce, et le Nazard.[318]

For the Basse de Tromp. or de Cromh. [...] on the grand Orgue petit Bourdon [8'] and Prestant. On the positif montre [4'] and Bourd. But for the basse de Cromh. one should use montre, Tierce and Nazard.

1703 – Gaspard Corrette

Basse de Trompette, On pousse les Claviers, Au Grand Jeu, Bourdon, Prestant, et Trompette, Au Positif, Bourdon, et Prestant ou Montre.

Basse de Trompette: the manuals are not coupled. On the Grand Jeu [= G.O.] Bourdon, Prestant and Trompette; on the Positif, Bourdon and Prestant or Montre [4'].

Basse de Cromhorne, On pousse les Claviers, au Grand Jeu, Montre et Bourdon, Au Positif, Prestant ou Montre, Nazar, Tierce, Doublette, Larigot, et le Cromhorne, point de Bourdon.[319]

Basse de Cromhorne: the manuals are not coupled. On the Grand Jeu [= G.O.] Montre and Bourdon; on the Positif Prestant or Montre [4'], Nazar, Tierce, Doublette, Larigot and Cromhorne, without Bourdon.

c. 1710/20 – Manuscrit de Tours

Trompette : Bourdon, Prestant, Trompette et Clairon.

Trompette: Bourdon, Prestant, Trompette and Clairon.

ou: basse de Cromorne pour basse seulement les 3 fonds, Nasard et Tierce.[320]

Or Basse de Cromorne: for the bass only the 3 fonds, Nasard and Tierce.

1737 – Michel Corrette

Basse de Cromhorne [...] On pousse le Grand Clavier. au G.j. Bourdon seul. au Positif. Cromhorne et Nazar seul.[321]

Basse de Cromhorne: the manuals are uncoupled. On the G.j. [= G.O.] Bourdon alone; on the Positif Cromhorne and Nazar alone.

Corrette's description of a *Basse de Trompette* deserves mention:

Basse de Trompette [...] On pousse le G. Clavier. au G.j. Trompette, Clairon et Grand Cornet.

Basse de Trompette [...] the manuals are not coupled. On the G.j. [= G.O.] Trompette, Clairon and Grand Cornet.

au Positif. Bourdon et Larigo le Tremblant a vent perdu.[322]

On the Positif Bourdon and Larigo; Tremblant à vent perdu.

In reality, the piece to which the registration refers (*Magnificat du 2e ton - 4e couplet*) is a *Dialogue*, despite the fact that the title is *Basse de Trompette*; this explains the presence of the *Grand Cornet*, a treble stop, that would otherwise have no function in a *Basse*:

Michel Corrette: *Basse de Trompette - Magnificat du 2ᵉ ton (Premier Livre d'Orgue)*

The registration requested by Corrette is similar to the *4ᵉ Couplet* of the *Gloria* from Couperin's *Messe pour les Paroisses*, the full title of which is *Dialogue sur les Trompettes, Clairon et Tierces du G.C. et le Bourdon avec le Larigot du Positif*. It should be noted that Boyvin and Michel Corrette, unlike their colleagues, call for the *Tremblant à vent perdu* for their *Basses de Trompette*.

The adjective most used to describe the performance of a *Récit de basse* (especially *de Trompette*) is *hardiment*, which can be translated: "with ardor, brilliant, resolutely". Several authors such as Lebègue, Raison or Jullien have often placed *gayement* at the beginning of their *Basses de Trompette*.

Here are the indications for playing a *Basse* contained in the different *livres d'orgue*:

1665 – Guillaume-Gabriel Nivers

Le Mouvem.ᵗ des [...] Basses Trompettes, [...] est plus guay.[323]	The pace of the [...] Basses de Trompettes [...] is gayer.

1676 – Nicolas Lebègue

La Basse de Trompette hardiment.[324]	The Basse de Trompette boldly.

1688 – André Raison

La Baße de Trompete, de Cromorne et de Tierce, se touche hardim.ᵗ et nettem.ᵗ. jl les faut beaucoup animer.[325]	The Basse de Trompete, de Cromorne and de Tierce is played boldly, with clarity and in a very animated way.

last quarter of 17ᵗʰ century – Manuscrit de l'Arsenal

La basse de Trompette chromorne et tierce [...] ce joüee fort hardiment et tres legerement et vivement mais netement et distinctement comme on fait le recit car ce nes autre chose qun recit ala basse qui est joué plus viste et plus hardiment et grand feu [...].[326]	The basse de Trompette, chromorne and tierce [...] is played very boldly, very lightly and quickly, but in a very clear and distinct manner, as one does for the récit, since it is none other than a récit on the bass, but played faster, more boldly and with great fire [...].

1695 – Lambert Chaumont

La Basse de Tromp et de Cromh. fort hardiment.³²⁷	The Basse de Trompette and de Cromhorne very boldly.

1700 – Jacques Boyvin

Les Basses de Trompettes & Cromhorne [veulent] une execution nette & hardie.³²⁸	The Basses de Trompettes and Cromhorne [demand] a clear and decisive performance.

1703 – Gaspard Corrette

La Basse de Trompette se touche hardiment avec imitation de Fanfare.	La Basse de Trompette is played boldly, as though imitating a Fanfare.
La Basse de Cromhorne imite les traits, les Cadences, les Batteries, et les vitesses de la Basse de Violle.³²⁹	La Basse de Cromhorne imitates the passages, Cadences, Batteries and fast notes of the Viola da gamba.

The term *Batteries* used here by Corrette indicates a line of arpeggios, broken chords and disjunct motion (i.e. leaps) that characterizes many *Basses de Trompette*, as in the following example:

Pierre du Mage: *Basse de Trompette* (*Livre d'Orgue*)

---

[310] Raison 1688, 31.
[311] Raison 1688, 31.
[312] Manuscrit de Bourges, 87.
[313] Dom Bédos 1766-1778, 205.
[314] Lebègue 1676, 14.
[315] Gravet 1996, 75.
[316] Raison 1688, 31.
[317] Boyvin 1690, 55.
[318] Chaumont 1695, 61.
[319] Corrette 1703, 122.
[320] Gravet 1996, 85.
[321] Corrette 1737, 160-161.
[322] Corrette 1737, 160-161.
[323] Nivers 1665, 177.
[324] Lebègue 1676, 14.
[325] Raison 1688, 31.
[326] Pruitt 1986, 249.
[327] Chaumont 1695, 61.
[328] Boyvin 1700, 92.
[329] Corrette 1703, 123.

NOTES INÉGALES

INÉGALITÉ ACCORDING TO THE *LIVRES D'ORGUE*

One of the recurring performance issues in the French classical repertoire is that of the *notes inégales*. The basic concept underlying this practice is that certain notes should be played with a different rhythm from that indicated in the score. A typical example:

notation ♪♪ = performance ♪.♪

Starting with Nivers (1665) and for a large part of the following century, numerous authors describe this practice. Nevertheless, the indications they give remain rather vague, making it impossible to establish the "correct interpretation" of the *notes inégales* with certainty. On the other hand, it is implicit in the nature of *notes inégales* that there is more than one possible "correct interpretation"; the choice is left – as often repeated in the sources – to the *bon goût* [*good taste*] of the player.

The earliest text addressing the subject seems to be *Le droict Chemin de Musique* of the French Loys Bourgeois, published in Geneva in 1550, and hence more than a century earlier than the writings of Nivers. The description given by Bourgeois is very clear:

La maniere de biē châter les demiminimes en ces signes diminués	The manner of singing well the quarter notes in these diminished time signatures

est de les châter cōme de deux en deux, demourant quelque peu de tēps d'avantage sur la premiere, que sur la seconde: cōme si la premiere avoit un poinct, & que la seconde fust une fuse. A cause que la premiere est un accord, & que la seconde est le plus souvent un discord, ou (cōme on dit) un faux accord [...]	is to sing them in groups of two, dwelling a little longer on the first of the two notes: as if the first one were dotted and the second were a quaver, because the first is a consonance [accord] and the second is most often a discord, or (as we say) a false chord [faux accord]

Il faudra faire le semblage des Fuses, en ces signes entiers:[330]	One should do the same for quavers with the following whole symbols:

Nivers writes in his first *Livre d'Orgue*:

Il y en a encore un autre particulier [mouvement] et fort guay, qui est de faire comme des demipoints apres la 1.ere, 3.me, 5. et 7. croche de chaque mesure, (Supposé qu'il y en ait huit) [...].[331]	There is still another particular and very gay [manner], which is to make semidots [demipoints] after the 1st, 3rd, 5th and 7th quaver of each measure (assuming there are eight) [...].

Some composers explicitly request *inégal* playing by providing a reference model, as in the case of Gilles Jullien:

Je n'ay mis les points apres les premieres croches, que dans la piece, quy Est aufolio 51 pour Servir d'Exemple apointer les autres de mesme [...].[332]	I have placed dots only after the first quavers of the piece on page 51, to serve as an example for dotting the others similarly [...].

Gilles Jullien: *Trio pour une Elevation* (Folio 51, 3e ton, Premier Livre d'Orgue)

Sometimes, the composer indicates the *inégalité* only at the beginning of the piece, leaving it to the player to continue intuitively, as in the following example by Boyvin:

Jacques Boyvin: *Grand Dialogue (Second ton, Premier Livre d'Orgue)*

In other cases, it is stated explicitly:

Jacques Boyvin: *Duo (Second ton, Premier Livre d'Orgue)*

Other authors – particularly Gigault – prefer to note *in extenso* the *inégalité*. In almost each one of the *"plus de 180 pieces"* contained in his *Livre de Musique pour Orgue* (1685), Gigault used the notation ♪♩ or, less frequently ♫♩. , to the extent that undotted passages are almost the exception.

A common thread running through the sources is that the *inégalité* should not simply be played as a mechanical succession of ♪ and ♪ but rather with varying rhythmic gradations, at the performer's discretion. Nivers (1665) writes in this regard:

[...] c'est a dire d'augmenter tant soit peu les dites croches, et diminuer tant soit peu et à proportion les suivantes [...] ce qui se pratique a discretion, et plusieurs autres choses que la prudence et l'oreille doivent gouverner.³³³	[...] that is to say, lengthen a little the aforesaid quavers and shorten a bit, in proportion, the following ones [...] this is done at one's discretion, as are several other things that should be guided by prudence and the ear.

Gilles Jullien (1690) puts the degree of *inégalité* in relation to the tempo and character (*mouvement*) of the passage:

[...] plus ou moins legerement selon le mouvement, quy y Sera marqué.³³⁴	[...] more or less strongly according to the tempo indicated.

INÉGALITÉ ACCORDING TO THE TREATISES

Etienne Loulié (1696) illustrates the different possibilities for performance, *égal* and *inégal*, and specifies that in some types of measure, particularly in ternary bars

[...] *les demy-temps s'executent de deux manieres differentes, quoy que marquez de la même maniere.*	[...] *the semi-beats [demy-temps] are performed in two different ways, although indicated in the same way.*
1° On les fait quelquefois égaux.	*1st They are sometimes played equal.*
Cette maniere s'appelle détacher les Nottes, on s'en sert dans les chants dont les sons se suivent par Degrez interrompus.[335]	*This way is called détacher les Notes, and is used in pieces where the notes proceed by leap.*

Like other authors, such as Hotteterre or François Couperin, Loulié recommends the avoidance of playing *inégal* when the musical line proceeds in disjunct motion (with leaps). Conversely, when lines proceed by stepwise movement (conjunct notes) he writes that

2° On fait quelquefois les premiers demy-temps un peu plus longs. Cette maniere s'appelle Lourer.[336]	*2nd Sometimes the first semi-beats are played a little longer. This manner is called Lourer.*

Note that in both cases Loulié is not dogmatic, specifying that these precepts apply "*quelquefois*" [*sometimes*]. He then explains:

Il y a encore une troisiéme maniere, où l'on fait le premier demi-temps beaucoup plus long que le deuxiéme, mais le premier demi-temps doit avoir un point. On appelle cette 3. maniere Piquer, ou Pointer.[337]	*Then there is a third way, where the first semi-beat is played much longer than the second, but the first semi-beat must have a dot. We call this third way Piquer or Pointer.*

Other theorists such as Monsieur de Saint Lambert (1702) speak of an alternation of long and short notes:

On a coûtume d'en faire une [croche] longue & une bréve successivement, parce que cette inégalité leur donne plus de grace.[338]	*There is the custom of playing first a long [quaver] and then a short one, because this inegalité gives them more grace.*

Also stating:

Quand on doit inégaliser les Croches ou les Noires; c'est au goût à décider si elles doivent être peu ou beaucoup inégales. Il y a des Pièces où il sied bien de les faire fort inégales, & d'autres où elles veulent l'être moins. Le goüt juge de cela comme du mouvement.[339]	*When quavers or crotchets are to be played inégales, it is up to one's taste to decide whether they should be little or very inégales. There are pieces where it is good to play them very inégales, and others where they are better played less. Taste dictates this as [also] the tempo.*

Michel Pignolet de Montéclair uses similar words in his *Nouvelle méthode pour apprendre la musique*, published in Paris in 1709 and dedicated *"à Monsieur Couperin"*:

> Il est tres difficile de donner des principes generaux sur l'égalité ou sur l'inégalité des nottes, car c'est le gout des Pieces que l'on chante qui en decide.[340]

> It is very difficult to give general principles about the égalité or inégalité of notes, since it is the affect [le gout] of the pieces being sung that decides it.

DEGREE OF *INÉGALITÉ*

According to numerous texts, the degree of *inégalité* is always to be considered in relation to the tempo, character and *affect* of the passage or work concerned. Nivers is one of the very few authors to use, in addition to the models ♩♩ and ♩.♪ , the irrational rhythm ♩♪ , which would seem to suggest a softer degree of *inégalité*:

Guillaume-Gabriel Nivers: *La Prose de la feste du tres sainct Sacrement, A Sumente* (2ème *Livre d'Orgue*)

Bénigny de Bacilly (1668) also recommends a "smooth rhythm" in the execution of the dotted notes:

> Quoy que ie die qu'il y a dans les Diminutions des Poincts alternatifs & supposez, c'est à dire que de deux Nottes il y en ait d'ordinaire une pointée, on a jugé à propos de ne les pas marquer, de peur qu'on ne s'accoustume à executer par sacades, [...] Il faut donc faire ces sortes de Nottes pointées si finement [...].[341]

> Although I said that in diminutions there are alternating and implicit dots (dotted notes), i.e. of two notes usually one is dotted, we considered it appropriate not to indicate them, for fear that one would become used to performing them in a jerky manner, [...] One should therefore perform such dotted notes very finely [...].

By contrast, at the beginning of the *Christe* of the *Messe du Troisiesme ton*, Raison calls for a very pronounced *inégalité*, using the double dot. One would assume that the same principle also applies to similar figures later on, where the single dot appears (bar 8 onwards):

André Raison: *Duo* (*Christe, Messe du Troisiesme ton*)

According to the sources, the *inégalité* should be understood at two different "levels": i) that which is played is different (*inégal*) from what is written, and ii) simultaneously, in the course of any given piece, that there are different degrees of *inégalité*. Marie-Dominique-Joseph Engramelle, author of the treatise *La Tonotechnie ou l'art de noter les Cylindres* (1775), is explicit about this:

[...] car il est bien des endroits où ces inégalités varient dans le même air: c'est au bon goût seul à apprécier cette variété dans ces inégalités. Quelques petits essais feront rencontrer le bon & le meilleur, ou pour l'égalité, ou pour les inégalités: l'on verra qu'un peu plus ou un peu moins d'inégalité dans les croches change considérablement le genre d'expression d'un air.[342]	[...] there are many places where these inégalités vary within the same piece: it is a matter only of good taste to appreciate this variety within the inégalités. A few small trials will help decide whether it is good and better to opt for égalité or inégalités: one will see that a little more or a little less inégalité in the quavers considerably changes the affect of an air.

Although the treatise by Engramelle appeared some decades later than most of the classical *livres d'orgue*, it is worthy of consideration owing to its precise mathematical references to *inégalité*. A technical treatise for craftsman on the construction of a revolving cylinder – whether for carillon, musical clock or automatic organ – would normally be of limited importance to musicians. However, Engramelle's precise measurements for the positioning of the pins on the cylinder, in order to produce sound, indirectly provide valuable clues with regard to the execution:

[...] il faut exécuter les premières comme si elles étoient croches pointée, & les secondes doubles croches: d'autres où la différence est d'un tiers, comme si la première valoit deux tiers de noir, & la seconde l'autre tiers, d'autres enfin où cette différence, moins sensible, doit être comme de 3 à 2; ensorte que la première vaudra 3 cinquiémes de la noir & la seconde 2 cinquiémes.[343]	[...] one should perform the first notes as if they were dotted quavers and the second as semiquavers; others where the difference is one-third, as if the first represented two-thirds of a crotchet and the second the remaining third; others, finally, where this difference, less sensitive, is like 3 to 2, so that the first one represents 3-fifths of a crotchet and the second 2-fifths.

Later on in the text, Engramelle also speaks of the ratios 5:3, 7:5, 9:7 and – of no less importance – *&c.* (= *etcetera*), thus leaving room for further rhythmic ratios.

The following graphical representation gives greater clarity to the varying relationship between the first and second notes. The 3:1 ratio indicates the proportion of a normal dotted note (e.g. ♩⋅ followed by ♪) while the last ratio, 1:1, indicates – used here only for reference – the length of two equal notes (two ♪), i.e. not *inégales*. By comparing the different ratios indicated by Engramelle, one can see the rich nuances of *inégalité*, ranging from a normal dotted rhythm to a slightly differentiated equal-note rhythm, in the case of the 9:7 ratio.

3 : 1   1st note ———————————————————————— 2nd note ————

2 : 1   1st note ———————————————————————— 2nd note ————————

5 : 3   1st note ———————————————————————— 2nd note ————————————

3 : 2   1st note ———————————————————— 2nd note ————————————————

7 : 5   1st note —————————————————— 2nd note ——————————————————————

9 : 7   1st note ———————————————— 2nd note ————————————————————————

1 : 1   1st note —————————— 2nd note ——————————————————————————————

Hence, it is precisely the variety of rhythmic ratios between first and second notes, the choice of which depends on the player's *bon goût*, that forms and shapes the *jeu inégal*.

Loulié spoke of another type of *inégalité*, i.e. the so-called *Lombardic rhythm* ♬⋅ . Referring specifically to the *Mesures de trois Temps*, he stated:

[...] les premiers demi-Temps s'executent encore d'une quatriéme maniere, sçavoir en faisant le 1. plus court que le 2. Ansi.[344]	[...] the first semi-beats are performed in yet a fourth way, that is, making the first [note] shorter than the second. Like this:

Although used less than the more frequent ♩.♪, the rhythm ♬⋅ is often found *in extenso* in the repertoire. The rather pedantic manner in which Gigault notated *notes inégalés* in his 183 pieces for organ illustrates the use of this rhythmic figure:

Nicolas Gigault: *Recit a 3 parties du 8ᵉ et 6ᵉ Ton* (*Livre de Musique pour l'Orgue*)

A slur added to pairs of notes, as in the example below, indicates a subtle, *lombardic* execution:

Louis Marchand: *Duo* (*Pièces d'Orgue, 2ᵉ Livre*)

LEVEL OF *INÉGALITÉ*

In most cases, the *inégalité* is to be applied to the ♪. In defining the *Mesure du Triple Simple*, Hotteterre explains (1719):

Les croches sont presque toujours pointées dans la musique françoise.[345]	The quavers are almost always dotted in French music.

In reality, *inégalité* can also be applied, albeit less frequently, at the level of ♩ or ♫. Here is an example from the *Livre de Musique pour Orgue* (1685) by Nicolas Gigault:

Nicolas Gigault: *Fugue a 3 du 6ᵉ Ton* (*Livre de Musique pour l'Orgue*)

In general, the time signature defines the note value to which the *inégalité* should be applied. In his in-depth study on *notes inégales*, David Ponsford draws a relationship between the time signature and level of *inégalité*, which can be summarized as follows:[346]

- in the **3/2** time signature, the *inégalité* usually applies to the ♩
- in the time signatures: **2, ₵** in two beats, **3, 3/4, 6/4** and **9/4**, the *inégalité* usually applies to the ♪
- in the time signatures **C, ₵** in four beats, **2/4** and triple meter signatures (in ♪), the *inégalité* usually applies to the ♬

A confirmation of the latter principle – i.e. that in a piece in **C**, the *inégalité* is to be applied to the ♬ and, consequently, that the ♪ are to be performed *égales* – can be found in a late source, the *Dictionnaire de Musique* by Jean-Jacques Rousseau, published in 1768:

[...] on ne fait les Croches exactement égales que dans la Mesure à quatre Tems: dans toutes les autres, on les pointe toujours un peu à moins qu'il ne soit écrit Croches égales.[347]	[...] the quavers are played égales only in four-four measure; in all the others they are always a little dotted, unless there is written: Croches égales [equal quavers].

In fact, most authors appear to imply that, if in one piece the *inégalité* is applied to a specific level (e.g. to the ♪), the other rhythmic values (e.g. ♩ and ♬) are to be played *égal*.

A further question – although not strictly related to the *jeu inégal* – concerns if and when to synchronize the execution of short notes of conflicting duration in different voices. Taking as an example the two notes of alto (A) and soprano (F♯) in the second quarter of bar 16 in the passage below (see arrows)

Nicolas Gigault: *1.er ton prelude* (*Livre de Musique pour l'Orgue*)

it was the author himself who suggested their synchronization:

Lors qu'il y aura vne double croche au dessus d'vne croche jl les faut toucher ensemble.[348]	When there is a semiquaver over a quaver, one must play them together.

EXCEPTIONS

Starting with Nivers and for much of the following century, the practice of playing *inégal* seems to have been the norm. Exceptions were few, and were clearly indicated by the composer. Gilles Jullien explicitly requested *égal* execution in the *Fugue renverseé* of his *Premier Livre d'Orgue*:

Gilles Jullien: *Fugue renverseé* (8ᵉ ton, Premier Livre d'Orgue)

As mentioned earlier, Nicolas Gigault explicitly marked the *jeu inégal* by using a continuous ♫ notation. One of the very few exceptions is the *Fugue du 1ᵉʳ ton poursuivie à la maniére italienne à 4 parties*, in which, despite the notation, a *jeu égal* was desired:

N. Gigault: *Fugue du 1ᵉʳ ton poursuivie à la maniére italienne à 4 parties* (*Livre de Musique pour l'Orgue*)

In the title of the piece, Gigault alludes to the Italian custom, different from that in France, of using dotted notation to indicate notes that are to be played as such. This is also confirmed by François Couperin in *L'Art de Toucher le Clavecin*:

[…] nous ècrivons dif̀feremment de ce que nous excècutons: ce qui fait que les ètrangers jouent notre musique moins bien que nous ne fesons la leur.	*[…] we write differently from the way we perform: this means that foreigners play our music less well than we play theirs.*
Au contraire les Italiens ècrivent leur musique dans les vrayes valeurs qu'ils l'ont pensée, par exemple nous pointons plusieurs croches de suites par degrés=conjoints; et cependant nous les marquons ègales![349]	*On the contrary, Italians write their music using to the true note-values that they intend; for example we play in a dotted way several quavers in stepwise succession, and yet we write them égales!*

The presence of a dot placed above or below the note (*staccato* dot) also implies that such notes should not be played *inégales*.

In the *Avertissement* to the *Deuxième Livre de Pièces de Viole* (1701), Marin Marais wrote:

Les points qui sont au dessus des nottes non Liéés	Dots placed above untied notes

Exemple
12.ᵉ Couplet des Folies d'espagne

signifient quil faut faire chaque notte égalle, au lieu qu'on les pointe ordinairement de la premiere a la seconde.[350]	signify that one must play each note égal, instead of playing them, as usual, with the first of each pair dotted.

Summarizing what we know from the sources, it can be said that *inégal* playing was common practice and should be applied systematically. The exceptions to this rule are as follows:

- when the composer expressly indicates *notes égales, notes égales et detachées, les croches (les noires) égales* and similar
- when a *staccato* dot is placed above the notes
- when there are triplets in succession

Situations for which an execution *égal* is generally preferable:

- melodic lines that proceed mainly by disjunct motion
- repeated notes
- in works of clear Italian derivation

---

[330] Bourgeois 1550, C8r and C8v.
[331] Nivers 1665, 177.
[332] Jullien 1690, 50.
[333] Nivers 1665, 177.
[334] Jullien 1690, 50.
[335] Loulié 1696, 34.
[336] Loulié 1696, 34.
[337] Loulié 1696, 35.
[338] Saint-Lambert 1702, 60.
[339] Saint-Lambert 1702, 61.
[340] Michel Pignolet de Montéclair: *Nouvelle méthode pour apprendre la musique* (1709), in Ponsford 2011, 25.
[341] Bacilly 1668, 232.
[342] Engramelle 1775, 280.
[343] Engramelle 1775, 221.
[344] Loulié 1696, 62.
[345] Hotteterre 1719, 58.
[346] Ponsford 2011, 29-32.
[347] Rousseau 1768, 387.
[348] Gigault 1685, 26.
[349] Couperin 1716, 39.
[350] Marais 1701, Avertissement, without page number.

TEMPO

TIME SIGNATURES

In most writings of the period, questions of tempo are based on the following premises:

- the time signature ¢ or **2** indicates two beats
- time signatures in simple ternary time indicate three beats
- the time signature C indicates four beats

Generally speaking, the same note values (e.g. ♩) between a piece in ¢ and one in C have a ratio of 1:2. In the Renaissance, binary time was usually indicated with the *alla Breve* ¢ sign. In the preface to the *Hymnes de l'Eglise* (1623), Titelouze explains the meaning of the sign *alla Semibreve* C :

Pour la mesure, le demy cercle sans barre que j'y ay aposé, fait la loy d'alentir le temps & mesure comme de la moytié, qui est aussi vn moyen de facilement toucher les choses les plus dificiles.[351]	*For the measure, the semicircle without a line through it that I have employed is for the purpose of slowing down the tempo and the bar as if by half [i.e. the speed is quasi halved]; this also helps to play the most difficult things easily*

It is unlikely that Titelouze is speaking here of an exact mathematical proportion, preferring a more vague definition of the relationship („*as if by half*"). Analyzing the versets in the *Magnificats* by Titelouze, printed three years after the *Hymnes*, one can observe an extensive use of both signs: in the pieces marked in ¢ the use of o 𝅗𝅥 𝅘𝅥 𝅘𝅥𝅮 prevails (𝅘𝅥𝅯 notes are an exception) while, in pieces in C 𝅘𝅥 𝅘𝅥 𝅘𝅥𝅮 𝅘𝅥𝅯 prevail.

Forty years later, Nivers illustrated in his first *Livre d'Orgue* the different types of measure:

Ordinairement l'on admet trois sortes de mesures, la mesure du signe maieur **C**, *a quatre temps, celle du signe mineur* ¢, *ou du signe binaire* **2** *a 2 temps, et celle du signe trinaire* **3** *a 3 temps.*[352]	Normally three types of measures are admitted, the bar with the major sign **C** with four beats, the bar with the minor sign ¢ or with the binary sign **2**, both with 2 beats, and the bar with the ternary sign **3** with 3 beats.

He then defined the reciprocal relationships:

Les 2 temps du signe mineur [¢ *] ou du signe binaire [* **2** *] ne valent pas plus ordinairement que deux temps du signe maieur [* **C** *].*[353]	The 2 beats of the minor sign [¢] or of the binary sign [**2**] are not ordinarily longer than two beats of the major sign [**C**].

In triple time signatures the duration of the single beat varies according to the notation employed, but remains related to duple time signatures. To better illustrate the different cases, Nivers gives some examples from the aforementioned volume. In the first case, in particular, numerous 𝅘𝅥𝅮 and 𝅘𝅥𝅯 notes are present:

Les trois temps du signe trinaire (ou du signe de triple) quād il y a plusieurs croches à la mesure valent 3 temps du signe maieur [...].[354]	The three beats of the ternary signature (or triple signature), when there are several quaver notes in the bar, equal 3 beats of the major signature [...].

Guillaume-Gabriel Nivers: *Basse Trompette (6 Ton transposé en A, Premier Livre d'Orgue)*

i.e., given the prevailing notation of 𝅘𝅥𝅮 and 𝅘𝅥𝅯, when moving from 3/4 into C (or vice versa) the relationship is 𝅘𝅥 = 𝅘𝅥 .

In the second case, 𝅘𝅥 or 𝅘𝅥/𝅘𝅥𝅮 notes prevail:

Quand il n'y a que des noires ou quelque noire et quelque croche à la mesure, pour lors ces 3 temps ne valent que la moitié des trois temps du signe maieur [...].[355]	When there are only crotchets, or some crotchets and some quavers in the bar, these 3 beats are equal to only half of the three beats of the major sign [...].

Guillaume-Gabriel Nivers: *Grand Jeu* (*3ᵉ Ton, Premier Livre d'Orgue*)

i.e., given the prevailing notation of ♩ and ♪, when moving from ¢ into 3/4 (or vice versa), the relationship is as follow: 3 beats in a triple time signature are equal to the half of 3 beats in C (*signe majeur*); however, as the sign used in the given example is the ¢ (*signe mineur*) the resulting relationship is ♩ = ♩.

The *Duos* marked in **3** are to be played even more quickly:

*Mais les 3 temps du signe trinaire aux Duos, […] sont encore une fois plus vistes que le precedens, et ainsy cette mesure est fort prompte.*³⁵⁶	But in the Duos, the 3 beats of the ternary signature […] are twice as fast as the previous ones, and thus this type of measure is very rapid.

Guillaume-Gabriel Nivers: *Duo* (*7ᵉ Ton, Premier Livre d'Orgue*)

Irrespective of the tempo indications, the speed can then vary considerably according to the notation and musical context. This concept was reiterated twenty years later by Raison in his *Livre d'Orgue* (1688):

*Il faut observer le signe de la Piece que vous touchez et considerer si il a du rapport à une Sarabande, Gigue, Gavotte, Bourrée, Canaris, Passacaille et Chacone, mouvement de Forgeron, &c. y donner le mesme air que vous luy donneriez sur le Clavessin, excepté qu'il faut donner la cadence un peu plus lente à cause de la Sainteté du Lieu.*³⁵⁷	One must observe the time signature of the piece one is playing and consider whether it is related to a Sarabande, Gigue, Gavotte, Bourrée, Canaris, Passacaglia and Chacone, tempo of Forgeron [= Blacksmith], etc., and give it the same rhythmic flow [poise] as on the harpsichord, except that one should play a little bit slower because of the holiness of the place.

The fact that Raison refers to pieces of the harpsichord tradition in a *livre d'orgue* is not so strange, since dances were well known to most musicians. As a matter of fact, many organ pieces were *Courants*, *Sarabandes*, and similar. In the *Traité d'Acompagnement pour le Théorbe, et le Clavessin* (1690), Denis Delair echoes the same concepts already expressed by Nivers but using different symbols to better specify the desired pace:³⁵⁸

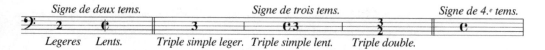

Later he spoke about the tempo relationship that should be maintained between ternary and binary time:

La valeur des notes, ne se fixe que sur la mesure de deux ou de quatre tems,[359] *[...]*

La mesure de trois tems simple se raporte à la mesure de quatre tems, en ce que l'on fait une noire, ou valeur, pour chaque tems, en l'une et en l'autre mesure, et la mesure triple double, se raporte à la mesure de deux tems, en ce que l'on fait une blanche ou valeur pour chaque tems, elles ne diferent qu'en ce que les mesures triples ont un tems de plus, ou demoins, que le mesures de deux, ou de quatre tems.[360]

The value of the notes is established only in reference to the two- or four-beat measure, [...]

The bar of three in simple time has as its reference the bar of four, i.e. the crotchet note or equivalent value for one or other are the same; the 3/2 time [mesure triple double] has as its reference the two-beat bar, i.e. a minim or equivalent value for each beat; the only difference is that in ternary time there is one beat more than in a two-beat bar, or one beat less than in a four-beat bar.

What Delair stated can be summarized in the following table:

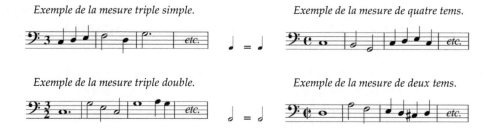

Analogously to Delair's use of the time signature for the *Triple simple lent,* Loulié, too, defined the speed of the individual tempi of the various types of triple meters by placing the sign 𝐂 or 𝄵 in front of the time value. These indicate, respectively, a slow and a fast pace:

On se sert du C Simple pour le Signe de la Mesure à quatre Temps; on s'en sert encore en le joignant avec les chiffres ou Signes des autres Mesures, pour marque que les Battements ou Temps en sont aussi lents qu'à quatre Temps lents. Ainsi:[361]

We use the simple C time-signature for the bar of four; this sign [C] is also used together with the numbers or symbols of other time-signatures, to indicate that the beats are just as slow as in slow four-beat tempo. Thus:

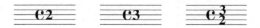

On se sert du C Barré pour le Signe de la Mesure à quatre Temps vistes, ou deux Temps lents; on s'en sert encore en le joignant avec les chiffres ou Signes des autres Mesures, pour marque que les Battements en sont aussi vistes qu'à quatre Temps vistes. Ainsi:[362]	We use the barred C as a time-signature for a fast bar of four or a slow bar of two; it is also used together with numbers or symbols of other time-signatures to indicate that their beats are as fast as in a fast bar of four. Thus:

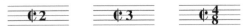

Until the end of the 17th century, the time signatures **3/8** and **6/8** (of Italian origin) were seldom used. For this reason Jullien, in 1690, used a bizarre notation of **8/6**, which he explained as follows:

Les personnes éloigneés se trouveront peut estre embarasseés pour bien entrer dans le mouvement de certaines pieces de ce livre, mais cela sera tres facile en remarquant que le mouvement de huit six, se bat a deux temps, scavoin un coup pour trois croches, et ceux qui sont peu usitéz à cette mesure, doivent se figurer que ces croches sont autant de noires en mesure de triple simple, par exemple au folio 27.[363]	People far away [from the city, i.e. "en province"] may be in doubt about the tempo of some pieces in this volume; but the solution is very simple if one considers that the bar in 8/6 has two beats, i.e. one beat for every three quavers; those who are not accustomed to this time-signature must imagine that the quaver notes are like the crotchet notes in a simple triple-time measure, for example as in folio 27:

He then gave, as an example, the first bars of the *Prelude du 2ᵉ ton* and the *Duo du 1ᵉʳ ton* followed by the corresponding "transcriptions" in **3** (i.e. **3/4**):

Prelude du 2ᵉ ton

Duo du 1ᵉʳ ton

Still more creative is Chaumont (1695), who even invented a special symbol for very fast binary time:

Le **C** sans barre lentement. Le **₵** barré gayement. Le **€** avec deux point tres gayement comme un mouvement de ballet.³⁶⁴	The unbarred **C**: slowly. The **₵**: gaily. The **€** with two dots: very quickly, like a ballet tempo.

In the very first years of the 18th century, Saint-Lambert devoted much space to the question of the relationship between time signature and tempo. In *Les Principes du Clavecin* (1702) he compared the speed of the ♩ to the steps of a man who walks five quarters of a (Parisian) league – i.e. approx. 4.8 km – in one hour, specifying that this should only be taken as a approximate indication:

[...] les Noires devoient se mesurer sur les pas d'un Homme, qui fait cinq quarts de lieuë dans une heure, & que les autres valeurs se conduisoient, à proportion de la Noire: Mais ce que j'ay dit en cet endroit-là, n'est pas une regle qui doive s'appliquer à toutes sortes de Pièces: [...].³⁶⁵	[...] the crotchets should be measured in terms of the steps of a man who walks five quarters of a league in an hour, and the other note-values are in proportion to the crotchet. But what I affirm here is not a rule to be applied in all kinds of pieces: [...].

Speaking then of the *Signe majeur* **C** (*Mesure à quatre temps*) he continued:

La Mesure à quatre temps est fort grave; les temps s'en doivent mesurer sur les pas d'un Homme qui se promene, & même assez lentement. Je compare toûjours les temps de la Musique aux pas d'un Homme, parce que les pas d'un Homme étant égaux entre eux, sont fort propres à donner une juste idée des temps & de leur égalité.³⁶⁶	The four-beat bar is very slow [grave]; the tempo must be measured in terms of the pace of a man who is walking, and even rather slowly. I always compare the beats of music to the step of a man, because, as the steps of a man are equal to each other, they are highly suitable to give a good idea of the beats and their equality.

Like other authors, he also implied a doubling of the speed when using the *Signe mineur* **₵** :

[...] dans les Pièces marquées du Signe mineur, les Notes vont une fois plus vîte que dans celles qui sont marquées du Signe majeur;³⁶⁷	[...] in the pieces marked with the minor sign, the notes go twice as quickly as in those marked with the major sign;

N.B.: *une fois plus vîte* would be translated as "twice as fast", i.e. double the speed

A similar ratio of "double velocity" may be seen in the relationship of the *alla Breve* signature [**₵**] to the *Signe binaire* **2**:

[...] les temps du Signe binaire doivent aller une fois plus vîte que ceux du Signe mineur.³⁶⁸	[...] the beats of the binary sign must go twice as quickly as those of the minor sign.

A further doubling of speed is to be understood as the ratio between measures marked in **2** and in **4/8**: *ainsi cette Mesure est très vîte*[369] [hence, this latter measure is very fast]. With regard to the relations with ternary times signatures, Saint-Lambert was of the same opinion as other authors:

Pour le Signe de trois pour deux **3/2**

La Mesure de trois pour deux contient trois Blanches, & l'on en met une, ou sa valeur, sur chaque temps lesquels doivent être graves, c'est-à-dire lents, & tout pareils à ceux de la Mesure à quatre temps.[370]

The 3/2 bar contains three minims, and each one, or its equivalent value, occupies a beat, and the beats must be grave, that is slow, exactly the same as those of the bar of four.

Pour le Signe trinaire **3**

Aux Pièces marquées du Signe Trinaire, la Mesure se bat à trois temps comme à la précédente, excepté qu'en celles-cy les temps doivent aller une fois plus vîte, parce que la Mesure n'est que de trois Noires, & qu'on n'en met qu'une ou sa valeur pour chaque temps.[371]

In pieces marked with the ternary sign, the bar is beaten in three like the previous one, except that the beats are twice as fast, because the bar consists only of three crochets; each crotchet, or its equivalent, corresponds to one beat.

Pour le Signe de trois pour huit **3/8**

[…] cette Mesure n'étant composée que de trois Croches, & ny en ayant qu'une à mettre sur chaque temps, ils doivent aller encore une fois plus vîte que ceux du Signe Trinaire, c'est-à-dire très vîte.[372]

[…] since this bar is composed of only three quavers, one for each beat, they must go twice as fast as those within the ternary sign, i.e. very quickly.

As for the *six pour quatre* **6/4**, Saint-Lambert specified that this kind of bar may be of two types: in two movements (♩♩♩ + ♩♩♩) or in three (♩♩ + ♩♩ + ♩♩). In the second case

[…] la Mesure se bat à trois temps; non pas à trois temps lents en mettant deux Noires sur chaque temps comme dans la Mesure de trois pour deux, mais à trois temps gais; […].[373]

[…] the bar has three beats; not three slow beats with two crochets on each beat as in the 3/2 bar, but three quick beats; […].

Returning to the first case, i.e. ♩♩♩ + ♩♩♩ , Saint-Lambert added:

[…] les Notes passent beaucoup plus vîte: car ces deux temps doivent être du moins aussi pressez que ceux du Signe binaire.[374]

[…] the notes proceed much more quickly: since these two beats must be at least as fast as those of the binary sign.

With the *Signe de six pour huit* **6/8**, there is a further doubling of speed:

[…] les temps de six pour huit doivent aller une fois plus vîte que ceux de six pour quatre, […].

[…] beats in 6/8 must go twice as fast as those in 6/4, […].

Les Musiciens appellent ce temps le FRAPPÈ, parce qu'en effet ceux qui battent la Mesure dans un Concert, ont coûtume de frapper ce temps dans leur main, ou sur une table avec un papier roulé.[375]

Musicians call this tempo FRAPPÈ [= beaten], because in fact those who beat the bar in a concert have the habit of beating time with their hands or on a table with a roll of paper.

He then concluded his extensive discourse on tempo, specifying that musicians themselves frequently do not apply the aforementioned rules:

De tout cecy je conclus que, puisque dans la Musique on est si peu exact à observer les regles des Signes & des mouvemens, le Lecteur qui étudie icy les principes du Clavecin, ne doit pas beaucoup s'arrêter à tout ce que j'ay dit sur cette matiére; qu'il peut user du privilege des Musiciens, & donner aus Pièces tel mouvement qu'il luy plaira, sans avoir que très peu d'égard au Signe qui le marque; pourvû qu'il ne choisisse pas pour une Piéce un mouvement directement opposé à celuy que demande le Signe, ce qui pourroit ôter la grace de la Piéce; […].[376]

From all this I conclude that, since in music there is such little precision in observing the rules of signs and tempi [and rhythmic flow], the reader who is studying the principles of the harpsichord here should not adhere too closely to all that I have said on this matter; he may take advantage of musicians' privilege and give each piece the tempo he wishes, caring but little about the sign used; provided he does not choose a tempo for a piece completely contrary to that indicated by the sign, as this could destroy the grace of the piece; […].

As an example, he made reference to Jean-Baptiste Lully:

[…] souvent le même Homme marque du même Signe, deux Airs d'un mouvement tout different: comme par exemple, Mr. de Lully, qui fait joüer la reprise de l'ouverture d'Armide très vîte, & l'Air de la page 93 du même Opera très lentement, quoy que cet Air & la reprise de l'ouverture soient marquez tout deux du Signe de six pour quatre; […].[377]

[…] often the same person uses the same sign for two Arias with very different tempi: as for example Mr. de Lully, who wants the da Capo of the Armide ouverture to be played very quickly, while he wants the Aria on page 93 of the same Opera to be played very slowly, notwithstanding that this Aria and the da Capo of the ouverture are both indicated with the sign 6/4; […].

Attempts to precisely determine the speed of performance were made by several authors, following Étienne Loulié's presentation in 1696 of his *Chronomètre*, a mechanical device that refers to Galileo Galilei's pendulum and which can be considered as the precursor of the modern metronome (see illustration alongside). In the ensuing years, several French musicians and inventors dealt with the question of instruments for measuring time in music:[378]

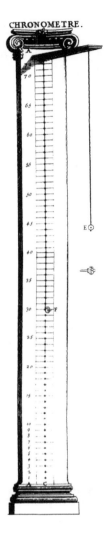

- ❖ Michel L'Affilard:
  Principes très faciles pour bien apprendre la musique (1705)

- ❖ Louis-Lëon Pajot-D'Ozembray:
  Description et usage d'un métromètre ou machine pour battre les mesures et les temps de toutes sortes d'airs (1732)

- ❖ Jacques-Alexandre de La Chapelle:
  Les vrais principes de la musique exposez par gradation de leçons (1737)

- ❖ Henri-Louis Choquel:
  La musique rendue sensible par la méchanique (1762).

The *Chronomètre* indications provided by these authors are not always very consistent and mainly related to dance forms such as *Allemande, Bourrée, Gaillarde, Gavotte, Gigue* and forth. No organ pieces of the period bear tempo indications referring to the *Chronomètre*.

More detailed information on this topic can be found in the essay by Olivier Latry (see page 6).

TEMPO INDICATIONS

Despite his effort to illustrate in quasi-mathematical terms the tempo relationships between the various time-signatures, and after a long disquisition between theory and what actually happens in practice, Saint-Lambert stated:

Les Signes ne marquent donc le mouvement des Pièces que très imparfaitement; & les Musiciens qui en sentent le défaut, ajoûtent souvent au Signe dans les Pièces qu'ils composent, quelqu'un de ces mots, LENTEMENT, GRAVEMENT, LEGEREMENT, GAYE-	The signs, therefore, indicate the tempo of the pieces only in a very imperfect manner; and musicians, aware of this, often add to the sign in their compositions some words such as LENTEMENT, GRAVEMENT, LEGEREMENT, GAYEMENT, VÎTE, FORT VÎTE and

MENT, VÎTE, FORT VÎTE, & semblables, pour suppléer par-là à l'impuissance du Signe, à exprimer leur intention.[379]	the like, to compensate for the sign's inability to express their intention.

In fact, from the 18th century onwards, the indications (of tempo but, at the same time, also of character) given by authors at the start of their pieces became more and more common, precisely in order to define the desired tempo with greater clarity. Within three decades after the writings of Saint-Lambert, this practice had become routine, as quoted by Pignolet de Montéclair (1736):

Pour prouver que tous ces differents signes ne sont pas capables de determiner absolument le veritable degré de lenteur ou de vitesse du mouvement desiré, c'est qu'on trouve presque toujours à la teste d'une piece de Musique, l'un des termes suivants:	As proof of the fact that all these different signs are incapable of determining in an absolute sense exactly how slow or fast the desired tempo should be, one of the following terms is almost always placed at the beginning of a piece of music:

> Jtalien. Grave, Largo, Adagio, Moderato, Allegro, Presto, Prestissimo
> François. Grave, Lent, Aisément, Moderé, Gay, Leger, vite, Tres vite   } &c.[380]

A year after de Montéclair, Michel Corrette in his *Premier Livre d'Orgue* took care to provide a French translation of the Italian terms he used in his book:

Explication des Termes Italiens usitez dans ce Livre.	Explanation of the Italian Terms used in this Book.
Adagio veut dire très lentement.	**Adagio** means very slowly.
Affettuoso veut dire tendrement.	**Affettuoso** means tenderly.
Allegro veut dire legerment, mais d'un mouvement Modèré.	**Allegro** means quick, but with a moderate pace.
Gracioso veut dire d'une maniere gracieuse et agreable.	**Gracioso** means in a graceful and pleasant manner.
Largo veut dire lentementet avec goût.	**Largo** means slowly and tastefully.
Presto veut dire vite avec rapidité.	**Presto** means fast and rapid.
Vivace avec vivacité mais plus modèré que l'Allegro.[381]	**Vivace** with vivacity but more moderate than Allegro.

What the French terms used at the time actually meant does not always correspond to the modern translation. *Doucement*, for example, could have signified "gently" (i.e. the modern translation), but also *con affetto* or *liberamente* (freely). *Legerement* (*légèrment*) could have signified "lightly" but at the same time *veloce* or *vivace* (fast or lively). In his *Dictionaire de Musique* (1703), Sébastien de Brossard, under the definition of *Légèrement*, wrote:

> Legerement: V. ALLEGRO, LEGGIADRO, BRILLANTE, VIVACE &c.[382]

General indications concerning tempo within the context of music in the liturgy are found in various documents of the time. A common element of these writings is that the organ had to adapt to the degree of solemnity of the liturgical celebration and that – generally speaking – a slow tempo should prevail. Martin Sonnet's *Caeremoniale Parisiense* of 1662, probably the most important and influential French ceremonial, prescribes that the organ be played

[...] ad modulos, graviter, suaviter, dulciter & modulatè, [...].[383]	*[...] with expression, gravity, gentleness, sweetness and harmony, [...].*

Particularly in the important festivities, a great deal of gravity was required in the sound of the organ, as attested to by the *Ceremonial Monastique des Religieuses de l'Abbaye Royale de Montmartre lez Paris* (1669):

Mais sur tout les Organistes seront soigneuses d'observer la qualité des jours, en sorte qu'elles touchent plus gravement aux grandes Festes, & plus legerement aux moins solemnelles, comme il doit estre aussi observé à la Psalmodie.[384]	But above all organists should pay careful attention to observe what kind of [liturgical] day it is, so that they play more slowly [*plus gravement*] on the big feasts, and faster [*plus legerement*] on the less solemn ones; the same should also be observed in the psalmody.

The *Manuscrit de l'Arsenal* also calls for a serious and solemn pace:

Il faut prendre garde aussi au service de leglise qui se fait et qui se dit et aux mysteres qui sy pratiquent et aux petites et aux grandes feste les plus solemnelles comme quand le St Sacrement est expose et apres levelation de la S.^{te} hostie, il faut sans doute que les pieces soient plus graves et non point precipitées et qui ayent du recueillement et qui attirent les ames a devotion et qui excitent le coeur a louer dieu Interieurement.[385]	One must also consider the church service that is taking place and the mysteries being celebrated, and whether the Feast day is a lesser one or a highly solemn one. Also, when the Blessed Sacrament is exposed and after the elevation of the Sacred Host, there is no doubt that the pieces should be more solemn and not hurried, should be meditative, and draw souls to devotion and inspire the heart to praise God inwardly.

A little further on in the same text, it is stated that fast tempos are appropriate for the comedy or opera, but not suited to the dignity of the Church:

[...] des autres grandes festes comme pasque pentecoste lascension, noel lassomption et les autres festes de la bonne vierge comme ce sont des festes et des mysteres de joye on ne scavroit jouer trop gayement et cependant modestement qui sente touiours l'Eglise et non point la comedie ou lopera.[386]	As for the great Feast days such as Easter, Pentecost, Ascension, Christmas, Assumption and the other feasts of the Holy Virgin, as these are feasts and mysteries of joy one cannot err in playing too gaily and yet with a modesty that is proper to the Church, and not Comedy or Opera.

FLEXIBILITY OF TEMPO

Sections of the same piece to be played with different tempos are usually indicated by the composer very clearly, as in the following example by Raison:

André Raison: *Agnus Dei* (*Messe du huictiesme ton, Livre d'Orgue*)

In some cases it is legitimate to question whether the tempo of a section should start abruptly, or whether, instead, there should be a gradual modification of pace, e.g. by slowing down the previous bar. In bar 38 of the following piece, which connects the central section (indicated in **2** and with the words *Viste*, i.e. *veloce*) to the final section (in ¢ and with the words *Plus doucement et louré*, i.e. *con affetto e pesante:*), a gradual modification would seem appropriate:

Louis Marchand: *Duo* (*Pièces choisies pour l'Orgue*)

In this regard, see the comments on two compositions by de Grigny in the paragraph *"Italian influence"* (pages 8-9). Similar cases are to be found at the end of numerous pieces, where the author requires a different tempo for the concluding bars, often *Lentement* or *Fort lentement*.

Concerning flexibility of tempo – in relation to the whole piece in general, not just a short passage or a *rallentando* – François Couperin spoke explicitly in *L'Art de Toucher le Clavecin* concerning *Préludes*:

Quoy que ces Préludes soient ècrits mesurés, il y à cependant un goût d'usage qu'il faut suivre [...] joüent d'une maniere aisée sans trop s'attacher à la précision des mouvemens.[387]	Although these *Préludes* are written in bars [*mesurés*], there is however a custom that one should follow [...], i.e. to play them with a certain freedom [*d'une maniere aisée*] without depending too much on the precision of the tempo.

The quote alludes to the genre of the *Prélude non mesuré* (see below), well known to Couperin from 17th century harpsichord repertoire but unrelated to that of the French *livres d'orgue*. Couperin wrote his only organ music at the close of the 17th century, while his harpsichord music clearly remains a product of the 18th century.

Three years before publishing *L'Art de Toucher le Clavecin*, Couperin stated in the preface to the *Pieces de Clavecin* (1st book) that he was much more interested in an expressive performance than in a show of virtuosity:

L'usage m'a fait connoître que les mains vigoureuses, et capables d'exécuter ce qu'il y a de plus rapide, et de plus léger, ne sont pas toûjours celles qui reüssissent le mieux dans les pièces tendres, et de sentiment, et j'avoüeray de bonne foy, que j'ayme beaucoup mieux ce qui me touche, que ce qui me surprend.[388]	Experience has taught me that vigorous hands, capable of executing the quickest and fastest pieces, are not always the ones that succeed best in tender pieces and those of feeling; I avow with sincerity that I much prefer that which moves me to than which astonishes me.

The taste for flexibility of tempo had its roots in the *seconda pratica*; a practice that became widespread in France through the numerous contacts between Italy and France during the 17th and 18th centuries (see page 7).

The peak of this flexibility of tempo was reached in France with the *Préludes non mesurés* for harpsichord. In such compositions – usually notated in *semibreves* (whole notes) and with slurs defining the musical gestures – the author completely renounced the writing of precise note-values.

Louis Couperin seems to have been the first composer in France to use this notation for the harpsichord. One example in the *M[s.] de Parville* – the "*Prélude à l'imitation de Mr. Froberger*" – indicates that the genre originated with Frescobaldi's pupil Johann Jacob Froberger, who was well known in Paris and personally acquainted with Louis Couperin.[389] Pieces written in *non-mesuré* form have also been composed for lute.

Here is an example of a *Prélude non mesuré* for harpsichord by Louis Couperin taken from the *Manuscrit Bauyn*:

Louis Couperin: *Prelude de M.ʳ Couperin* (*Manuscrit Bauyn*)

Lebègue adopts a similar principle in some of the *Pieces de Clavessin* of 1677, using a metrically more precise notation but without bar lines, and in the same spirit as the *Préludes non mesurés*:

Nicolas Lebègue: *Prelude en d la re sol* (Pieces de Clavessin 1677)

Although several composers, from Louis Couperin to Rameau, wrote *Préludes non mesurés*, no work explicitly composed for organ with such notation exists.

[351] Titelouze 1624, 15.
[352] Nivers 1665, 176.
[353] Nivers 1665, 176.
[354] Nivers 1665, 176.
[355] Nivers 1665, 176.
[356] Nivers 1665, 176-177.
[357] Raison 1688, 30.
[358] Delair 1690, 47.
[359] Delair 1690, 47.
[360] Delair 1690, 48.
[361] Loulié 1696, 60.
[362] Loulié 1696, 60-61f.
[363] Jullien 1690, 51-52.
[364] Chaumont 1695, 61.
[365] Saint-Lambert 1702, 42.
[366] Saint-Lambert 1702, 43.
[367] Saint-Lambert 1702, 44.
[368] Saint-Lambert 1702, 45.
[369] Saint-Lambert 1702, 45.
[370] Saint-Lambert 1702, 46.
[371] Saint-Lambert 1702, 46.
[372] Saint-Lambert 1702, 46.
[373] Saint-Lambert 1702, 47.
[374] Saint-Lambert 1702, 47.
[375] Saint-Lambert 1702, 48.
[376] Saint-Lambert 1702, 60.
[377] Saint-Lambert 1702, 59.
[378] Latry 2016, 9.
[379] Saint-Lambert 1702, 58.
[380] Montéclair 1736, 117.
[381] Corrette 1737, 161.
[382] Brossard 1703, definition of term *Legerement*, without page number.
[383] Sonnet 1662, 172.
[384] Dom Pierre 1669, 179.
[385] Pruitt 1986, 250.
[386] Pruitt 1986, 250-251.
[387] Couperin 1716, 60.
[388] Couperin 1713, Preface, without page number.
[389] Kind communication of Brett Leighton.

ORNAMENTS*

DIMINUTION & *AGRÉMENT*

Before the diffusion of the characteristic Baroque *agréments*, the most common type of ornamentation was the *diminution*. Conceived as part of the *intavolatura* practice, it consists of connecting the main (structural) notes of a composition by means of notes of shorter value.

There are numerous treatises on the art of diminution published in Italy in the 16th and 17th century: *Fontegara* (Silvestro Ganassi, 1535), *Il vero modo di diminuir con tutte le sorti di stromenti* (Girolamo Dalla Casa, 1584), *Selva dei vari passaggi secondo l'uso moderno, per cantare et suonare con ogni sorte de stromenti* (Francesco Rognoni, 1620) and many others.

---

* The issue of ornamentation is of primary importance in French Baroque music in general, and not only to the organ repertoire. A thorough investigation of the great wealth of information on ornamentation contained in all of the *livres d'orgue, livres de clavecin* and treatises is beyond the scope of this book. The aim of this chapter is simply to offer a general overview.

In France, Mersenne discussed the art of diminution in relation to keyboard instruments in 1636. He illustrated the technique in the *Livre Sixiesme* of the *Harmonie Universelle*. First, he presented a

Chanson composée par le Roy, & mise en tablature par le Sieur de la Barre, Epinette & Organiste du Roy & de la Reyne.[390]

Chanson composed by the King and set to tablature by Monsieur de la Barre, harpsichordist and organist of the King and Queen.

Then, taking as a model the first two bars of the *chanson*, he gave some examples of soprano *diminutions*:

Similarly, also in the tenor and bass voices:

Marin Mersenne: *Harmonie Universelle (Livre Sixiesme)*

Countless cases of passages featuring *diminutions* can also be found in later organ repertoire. While a small number of pieces are specifically entitled as such, e.g. Nivers' *Diminution de la basse* (see page 194), written out *diminutions* (*in extenso*) abound in keyboard repertoire. During the 17th century, the concept of the *agrément* gradually became established. *Agréments* were graphically expressed by a *Signe*, i.e. a specific sign for *tremblement, pincé, port de voix*, etc. This manner of embellishment would enjoy enormous popularity in the following decades. At the same time, authors like de Grigny – who typically used conventional symbols (*agréments*) for his embellishments – did not always refrain from using *diminutions* in order to highlight embellishments which were out of the ordinary, such as in the final bars of the *Basse de Trompette* (see page 9).

Composers often provided a wealth of information concerning ornamentation in the prefaces of their publications; first of all, Nivers in his *Livre d'Orgue* of 1665. Sometimes the number of embellishments is so great that they almost become an integral part of the musical discourse and deeply influence the *affect* of a piece.

Although the most used embellishments were the *Tremblement* (trill), the *Pincé* (mordant) and the *Port de voix* (appoggiatura), the large number of ornaments described by composers are clearly a testament to the importance of these extremely expressive devices. The presence of a large number of embellishments within the same piece – sometimes even in close succession – suggests that variety in their "expressive qualities", and execution, was desirable and contributed to the *bon goût* of the performance.

The number of ornamentation tables handed down through the *livres d'orgue* and treatises is remarkable. It is as if composers were competing to create new signs for their *agréments*.

Not infrequently one finds different names or symbols for the same ornament. Or, conversely, the same symbol is used for different embellishments. The sign + could mean a *Tremblement*, a *Pincé* or a *Port de voix*, depending on the composer or its context. The table of ornaments by Jean-Henry d'Anglebert (1689), for example, which is often taken as a reference – and which was also probably used as a model by Johann Sebastian Bach for the composition of the *Clavierbüchlein für Wilhelm Friedemann Bach* – differs from the other sources in terms of the notation of very common embellishments, such as the *Pincé, Port de voix, Tierce coulée* or *Arpège*:

Jean Henry D'Anglebert, *Pieces de clavecin* (Paris 1689)

It should be noted that this table is contained in the *Pieces de Clavecin*, a volume clearly intended for harpsichord, although in the preface there are references to the organ:

J'ay voulu donner aussi un échantillon de ce que j'ay fait autrefois pour l'Orgue, c'est pourquoy j'ay mis seulement cinq fugues sur un même sujet varié de differens mouvemens, et j'ay fini par un quatuor sur le Kirie de la Messe.[391]	*I also wished to give an example of what I have done in the past for the organ - this is why I included only five fugues on the same subject treated in different ways, ending with a quatuor on the Kyrie of the Mass.*

Another question arises concerning whether ornaments should be played *on the beat* or *before the beat*. If the "general rule" for the music of this period is that ornaments should be played on the beat – as specified in numerous sources or tables of embellishments – there are also numerous sources that attest to the performance of ornaments before the beat, as illustrated in the following chapters.

IMPROVISATION OF ORNAMENTS

The practice of improvising *ex tempore* ornaments or *diminutions* is part of the art of playing, and is as old as the art of playing itself. Countless writings and treatises testify to this practice. In older publications, such as the *Hymnes* by Titelouze (1623), no ornaments were indicated and the author left the improvisation of *accents* to the player's judgment:

La mesure & les accents sont recommandables tant aux voix qu'aux instruments, la mesure reglant le mouvement, & les accents animans le chant des parties. [...]	*Observation of bars and accents [ornaments] is recommended, as much for the voices as for the instruments: the bar regulates the tempo and the accents animate the melodic line of the different parts. [...]*
Pour les accents, la dificulté d'aposer des caracteres a tant de notes qu'il en faudroit m'en a fait raporter au jugement de celuy qui touchera, comme je fais des cadences qui sont communes ainsi que chacun sçait.[392]	*As for the accents, the difficulty of placing symbols for so many notes, as would be required, is such that I leave it to the judgment of the player, as I do for the cadences [trills] which are of a common sort, such as everyone knows.*

From Titelouze's words it is clear that abundant ornamentation was desired. It is likely that, here, Titelouze is using the term *accent* to refer to an ornament in the broad sense. Thirteen years later, Mersenne stated in reference to *Sieur de la Barre, Epinette & Organist du Roy & de la Reyne* (see beginning of this chapter):

Mais il seroit necessaire d'avoir plusieurs caracteres particuliers pour marquer les endroits des martelemens, des tremblemens, des battemens, & des autres gentillesses, dont cet excellent Organiste enrichit son jeu, lors qu'il touche le Clavier.[393]	*But it would be necessary to have several specific signs to mark the places of martelemens, tremblemens, battemens, and other similar gallantries, by which this excellent organist enriches his playing when he plays the keyboard.*

Strictly speaking, the *accent* was a vocal ornament that involved the insertion of an escape note (*note echappée*), or sometimes a passing note. Étienne Loulié gives some examples in the *Elements ou Principes de Musique* (1696):

L'Accent est une Elevation de la Voix d'un Son fort à un petit Son foible, & plus haut d'un degré. L'Accent se marque ainsi | .[394]

The Accent consists of an elevation of the voice, from a strong sound to a short weak sound one degree higher. The Accent is indicated thus: | .

In organ repertoire the symbol used by Loulié for the *accent* (|) was not used. On the other hand, the embellishment itself was often used and indicated as follows

or written out in full, as in the following passage by Gigault:

Nicolaus Gigault: *Petite Fug. sur veni creator à 4. partie* (*Livre de Musique pour l'Orgue*)

A practical example of the manner in which to add ornaments was provided by the same author in his *Livre de Musique dédié à la très Ste Vierge* (*Livre de Noëls*). In the last piece, Gigault presented an *Allemande par fugue*

and then *la mesme allemande avec les ports de voix* [*the same allemande with appoggiaturas*]:

Nicolaus Gigault: *Allamanda par fugue (Livre de Musique dédié à la très Ste Vierge)*

It should be noted that the *ports de voix* presented here by Gigault are to be played before the beat:

Il y a aussi plusieurs personnes qui seroient bien aises d'avoir quelque tendresse dans leur touché. Pour cela j'ay disposé une pièce Diatonique décrite en deux manieres, l'une simple & l'autre composée de ports de voix pour donner l'idée & l'usage de les appliquer à toutes autres sortes de pieces.[395]	There are also some people who it wouldn't hurt to play with some *tendresse*. For this reason I have included a diatonic piece in two versions: one simple and the other written with *ports de voix*, to give the idea of how to apply them to all other kinds of pieces.

Referring to other passages of the same volume, Gigault explained to those *qui n'ont pas encore la pratique* [*who are still inexperienced*] how to decide which notes to embellish, by providing examples that he indicated with little crosses:

J'ay marqué les tremblemens avec de petites croix pour les personnes qui n'ont pas encore la pratique de mettre où il faut.[396]	I have marked the *tremblements* with small crosses [+] for those who have not yet the experience to put them where needed.

The practice of improvising embellishments – beyond those already indicated in the piece – was first encouraged by Saint-Lambert (1702):

[...] on est extrêmement libre sur le choix des Agrémens; & dans les Pieces qu'on étudie, on peut en faire aux endroits même où ils ne sont pas marquez; retrancher ceux qui y sont, si l'on trouve qu'ils ne siént pas bien à la Piéce, & y en ajoûter d'autres a son gré. On peut même, si l'on veut, negliger tous ceux que j'ay enseignez icy (excepté seulement les essentiels) & en composer soy-même de nouveaux selon son goüt, si l'on se croit capable d'en inventer de plus beaux.[397]	[...] there is extreme freedom in the choice of ornamentation; and in the pieces studied, one can insert them in places where they are not marked, or suppress those indicated if one thinks they do not go well with the piece, and replace them with others at will. One can also, if one wishes, forget all those I've talked about so far (except the essential ones) and compose new ones according to personal taste, if one thinks to be capable of inventing more beautiful ones.

However, later in the text he seems to go back on his words:

[...] mais il faut cependant prendre garde à ne se pas donner trop de liberté sur ce sujet, surtout dans le commencement; de peur qu'en voulant rafiner trop tôt, on ne gâtât ce qu'on voudroit embellir:	[...] but one must nevertheless be careful not to allow oneself too much freedom in this matter, especially at the beginning; because, wanting to reach perfection too soon, one risks ruining what one wishes to embellish.
C'est pourquoy il est bon, & même necessaire, de s'assujettir d'abord aux Agrémens des autres, & de ne les faire qu'aux endroits où ils sont marquez dans les Pièces, jusqu'à-ce qu'on soit assez fort, pour juger sans se tromper, que d'autres n'y seront point de mal.[398]	For this reason it is good, and even necessary, to limit oneself first to the ornaments of others [= composers], and play them only in the places where they are marked, until one is confident to be able to judge without mistake that other [embellishments] would not be bad.

These conclusions were echoed twenty years later, in a much more strident tone, by François Couperin in the *Troisième Livre de Pièces de Clavecin* (1722):

Je suis toujours surpris (apres les soins que je me suis donné pour marquer les agrémens qui conviennent à mes Pièces [...]) d'entendre des personnes qui les ont aprises sans s'y assujétir. C'est une négligence qui n'est pas pardonnable d'autant qu'il n'est point arbitraire d'y mettre tels agrémens qu'on veut.	I am always surprised (after the care I took to mark the ornaments that are appropriate for my pieces [...]) to hear of people who studied the pieces without observing them [the written ornaments]. This is an unforgivable negligence, because it is not arbitrary [= up to one's taste] to put whatever ornaments one wants.
Je déclare donc que mes pieces doivent être exécutées comme je les ay marquées; et qu'elle ne feront jamais une certaine impression sur les personnes qui ont le goût vray, tant qu'on n'observera pas a la lettre, tout ce que j'y ay marqué, sans augmentation ni diminution.[399]	I therefore declare that my pieces must be executed as I wrote them; and that they will never make a certain impression on people who have true taste unless all that I have written is observed literally, without adding or taking away anything.

Reading Couperin's severe words, one may perhaps wonder whether these prescriptions were written in reaction to excesses that may have become a custom. That Couperin's *Messe pour les Paroisses* and *Messe pour les Couvents* should be interpreted with such rigidity can only be a matter of speculation. The two masses were not printed at the time: only the frontispiece was printed, but the interior was hand-written. According to David Ponsford, they did not, therefore, have the precise and rich ornamentation of printed publications, such as the various *livres d'orgue* or even the *Premier Livre de Pièces de Clavecin* by Couperin himself.[400] It should be noted that in the principal manuscripts of the two masses (*Ms. de Carpentras* and *Ms. de Versailles*) the use of ornamentation differs considerably. The pieces for harpsichord published by d'Anglebert in 1689 followed a similar pattern: they exhibit a greater amount of ornamentation than the manuscript copies.

In the *Principes de Musique* (1736), Michel Pignolet de Montéclair wrote about the addition of ornaments in the small chapter entitled *Passage*:

Le Passage se fait de plusieurs manieres differentes, comme on le verra cy dessous, et encoremieux dans les airs que les Anciens appelloient Doubles. [...] Les Passages sont arbitraires, chacun peut en faire plus ou moins, suivant son gout et sa disposition.[401]

The Passage can be done in different ways, as we will see below, and even better in the arias [airs] that our ancestors called Doubles. [...] The passages are ad libitum, one can play more or fewer of them in accordance with their own taste and inclination.

However, he added that excessive ornamentation can disfigure the nobility of the melody and become ridiculous:

Ils se pratiquent moins dans la Musique vocale que dans l'instrumentale, sur tout à present que les joüeurs d'instruments, pour imiter le gout des Jtaliens, defigurent la noblesse des chants simples, par des variations souvent ridicules.[402]

They are less used in vocal music than in instrumental music, especially nowadays that instrumentalists, to imitate the taste of Italians, disfigure the nobility of simple melodies with variations that are often ridiculous.

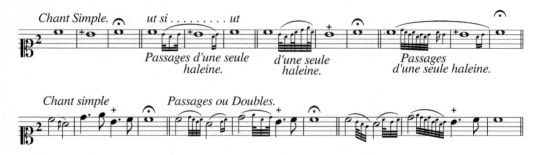

Michel Pignolet de Montéclair: *Principes de Musique (Troisieme partie, Cap. Passage)*

De Montéclair underlines that Jean-Baptiste Lully, the celebrated *Compositeur de la musique instrumentale* at the court of *Louis XIV*, was also vehemently opposed to excessive ornamentation:

L'incomparable Lulli, ce genie superieur dont les ouvrages seront toujours estimés des vrais connoisseurs, a preferé la melodie, la belle modulation, l'agréable harmonie, la justesse de l'expression, le naturel et enfin la noble simplicité, au ridicule des Doubles et des musiques heteroclites dont le merite pretendu ne consiste que dans les ècarts, dans les modulations detournées, dans la dureté des accords, dans le fracas, et dans la confusion. Tous ces faux brillants decellent la seicheresse du genie de l'autheur, et cependant ils ne laissent pas d'en imposer aux oreilles ignorantes.[403]	*The incomparable Lulli, this sublime genius whose works will always be appreciated by true connoisseurs, preferred melody, beauty of modulation, pleasant-sounding harmony, accuracy of expression, naturalness and, finally, noble simplicity to the ridiculousness of Doubles [with ornate passages] and extravagant pieces [heteroclites] whose presumed merit lies only in their departures [from the norm], distorted modulations, harshness of chords, and in a chaos of noise and confusion. All these false gems reveal the aridity of the author´s talent, and yet they do not fail to impress the ears of the ignorant.*

Also Georg Muffat in his *Florilegium Secundum* (1698), referring to Lully and advocating a style „*à la Françoise*", rails against those with a tendency towards excessive ornamentation:

Ceux qui sans discrétion décrient les agrémens, & ornemens de la methode Françoise, comme s'ils offusquoient l'air ou l'harmonie, & ne consistoient qu'en de seuls tremblemens; n'ont certes guere bien examiné cette matiere, ou n'ont Jamais entendu Jouër de vrais éleves, mais seulement peut être de faux Imitateurs de l'Ecôle de feu Mr. de Lully.[404]	*Those who, without discretion, vituperate the embellishments and ornaments in the French manner, as if they obfuscated the melody [Air] or harmony and consisted of nothing but tremblements, have certainly not well examined this matter, or have never heard true pupils of the school of the late M. de Lully play, but only perhaps false imitators.*

Another element that can influence the addition of ornaments is the touch of the instrument. Although the classical French organ is characterized by a remarkable lightness of keyboard action, it is, at the same time, clear that when *Positif* and *Grand Orgue* are coupled, the touch is heavier and, therefore, less suitable for playing music with a rich ornamentation. To this should be added the amount of reverberation of the church in which the music is performed: a *Grand plein jeu* based on 16' is less agile than a 8' *Petit plein jeu*, particularly in a large acoustic. These precepts seem to be confirmed, albeit indirectly, by numerous *Grands pleins jeux*, where the writing to be played on the *Grand Orgue* is clearly less ornate than that which is to be played on the *Positif*. Here is an example from Boyvin's *Suite du 4ᵐᵉ Ton*:

Jacques Boyvin: *Grand prelude a 5 parties, a 2 Chœurs* (4me ton, *Premier Livre d'Orgue*)

Lebègue also suggested the omission of some embellishments should the player find their execution difficult:

*Ceux qui auront peine à faire certains tremblemens où ils se rencontreront trop difficiles à toucher, pourront les passer, ne desirant pas que les mains soient contraintes en aucune maniere, mais plustost que les mouvemens soient observez fort exactement.*⁴⁰⁵	Those who struggle to perform certain tremblements where they will be found too difficult to play, can leave them out, since it is not desirable that the hands be constrained in any way, but rather it is the tempo that should be observed very precisely [= do not let trills alter the regularity].

Besides being opposed to excessive added ornamentation – i.e. not written but improvised – Saint-Lambert also underlined the importance of the graceful performance of embellishments, stating that it was better to omit them rather than to perform them ungracefully:

*Il importe cependant beaucoup de sçavoir bien éxécuter les Agrémens; car sans cela ils défigurent les Pièces au lieu d'en augmenter la beauté, & il vaudroit miex n'en point faire du tout que de les faire mal: […].*⁴⁰⁶	It is however very important to know how to perform well the ornaments, because without such attention they disfigure the pieces instead of increasing their beauty, and it would be better not to play them at all than to play them badly: […].

Finally, the quality of the wind supply – particularly where there is excessive instability – could be a critical factor to be taken into account when deciding whether or not to add ornamentation.

TREMBLEMENT

The term *Tremblement* refers to a trill beginning on the upper note and is indicated with the following sign:

It is also called *Cadence* by virtue of its frequent use in cadencial formulas. Nivers (1665) first states that it should be played quickly and in a regular manner:

Les Cadences ou Tremblemens se font en battant deux touches prochaines alternativement également et promptement.[407]	The Cadences or Tremblements are performed by playing two adjacent keys alternately, in an equal and rapid manner.

Demonstration de la Cadence.

However, later in the text he specifies that *Cadences* should be differentiated according to their *affect*:

[…] l'on voit leurs diverses expressions selon leurs diverses rencontres.[408]	[...] one can see their different expressions according to the different contexts.

He also points out that the number of notes indicated in the ornaments in his *Demonstrations* was intended simply as an example:

Toutes ces petites notes ne sont que pour exprimer le tremblement, la grosse note seule estant comptée, et sur la quelle comme principalle on demeure un peu apres le battement.[409]	All these short notes serve only to represent the tremblement, but it is only the long note [= on which the ornament is placed] that counts in terms of the time value; and on this main note one rests a little after the trill.

Boyvin (1690) added:

La Cadence ou tremblement se doit faire long, selon la notte & le temps ou on l'applique, On le fait ordinairement en descendant, on le commence a la notte d'audessus.[410]	The Cadence or Tremblement should be long, according to the note and the place to which it is applied. It is usually placed on a descending line and starts on the upper note.

In the *Manuscrit de l'Arsenal* (last quarter of the 17th century) one can read:

Le tremblement ou cadence ce doit faire egallement legerement vivement et tre longuement et on ne blamera jamais dela faire longue mais bien trop courte […].[411]	The tremblement or cadence should be performed in a uniform, light, rapid manner and should be very long. One will never be blamed for playing it long, but rather if it is too short [...].

Saint-Lambert (1702) first wrote that

Le Tremblement est une agitation de deux Touches, battuës alternativement le plus également & le plus promtement que l'on peut.[412]

The Tremblement is a tremor of two keys, played alternately as equally and rapidly as possible.

But further on he specified that

Quand le Tremblement doit être long, il est plus beau de le battre lentement d'abord, & de ne le presser qu'à la fin; mais quand il est court il doit toûjours être promt.[413]

When the Tremblement has to be long, it is better to start slowly and accelerate only towards the end; but when it is short it must always be fast [promt].

In *L'Art de Toucher le Clavecin* (1716) Couperin called for a controlled and very subtle acceleration:

Quoi que les tremblemens soient marqués ègaux, dans la table des àgrèmens de mon livre de pieces, ils doivent cependant commencer plus lentement qu'ils ne finissent: mais, cette gradation doit etre imperceptible.[414]

Although the tremblements are marked equal in the table of ornaments of my book of pieces, they should however start more slowly than they finish; but this gradation must be imperceptible.

D'Anglebert and Dandrieu termed this ornament *Tremblement simple* in order to differentiate it from the *Tremblement appuyé*. The latter calls for a significant lengthening of the first note

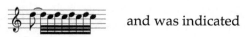 and was indicated

Couperin defined the three parts of a long trill:

Les tremblemens d'une Valeur un peu considerable renferment trois objets, qui dans L'execution ne paroissent qu'une même chose. 1.° L'appuy qui se doit former sur la note au dessus de L'essentièle. 2.° Les batemens. 3.° Le point=d'arèst.[415]

Tremblements placed on a note of rather long value consist of three elements, which in the execution appear to be one only: 1. The appuy [appoggiatura] which is placed on the upper note. 2. The repetitions. 3. The point of closure.

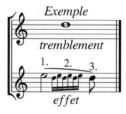

However, he added that in other cases, particularly in shorter *Tremblements*, the first and third elements could be omitted:

A L'egard des autres tremblemens ils sont arbitraires. Il y en à d'appuyés; d'autres si courts qu'ils n'ont ny appuy, ny point d'arrest. On en peut faire même d'aspirés.[416]

The other tremblements are ad libitum. There are some with *appuyés* [appoggiaturas], others so short that they have neither appoggiatura nor a point of closure. Some may also be followed by a short pause [Aspiration].

Besides the *Tremblement appuyé* there is also the *Tremblement lié*. It is indicated with a slur, and the first upper note of the trill is not repeated:

The decision of whether to play the first note of a *Tremblement lié* (in the previous example, the first D of the ♪ group) *appuyé* or not depends on the duration of the note on which the ornament is placed, as a short duration precludes this possibility. In the table of *Explication des Agrémens, et des Signes* contained in the *Premier Livre de Pièces de Clavecin* (1713), François Couperin expressly added a *Tremblement lié sans etre appuyé*.

Whether the *Tremblement* (here in facsimile) is intended to be played before the beat, by virtue of its graphic alignment, is a matter of controversy among musicologists.[417] Also noteworthy is the difference between *Tremblement lié* (left) and *Tremblement détaché* (right), exemplified by the presence or absence of a tie between the two notes.

In some cases, when the starting note of the *Tremblement* is anticipated in the score, the ornament actually starts before the beat. This occurs in numerous pieces by Nivers or Raison, particularly those of a moderate pace such as *Récits*. In such cases, there are often two ♪ notes before a *Tremblement* or *Pincé*: the second ♪ (the one immediately preceding the ornamented note) is the beginning of the embellishment which follows, as can be understood from the following two examples (see also page 247):

G.-G. Nivers: *Recit du 2ᵉ Ton (3. Livre d'Orgue)*

A. Raison: *Second Kyrie (1ᵉʳ Ton, Livre d'Orgue)*

This concept finds confirmation in the *Motets à voix seule, accompagnée de la basse continue* (1689) by Nivers:[418]

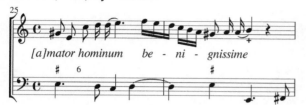

G.-G. Nivers: *Obsecro te Domine* (*Motets à voix seule*)

La simple Cadence & ordinaire, est exprimée par une petite croix posée directement dessus ou dessous la Note qu'il faut trembler.[419]

The simple and ordinary Cadence [= trill] is indicated by a small cross placed directly above or below the note on which to trill [trembler].

This type of notation, quite common among earlier authors, tends to disappear towards the end of the 17th century. Dandrieu (1739) and Rameau (in his *Pièces de clavecin*, 1724) instead used the slur of the *Tremblement lié* to indicate that the trill started on the main note:

For the trill with termination, an ascending tail is usually added to the trill sign; it can have different names:

Other authors indicate the termination by placing the two notes after the *Tremblement* sign. Nivers calls this ornament *Double Cadence*:

Interestingly, Raison explicitly asked that the *Cadence* be separated from its termination by means of a short break:

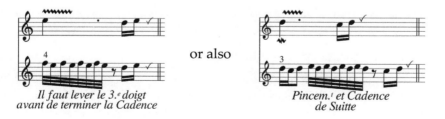

Even more unusual is the *Cadence particuliere,* in which Raison asked that the penultimate note of the resolution be tied to the final note:

It is legitimate to also ask whether Clérambault, a pupil of Raison, wished his *Cadences* to be executed according to these precepts. Variants to the normal *Tremblement,* i.e. with the head of the ornament modified in the manner of a *turn,* and called *Cadences,* are provided by d'Anglebert:

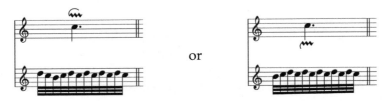

Finally, a very unusual and enigmatic type of trill is the one described by Chaumont (1695) as *Deffaut du Tremblement* [*defective trill*]:

PINCÉ

The *Pincé* or *Pincement* (or sometimes simply *Agrément*) corresponds to the mordant; it starts from the principal note and then touches the lower auxiliary:

 it is usually indicated by while d'Anglebert used the sign

Boyvin explained that

Le pincement se fait court, ordinairement en montant.[420]	The pincement is a short ornament usually placed on an ascending line.

Gaspard Corrette further specified that

Le Pincé se fait, ordinairement en montant par degré conjoint et par intervalle, quelque fois en descendant.[421]	The Pincé is usually placed on an ascending line of stepwise notes or intervals; sometimes it can be placed on a descending line.

Lebègue, Raison, Chaumont and Gaspard Corrette included in their tables of *agréments* only the *pincé* consisting of three notes, therefore touching the lower auxiliary only once. D'Anglebert presented two types of *pincé*, one short and one with repeated alternations

while Dandrieu presented only the *Pincé* with several alternations, despite referring to it as *Pincé simple*:

In *L'Art de Toucher le Clavecin*, Couperin also presented two types of *Pincé*, specifying that the difference is determined by the duration of the note on which a *Pincé* is placed and not by the sign, which, in fact, remains the same:

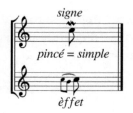 

| *C'est la valeur des notes qui doit, en general, dèterminer la durée des pincés=double, des ports=de=voix=double; et des tremblemens.*[422] | It is the length of the notes which, in general, should determine the duration of the pincés=double, of the ports=de=voix=double, and of the tremblements. |

He then explained that

| *Le pincé=double, dans le Toucher de L'orgue, et du clavecin, tient lieu du martèlement dans les instrumens à Archet.*[423] | The pincé=double, on the organ or harpsichord, takes the place of the martèlement in string instruments. |

At the time of Couperin, in contrast to later periods, the *Martèlement* of string instruments corresponded to a tremolo on a single note. Loulié used *Martellement* to describe various types of *Pincé* and provided a description in his *Elements ou Principes de Musique* (1696):

| *Le Martellement sont deux petits Sons fort legers en maniere de Chute, d'un degré plus bas l'un que l'autre, lesquels precedent la Notte sur* | The Martellement consists of two short, very light sounds in the manner of Chute, one note lower than the other, which precede the note on |

243

laquelle est marqué le Martellement. Le Martellement se marque ainsi V .[424]

which the Martellement is placed. The Martellement is indicated as: V .

On the other hand, according to Nivers and his pupil Jullien, this ornament – which they called *Agrément* – began on the lower auxiliary, in the manner of the *Pincé avec Port de voix* described below. Nivers designates it with a short undulating line [∼] without specifying whether it should be played on or before the beat:

PORT DE VOIX

The *Port de voix* (also called *Cheute* or *Coulé*) corresponds to the appoggiatura; it was described and played in different ways by different authors. Frequently it was indicated by a small note (and relative slur) before the note to which it applied:

Its duration should be in relation to the following note, as Boyvin outlined in the *Second livre d'orgue*:

[…] le port de voix long à proportion de la notte où il est placé.[425]

[...] the length of the port de voix is proportionate to the note on which it is placed.

Various sources confirm that the *Port de voix* could be played both on or before the beat. In this regard, Saint-Lambert in *Les Principes du Clavecin* (1702) wrote:

[…] il n'est pas bien décidé si c'est sur la valeur de la Note marquée que se doit prendre cette seconde, ou si c'est sur la valeur de la Note précédente.[426]

[...] it is not well established whether it should subtract value from the note on which it is placed, or from the preceding note.

Saint-Lambert, in fact, prefered the solution before the beat, and provided the following example:

[...] *celle qui prend cette seconde Note sur la précédente, est beaucoup plus convenable. C'est donc de la façon qui suit, que je voudrois exprimer les Ports de Voix cy devant.*[427]

[...] subtracting the value of this second note [i.e. the appoggiatura] from the previous note is better. So it is in this way that I would like to express the Ports de voix here below.

EXEMPLE.

En montant, en descendant.

EXPRESSION.

En montant, en descendant.

Earlier authors seem to have prefered playing the appoggiatura before the beat: by applying the slurs described by Nivers in the example below [*qu'il faut le plus couler*], we obtain *de facto* a pre-beat articulation:

Pour couler les notes, il faut bien les distinguer, mais il ne faut pas lever les doigts si promptement: cette maniere est entre la distinction et la confusion, ou participe un peu de l'une et de l'autre; et se pratique le plus ordinairement aux ports de voix et en certains passages dont voicy quelques exemples. De touttes ces choses on doit consulter la methode de chanter, par ce qu'en ces rencontres l'Orgue doit imiter la Voix.[428]

To "connect the notes", it is important to distinguish them well, but the fingers should not be lifted too quickly: this way of playing is between distinction and confusion, or a bit of both; and is more commonly practiced with the ports de voix and in certain passages as in the following examples. In all these things one should refer to the method of singing, because in these instances the organ must imitate the voice.

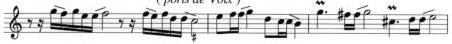

The two notes which must be played legato are marked here with an oblique stroke.

There are numerous examples of pre-beat appoggiaturas in Nivers. In his pieces he did not use the oblique stroke that he indicated in the explanation. The situations in which this procedure is applicable are, however, clearly identifiable in the pieces: the ♪ at the end of bar 8 and bar 11 in the following example are certainly to be understood as the *Ports de voix* described above:

Guillaume-Gabriel Nivers: *Récit de Cromhorne* (1*er* Ton, Premier Livre d'Orgue)

This practice is exemplified even more explicity in the *Motets à voix seule, accompagnée de la basse continue* (1689) by Nivers, in which it is obvious from both slurs (which actually transform the notes into *Ports de voix*) and from corresponding sung text that the appoggiatura begins on the upbeat:

Guillaume-Gabriel Nivers: 2. *Magnificat* (*Motets à voix seule*)

Raison and Chaumont also prefer a pre-beat execution of the *Port de voix*, indicating it with a slur and an inverted V respectively:

Raison explains that the *Port de voix* should be played with a good legato:

[...] jl ne faut lever le re qu'apres avoir posé l'ut.[429]	[...] one must lift the finger off D only after having depressed C.

Loulié (1696) differentiates the terminology for the descending and ascending appoggiaturas. In the case of the descending – as well as a leaping appoggiatura – Loulié used the term *Coulé* and preferred it to be played before the beat:

Le Coulé est une Inflexion de la Voix d'un petit Son ou Son foible, ou d'une petite durée, à un son plus bas & plus fort. Le Coulé se marque ainsi ɔ.[430]	The Coulé is an inflection of the voice which goes from a small or weak sound, or one of short duration, to a lower note and stronger sound. The Coulé is indicated as ɔ.

This type of ornament is also described by Hotteterre-le-Romain in his *Principes de la flûte traversière* (1707) and called *Coulement*. In the case of ascending appoggiatura – referred to by Loulié *Port de voix* and indicated with an oblique stroke – the author instead left open the possibility of playing it before or on the beat:[431]

Boyvin, D'Anglebert and Gaspard Corrette, on the other hand, specifically requested that it be played on the beat. D'Anglebert indicated the *Cheute ou Port de voix* with a small parenthesis placed before the note. The direction, ascending or descending, could be inferred from the previous note:

D'Anglebert

Gaspard Corrette used the *petite virgule* only for the ascending movement and asked that it be played on the beat: *[...] la petite notte touche precisement contre la Basse ou accompagnement.*[432]

[...] *the little note is played precisely together with the bass or accompaniment.*

G. Corrette

For the descending *Port de voix* Gaspard Corrette used a small cross placed before the note, always specifying that it be played on the beat [*"qu'elle frape directement contre la Basse"*].[433]

G. Corrette

Boyvin left open the possibility of playing in ascending motion:
[...] sur la notte d'ou l'on vien
[...] on the note from which we arrive
but he also specified that it was usually in descending motion:
qui est ordinairement en descendant.[434]

Boyvin

The *Cheute* was used by d'Anglebert not only for a melodic line but also within the chord:

The *Pincé avec Port de voix*, i.e. the fusion of appoggiatura and mordent – by Couperin in the *Premier Livre de Pièces de Clavecin* (1713) called *Port de voix simple* – is a very common embellishment in the French repertoire of the Baroque period. It is usually clearly indicated with two distinct signs:

D'Anglebert, Boyvin and Dandrieu indicated it in the following ways:

COULÉ

With the exception of Loulié and Hotteterre who called the descending appoggiatura *Coulé* and *Coulement* respectively, the term *Coulé* usually indicates a rapid passage between two notes.

The *Coulé* may occur within a chord or between two successive notes. In the first case, there are usually two notes placed at a distance of a third – hence the term *Tierce coulée* – thus creating a "harmonic" *Coulé*.

Most composers, including Lebègue and Gaspard Corrette, indicate this ornament with an oblique stroke placed between the two notes. D'Anglebert instead used a small, bracket-like vertical semicurve line:

| Lebègue | G. Corrette | D'Anglebert |

The *Coulé* is usually intended to be played on the beat and quickly, as recommended by Nivers:

| *Observez certaines tierces ou il y a une petite bare entre deux notes, c'est a dire qu il faut faire une coulade fort legere a la dite tierce, et tenir les deux notes extremes.*[435] | Observe some thirds where there is a small bar between two notes: this means that one has to make a very rapid coulade on that third, and hold the two outside notes. |

In the case of the "melodic" *Coulé*, which consists of a connection between two non-synchronous notes, the interval can be of a third or a fourth. Most authors – like Saint-Lambert in the example below – used an oblique stroke to show this, while D'Anglebert used a slur. D'Anglebert considered its performance either on or before the beat, as can be seen in the following examples:

| Saint-Lambert | D'Anglebert |

Many composers indicated this ornament with little notes written out in full. Loulié called this type of ornament *Coulade* and specified:

| *La Coulade n'a point de Caractere particulier, elle se marque par de petites Nottes.*[436] | The *Coulade* does not have a particular symbol, but is indicated by little notes. |

The note groupings in Loulié's examples of *Coulades* are notable, as is clearly evident in his example:

Other authors used both types of indication, i.e. symbols and notes written *in extenso*, as in the following example by Boyvin (cfr. bar 1 and bar 3):

Jacques Boyvin: *Fugue* (5ᵉ Ton, Second Livre d'Orgue)

DOUBLÉ

The *Doublé* or *Double cadence* (also *Tour de gosier*) corresponds to the *turn* which, according to the different authors, can be played – with different rhythmic variations – touching either both auxiliary notes or the third below the note on which it is placed:

It is often used together with other embellishments as a *double ornament* in cadential formulas:

Sometimes the *Double cadence* sign is placed between two notes. The example below presents two cases that produce a similar result but are conceptually different: the *Double cadence* at bar 5, during the second beat of the C, touches the upper (D) and lower (B) auxiliaries and then rises to the D as the beginning of the *Tremblement*; the one at bar 9 on the note D descends by a third (B) and then ascends to E:

Jacques Boyvin: *Dessus de cornet séparé ou de petite tierce* (3ᵉ *Ton, Second Livre d'Orgue*)

In many cases the *Double cadence* is not indicated by a specific sign but written out in full, as in the following example by Marchand, bars 4 and 7:

Louis Marchand: *Fugue* (*Pièces Choisies pour l'Orgue, 1ʳ Livre*)

ARPÈGE

The *Arpège* or *Harpègement* is an ornament of harpsichord derivation frequently cited and described in the various *livres d'orgue*. Boyvin stated

On ne fait guerre d'arpegement sur l'orgue on fait plus tost un petit tremblement a la notte d'audessous.[437]	One does not make much arpegement on the organ, but rather a little tremblement on the lowest note [of the chord].

Despite this, he gave some examples in his *Premier Livre d'Orgue* (1690):

In contrast to Boyvin, the *Manuscrit de l'Arsenal* suggested to play

[…] les harpagements tant dans les commancemens de chacque piece que dans les fins de chaque cadence.[438]	[…] harpègments both at the beginning of each piece and at the end of each cadence.

It also explained how they were to be performed:

[...] dune manierre prompte vive liée et imperceptible sant lever les mains ny les doist [...].[439]	[...] in a quick, lively, legato and imperceptible way, without lifting the hands or fingers [...].

The same manuscript stated that, in *Préludes* on the organ, arpeggios played with the left hand should be in descending motion:

De la main gaùche le harpagement ce commance toujours par le doit du pouce en suitte du segond doit qui suit le pouce et en fin du petit et dernier voila de la manierre que le harpagement du prelude de lorgue ce jouee de la main gauche [...].[440]	With the left hand the arpeggio always begins with the thumb, then the second finger after the thumb and finally the last, little finger; this is how one plays an arpeggio in a prelude on the organ with the left hand [...].

On the harpsichord they are first descending and then ascending:

[...] au clavesin il commance bien par le pouce mais ensuitte il desend aux petit doit et remonte au doit daupres du pouce et en suitte retourne au pouce; [...].[441]	[...] on the harpsichord the arpeggio starts also with the thumb and descends to the little finger; but then it remounts to the finger next to the thumb and then returns to the thumb; [...].

Arpeggios in the right hand are, instead, played with ascending motion:

[...] quand a la main droite il commance par le doit qui êst le plus proche du pouce et continué a celuy qui le suit et enfin va aux petit doit et êst semblable quand a la main droite au harpagemens du clavesin a la reserve que celuy de lorgue comme jay dit ailleurs doit être vif prompte et tres court et net et enfin imperceptible [...].[442]	[...] as for the right hand, it starts with the finger that is closest to the thumb and continues with the one that follows, and finally goes to the little finger; with the right hand it is therefore similar to arpeggios performed on the harpsichord, with the difference that on the organ, as I have already said elsewhere, the arpeggio must be lively, prompt and very short and clear, in the end imperceptible [...].

D'Anglebert indicates the *Arpège* with an oblique stroke above or below the chord:

Some authors use the arpeggio sign commonly used today, which – depending on the position – can indicate an ascending or descending arpeggio:

| Lebègue | Raison | Jullien | Chaumont |

Contrary to Boyvin (see above), Raison and his pupil Clérambault called occasionally for the use of arpeggios on the organ:

André Raison: *Premier Kyrie, Grand Plein Jeu* (Messe du Troisiesme ton)

Louis-Nicolas Clérambault: *Dialogue sur les grands jeux* (Suite du premier ton)

GEORG MUFFAT'S ORNAMENTATION
"À LA FRANÇOISE"

Published in Passau in 1698, the *Florilegium Secundum* by Georg Muffat contains valuable information on French-style ornamentation. The author, who, according to his own statements, came into contact with the best musicians of France during his six-year stay in Paris, often cites as a reference and mentor

| […] le genie de feu Monsieur Battiste de Lully, prise icy en sa pureté, & si recommandable par l'approbation des meilleurs Musiciens de l'Europe […].[443] | […] the genius of the late Monsieur Battiste de Lully, taken here in its purity, and so highly commended by the best musicians of Europe […]. |

Organ & interpretation: the French école classique

In the long preface (written in Latin, German, Italian and French) Muffat presents his

[...] Premieres Observations sur la belle methode de bien executer ces sortes d'airs Selon le goût de feu Monsr. Baptiste de Lully [...].[444]	*[...] First Observations on the beautiful method of performing well these kinds of arias [Airs] according to the style of the late Monsieur Baptiste de Lully [...]*

and at the end he emphasizes with vigor

[...] que tout le secret des ornemens du jeu à la françoise est contenu comme en un abbregé en ces dix regles, des quelles [...] dépend une douceur, vigueur, & beauté particuliere de cette methode, qui la fait distinguer des autres.[445]	*[...] that the whole secret of the ornaments "à la françoise" is contained, as in a compendium, in these ten rules on which [...] the suavity, strength, and unique beauty of this method depends, which makes it so distinct from the others.*

Although the volume does not include music expressly written for organ (these are eight *Suites* for strings and *basso continuo*), the description of the ornamentation is of great interest.[446]

Pincement, ou tremblement coupé

[...] commance & finit en sa propre note se servant de la prochaine touche d'au dessous pour trembler, ordinairement distante d'un semiton, [...]. Il se fait fort court, se contentant le plus souvent d'un seul tremoussement.	*[...] starts and ends on the note itself using the lower key to trill on, usually at a distance of a semitone, [...]. It is very short - most of the time a single beat [tremoussement] suffices.*

Tremblement, ou fredon

[...] commance d'une touche plus haut, & finit en sa note.	*[...] starts on the upper key, & ends on its note.*

Tremblement Reflechissant

[...] lors qu'il y mesle une seule fois la touche d'au dessous, puis se repose un peu sur sa note.	*[...] when it touches the lower key once only, and then rests a little on its note.*

Tremblement Roulant

[...] qui ne differe du Reflechissant qu'en ce qu'il ne s'arrête point sur sa note, mais roule tout d'un coup à la suivante, & se connoit	*[...] which only differs from the Reflechissant in that it doesn't rest on the note but immediately rolls to the next, and it is often recognized by*

souvent aux deux doubles crochuës, qui accompagnent sa note. C'est ce que les Jouëurs de Clavecin appellent double cadence.

the presence of two semiquavers, which accompany its note. This is what the harpsichord players call double cadence.

Accentuation

[...] met une seule touche devant ou apres sa note. Il y en a six especes: trois, qui se mettent devant, & trois qui se mettent apres la note.

Celles de devant sont le Sur-accent (1), le Sous-accent (2), & le Sursaut (3); dont le premier prend la prochaine au dessus, le seconde la prochaine au dessous, & le troisiéme une touche de tierce plus haut par avance.

[...] puts a single [ornamental] note before or after the [ornated] note. There are six kinds: three that are placed in front, and three placed after the note.

The ones in front are the Sur-accent (1), the Sous-accent (2), and the Sursaut (3); the first adds the upper note, the second the note below, and the third one adds a third higher.

Celles d'apres sont l'Accent ou la Superficie (4), Le Relâchemènt (5), & la Dispersion (6). L'Accent adjoute la prochaine au dessus, le Relâchement la prochaine au dessous, & la Dispersion la tierce, ou autre saut au dessus de sa note.

Then follows the Accent or Superficie (4), the Relâchemènt (5), and the Dispersion (6). The Accent adds the upper note, the Relâchement adds the note below, and the Dispersion adds the third or other interval above its note.

Port de voix

[...] embrassant les trois premieres especes d'accentuations, de deux notes, fait retoucher avant la seconde la touche de la premiere.

[...] embracing the first three kinds of accentuations, consists of two notes, and one has to replay the first note before playing the second.

Préoccupation

La Préoccupation au contraire, qui se sert des trois dernieres accentuations, adjoute à la note precedente, la touche de la suivante.

The Préoccupation, on the contrary, drawing on the last three accentuations, adds the note following to the preceding one.

Coulement

Le coulement fait couler deux ou plusieurs notes sous un même coup d'archet. [...]. Le coulement simple marqué dans la composition même, n'adjoute rien.

The coulement ties two or more notes under the same bow. [...]. The 'coulement simple' marked in the composition itself, adds nothing.

Coulement droit

[...] coule de suitte Jusqu'a la note au lieu d'y sauter, en adjoutant les touches d'entre deux.

[...] indicates to go from one written note to the other by playing the consecutive notes in between, instead of leaping from one to the other.

Tournoyant

[...] coule indifferemment ça. & la.

[...] indicates to play [around the note] indifferently here and there.

Exclamation ⁒

L'Exclamation est une éspece de coulement, montant par trois touches de suitte. Elle est ou accessive, ou superlative.

L'Accessive (a) monte à sa note; La superlative (b) monte apres sa note

The Exclamation is a kind of coulement, ascending by three consecutive notes. It is either Accessive, or Superlative.

The Accessive (a) ascends to the note; the Superlative (b) ascends after the note

(a):  (b):

Involution ∾

L'Involution, que quelques uns appellent agrément est une autre éspece de coulement qui envelopppe trois touches comme en rond, tantôt simplement (a), & tantôt avec un tremblement (b).

The Involution, which some call agrément, is another kind of coulement which envelops three notes as in a circle, sometimes simply (a), and sometimes with a tremblement (b).

(a):  (b):

Petillement

[...] differe du coulement, en ce qu'il exprime les notes distinctement, en les faisant craqueter sous un même trait d'Archet.

[...] differs from the coulement, in that the notes are played distinctly, making them hop under the same bow.

Diminution

[...] au lieu de sa note lente, en adjoute plusieurs autres petites convenables à l'accord, chacune ayant souvent son trait d'archet.

[...] instead of the slow [written] note, it adds several other small notes suitable to the chord, each often having its own bow.

Tirade, ou Course

[...] court à la note, ou elle butte par plusieurs touches de suitte avec rapidité, & extreme vitesse de l'archet.

[...] runs to the note with great rapidity, with a flourish of several consecutive notes, and extreme speed of the bow.

Even more interesting is the advice given by Muffat on the use of ornamentation. The author indicates precisely when it is appropriate to perform or add a specific type of embellishment:[447]

I. Les pincemens, ou tremblemens coupez, se peuvent faire presque par tout, hormis aux seules notes d'extreme vitesse; & rien n'empeche d'en faire deux, ou plus de suitte, pour peu que l'on n'aille pas trop vite:

I. The pincements, or tremblements coupez, can be done almost everywhere, except only on extremely fast notes; and nothing stops one from doing two or more consecutively, as long as one does not go too fast:

II. On n'approuvè que rarement de commancer une piece, ou une de ses periodes, une montée, ou une descente par un tremblement, excepté aux mi, ou diêses #, ou l'on se sert souvent du tremblement soit simple, ou Reflechissant; même en commançant:

II. It is seldom acceptable to start a piece, or part therof, or an ascending line, or a descending line with a tremblement, except on the E, or sharp # [i.e. within a semitone], where the tremblement - either simple, or Reflechissant - is often used, even when starting:

III. En montant conjointement on va à la bonne note par le port'de voix seul (7) ou joint au pincement (8). Si les notes vont trop vite cet ornement se reserve Jusqu'a la premiere bonne note un peu plus lente, qui viendra ensuitte (9). Quant la chetive ne monte pas trop vite on luy donne quelquefois le tremblement reflechissant seul (10), ou préoccupé d'un accent (11), auquel on peut élegamment joindre le port de voix (12), ou bien le roulant (13). Il est rude de donner le tremblement à une bonne note en montant. Que si on est quelque fois obligé de le faire, il le faut adoucir par la préoccupation (14). On en excepte les mi & les dièses ♯, qui bonnes, ou chetives, pour vu qu'elles ne passent pas extrémement vite, s'ornent presque toujours d'un tremblement (15):

III. Ascending stepwise, one reaches the good note with a port de voix alone (7) or together with a pincement (8). If the notes are too fast, this ornament should be reserved for the first good note following that is a bit longer (9). When the bad note doesn't ascend too fast, one can sometimes add a tremblement reflechissant alone (10), or with a préoccupation with an accent (11), to which a port de voix can be elegantly added (12), or else a roulant (13). It sounds harsh doing a tremblement on a good note when ascending. If, sometimes, one is obliged to do so, it should be softened by a préoccupation (14). An exception is made for E, and sharps ♯, that – whether they are good or bad notes, as long as not extremely fast – are almost always adorned with a tremblement (15):

IV. En descendant conjointement on fait aisément quelques tremblemens par cy, par là aux bonnes notes, sur tout à celles qui ont un point apres elles (16). Quelques fois aussy de chetives qui descendent moderément le reçoivent agréablement seul (17), ou préoccupant avec le Relâchement (18). En descendant plus vite on ne fait des tremblemens, que dispersément sur quelques bonnes notes (19):

IV. In descending stepwise it is nice to do some tremblements here and there on good notes, especially those that are dotted (16). Sometimes also bad notes which descend moderately can receive a trill, either alone (17), or with a préoccupation with a Relâchement (18). When descending faster, one only does a few tremblements scattered here and there over some good notes (19):

V. En sautant en haut On va à la bonne note par un port de voix seul (20), ou avec le pincement (21). Quelques fois pour exciter l'harmonie on se sert du coulement droit seul (22) ou enveloppé du tremblement roulant, ce qui est encore plus beau (23). La tirade est la plus vive de toutes les figures, dont il se faut servir quelques fois, mais sobrement (24). En sautant en haut par tierce, on adoucit tres bien le Jeu par l'exclamation accessive (25) dont les Lullistes ne se servent ordinairement qu'en cette rencontre, & presque Jamais ailleurs. Quoyque de sauter au tremblement passe pour defaut, Il se permet neant moins fort souvent aux mi & dièses ♯ (26):

V. Ascending to a good note by a leap, one uses a port de voix, either alone (20) or with a pincement (21). Sometimes to enliven the harmony one can use the coulement droit, alone (22) or enveloped by the tremblement roulant, which is even more beautiful (23). The tirade is the liveliest of all the figures, which can be used sometimes, but occasionally (24). In upward leaps by a third, one can very successfully soften the playing with an 'exclamation accessive' (25) which the Lullists usually do not use except on this occasion, and almost never elsewhere. Although leaping to a tremblement is considered bad, it is however very often permitted on E and sharps ♯ (26):

VI. En sautant en bas, Il ne se fait guere de tremblemens, si ce n'est en sautant par tierce (27), ou sur un mi, ou sur une dièse (28): Car alors il en faut presque toujours soient de simples, ou de Reflechissans. Au reste le saut en bas s'insinue Joliment par la préoccupation (29), ou par le coulement (30), ou par le petillement (31): Vivement par la Tirade (32); Mais le plus agréablement du monde par le coulement avec un tremblement tendre sur la penultième de la descente (33):

VI. In descending leaps, tremblements are not much done, except for intervals of a third (27), or E, or a sharp (28): in these cases one almost always does a [tremblement] simple or Reflechissant. In other cases, downward leaps can be embellished either with a préoccupation (29), or a coulement (30), or a petillement (31): vivaciously with a Tirade (32); but most pleasantly of all with a coulement with a tender tremblement on the penultimate note of the descent (33):

VII. Il y a dans les cadences de certaines notes qui demandent le tremblement, & d'autres qui le refusent. On n'en fait guere sur celle qui termine la cadence à moins qu'on n'y saute par tierce en bas (34), ou qu'on ne descende conjointement (35) ou par préoccupation (36) sur un mi, ou sur une dièse ♯ :	VII. In the cadences there are certain notes which call for a tremblement, and others which refuse it. It should never be done on the last note of a cadence unless reaching it by a downward leap of a third (34), or by a stepwise descent (35) or by a préoccupation (36) or on E, or a sharp ♯:

Interesting is the warning to avoid trills in succession:

IX. On n'approuve guere deux tremblemens de suitte; Neantmoins ils sont permis en y entremeslant une accentuation (37); ou lorsque s'en étant dû faire un sur une note selon la teneur de ces Regles, celle d'ensuitte se treuve en un mi, ou en une dièse ♯ plus dure que la precedente (38):	IX. Two tremblements in succession are hardly ever acceptable; nevertheless, they are permitted when there is an 'accentuation' in between (37); or if the note calls for it according to these rules - the following note is an E, or a sharp ♯ harder than the precedent note (38):

At the end of the chapter, Muffat describes the four errors that can be committed through an improper use of ornamentation, i.e.:

[...] par omission, par improprieté, par excés & par inhabilité. Par omission la melodie & l'harmonie en deviennent nuës, & sans ornement. Par improprieté le jeu se rend rude & barbare; par excés, confus & ridicule; & par inhabilité, lourd & contraint. C'est pourquoy il faut user de tant d'assiduité à faire ces precieux ornemens de la Musique toutes les fois qu'il en est besoin: de tant de circonspection à en connoître les vrais endroits: & de tant de dexterité a les bien exprimer [...].[448]	[...] by omission, impropriety, excess and inability. By omission, the melody & harmony result nude, and without ornament. By impropriety, the playing results rough and barbarous; by excess, confused and ridiculous; & by inability, heavy & constrained. This is why much diligence is required to do these precious musical ornaments whenever they are needed: much circumspection to know the right places [where they should be]: and much dexterity to express them well [...].

[390] Mersenne 1636, 107.
[391] D'Anglebert 1689, 47.
[392] Titelouze 1624, 15.
[393] Mersenne 1636, 108.
[394] Loulié 1696, 69.
[395] Gigault 1682, 21.
[396] Gigault 1682, 21.
[397] Saint-Lambert 1702, 123-124.
[398] Saint-Lambert 1702, 124.
[399] Couperin 1722, Préface, without page number.
[400] Ponsford 2011, 59f.
[401] Montéclair 1736, 86.
[402] Montéclair 1736, 86.
[403] Montéclair 1736, 86-87.
[404] Montéclair 1736, 86-87.
[405] Lebègue 1676, 15.
[406] Saint-Lambert 1702, 124.
[407] Nivers 1665, 176.
[408] Nivers 1665, 176.
[409] Nivers 1665, 176.
[410] Boyven 1690, 56.
[411] Pruitt 1986, 244.
[412] Saint-Lambert 1702, 94.
[413] Saint-Lambert 1702, 96.
[414] Couperin 1716, 23.
[415] Couperin 1716, 24.
[416] Couperin 1716, 24.
[417] Neumann 1993, 386 and Ponsford 2011, 78.
[418] Kind communication of Christophe Mantoux.
[419] Nivers 1689, Observations, without page number.
[420] Boyvin 1690, 56.
[421] Corrette 1703, 123.
[422] Couperin 1716, 19.
[423] Couperin 1716, 19.
[424] Loulié 1696, 72.
[425] Boyvin 1700, 92.
[426] Saint-Lambert 1702, 109.
[427] Sain-Lambert 1702, 109.
[428] Nivers 1665, 177.
[429] Raison 1688, 31.
[430] Loulié 1696, 68.
[431] Loulié 1696, 69.
[432] Corrette 1703, 123.
[433] Corrette 1703, 124.
[434] Boyvin 1690, 57.
[435] Nivers 1665, 177.
[436] Loulié 1696, 74.
[437] Boyvin 1690, 58.
[438] Pruitt 1986, 239.
[439] Pruitt 1986, 239.
[440] Pruitt 1986, 239.
[441] Pruitt 1986, 239.
[442] Pruitt 1986, 239.
[443] Muffat 1698, 51f.
[444] Muffat 1698, 49.
[445] Muffat 1698, 89.
[446] Muffat 1698, 79-83 and 96-97.
[447] Muffat 1698, 83-90.
[448] Muffat 1698, 89-90.

FINGERING

FINGERING IN FRENCH ORGAN MUSIC

Information concerning fingerings in texts expressly pertaining to the organ is contained in the following publications:

- ❖ 1665 - Guillame-Gabriel Nivers: *[Premier] Livre d'Orgue*
- ❖ 1688 - André Raison: *Livre d'Orgue*
- ❖ 1700 - Jacques Boyvin: *Second Livre d'Orgue*
- ❖ 1714 - André Raison: *Second Livre d'Orgue*

In the case of Nivers, these are rules presented in the form of a treatise at the beginning of the volume, while in the other three sources, fingerings are to be found in some of the pieces contained in the respective *livres d'orgue*. Further information is included in some harpsichord treatises, in particular:

- ❖ 1702 - Mr de Saint-Lambert: *Les Principes du Clavecin*
- ❖ 1716 - François Couperin: *L'Art de Toucher le Clavecin*
- ❖ 1724 - Jean-Philippe Rameau: *Pièces de Clavessin*

In the case of Rameau, however, it should be emphasized that this is the preface to the volume of the *Pièces de Clavessin* entitled *Méthode pour la Mechanique des Doigts* in which the position to be adopted by the hand and fingers is amply illustrated, but no real fingerings are described. The reference to the latter is limited to a brief musical example – a *Menuet en Rondeau* – where it is clear that the fingering used moves away from the concept of *good* and *bad fingers,* and thus, can already be called "modern":

Jean-Philippe Rameau: *Méthode pour la Mechanique des Doigts* (1724)

Although the aforementioned texts give precise information on the fingerings to be adopted, it should be remembered – and not only in respect of French music – that treatises often provide general information targeted mostly at the beginner musician who requires basic guidance. It is therefore evident that such "rules" are not to be considered as exclusive and absolute.

This axiom is very evident in the Nivers' introductory words to the fingering examples (*De la position des doigts*) contained in the preface to his *Livre d'orgue* of 1665. Here, he underlined the importance of playing in a straightforward and comfortable manner:

Pour toucher agreablement, il le faut faire facilement; pour toucher facilement, il le faut faire commodément; et pour cet effet disposer les doigts sur le clavier de bonne grace, avec convenance et egalité en courbant un peu les doigts principalement les plus longs pour les rendre égaux aux plus petits: […].[449]	*To play with elegance one has to play with ease; to play with ease, one has to play comfortably; for this purpose the fingers must be positioned on the keyboard with grace, in a comfortable and uniform manner, slightly curving the fingers, especially the longer ones, to make them equal to the shorter ones: […].*

Later, he highlights the great importance of using fingerings that are comfortable for the player:

[…] et choisissant les doigts les plus commodes pour les passages et accords differents […].[450]	*[…] and choosing the most comfortable fingers for the different passages and chords […].*

The writer of the *Manuscrit de l'Arsenal* also left freedom of choice regarding the fingering:

[…] il ne faut pas que rien contraine les mains et les doist mais il faut ce servir de ceux qui sont les plus commode et les plus proche […].[451]	*[…] one should avoid in any way constraining the hands and fingers, rather one should use the fingers that are most comfortable and nearest […].*

In the *Principes du Clavecin* (1702), a treatise explicitly addressed to beginners, Saint-Lambert opened the chapter on fingerings with the following statement:

Il n'y a rien de plus libre dans le Jeu du Clavecin, que la position des doigts. Chacun ne recherche en cela que la commodité & la bonne grace.[452]	*There is nothing freer in playing the harpsichord than the positioning of the fingers [= choice of fingerings]. In this one should seek only what is most comfortable and graceful.*

He then presented the convenient fingerings for ascending and descending scales (see below) but, at the same time, added:

En toute autre occasion on employe les doigts comme on le juge à propos. [...] Bien ou mal, selon qu'on a de jugement & de goût pour la chose. La commodité de celuy qui joüe est la premiére regle qu'il doit suivre; [...].[453]	*In all other cases, one should use the fingers that one finds best. [...] Good or bad, according to one's judgment and taste in the matter. The player's own comfort is the first rule to be followed; [...].*

Similar instructions can also be read in the preface of Couperin's *L'Art de Toucher le Clavecin*:

La façon de doigter sert beaucoup pour bien joüer; mais, comme il faudroit un volume entier de remarques, & de passages variés pour démontrer ce que je pense; et ce que je fais pratiquer a mes élèves, je n'en donneray icy qu'une notion generale.[454]	*The fingering is very important for playing well; but since an entire volume with indications and varied passages would be needed to illustrate what I think and what I make my students practise, I will give here only some general notions.*

Furthermore, regarding the fingerings to be used for the ornaments, Couperin left it up to the player (the student), i.e. to his teacher:

Il seroit tres utile de pouvoir exercer les jeunes personnes a faire des tremblemens de tous les doigts: mais comme cela dépend en partie de la disposition naturèle, et que quelques unes ont plus ou moins de liberté, et de force, de certains doigts, il faut laisser ce choix aux personnes qui les instruisent.[455]	*It would be very useful to let young people practice doing tremblements with all the fingers; but since this depends in part on the natural disposition, and the fact that some [people] have more or less freedom and strength in certain fingers, this choice should be left up to those who teach them.*

FINGERINGS FOR SCALES

Taking into consideration the three texts that methodically illustrate the fingering to use in ascending and descending scales – Nivers, Saint-Lambert and Couperin – some differences emerge.

Nivers presents some *Exemples les plus cōmunes et generales*. One can see a certain affinity with the fingerings by Girolamo Diruta, above all in the use of the 2nd and 4th finger - the treatise *Il Transilvano* was well known even outside Italy. However, from the examples given it is clear that in Nivers, differently from Diruta, there was not a strict rule of division between *good fingers* and *bad fingers*:[456]

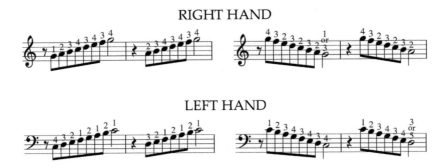

In part similar to those by Nivers are the fingerings for scales suggested by Saint-Lambert:[457]

In the chapter *Pour les Diminutions* towards the end of the treatise, Saint-Lambert seems however to be open to other solutions:

[…] quand on a une Diminution à faire de la main droite, si les Notes vont toûjours en descendant, l'usage est d'y employer le second & le troisiéme doigt alternativement, ainsi que je l'ay marqué au Chapitre de la Position des doigts, mais j'ajoûte icy que cet usage ne me paroît pas encore bien établi, & que le pouce & le second doigt conviendroient mieux à ces sortes de passages, que le second & le troisiéme, parce que le pouce étant plus court que les autres doigts, il est plus aisé à retirer de dessous le second, que le second n'est aisé à retirer de dessous le troisiéme, […].[458]	*[...] when there is a Diminution in the right hand, if the notes constantly proceed by descending motion, the custom is to use alternately the second and third fingers, as I indicated in the chapter on the positioning of the fingers, but I add here that this custom does not seem to me well established yet, and that the thumb and the second finger would be more suited to these kinds of passages than the second and third, because the thumb, being shorter than the other fingers, is easier to pass under the second, than the second is to pass under the third, [...].*

He added that the same criteria can be applied to similar passages in the left hand:

La même raison qu'on a pour employer le pouce dans les Diminutions en montant de la main	*The same reason for which one should use the thumb in ascending Diminutions of the left*

gauche, doit determiner à l'employer aussi dans les Diminutions en descendant de la main droite.[459]

hand should also determine its use in descending Diminutions of the right hand.

Couperin provided fingerings only for the right hand, which – in the case of diatonic scales – were identical to those by Saint-Lambert:[460]

In addition, he provided a *Manière plus commode pour les tous dïesès, et bèmolisès* (a more comfortable mode for playing sharps and flats):

FINGERINGS FOR CHORDS

The fingerings for chords are logically influenced by the physical conformation of the hand and there is, therefore, less difference from author to author. The examples by Nivers and Saint-Lambert are compared here. For the right hand, Saint-Lambert provided a different fingering for large and small hands (*pour les grandes mains* and *pour les petites mains*):

Two-note chord - LEFT HAND

Nivers:

Two-note chord - RIGHT HAND

Nivers:

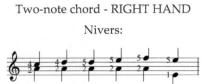

Saint-Lambert - *Pour les grandes mains*:

Saint-Lambert:

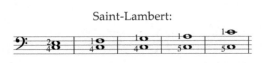

Saint-Lambert - *Pour les petites mains*:

Three/four-note chord - LEFT HAND

Nivers:

Three/four-note chord - RIGHT HAND

Nivers:

Saint-Lambert - *Pour les grandes mains*:

Saint-Lambert:

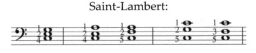

Saint-Lambert - *Pour les petites mains*:

Saint-Lambert
Pour les grandes & les petites mains:

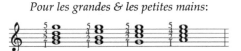

Saint-Lambert then gave some examples of chords containing chromatic keys, explaining that in such cases one must change the position of the fingers to avoid playing with the thumb on sharp and flat keys:

Main droite, grande ou petite

Main gauche, grande ou petite

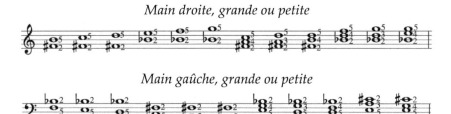

Couperin did not provide chord fingerings but focused his attention on passages with thirds in succession:

Manière ancienne de faire plusieurs tierces de suitte.[461]

Old manner of playing several thirds in succession:

Cette Manière ancienne n'avoit nulle Liaison. Celle qui suit est la vraye. Façon Moderne pour couler ces mêmes tièrces.

This old manner did not permit any legato. The following is the right one. Modern way to play the same thirds legato:

And he continued:

Je suis persuadé que peu de personnes dans Paris restent entêtès des Vielles maximes: Paris étant le centre du bon.

I am convinced that few people in Paris remain rigidly bound to the old maxims: Paris being the center of what is good.

Finally, he added a further example of fingerings for passages consisting of ascending and descending thirds ("*Other progression of legato thirds*"):

Autre progrès de tierces coulées

OTHER FINGERINGS

Analyzing the fingerings occasionally present in some pieces in Raison's *Livre d'Orgue*, it is difficult to discern an underlying logic. The use of the fourth finger, first on a *good note* and in the following bar on a *bad note* (bars 7 and 8 of the following example) would seem to contradict the system of *good fingers* and *bad fingers* advocated – with some liberty – by Nivers and Saint-Lambert:

André Raison: *Benedicimus te (Messe du Sixiesme ton)*

Also other fingerings in the same piece do not appear to be exactly conventional:

André Raison: *Benedicimus te* (*Messe du Sixiesme ton*)

The use of the same finger on two adjacent notes, even of very short duration, is documented in several cases:

André Raison: *Premier Kyrie* (*Messe du Sixiesme ton*)

André Raison: *Glorificamus te* (*Messe du Huictiesme ton*)

A. Raison: *Premier Kyrie* (*Messe du 1er ton*)

(however, in the latter case it cannot be ruled out *a priori* that this could be a printing error).

In the following example, the use of the same finger on two non-adjacent notes has an inevitable influence on the articulation:

André Raison: *Tu solus altissimus* (*Messe du Huictiesme ton*)

In the *Amen* that concludes the *Gloria* of the *Messe du Huictiesme ton*, the passing of the thumb under the second finger seems to be indicated, although this technique was not commonly used at this time. The fingering indicated at bars 26 and 27 for the alto voice does not, however, prove with certainty whether what is meant is really the passing of the thumb under the second finger or instead a change of hand position:

André Raison: *Tu solus altissimus* (*Messe du Huictiesme ton*)

Only in the following decades would the technique of the passing under of the thumb become commonplace. Rameau described it and strongly recommended its use in the *Méthode pour la Mechanique des Doigts* which opens the collection of *Pièces de Clavessin* of 1724:

Pour continuer un roulement plus étendu que celui de la Leçon, il n'y a qu'à s'accoutumer à passer le 1. par-dessous tel autre doigt que l'on veut, & à passer l'un de ces autres doigts par-dessus le 1. Cette maniere est excellente, surtout quand il s'y rencontre des Diézes ou des Bemols; [...].[462]

To continue a more extensive roulement [= rapid passage] than that of the lesson, one only needs to get used to passing the first [= thumb] under any other finger that one wants and passing any [of] these other fingers over the thumb. This manner is excellent, especially when there are sharps or flats in the passage; [...].

The fingerings contained in the other two *livres d'orgue* referred to at the beginning of the chapter are somewhat fewer in number. In the volume published in 1714, Raison made frequent use of the fifth finger, including in succession in the same voice, as in the following example:

André Raison: *Ou s'en vont ces gais Bergers* (Second Livre d'Orgue)

In the *L'Art de Toucher le Clavecin*, François Couperin seems to take a progressive look ahead as far as fingering is concerned. In reference to the performance of ornaments, he urged the reader to abandon the "old fingerings":

[…] sans aucun égard a l'ancien usage de doigter, qu'il faut quiter, en faveur du bien=joüer d'aujourd'hui.[463]	*[…] regardless of the old manner of fingering, which must be abandoned in favor of today's mode of "playing well".*

In the same source he described *finger substitution*, i.e. the silent changing of fingers on a key while said key remains depressed:

On connoitra par la pratique, combien le changement d'un doigt a un autre, sur la même note, sera utile; et quelle liaison cela donne au jeu.[464]	*One will know from practice just how useful finger substitution on the same note is, and what [a nice] legato it gives to the playing.*

To this end, Couperin also provided some musical examples ("*Succession of tremblements, using the substitution technique*"):

Progrès de tremblemens enchaînés,
par la manière de changer de doigt sur une même note.[465]

On the other hand, in other cases Couperin referred to the past, using the same finger for two adjacent notes or using the technique of the lateral shift of the hand.

In the first example below – concerning a passage taken from the *Premier Livre de Clavecin* but cited as an example of fingering in the *L'Art de Toucher le Clavecin* – the same finger (the third) is used between the second and third eighth note as well as between the sixth and seventh:[466]

François Couperin: *Silvains, seconde partie*
(*Premier Livre de Clavecin*)

In the following example, taken from the same piece, the technique of the lateral shift of the hand is used in order to play the same passage with the same fingering:[467]

François Couperin: *Silvains, Arpègement (Premier Livre de Clavecin)*

Progressive ideas and elements of the *ancien usage* would coexist for a certain time: in his *Dictionnaire de Musique* of 1768 – i.e. published half a century after the treatise by Couperin – Jean-Jacques Rousseau first established

De ne point porter successivement le même doigt sur deux touches consécutives, mais d'employer tous les doigts de chaque main.[468]	Not to use the same finger successively on two consecutive keys, but to use all the fingers of each hand.

A few paragraphs later he also wrote:

Evitez, autant qu'il se pourra, de toucher du pouce ou du cinquieme doigt une touche blanche, surtout dans les roulemens de vitesse.[469]	Avoid, as far as possible, using your thumb or fifth finger on a chromatic key, especially in fast passages.

[449] Nivers 1665, 176.
[450] Nivers 1665, 176.
[451] Pruitt 1986, 240.
[452] Saint-Lambert 1702, 89.
[453] Saint-Lambert 1702, 93.
[454] Couperin 1716, 10.
[455] Couperin 1716, 22.
[456] Nivers 1665, 176.
[457] Saint-Lambert 1702, 93.
[458] Saint-Lambert 1702, 138.
[459] Saint-Lambert 1702, 138.
[460] Couperin 1716, 29.
[461] Couperin 1716, 29.
[462] Rameau 1724, 5.
[463] Couperin 1716, 11.
[464] Couperin 1716, 14-15.
[465] Couperin 1716, 31.
[466] Couperin 1716, 47.
[467] Couperin 1716, 47.
[468] Rousseau 1768, 170
[469] Rousseau 1768, 170

PRINCIPAL COMPOSERS

GENERAL OVERVIEW

This chapter includes those authors whose contribution to the organ repertoire was of significant importance. The profile of each includes a brief, essential biography, a list of extant organ compositions, and also, when known, a description of the organs of which they were *titulaires*.*

The following page shows a chronological table of the main composers of organ works in France from the beginning of the 17th to the middle of the 18th century.

---

* The information contained in this chapter, unless otherwise indicated, has been compiled from the following sources:
  - Fuzeau facsimiles concerning the different composers (see paragraph: *Musical works and editions*, p. 352)
  - *The New Grove Dictionary of Music and Musicians* (Reprint, Macmillan Publishers Limited, 1998)
  - *MGG: Die Musik in Geschichte und Gegenwart* (2. Ausgabe, Bärenreiter 1994-2007)
  - *Lexikon der Orgel* (3. Auflage, Laaber Verlag 2010)

Organ & interpretation: the French *école classique*

1550 60 70 80 90 **1600** 10 20 30 40 **1650** 60 70 80 90 **1700** 10 20 30 40 **1750** 60 70 80 90 **1800**

```
    Eustache du Caurroy
          Jehan Titelouze
             Charles Guillet
              Charles Racquet
              Étienne Richard
                François Roberday
                L. Couperin
                     Nicolas Gigault
                     Jean-Henry d'Anglebert
                      Lambert Chaumont
                      Nicolas Lebègue
                        Guillame-Gabriel Nivers
                        Jean-Nicolas Geoffroy
                          André Raison
                          Gilles Jullien
                          Jacques Boyvin
                                Pierre Dandrieu
                                François Couperin
                                Louis Marchand
                                Charles Piroye
                                Gaspard Corrette
                            N. de Grigny
                                    Pierre Du Mage
                                  Louis-Nicolas Clérambault
                                  Jean-Adam Guilain
                                    Jean-François Dandrieu
                                         François D'Agincourt
                                         Louis Antoine Dornel
                                           Louis-Claude Daquin
                                              Michel Corrette
                                                Claude-Bénigne Balbastre
```

276

EUSTACHE DU CAURROY
1549 - 1609

Born in 1549 in Hauts-de-France, he began his musical career as *Haute-contre* (alto) at the *Chapelle du Roi* before being appointed *Maître de Chapelle* and composer of the *Chambre du Roi*. Over the course of his twenty-year career at the *Chapelle du Roi* he accumulated numerous honours and enjoyed great esteem as a composer.

Even 36 years after his death he was still remembered by Du Peyrat (*Antiquitez de la musique de la chapelle royale*) as one of the greatest musicians of Europe. His five-part *Messe pour les deffuncts* was sung at the funerals of French Kings until the end of the 18th century.

Although Du Caurroy was not active as an organist and composed nothing explicitly for organ, his *Fantasies* were probably used as a model by pre-classical composers such as Titelouze. They were so-called *"pure music"*, i.e. compositions without a specific instrumental designation and characterized by great contrapuntal rigour.

WORKS

Fantasies a III. IIII. V. et VI. parties par Eustache de Caurroy,
Maistre de Musique de la Chappelle du Roy.
A Paris, Par Pierre Ballard, Imprimeur de la Musique du Roy.

– 1610 –

The *Fantasies a III. IIII. V. et VI. parties* were published by his nephew André Pitard in 1610, a year after the death of Du Caurroy. They were printed in separate parts to facilitate their use by instrumental *ensembles*. They could therefore be performed by families of homogeneous instruments (flutes, strings, cornets, etc.) or by a *Consort misto*, i.e. instruments of different types; the latter better enabled one to follow the single voices in the contrapuntal structure.[470]

The practice of *entabulating* vocal or instrumental pieces for keyboard instruments has been documented since the 15th century. In the case of the *Fantasies* by Du Caurroy, the required compass sometimes exceeds the reach of the hands: in such cases the pedal can be used as a *Spielhilfe* (= as an aid to playing) or – as Raison suggested 70 years later – with the help of a *third hand*, i.e. that of another person.

Fantasies a Trois

Premiere Fantasie	*Dessus*
Seconde Fantasie	*Hautecontre*
Troisiesme Fantasie sur, Regina Cœli	*Taille*
Quatriesme Fantasie sur, Conditor Alme Syderum	
Cinquiesme Fantasie	
Sixiesme Fantasie	
Septieme Fantasie	

Fantasies a Quatre

Huitiesme Fantasie	*Dessus*
Neuviesme Fantasie	*Hautecontre*
Dixiesme Fantasie sur, Requiem Æternam	*Taille*
Unziesme Fantasie	*Basse-Contre*
Dousiesme Fantasie a l'imitation de Cunctipotens Genitor	
Treisiesme Fantasie a l'imitation de Salve Regina	
Quatorziesme Fantasie sur, Ave Maris Stella	
Quinziesme Fantasie a l'imitation d'Ave Maris Stella	
Seisiesme Fantasie	
Dixseptiesme Fantasie	
Dixhuictiesme Fantasie a l'imitation de, Que n'ay-ie des ailes mon Dieu	
Dixneusiesme Fantasie a l'imitation de, Conditor Alme Syderum	
Vingtiesme Fantasie	
Vingtuniesme Fantasie a l'imitation de, Iste Confessor	
Vingtdeuxiesme Fantasie	
Vingtroisiesme Fantasie	
Vingtquatriesme Fantasie	
Vingtcinquiesme Fantasie sur, Le Seigneur des qu'on nous offense	
Vingtsixiesme Fantasie	

Fantasies a Cinq

Vingtseptiesme Fantasie	*Dessus*
Vingthuictiesme Fantasie sur, Ad Cœnam Agni Providi	*Hautecontre*
Vingtneufiesme Fantasie a trois sur, Une Ieune Fillette	*Taille*
Trentiesme Fantasie a trois, seconde partie	*Basse-Contre*
Trenteuniesme Fantasie a quatre, troisiesme partie	*Quintus*
Trentedeuxiesme Fantasie a quatre, quatriesme partie	
Trentetroisiesme Fantasie a Cinq, derniere partie	
Trentequatriesme Fantasie a l'imitation de, Pange Lingua	
Trentecinquiesme Fantasie sur, Conditor Alme Syderum	
Trentesixiesme Fantasie	
Trenteseptiesme Fantasie	
Trentehuictiesme Fantasie, a l'imitation des six monosyllabes	

Fantasies a Six

Trenteneufiesme Fantasie	*Dessus*
Quarantiesme Fantasie sur, Cœco Claudiiturde Beato Vincentio	*Hautecontre*
Quaranteuniesme Fantasie suitte, sur Alloquio Privatur	*Taille*
Quarantedeuxiesme Fantasie sur, Ie Suis Desheritee	*Basse-Contre*
	Quintus & Sextus

JEHAN TITELOUZE
c. 1563 - 1633

Titelouze was born c. 1563 in Saint-Omer (in the then Spanish Netherlands). Nothing is known about his musical education. In c. 1585, upon completion of his training for the priesthood, he moved to Rouen where he became a French citizen and took the position of organist at the church of *Saint-Jean*. Three years later he became organist of the Cathedral of the same city; a position he retained until his death.

In addition to being a well-respected organist, he also collaborated as *expert d'orgue* with organ builders such as Nicolas Barbier and Crespin Carlier. There was also an intense correspondence with Marin Mersenne, and it has been suggested that some of the registrations presented in the *Proposition XXXI* of the *Harmonie Universelle* were written by Titelouze.

A learned and knowledgeable man, he was also a writer, earning literary prizes for his poems by the *Académie des Palinods* in Rouen. He died in 1633 at the age of approximately 70 years.

Apart from the *Fantasies* by the Flemish Charles Guillet of 1610 (published in Paris), Titelouze is the first major composer to have left important collections expressly designated for the organ. His two books of *Hymnes* (1623) and *Magnificat* (1626) traditionally mark the beginning of organ literature within the French classical school.

WORKS

Hymnes de l'Eglise pour toucher sur l'orgue,
avec les Fugues et Recherches sur leur plain-chant.
Par I. Titelouze, Chanoine, & Organiste de l'Eglise de Rouën.

– 1623 –

The *Hymnes de l'Eglise* were published in 1623 and were reprinted the following year. The versets of the hymns, as well as those of the *Magnificat*, are composed on the model of the *Fantaisie* and are without indications of registration.

Each of the twelve hymns consists of three or four *couplets*, while the *plainchant* is treated in a diverse manner (see page 30). Worthy of note are two versets, constructed entirely over a long pedal point; in particular the third verset of the hymn *Annue Christe* (*Amen*), in which an e" is sustained for all 55 bars of the piece.

I. *Ad cænam agni providi*	4 couplets	
II. *Veni Creator Spiritus*	4 couplets	Verset 3: *Canon in Diapason*
III. *Pange lingua gloriosi*	3 couplets	
IV. *Ut queant laxis*	3 couplets	
V. *Ave maris stella*	4 couplets	Verset 3: *Canon in Diapente*
VI. *Conditor alme siderum*	3 couplets	Verset 2: *Canon in Diapente*
VII. *A solis ortus cardine*	3 couplets	
VIII. *Exultet cælum laudibus*	3 couplets	
IX. *Annue Christe*	3 couplets	Verset 3: *AMEN*
X. *Sanctorum meritis*	3 couplets	
XI. *Iste confessor*	3 couplets	
XII. *Urbs Jerusalem*	3 couplets	

Le Magnificat, ou Cantique de la Vierge
pour toucher sur l'Orgue, suivant les huit tons de l'Eglise.
Par I. Titelouze, Chanoine, & Organiste de l'Eglise de Rouën.

– 1626 –

The structure of the eight *Magnificats* is extremely regular: each consists of six *couplets*, corresponding to the odd-numbered versets of the canticle, to which an *alio modo* is added for the verset *Deposuit potentes*. In the preface *Au Lecteur* Titelouze explains that he composed the *Magnificats* in such a way that they are simpler to play than the *Hymnes*.

Magnificat Primi Toni	- *Magnificat*
Magnificat Secundi Toni	- *Quia respexit*
Magnificat Tertii Toni	- *Et misericordia eius*
Magnificat Quarti Toni	- *Deposuit potentes*
Magnificat Quinti Toni	[Alter Ver.] *Deposuit potentes*
Magnificat Sexti Toni	- *Suscepit Israel*
Magnificat Septimi Toni	- *Gloria Patri et Filio*
Magnificat Octavi Toni	

ORGAN

The precise specification of the organ played by Titelouze in the Cathedral of Rouen is not verifiable. In 1600 the instrument underwent an important restoration by Crespin Carlier; six years later the same organ builder modified the two divisions *Grand Orgue* and *Positif* so that one could play with coupled manuals. On the basis of subsequent documents the following disposition has been reconstructed:[471]

Grand Orgue		Positif	Pédale
Montre 16	*Petit Nazard 1 1/3*	*Montre 8*	*Flûte 8*
Montre 8	*Larigot*	*Prestant 4*	*Flûte 4*
Bourdon 8	*Flageolet*	*Flûte 4*	*Trompette 8*
Prestant 4	*Cornet*	*Nazard*	
Flûte 4	*Fourniture V*	*Quarte*	
Quintadine	*Cymbale III*	*Sacqueboute*	
Nazard	*Trompette 16*		
Doublette 2	*Trompette 8*		
Petite flûte	*Clairon*		
Tierce étroite 1 3/5	*Vox humaine*		

Errors in the above specification, including that certain stops on the *Grand Orgue* may have been intended for the *Positif*, cannot be ruled out.

CHARLES GUILLET
c. 1575 – 1654

Charles [Karel, Carolus] Guillet was born in Bruges (Flanders) around 1575. Although not born in France, Guillet is closer stylistically to composers such as Du Caurroy and Titelouze than to Sweelinck. It was in Bruges for the most part that Guillet was active as a composer, theorist, organist and also as a municipal councillor and, later, alderman.

Although Guillet was not born in France, his *Vingt-Quatre Fantasies, a Quatre Parties* were published in Paris by Pierre Ballard in 1610. Unlike the *Fantasies a III. IIII. V. et VI. Parties* by Du Caurroy (published in the same year), Guillet's compositions were explicitly intended for the organ, thirteen years ahead of the *Hymnes* by Titelouze published in 1623.

COMPOSITIONS

Vingt-Quatre Fantasies, a Quatre Parties, disposees selon l'ordre des douze Modes. Par C. Guillet natif de Bruges en Flandres. A Paris, par Pierre Ballard, Imprimeur de la Musique du Roy, demeurant rue Sainct Iean de Beauvais, à l'enseigne du Mont Parnasse.

– 1610 –

In the words of Guillet himself, the *Vingt-Quatre Fantasies* were aimed at clarifying the nomenclature of the modes: rather than *"les anciens"*, Guillet adopted the classification of modes *en Ut* [in C] illustrated in the *Dimostrationi harmoniche* by Zarlino, and also used by Salinas and Cerone. His aim was also to present pieces to be performed on the organ, although printed in separate part books:

Bien que ce ne fut pas mon intention de produire ces Fantasies à la veuë du public [...] je me suis resolu de leur [= mes amis] complaire, esperant apporter quelque commodité à ceux qui s'estudient à la Musique, & aussi à ceux qui apprennent à joüer des Orgues; à ceux-cy leur donnant dequoy s'exercer les doigts sur le clavier, & à tous les deux ensemble leur frayant (par ces Fantasies qui serviront d'exemple) le chemin pour venir plus facilement à la cognoissance des Modes.[472]	*Although it was not my intention to produce these fantasies for the public [...] I decided to appease them [= my friends], hoping to help in some way those who study music and also those learning to play the organ; the latter by giving them a means to exercise their fingers on the keyboard, and for both [musicians in general and organists] (as these Fantasies will serve as an example) a way to more easily get to know the modes.*

These are four-part compositions (*Dessus, Haute-Contre, Taille, Basse-Contre*) built on the model of the monothematic *ricercare*, in which the author uses diverse contrapuntal procedures and, at the same time, characterizes the different *modes* by attaching to each its own cadential formula. The collection includes 12 pieces written in natural modes and 12 transposed:

Les Modes Naturels

Premiere Fantasie	*Mode Dorien, Autentique, contenu dans la premiere espece de Diapason divisee Harmoniquement: Premier des modernes, Unziesme des anciens.*
Seconde Fantasie	*Mode Sous-Dorien, Plagal, contenu dans la cinquiesme espece de Diapason divisee Arithmetiquement: Second des modernes, Douziesme des anciens.*
Troisiesme Fantasie	*Mode Phrigien, Autentique, contenu dans la seconde espece de Diapason divisee Harmoniquement: Troisiesme des modernes, Premier des anciens.*
Quatriesme Fantasie	*Mode Sous-Phrygien, Plagal, contenu dans la sixiesme espece de Diapason divisee Arithmetiquement: Quatriesme des modernes, Seconde des anciens.*
Cinquiesme Fantasie	*Mode Lydien, Autentique, contenu dans la troisiéme espece de Diapason divisee Harmoniquement: Cinquiéme des modernes, Troisiéme des anciens.*
Sixiesme Fantasie	*Mode Sous-Lydien, Plagal, contenu dans la septiesme espece de Diapason divisee Aritmetiquement: Sixiesme des modernes, Quatriesme des anciens.*
Septiesme Fantasie	*Mode Mixolydien, Autentique, contenu dans la quatriesme espece de Diapason divisee Harmoniquement: Septiesme des modernes, Cinquiesme des anciens.*
Huictiesme Fantasie	*Mode Sous-Mixolydien, Plagal, contenu dans la premiere espece de Diapason divisee Arithmetiquement: Huictiesme des modernes, Sixiesme des anciens.*
Nevfiesme Fantasie	*Mode Ionien, Autentique, contenu dans la cinquiesme espece de Diapason divisee Harmoniquement: Neufiesme des modernes, Septiesme des anciens.*
Dixiesme Fantasie	*Mode Sous-Ionien, Plagal, contenu dans la seconde espece de Diapason divisee Arithmetiquement: Dixiesme des modernes, Huictiesme des anciens.*
Unziesme Fantasie	*Mode Eolien, Authentique, contenu dans la sixiesme espece de Diapason divisee Harmoniquement: Unziesme des modernes, Neufiesme des anciens.*
Dousiesme Fantasie	*Mode Sous-Eolien, Plagal, contenu dans la troisiesme espece de Diapason divisee Arithmetiquement: Dousiesme des modernes, Dixiesme des anciens.*

Les Modes Transposez

Treziesme Fantasie	*Mode Dorien, Autentique, contenu dans la premiere espece de Diapason divisee Harmoniquement: Premier des modernes, Unziesme des anciens.*
Quatorsiesme Fantasie	*Mode Sous-Dorien, Plagal, contenu dans la cinquiesme espece de Diapason divisee Arithmetiquement: Second des modernes, Douziesme des anciens.*
Quinsiesme Fantasie	*Mode Phrigien, Autentique, contenu dans la seconde espece de Diapason divisee Harmoniquement: Troisiesme des modernes, Premier des anciens.*
Seisiesme Fantasie	*Mode Sous-Phrygien, Plagal, contenu dans la sixiesme espece de Diapason divisee Arithmetiquement: Quatriesme des modernes, Seconde des anciens.*
Dixseptiesme Fantasie	*Mode Lydien, Autentique, contenu dans la troisiéme espece de Diapason divisee Harmoniquement: Cinquiéme des modernes, Troisiéme des anciens.*
Dixhuictiesme Fantasie	*Mode Sous-Lydien, Plagal, contenu dans la septiesme espece de Diapason divisee Aritmetiquement: Sixiesme des modernes, Quatriesme des anciens.*
Dixneufiesme Fantasie	*Mode Mixolydien, Autentique, contenu dans la quatriesme espece de Diapason divisee Harmoniquement: Septiesme des modernes, Cinquiesme des anciens.*
Vingtiesme Fantasie	*Mode Sous-Mixolydien, Plagal, contenu dans la premiere espece de Diapason divisee Arithmetiquement: Huictiesme des modernes, Sixiesme des anciens.*
Vingt-uniesme Fantasie	*Mode Ionien, Autentique, contenu dans la cinquiesme espece de Diapason divisee Harmoniquement: Neufiesme des modernes, Septiesme des anciens.*
Vingt-deuxiesme Fantasie	*Mode Sous-Ionien, Plagal, contenu dans la seconde espece de Diapason divisee Arithmetiquement: Dixiesme des modernes, Huictiesme des anciens.*
Vingt-troisiesme Fantasie	*Mode Eolien, Authentique, contenu dans la sixiesme espece de Diapason divisee Harmoniquement: Unziesme des modernes, Neufiesme des anciens.*
Vingt-quatriesme Fantasie	*Mode Sous-Eolien, Plagal, contenu dans la troisiesme espece de Diapason divisee Arithmetiquement: Dousiesme des modernes, Dixiesme des anciens.*

CHARLES RACQUET
1597 - 1664

Racquet was a distinguished member of an important family of organists active in Paris in the 17th century. In 1618, at the age of 21, he was appointed *titulaire* of *Notre-Dame*, a position he held for most of his life. At a young age he made an important journey abroad from which he returned with important honours, including seven medallions and a silver crown. He was also *Organiste ordinaire de la chambre* of Maria de Medici. Mersenne considered him to be one of the best composers of his time and he was praised by many contemporaries. His collaboration with important organ builders is also documented; among them Pierre Thierry. Racquet died in Paris on January 1st, 1664.

WORKS

Despite the fame and esteem that Racquet enjoyed during his lifetime, the only known compositions for organ in print are the *12 versets de psaume en duo,* based on Psalm 146 and contained in the *Livre cinquiesme de la composition de musique* in Mersenne's *Harmonie Universelle.* A further manuscript work – untitled, belonging to the genre of the *Fantaisie* – is contained in Mersenne's personal copy of his *Harmonie Universelle,* a piece solicited by Mersenne and written by Racquet *"pour montrer ce qui se peut faire à l'orgue"* [*to show what can be done on the organ*]. It is a large contrapuntal composition of over 100 bars in *Brevis* that goes beyond the typical schemes of the French school and rather resembles the compositional style of Jan Pieterszoon Sweelinck.

ORGAN

The specification of the organ of *Notre-Dame* Cathedral during the time of Charles Racquet is shown on page 57.

FRANÇOIS ROBERDAY
1624 - 1680

Roberday was born in 1624 in Paris into a family of goldsmiths and musicians. His father had a *Cabinet d'orgue* and François was brother-in-law to Jean-Henri d'Anglebert. Upon his father's death, François succeeded him as *Orfèvre du roi* (goldsmith to the King) and *Valet de Chambre* of the Queen. At the same time he also worked as an organist in several Parisian churches, in particular in *Notre-Dame-des-Victoires.*

In the following years, however, his financial situation deteriorated, leaving Roberday in difficulties. He died in 1680 following an epidemic. It has been hypothesized that Jean-Baptiste Lully was numbered among his students.

WORKS

Fugues, et Caprices, a Quatre Partie mises en partition pour l'Orgue.
Dediez aux amateurs de la Musique.
Par Francois Roberday, Valet de Chambre de la Reyne.

– 1660 –

Roberday published his works for organ in open score (on four staves) because, as he himself explained in the initial preface, it is *"la maniere d'escrire la plus utile & la plus avantageuse"* [*the most useful and convenient mode of writing*]. Although the pieces were composed primarily for organ, the author suggested that they could also be played *"sur des Violles ou autres semblables Instruments, chacun y trouvera sa Partie destachée des autres"* [on viols or other similar instruments, each player will find his part distinct from the others]. Published five years before Nivers' first *Livre d'orgue* and structurally linked to the contrapuntal tradition, Roberday's pieces also anticipate a more modern language, as Roberday himself stated:

Il se trouvera dans cet ouvrage quelques endroits peut-estre un peu trop hardis aux sentimens de ceux, qui s'attachent si fort aux anciennes regles qu'ils ne croyent pas qu'il soit iamais permis de s'en départir.	One will find in this work some places that are perhaps a little too daring for the likes of those who are so strongly bound to the old rules that they believe one should never be allowed to abandon them.
Mais il faut considerer que la Musique est inventée pour plaire a l'oreille [...].[473]	But one must consider that music is composed [inventée] to please the ear [...].

In fact, Roberday sought to approach the compositional features of the *seconda pratica*, including for this reason one piece *"composée par l'illustre Frescobaldy"*, another *"de Monsieur Froberger"* and a third by Wolfgang Ebner (1612-1665), further specifying

[...] que les Caprices se doivent (quant à la mesure) joüer à discretion & fort l'entement, quoy qu'ils soyent Nottez par des crochuës & doubles crochuës [...].[474]	[...] that the Caprices should be played (as far as the measure is concerned) with discretion [= freedom] and very slowly, despite the fact that they are written in quavers and semiquavers [...].

Fugue
Caprice sur le mesme sujet
Fugue 2.me
Caprice sur le mesme sujet
Fugue 3.me
Caprice sur le mesme sujet
Fugue 4.[me] - *Fugue, revers, & 2 autres sujets*
Fugue 5.me
Fugue 6.me
Caprice sur le mesme sujet
Fugue 7.me
Fugue 8.me
Caprice sur le mesme sujet
Fugue 9.me
Caprice sur le mesme sujet
Fugue 10.me
Fugue 11.me
Fugue 12.me

LOUIS COUPERIN
c. 1626 - 1661

Louis Couperin was born around 1626. Together with his two younger brothers François and Charles (the future father of François Couperin *le Grand*) the very young Louis gave a short concert for Jacques Champion de Chambonnières, organist of the *Chapelle Royale* and court harpsichordist of *Louis XIV*. Under the guidance of de Chambonnières, Louis Couperin perfected his musical studies and was appointed titular organist at *Saint-Gervais* in 1653. For the next 174 years, the post of *titulaire* of *Saint-Gervais* would be held by members of the Couperin family.

In Paris, Louis Couperin distinguished himself as an excellent harpsichordist and viol player. Through the compositions (and probably personal acquaintance) of Froberger he came into contact with the Italian keyboard repertoire (in mid-17th century Paris, Italian music and, in particular, Italian singers and violinists enjoyed enormous popularity). This aspect is very evident in the *Préludes* for harpsichord – influenced by Froberger – as well as in the *Duretez fantaisie* which opens the manuscript for organ. His compositional output includes about 130 pieces for harpsichord, some *Symphonies* and *Fantaisies* for oboe or viol and 70 pieces for organ. None of the works was printed during the short life of Louis Couperin, who died in 1661 at the age of about 35 years.

WORKS

Pièces d'Orgue

– mid 17th century –

The seventy organ compositions by Louis Couperin came to light at a public auction in 1960, when they were bought by the British collector Guy Oldham who waited more than 40 years to publish them (2003, *Éditions de l'Oiseau-Lyre*). Many of the pieces carry the date of composition; all of them between 1650 and 1659.

Unlike most of the *livres d'orgue*, the *Pièces d'Orgue* in Louis Couperin's manuscript were not ordered by mode; most of them were composed in the *Dorian* and, especially, *Phrygian* mode. It should be emphasized that seven of the fifteen trio pieces linked to a *cantus firmus* were written on two staves (indicated below as "3 voices"), while the remaining eight are on three staves (indicated below as "on 3 staves"). In some of them, the *cantus firmus* – usually placed in the middle voice – can be played *pedaliter* while, in other cases the intended performance was clearly *manualiter*. Six pieces of the collection contain registrations.

Principal composers

Alongside the original titles the following table provides some brief information.

1	*Duretez fantaisie*	Toccata di durezze
2	*Fantaisie*	in 12/8, last eight bars in ₵
3	*Fugue grave sur Urbs beata Jherusalem*	in C
4	*Autre fugue grave sur Le mesme subject*	in C
5	*Urbs beata Jherusalem en haulte Contre avec le poulce droict ou en trio*	3 voices, ornamented c.f. in alto voice
6	*Conditor en haultecontre avec le poulce droict en trio*	3 voices, semi-ornamented c.f. in alto voice
7	*Conditor*	3 voices, ornamented c.f. in alto voice
8	*Conditor a 2 dessus*	on 3 staves, ornamented c.f. in soprano
9	*Ave Maris Stella*	Plein jeu type, c.f. in o in bass voice
10	*Ave Maris Stella trio*	on 3 staves, ornamented c.f. in alto voice
11	*Fugue*	in o
12	*Fantaisie*	recte: *Récit de basse*
13	*Fantaisie*	recte: *Récit de basse*
14	*Duo*	bars 1-24 in C – bars 25-61 in 3/4
15	*Fantaisie*	recte: *Récit de basse*
16	*Duo*	bars 1-31 in 12/8 – bars 32-43 in 2
17	*Fugue*	in ₵
18	*[Fugue]*	in ₵, *Fugue grave* type
19	*Fugue*	in C
20	*Fugue sur le Cromhorne*	in ₵, *Fugue grave* type
21	*Fantaisie*	in C
22	*Fantaisie*	in C
23	*Fantaisie*	in C
24	*Fantaisie*	in C
25	*Fantaisie*	in C
26	*Fantaisie*	in C, pedal point at the end (5 bars)
27	*Fantaisie*	in C
28	*Fugue*	in C
29	*Fugue quil fault Jouer dun mouvement fort lent sur la tierce du Grand Clavier avec le tremblant lent*	in C
30	*Fantaisie*	in C
31	*Ut queant Laxis*	on 3 staves, semi-ornamented c.f. in alto
32	*Ut Queant Laxis*	on 3 staves, semi-ornamented c.f. in alto
33	*Iste Confessor*	on 3 staves, semi-ornamented c.f. in alto
34	*Pange Lingua en basse*	*Plein jeu* type, c.f. in o in bass voice
35	*Pange lingua*	on 3 staves, ornamented c.f. in alto voice
36	*Pange lingua*	3 voices, c.f. in ♩ in alto voice
37	*Beata nobis gaudia*	*Plein jeu* type, c.f. in o and ♩ in bass voice
38	*Beata nobis gaudia, Trio*	on 3 staves, semi-ornamented c.f. in alto
39	*Jesu Salvator Sæculi*	*Plein jeu* type, c.f. in o and ♩ in bass voice
40	*Tristes erant Apostolj*	*Plein jeu* type, c.f. in o and ♩ in bass voice
41	*A Solis. En taille*	*Plein jeu* type, c.f. in ♩ in tenor voice
42	*A Solis en haultre Contre*	3 voices, c.f. (in ♩) in alto voice
43	*A Solis, Trio*	on 3 staves, semi-ornamented c.f. in alto
44	*A Solis, En basse*	*Plein jeu* type, c.f. in o in bass voice
45	*A Solis, En triple. A la haulte Contre*	3 voices, c.f. in ♩. in alto voice
46	*Prelude autre livre grand livre dOrgue. Il fault Jouer cecy dun Mouvemen fort lent*	in C
47	*Fantaisie*	in C

48	*Fantaisie*	in ₵
49	*Fantaisie*	in ₵
50	*Regina cœli*	*Plein jeu* type, c.f. in ♩ in bass voice
51	*Invitatoire po.ʳ le Jour de pasques*	*Plein jeu* type, c.f. in ♩ in bass voice
52	*Invitatoire de la trinité*	*Plein jeu* type, c.f. in ♩ in bass voice
53	*Invitatoire de la feste Dieu*	*Plein jeu* type, c.f. in ♩ in bass voice
54	*Ad Cœnam agni providi co[mme] Il se chante a montmartre*	*Plein jeu* type in 3/2, c.f. in 𝅝 and ♩ in bass voice
55	*[Ad Cœnam Agni Providi] 3.ᵉ Verset*	3 v., ornamented c.f. in sopr., *4ᵃ vox* at the end
56	*Fantaisie 2ᵐᵉ Livre*	in ₵
57	*Fantaisie sur le Cromhorne*	in ₵
58	*Fantaisie sur La tierce du Grand Clavier avec le tremblant Lent*	in ₵
59	*Fantaisie*	in ₵
60	*Fugue Renversée*	in ₵
61	*Fugue*	in ₵
62	*Fugue*	in ¢
63	*Fugue sur la tierce du Grand Clavier*	in ₵
64	*Fugue sur La tierce*	in ₵
65	*Fugue sur le Cromhorne*	in ¢
66	*Fantaisie*	in ₵
67	*Fantaisie*	in ¢
68	*Fantaisie*	in ¢, recte: *Récit de basse*
69	*Fantaisie*	in ¢, recte: *Récit de basse*
70	*Fantaisie*	in ¢, recte: *Récit de basse*

ORGAN

The specification of the *Saint-Gervais* organ at the time of Louis Couperin is given on page 57.

NICOLAS GIGAULT
c. 1627 – 1707

Gigault was born around 1627 into a family of modest means. In a document dated 1648 it is written that, together with his brothers, he renounced his paternal inheritance in order to avoid taking on debts. Nothing is known of his musical education; it has been hypothesized that he was a student of Charles Racquet.

Thanks to his remarkable musical skills, he soon managed to improve his financial situation: in the contract relating to his first marriage, it emerges that he possessed various keyboard instruments (including an organ, several harpsichords, spinets and clavichords) as well as stringed instruments. In the tax register of 1695 his name appeared among the keyboard musicians of *1.ᵉʳ Classe*, alongside d'Anglebert and François Couperin. Gigault served as an organist in several Parisian churches, including *Saint-Nicolas-des-Champs*, for 55 years, from 1652 until his death.

WORKS

Livre de musique dédié à la très Ste Vierge par Gigault organiste de S. Nicolas des Champs à Paris contenant les cantiques sacrez qui se chantent en l'honneur de son divin enfantement; diversifiez de plusieurs manières à II. III. et IV. parties qui peuvent estre touchez sur l'orgue et sur le clavessin, comme aussi sur le luth, les violes, violons, flûtes et autres instruments de musique. Une pièce diatonique en forme d'Allemande marquée simple, et avec les ports de voix pour servir de guide et d'instruction pour les former et adapter à toutes sortes de pièces le tout divisé en deux parties.
Achevé d'imprimer pour la première fois le 5e jour de décembre 1682

– 1682 –

The *Livre de musique* of 1682 is a collection in two parts of 17 "*cantiques sacrez qui se chantent en l'honneur de son divin enfantement*" (*Noëls*) that can be played "*sur l'orgue et sur le clavessin, comme aussi sur le luth, les violes, violons, flûtes et autres instruments de musique*" [on the organ and on the harpsichord, as well as on the lute, the viols, violins, flutes and other instruments] as stated in the title. It is probably the first collection of *Noëls* with variations that appeared in France. The cycle closes with an *Allemande*, first presented in its simple form and then enriched with ornaments (*Ports de voix*). In the preface Gigault also provided a summary of registrations:

À l'égard des trios à deux dessus, l'on peut se servir des pédales de Flûte.	Concerning the Trios à deux Dessus, one can make use of the Flûte of the pedal.
Ceux qui voudront pour les dialogues, il faut faire régner le sujet sur le jeu le plus éclatant.	In the Dialogues, those who so desire can highlight [faire régner] the subject with he most imposing registration.
Les pièces à deux chœurs, les changements des claviers sont marqués par deux rais.[475]	In double-chorus pieces [à deux chœurs], manual changes are indicated with two dashes.

1.re partie:	2.me partie:
Conditor - Noël, Noël	Conditor
Quand par ton orgueil Lucifer	Prosa - Mittit ad Virginem
À la venue de Noël	Laissez paistre vos bestes
Voicy le Jour Solemnel	Où s'en vont ces gays bergers?
Une vierge pucelle	Chantons, je vous prie, Noël
Or nous dites Marie	Noël pour l'amour de Marie
Or voyla Noël passé	Tous les bourgeois de Chastres
Estant Cesar Auguste	Vous qui désirez sans fin
Peuples catholiques	Allemande par fugue/La mesme avec les ports de voix

> *Livre de Musique pour l'Orgue, composées par Gigault
> Organiste du St Esprit,et des Eglise St Nicolas et St Martin des Champs a Paris,
> Conten.^{t} plus de 180. pieces de tout les caracteres du touché qui est presentement en usage pour servir sur tous les jeux a 1.2.3. et 4. Claviers et pedalles en basse et en taille sur des mouvements jnusitez a 2.3.4. et 5. parties, ce qui n'a point encore esté mis au jour que par l'Auteur, le tout pour servir aux huit tons de l'Eglise, sur chacun desquels on trouvera plusieurs pieces, avec la maniere d'en transposer une grande partie plus haut, ou plus bas, pour la comodité des voix de Chœur.*

– 1685 –

The voluminous *Livre d'Orgue* of 1685, containing *"plus de 180 pieces"*, begins by presenting two versions of the usual *Missa Solemnis* for the *Fêtes doubles* based on the gregorian melody *Cunctipotens Genitor Deus*. The first, in particular, contains several 5-voice *Pleins jeux* (with *cantus firmus* in the pedal), for which an *Alio modo Manualiter* is also provided. Between the two masses are some 3-voice versets that require the *Trompette* for the *plainchant* in the bass voice. Then follow numerous *couplets*, grouped according to the most commonly used modes, as well as some hymns; the latter contain only a very few versets. A complete cycle of the *Te Deum* closes the book, for which some *Alio modo* versets are also provided.

In order to make the distribution of the pieces clearer the *Hymnes* are grouped together at the end of the list in the following table.

1.re Messe

Kyrie	Kyrie double a 5. parties
	Kyrie a 4. parties point simple || alio modo: Fugue sur le Kyrie a 4. parties
	Fugue a 2. pour le Christé
	Fugue a 3. du 1.er ton pour la basse, trompette, tierce, clairon, cromorne, où autre jeu
	Dernier Kyrie à 5. parties || alio modo: Dernier Kyrie contre point simple
Gloria	Et in terra pax a 5. parties || alio modo: Et in terra pax a 4. contre point simple
	Benedicimus te Fugue a 2. || alio modo: Autre benedicimus te
	Recit a 3. glorificamus || alio modo: Autre glorificamus
	Fugue a 3. pour Domine Deus
	Fugue à 3. sur Domine deus pour la basse tromp. ou de tierce
	Qui tollis a 5. parties || alio modo: Qui tollis contre point sincopé
	Fugue a 2. pour Quoniam tu solus || alio modo: Autre quoniam tu solus
	Tu solus altisimus a 2. et 3. cœurs
	In gloria dei patris a 5. parties || alio modo: In gloria a 4. contre point simple
Sanctus	Sanctus a 5. parties || alio modo: Sanctus contre point simple a 4. parties
	Recit a 3. pou.le 2.' Santus
Agnus Dei	Agnus dei a 5. par. || alio modo: Agnus dei a 4 parties contre point simple
	Fugue Pour l'agnus dei à 3. parties

Les plainchant de la Messe a 3. partyes en baße Trompette

Kyrie
Premier Kyrie a 3.
Dernier Kyrie a 3.

Gloria
Et jn terra pax a 3.
Qui tollis a 3.
In gloria dei a 3.

Sanctus
Sanctus a 3.

Agnus
Agnus dei a 3.

2.*me* Messe

Kyrie
Kyrie double a 4.
Fugue grave recherchée sur le Kyrie a 4.
Recit a 3. parties. Christe
Fugue à 2. sur le Kyrie
Dernier Kyrie a 4.

Gloria
Et in terra pax. a 4.
Benedicimus te a 3.
Glorificamus te a 3.
Fugue a 3. parties. Domine Deus
Fugue a 2 partyes Domine Deus
Qui tollis a 4.
Quoniam [Récit de Dessus]
Fantesie a 2. pour tu solus altissimus
In gloria dei patris a 4.

Sanctus
Santus a 4.
Santus dominus
Benedictus [Récit de Cromorne]

Agnus Dei
Agnus Dei [à 4]
Fugue a 3. sur lagnus prise de pres

Amen
Amen où deo gratias du premier ton

Couplets (grouped by mode)

1.*er* ton
Prelude
Prelude du 1.er ton a 4.
Prelude du 1.er ton a 4.
Fugue du premier ton a 4. parties
Fugue a 2. parties du 1.er ton
Fugue a 2. parties du premier ton d'un mouvement gay
Fugue a 2. du 1.er ton
Fugue a 2 du premier ton
Petit prelude du 1.er ton a 4.
Recit du 1.er ton pour le dessus de tierce où autre jeux

	Diminution pour le Cornet ou flajolet du premier ton a 3.
	Fugue a 3. du 1.er ton pour la basse de tierce ou trompe.
	Fugue du 1.er ton. Dialogue pour la main gauche et main droit l'un apres l'autre
	Trio. Fugue a 3. du 1.er ton
	Diminution pour la basse de tierce oû trompette du 1.er ton
	Recit en diminution pour le grand Cornet et pour le Cornet d'Éscho. En dialogue à 3 p. du 1.er ton.
	Fugue a 2. du premier ton.
	Recit à trois
	Pour toucher a 2. 3. ou 4. clavier si l'on veut
	Tierce en taille
	Pour toucher a 2. 3. et 4. Cœurs sur auta.^{t} de claviers
	Fugue du 1.er ton poursuivié à la maniere Jtalienne a 4. parties
	Le mesme subjet dun autre mouvement
2. ton	*Prelude a 4. parties [du] 2. ton, 4. et 7. ainsi du reste*
	Fugue grave du 2.e ton
	Fugue a 2. du 2.e ton qui faut toucher gayement
	Prelude du 2.e ton a 4.
	Fugue a 2. parties du 2. ton
	Fugue a 2. partyes du 2.^{e} ton
	Recit pour un ou 2 Cornet ou autres jeu
	Petit prelude du 2. ton
	Recit a 3. partyes du 2.^{e} ton pour le dessus de Cromorne oû autre jeu
	Prelude a 4
	Fugue a 3. parties du 2. ton pour la basse de tierce ou tromp.
	Fugue a 3. du 2.^{e} ton
	Fugue a 3. parties pour les mains l'une apres l'autre
	Cromorne Recit en taille a 4. du 2.^{e} ton
	Pour toucher sur 2. 3. et 4. claviers du 2.^{e} ton
	Autre piece a 2. 3. et 4. Cœurs du 2.^{e} ton d'un mouvem.^{t} prest
3. et 4. ton	*Prelude a 4. 2. et 7. ainsi du reste*
	Petit prelude du 3. et 4. ton a 4.
	Prelude du 3. et 4. ton
	Fugue du 3. ton a 4.
	Fugue a 2. du 3. et 4. ton
	Fugue du 3. et 4. ton a 2. parties
	Fugue a 2. parties du 3. et 4. ton preste et viste
	Dessus de Cromorne oû autre jeu a 3. partyes du 3. et 4. ton
	Fugue a 3. parties du 3. et 4. ton
	Fugue a 2. du trois et 4. ton
	Fugue. Dialogue pour les mains l'une apres l'autre du 3. et 4. ton a 3.
	Fugue du 3. et 4. ton pour la basse de tierce ou tromp. a 3. parties
	Tierce en taille du 3. et 4. ton a 4. parties
	A 2. 3. et 4. cœurs du 3. et 4. ton
	A 2. 3. et 4. Cœurs du 3. et 4. ton
5. ton	*Caprice du 5. ton &c.*
	Prelude a 4. p.^{ties}
	Fugue grave a 4. parties du 5. ton
	Fugue a 2. du 5. ton et peut servir au 8.
	Prelude du 5. et 8 ton a 4.

	Fugue a 2. du 5. ton qui peut servir du 8. ton auβi
	Fugue a 3. parties du 5. et 8. ton
	Fugue a 3. du 5. et 8. ton po.ʳ la voix humaine avec le pouce de main droite sur le jeu doux
	Fugue a 3. pour la basse de tromp. ou de tierce
	Recit a 3. du 5. &c.
	Escho a 3. parties Lisez l'jnstructiõ du livre. Grand cornet ou corn.ᵗ separé.
	Prelude du 5. ton
	Cromorne en taille du 5. ton &c.
	A 2. 3. et 4. Cœurs s'y l'on veut du 5. et 8. ton
	A 2. 3. et 4. Cœurs du 5. et 8. ton
	Petit Fug. sur veni creator à 4. partie
	Petite Fugue à 2. de même
6. ton	*Prelude*
	Prelude du 6. ton a 4. parties
	Fugue a 2. parties du 6. ton
	Fugue a 2. du 6.ᵉ ton
	Fugue a 2. du 6. ton
	Fugue a 2. du 6. ton
	Fugue du 6. ton a 4.
	Fugue a 3. du 6. ton
	Prelude du 6. ton a 4.
	Recit a 3. parties du 6. ton dessus de cromor ou autre Ieu
	Fugue a 3. du 6. ton pour la basse tromp. oû autre Jeu
	Fugue a 3. du 6. ton dialogue pour toucher les 2. mains l'une apres l'autre
	Tierce en taille a 4. parties du 6. ton
	A 2. 3. et 4. cœurs du 6. ton
	A 2. 3. et 4. Cœurs du 6. ton
8. ton	*Du 8. ton prelude et 6. par ♮ si l'on veut*
	Prelu. gra a 4. parties du 8. ton et six si on veut par ♮
	Fugue a 4. parties du 8. et 6. ton
	Fugue a 2. du 8. et 6. ton
	Fugue a 2. du 8. et 6. ton par ♮
	Fugue a 2. parties du 8. et 6. ton
	Petit prelude du 8. et 6. ton
	Fugue a 3. du 8. et 6. ton
	Recit a 3. parties du 8. et 6. ton
	Fugue a 3. Dialogue pour les 2. mains l'une apres l'autre du 8. et 6. ton par ♮ d'un mouvement gay
	Fugue a 3. du 8. et 6. ton par ♮
	A 2. 3. et 4. cœurs du 8. et 6. ton d'un mouvem.ᵗ gay
	Cromorne en taille
	A 2. 3. et 4. Cœurs du 8. et 6. ton dune mesure legere
	Prelude a 4. du 8. en f. ut. fa
	Fugue du 8. ton en f ut fa
	Fugue pour le hui.ᵉ ton à 2 parties
	A 2. 3. et 4. cœur du 8. ton en f. ut. fa.

Hymnes

Tantum ergo	*Tantũ ergo Sacramentum. Escho a 2. parties avec la basse continüe*
Pange lingua	*Pange lingua a 3. parties*

	Pange lingua, à 4. parties
	Fugue sur pange lingua à 4. parties ou les Fugues des vers sont poursuivie
Veni Creator	*Veni Creator Spiritus a 4. parties*
Te Deum	*Te dominum à 3. parties || alio modo: Te domĩ a 4 || Te dominum à 5. parties / Tibi omnes Angeli. Fugue a 4. / Santus a 3. partie || alio modo: Santus a 4 partie || Santus à 5 parties / Sanctus dominus. Fugue à 2. / Te gloriosus. Prelude à 4. / Te martirum. Recit à 3. / Patrem jmmensœ. Fugue à 2. / Santum quoque. Prelude a 4. / Tu patris. Recit pour la basse à 3. / Tu devicto. Fugue a 3. recherché / Judex crederis. Recit a 3 / Æterna fac. Prelude Fantesie a 4. / Et rege eos. Dialogue à 3. / Et laudamus. Fugue a 2. / Miserere nostri. Fugue a 4. prise de pres recherchés / In te domine. Prelude a 4*

ORGAN

In *St- Nicolas-des-Champs* in 1632 – thirty years before Gigault was appointed – an organ was built by Crespin Carlier; the only known organ in Paris (and perhaps in France) which had the split-keys D♯/E♭ and G♯/A♭ for the three higher octaves. The presumed specification is as follows:

Grand Orgue	**Positif**	**Récit**
Montre 16	*Bourdon 8*	*Cornet*
Bourdon 16	*Montre 4*	
Huit pieds ouvert	*Flûte 4*	
Bourdon 8	*Nasard II (avec la Quarte)*	**Pédale** (Do$_1$ Re$_1$ – Fa$_3$)
Prestant 4	*Doublette*	*Flûte 8*
Flûte 4	*Tierce de grosse taille coupée*	*Flûte 4*
Nasard	*Larigot*	*Sacqueboutte 8 (Trompette)*
Doublette	*Forniture IV*	
Quarte	*Cymbale III*	
Tierce 1 3/5 (étroite)*	*Cromorne*	
Tierce 1 3/5 (large)**	*Voix Humaine*	
Flageolet 1		
Fourniture V		
Cymbale III	* narrow scaled	
Cornet V	** wide scaled	
Trompette		
Clairon		
Cromorne		
Vox humaine		

In 1688 Gigault had some changes made by the organ builder Antoine Vincent, including the possible addition of a *Tierce étroite* in the *Plein Jeu*, a $3^{1/5}$ *Double-Tierce* to the *Grand Orgue*, a *Clairon 4* to the pedal and *Ravalement* down to AA, as well as the addition of an *Écho* consisting of two stops and perhaps also of a fifth manual.[476]

NICOLAS-ANTOINE LEBÈGUE
c. 1631 - 1702

Lebègue was born in Laon, probably in 1631, into a family of humble origins. Nothing is known about his musical education. Around 1656 he settled in Paris. His name appears for the first time in 1661 on the occasion of his musical performance in Troyes, where he was defined as *"fameux organiste de Paris"*. In 1664 he became organist of the church of Saint-Merry (St. Médéric), a position that he would hold for the rest of his life, and fourteen years later, in 1678, he was also one of the four *Organistes du Roi* in Versailles.

The number of publications and reprints between 1676 and 1698, as well as the many important students – among them de Grigny, d'Agincourt, Geoffroy and perhaps also Jullien – attest to the renown achieved by Lebègue in his years of maturity. His fame as organ consultant is also attested to on several occasions; not only in Paris but also in Bourges, Chartres, Soissons and Troyes. In addition to the three *Livres d'Orgue*, he published two collections of music for harpsichord and vocal music. Several of his organ pieces have also survived in manuscript form. He died in Paris in 1702.

WORKS

Les Pieces d'Orgue Composées par N. Le Begue Organiste de St Mederic avec les Varietez, les agréements, et la maniere de toucher l'Orgue a present Sur tous les Jeux, et particulierement ceux qui Sont peu en Usage dans les provinces Comme la Tierce et Cromorne en Taille: Les Trio a deux dessus, et autres a trois Claviers avec les Pedalles: les Dialogues, et les Recits.

– 1676 –

The first *Livre d'Orgue* by Lebègue consists of eight cycles of versets corresponding to the usual *huit tons de l'église*; each cycle with the number of *couplets* varying between eight and twelve.

1. ton		2. ton	
	Prelude du I. Ton		Prelude du 2 Ton
	Duo		Cornet
	Cromhorne en taille		Trio a deux dessus
	Basse de Trompette		Duo
	Trio a 3 claviers		Cromhorne ou Tierce en Taille
	Dessus de Cromhorne		Trio a 3 Claviers
	Tierce en Taille		Dessus de Cromhorne ou de Trompette
	Recits de voix humaine		Dialogue
	Trio a 2 dessus		Plein Jeu
	Dialogue		
	Fugue grave		
	Plein Jeu		

3. ton	Prelude du 3 Ton	4. ton	Prelude du 4. Ton
	Basse de Trompette		Fugue
	Tierce En Taille		Duo
	Dessus de Cromhorne ou de Trompette		Basse de Trompette
	Voix humaine		Dessus de Tierce ou Cornet
	Trio a 2 dessus		Trio a 3 Claviers
	Dialogue		Cromhorne ou Tierce En Taille
	Plein Jeu		Dialogue
			Plein Jeu
5. ton	Prelude du 5 Ton	6. ton	Prelude du 6 Ton
	Dessus de Cromhorne ou de Trom.		Duo
	Tierce En Taille		Fugue grave
	Duo		Echo
	Trio a 2 dessus		Trio a 2 dessus
	Basse de Trompette		Tierce En Taille
	Echo		Basse de Trompette
	Dialogue		Dessus de Cromhorne
	Plein Jeu		Dialogue
			Plein Jeu
7. ton	Prelude du 7 Ton	8. ton	Prelude du 8 Ton
	Dessus de Tierce ou Cornet		Fugue grave
	Voix humaine		Duo
	Duo		Voix humaine
	Cromhorne En Taille		Cornet
	Basse de Trompette		Tierce En Taille
	Dialogue		Trio a 3 Claviers
	Plein Jeu		Dessus de Tierce
			Dialogue
			Plein Jeu du positif

Second Livre d'Orgue de Monsieur Le Begue Organiste du Roy et de St Mederic Contenant des Pieces courtes et faciles sur les huit tons de l'Eglise et la Messe des festes Solemnelles.

– 1678 –

In the *Preface* to the *Second Livre d'Orgue* we read that – unlike the first book written *particulierement pour les Sçavans* (the learned) – the second, easier one is aimed at those who have *une Science mediocre* (average knowledge). Here we find the usual *Messe des festes Solemnelles* (based on the *Missa IV: Cunctipotens Genitor deus*) and nine *Magnificats* (the traditional eight plus a 6.me *Ton* transposed); the number of *couplets* constituting each single *Magnificat* varies from seven to eight.

Messe [*Cunctipotens Genitor Deus*]

Kyrie	1.er Kyrie [c.f. al basso]
	2.me Kyrie fugue
	Duo pour le Christe
	4.^{e} Kyrie Recit au dessus
	Dernier Kyrie plein Jeu

Gloria	Et in terra pax [c.f. al basso] Benedicimus te petit plein Ieu Glorificamus te Ieu doux Cornet Domine deus Domine deus Agnus dej [Dialogue de] voix humaine Qui tollis [3 v. - c.f. al basso] Duo du 4.^{e} Quoniam tu solus Trio du 4.^{e} Tu Solus In gloria [4 v., tipo Petit plein jeu]
Sanctus	J.^{r} Sanctus [c.f. al basso] 2.^{e} Sanctus fugue Trio pour l'Elevation
Agnus Dei	Agnus Dei [c.f. al basso] Fugue pour le 2.^{e} Agnus

Magnificat

Magnificat 1. ton	Prelude du j.^{r} ton Duo du premier Recit pour le Cromhorne Basse de Trompette Trio du j.^{er} ton Dialogue du Premier Plein Ieu	Magnificat 2. ton	Prelude du 2.me ton Duo du 2. Basse de Trompette du 2. Recit [de dessus] du 2. Trio du 2. Cornet du 2. Dialogue du 2. Plein Ieu
Magnificat 3. ton	Prelude Fugue du 3.^{e} Duo du 3. Trio du 3.^{e} [Dialogue de] Voix humaine Recit du 3. Dialogue du 3.^{e} Dernier plein Ieu du 3.^{e}	Magnificat 4. ton	Prelude Duo du 4.^{e} Trio du 4.^{e} Cornet du 4.^{e} Basse de Trompette du 4.^{e} Dialogue du 4.^{e} Plein Ieu du 4.^{e}
Magnificat 5. ton	Prelude Recit du 5.^{e} Cornet du 5.^{e} Duo du 5.^{e} Basse de Trompette du 5. Trio du 5.^{e} Dialogue du 5. Dernier plein Ieu	Magnificat 6. ton	Prelude Duo du 6.^{e} Recit du 6.^{e} Trio du 6.^{e} Dessus de Tierce ou de Cornet Dialogue du 6.^{e} Prelude du 6.^{e}
Magnificat du 6.^{e} en g re sol ♮	Prelude Duo Cornet du 6.^{e} en g re sol ♮ Basse de Trompette du 6^e en G♯ Recit de Cromorne Dialogue du 6.^{e} en G♯ Plein Ieu	Magnificat 7. ton	Prelude 2.^{e} Verset Dessus de Trompette 3.^{e} Verset Trio Duo du 7^e Cornet du 7.^{e} 6.^{e} Verset Dialogue Dernier verset plein Ieu

Magnificat 8. ton	Prelude
	2.*e* Verset Duo
	3.*e* Verset Basse de Trompette
	4.*me* Verset Recit dessus de Crom.
	5.*me* Verset Cornet
	6.*me* Verset Dialogue
	Dernier Verset Plein Ieu

Troisieme Livre d'Orgue de M.ʳ le Begue Organiste du Roy et de S.ᵗ Mederic Contenant des grandes Offertoires et des Elevations; Et tous les Noëls les plus connus, des Symphonies et les Cloches que peut joüer Sur l'Orgue et le Clavecin.

– 1685 –

The third book departs from the tradition of the *Livres d'Orgue* and presents not only individual pieces for the Mass (*Offertoires* and *Élévations*) but also four *Simphonies* (stylistically close to the *Ouvertures* of Lully) and several *Noëls*; including an onomatopoeic piece entitled *Les Cloches*. The *Offertoires* were built on the usual model of the *Dialogue* between *Basse et Dessus*, sometimes with the use of the *Écho*.

Offertoires	Offertoire Ex D.
	Offertoire en g b[emolle]
	Offertoire du 3.*e* ton
	Offertoire du 5.*e* Ton
	Autre Offertoire en C
	Offertoire en g ♮
	Offertoire En b fa
	Offertoire En C sol ut b[emolle]
	Offertoire En f ut fa Sur le stabat Mater
	Offertoire sur le Chant d'O filij et filiæ
Symphonies	Simphonie sur le b fa
	Simphonie en g re sol ♮
	Simphonie en C sol ut
	Simphonie en d la re ♮
Noëls	Premier Noël. A la Venue de Noël
	Une Vierge Pucelle
	Noël pour l'Amour de Marie
	Noël cette Journée
	Ou nous ditte Marie. Pour la voix humaine
	Puer Nobis Nascitur
	Les Bourgeoises de Chatre
	Ou s'en Vont Ces gays Bergers
	Laissez Paistre Vos Bestes
	Les Cloches
Élévations	Premiere Elevation. [Récit en Dialogue: tierce/fluttes]
	Elevation En g ♮ [Récit en Dialogue: Cornet/Cromhorne]
	Elevation en E la mi. Trio
	Elevation en A♯. Dialogue
	Elevation en b fa pour la v. hu. [Dialogue pour la voix humaine]
	Elevation en g sol ♮ [Récit en Dialogue: Cornet ou Cromhorne/les fluttes]
	Petitte Elevation en A ♮. Trio

ORGAN

The origins of the *Saint-Merry* organ, where Lebègue served for 38 years, went back to the Renaissance. In the 17th century various modifications took place. During his first years of activity at the instrument, Lebègue requested some alterations, including the enlargement of *Grand Orgue* and *Positif* from 48 to 50 keys (CD-d''') and the addition of a *"Tremblant lent pour jouer les voix humaines"*. The contract also describes a *Trompette* on the 3rd manual *"pour imitier le hautbois demandé par Monsieur Lebègue"*.[477]

Grand Orgue	Positif	Récit (29 note)	Echo (34 note)
Montre 16	Bourdon 8	Cornet	Bourdon 8
Bourdon 16	Montre 4	Trompette	Flûte 4
Montre 8	Flûte		Nazard
Bourdon 8	Nasard		Doublette
Prestant	Doublette		Tierce
Flûte	Tierce		
Nasard	Larigot		
Doublette	Fourniture IV		
Quarte de Nasard	Cymbale III		
Tierce (étroite)	Cromorne		Pédale (18 note)*
Tierce			Flûte 8
Fourniture V			Flûte 4
Cymbale IV			Trompette 8
Dessus de Cornet			
Trompette			
Clairon			*Ravalement to AA
Vox humaine			

GUILLAUME-GABRIEL NIVERS
c. 1632 - 1714

Born in Paris around 1632 into a wealthy family, nothing is known about Nivers' musical education. At the age of twenty he became organist at *Saint-Sulpice*, a post he held until his death; later he added other highly remunerative positions: from 1678 he was one of the four organists of the *Chapelle Royale*, in 1681 he replaced Du Mont as *Maître de musique de la Reine*, and in 1686 he became the first organist and *Maître du chant de la Maison Royale Saint-Louis de Saint-Cyr*.

He published numerous works: in addition to the three *Livres d'Orgue*, there is also an important *Traité de composition* (1667) which was to retain its importance in the following century, a *Dissertation sur le chant grégorien* (1683) and also much vocal music. He also edited the *Graduale romanum - Antiphonarium romanum* (1687). His will, drawn up in 1711, shows the affluence of his last years of life, demonstrating his success as a musician: on his death, in 1714, he left a sizeable fortune (200,000 *livres*) as well as land holdings.

WORKS

Livre d'Orgue Contenant Cent Pieces de tous les Tons de l'Eglise.
Par le Sr Nivers Me Compositeur en Musique
et organiste de l'Eglise St Sulpice de Paris.

– 1665 –

The publication of this *Livre d'Orgue* conventionally marks the beginning of the French classical organ school. In the following ten years, two further important *livres d'orgue* came to light. The volume of 1665 contains a total of 100 versets, subdivided into eight cycles corresponding to the usual ecclesiastical modes plus four other cycles of transposed modes.

1er Ton	Prelude du 1. Ton	2e Ton	Prelude du 2. ou du 1. transposé
	Fugue		Basse Trompette
	Diminution de la Basse		Fugue
	Recit de Voix humaine		Cornet
	Duo		Duo
	Recit de Cromhorne		Recit de Cromhorne
	Fugue grave		Fugue grave
	Echo		Echo
	A 2. Cœurs		A 2. Cœurs
	Plein Jeu		Plein Jeu
3e Ton	Prelude du 3. Ton	4e Ton	Prelude du 4. Ton
	Fugue		Fugue
	Recit de Cromhorne		Duo
	Basse Trompette		Diminution de la Basse
	Cornet		Recit de Voix humaine
	Duo		Fugue
	Grand Jeu		Cornet
	Plein Ieu		Plein Ieu
5e Ton	Prelude du 5. Ton	6e Ton	Prelude du 6. Ton ou du 5. transposé
	Diminution de la Basse		Fugue
	Fugue en Basse de Voix humaine		Duo
	Duo		Recit de Cromhorne
	Recit de Cromhorne		Basse Trompette
	Cornet		Cornet
	Grand Jeu		Grand Ieu
	Plein Ieu		Plein Ieu
7e Ton	Prelude du 7. Ton	8e Ton	Prelude du 8e Ton
	Fugue grave		Fugue
	Recit de Cromhorne		Duo
	Diminution de la Basse		Recit de Cromhorne
	Echo		Basse Trompette
	Duo		Echo
	A 2. Cœurs		A 2. Cœurs
	Plein Ieu		Plein Ieu

1er Ton   Prelude du 1. transposé en C transposé
transposé en C   Fugue grave
ou du 4. a la   Diminution de la Basse
dominante   Cornet
   Duo
   Recit de Cromhorne
   Grand Ieu
   Plein Ieu

1er Ton   Prelude du 1. transposé en E
transposé en E   Fugue
   Basse Trompette
   Cornet
   Fugue grave
   Duo
   Recit de Voix humaine
   Plein Ieu

6e Ton   Prelude du 6. transposé en G
transposé en G   Fugue
   Diminution de la Basse
   Recit de Cromhorne
   Duo
   Cornet
   Grand Jeu
   Plein Ieu

6e Ton   Prelude du 6. transposé en A
transposé en A   Fugue
   Basse Voix humaine
   Duo
   Recit de Cromhorne
   Basse Trompette
   Dialogue de Voix humaine et de Cornet.
     Ou Recit continú de Voix humaine,
     ou de Cromhorne
   Plein Ieu

---

2. *Livre d'Orgue Contenant la Messe et les Hymnes de l'Eglise.*
Par le Sr Nivers Me Compositeur en Musique
et organiste de l'Eglise St Sulpice de Paris.

– 1667 –

Unlike the volume of 1665, in which the versets are free and grouped according to the ecclesiastical modes, in the second *Livre d'Orgue* the versets are preorganized, offering material for a mass, numerous hymns and three sequences. The volume includes twelve *Petite Pleins Jeux* composed for the *Amen* or for the *Deo Gratias*.

Messe

Kyrie   [Plein Jeu]
     Fugue
     Recit de Cromhorne
     Duo
     A 2 Cœurs

Gloria   [Plein Jeu]
     Jeu doux
     Fugue
     Recit de Voix humaine
     Duo
     Fugue grave
     Echo
     Diminution de la Basse
     Plein Jeu

Offerte et fugue et Dialogue	*[Dialogue sur les Grands Jeux]*
Sanctus	*Plein Jeu* *Fugue [recte: Basse de Trompette]* *Benedictus. Recit de Cromhorne*
Agnus Dei	*Plein Jeu. Le plain chant en Taille / A 2 Cœurs*

Hymnes

Christe redemptor omnium	*[Plein Jeu]* *Recit de Voix humaine ou de Cromhorne*
A solis ortus cardine *(Hostis Herodes impie)*	*[Plein Jeu]* *Recit de Voix humaine ou de Cromhorne* *Fugue sur le Sujet de l'Hymne precedente*
Ad cœnam agni providi	*[Plein Jeu]* *Variation sur le Cornet*
Iesu nostra redemptio	*[dessus:] Plein Jeu [basse:] Basse Trompette* *Fugue grave sur le sujet de l'hymne precedente*
Veni creator Spiritus (*)	*[Plein Jeu]* *Fugue sur le sujet de l'hymne precedente* *Recit de Voix humaine, gravement: ou de Cromhorne, plus legeremen*
Jam Christus astra *(Beata nobis gaudia)*	*[dessus:] Petit plein jeu [basse:] Basse de Trompette* *Fugue en Variation de Cornet sur l'hymne precedente*
O lux beata Trinitas	*[Plein Jeu]* *Fugue sur le sujet de l'hymne precedente*
Pange lingua (*)	*1°:[Plein Jeu] 2°: [d.] petit plein jeu [b.] Basse Trompette* *1°: Fugue sur le sujet de l'hymne precedente 2°: Recit de Voix humaine* *1°: Recit de Voix humaine 2°: Recit de Cromhorne ou de Cornet*
Sacris solemniis	*[dessus:] petit plein jeu [basse:] Basse de Trompette* *Fugue sur le sujet de l'hymne precedente* *Variation de Cornet*
Verbum supernum prodiens (*)	*[dessus:] petit plein jeu [basse:] Basse de Trompette* *Fugue grave sur le sujet de l'hymne precedente, en Recit de Voix humaine*
Ave maris stella	*[Plein Jeu]* *Fugue sur le sujet de l'hymne precedente* *Recit de Voix humaine*
Quem terra	*Plein Jeu* *Fugue sur le sujet de l'hymne precedente*

Christe redemptor omnium	*[Plein Jeu]*
	Fugue sur le sujet, et Recit de Voix humaine
Exultet coelum laudibus	*[Plein Jeu]*
	Fugue sur le sujet de l'hymne precedente
Tristes erant apostoli	*Plein Jeu*
	Variation de Cornet
Deus tuorum militum	*[dessus:] Plein jeu [basse:] Basse Trompette*
(Iesu corona virginum)	*Fugue grave sur le sujet de l'hymne precedente*
	Variation de Cornet
Iste confessor	*[Plein Jeu]*
	Fugue sur le sujet de l'hymne precedente, et en Recit de Cromhorne
	A 2 Coeurs
Te deum laudamus	*Plein Jeu / Dessus de Trompette / Dessus de Voix hum. / Dessus de Tierce / Basse Trompette / Recit de Cromhorne / Duo / Fugue grave / Fugue legere / Basse de Voix humaine / Echo / Fugue de Cromatique / Diminution de la Basse (Basse de Tierce) / Dialogue de Voix h., et de Cornet ou de Cromh.: Ou Recit continù de Cromh. / A 2 Cœurs / Plein Jeu*

Varia

Victimæ Paschali laudes	*[dessus:] Petit plein jeu [basse:] Basse Trompette*
	[dessus:] petit plein jeu [basse:] Basse de Tierce
	(°) sur le dessus de la Trompette ou de Cromhorne
	(°) sur le Cornet
Veni Sancte spiritus	*Plein Jeu*
	Dessus de Trompette
	Cornet
	Basse de Trompette
	Grand Jeu
Lauda Sion Salvatorem	*Plein Jeu*
(*)	*[dessus:] petit plein jeu [basse:] basse Trompette*
	Dessus de Trompette / [basse:] petit plein jeu
	Cornet
	[dessus:] plein jeu [basse:] Trompette
	[dessus:] Plein Jeu / Basse de grosse Tierce
	Dessus de Cromhorne
	Dessus de Tierce
	[dessus:] plein jeu [basse:] Trompette
	[dessus:] plein jeu [basse:] Grosse Tierce
	[Recit de] Voix humaine
	Fugue sur le Sujet

Amen ou Deo gratias de tous les Tons Pour le petit plein Jeu (12 versets)

(*) = two versions, one of which is transposed
(°) = same musical material but with different registrations

---

3. Livre d'Orgue Des Huit Tons de l'Eglise. Par le S.ʳ Nivers M.ᵉ Compositeur en Musique et Organiste de l'Eglise S.ᵗ Sulpice de Paris.

– 1675 –

In the 3. *Livre d'Orgue* Nivers took up the scheme of the first book, presenting eight cycles of free versets, i.e. not linked to a *cantus firmus*; each cycle consisted of 13 couplets.

1ᵉʳ Ton	Prelude du 1. Ton	1ᵉʳ Ton	Prelude du 1. en E
	Fugue	en E	Fugue grave
	Recit		Recit
	Duo		Duo
	Basse		Basse
	Echo		Cornet
	Dialogue a 2. Chœurs		Dialogue a 2 Chœurs
	Fugue grave		Fugue
	Recit		Recit
	Duo		Duo
	Basse		Basse
	Dialogue de Recits (Crom. / Cornet)		Dialogue de Recits (Cromhorne / Cornet)
	Dialogue à 2 Chœurs		Dialogue a 2 Chœurs
2ᵉ Ton	Prelude du 2 Ton, ou du 1. transposé	3ᵉ Ton	Prelude du 3. Ton
	Fugue		Fugue
	Recit		Recit
	Duo		Basse
	Basse		Duo
	Echo		Cornet
	Dialogue à 2 Chœurs		Dialogue a 2 Chœurs
	Fugue grave		Fugue
	Basse		Recit
	Recit		Duo
	Duo		Basse
	Dialogue de Recits (Cromhorne / Cornet)		Cornet
	Dialogue à 2 Chœurs		Dialogue a 2 Chœurs
4ᵉ Ton	Prelude du 4. Ton	5ᵉ et 7ᵉ Ton	Prelude du 5. et 7. Ton
	Fugue		Fugue
	Recit		Recit
	Duo		Duo
	Basse		Basse
	Echo		Dialogue de Voix humaine et de Cornet
	Dialogue à 2 Chœurs		Dialogue à 2 Chœurs
	Fugue grave		Fugue
	Recit		Recit
	Duo		Basse
	Basse		Duo
	Cornet		Echo
	Dialogue a 2 Chœurs		Dialogue à 2 Chœurs

6ᵉ Ton	*Prelude du 6. Ton, ou du 5. transposé*	*6ᵉ Ton en G*	*Prelude du 6. en G. ou du 8*
	Fugue	*ou 8. Ton*	*Fugue*
	Recit		*Recit*
	Duo		*Duo*
	Basse		*Basse*
	Cornet		*Cornet*
	Dialogue à 2 Chœurs		*Dialogue à 2 Chœurs*
	Fugue		*Fugue*
	Recit		*Recit*
	Duo		*Duo*
	Basse		*Basse*
	Echo		*Dialogue de Recits (Cromhorne / Cornet)*
	Dialogue à 2 Chœurs		*Dialogue a 2 Chœurs*

ORGAN

Nivers was organist in three churches: *Saint-Sulpice* (c. 1651-1702), the *Maison Royale Saint-Louis de Saint-Cyr* (c. 1686-1714) and the *Chapelle Royale*. The organ of *Saint-Sulpice*, restored and extended in 1675 by François Ducastel under the direction of Nivers himself, had the following specification at the time:[478]

Grand Orgue	**Positif**	**Écho**
Montre 8	Montre 8	Cornet
Bourdon	Bourdon 8	
Prestant 4	Prestant 4	
Doublette	Flûte 4	**Pédale**
Nasard	Doublette	Flûte 8
Tierce	Nasard	Trompette 8
Flageolet	Tierce	
Fourniture	Forniture	
Cymbale	Cymbale	
Cornet	Cromorne	
Trompette		Tirasse Grand Orgue
Clairon		2 Tremblants
Vox humaine		

LAMBERT CHAUMONT
c. 1630 – 1712

Chaumont was probably born between 1630 and 1635. Little is known of him. As a musician, Chaumont was self-taught. Although he spent most of his life between Liège and Huy (today in Belgium), the style of his *Pièces d'orgue sur les huit tons* is clearly influenced by the French classical school. His principal occupation was that of a priest, first in *Saint-Martin* of Huy, then, from 1688, as parish priest of *Saint-Germain* and *Pater* of the Carmelites of the same city. Nevertheless he managed to be active as an organist, to publish a *Livre d'Orgue* (there was also a previous musical publication, now lost) and to take an interest in matters related to tuning; including formulating his own temperament (although it is based on that described by Mersenne half a century earlier). Chaumont died in Huy in 1712.

WORKS

Pieces D'Orgue sur les 8 Tons Avec leurs varieté leurs Agreemens leurs Mouvemens et le Melange des Jeux propres a chaque espece de verset.
On Trouvera a la fin Un Petit Traité de l'Accompagnement Une Regle generale pour toucher le Contrepoint Et la Methode daccorder le Clavessin.

– 1695 –

Chaumont's eight *Suites* have a variable number of *couplets*, between ten and thirteen. Each of them is followed by one or two pieces in the form of a dance (*Allemande, Chaconne Gigue,* etc.) in harpsichord style and thus not belonging to the classic organ repertoire.

1er Ton	Prélude		2e Ton	Prélude
	2e Prélude			Fugue gaÿe
	Duo			Cornet
	Trio			Fugue grave
	[Dialogue de] Voix humaine			Récit
	Récit			Voix humaine
	Fugue à 3			Duo
	2e Fugue			Basse de Cromhorne
	Basse de Tierce			Dialogue
	Cornet			Plein Jeu
	2e Cornet			Allemande
	Cornet et Écho			Chaconne grave
	Plein Jeu			
	Allemande en mi			
	Gigue			
3e Ton	Prélude		4e Ton	Prélude
	Duo			Fugue gaye
	2e Duo			Récit
	Trio			Duo
	Fugue			Basse de Cromhorne ou Trompette
	Le même sujet Basse de Cromhorne			Trio
	Récit			Cornet
	Fugue			Dialogue
	Contrefugue chromatique			Tierce ou Cromhorne en Taille
	Cornet			Voix humaine
	Écho			Plein Jeu
	Plein Jeu			Allemande
	Récit de Cornet ou de Cromhorne			Duo en gigue
	Allemande			

5ᵉ Ton	Prélude	6ᵉ Ton	Prélude
	Duo		Fugue grave
	2e Duo		Trio par Contrefugue
	Trio		Cornet
	Récit		Duo
	Fugue légère		Duo en gigue
	2e Fugue légère		Dessus de Tierce ou Cornet
	Cornet		Basse de Cromhorne
	Basse de Trompette		Écho
	Basse de Cromhorne		Tierce en Taille
	Dialogue		Dialogue
	Trio è 3 Claviers		Plein Jeu
	Cornet et Écho partout		Chaconne en la
	Plein Jeu au Positif		
	Allemande		
7ᵉ Ton	Prélude	8ᵉ Ton	Prélude
	Fugue Grave		Fugue gaÿe
	Duo		Basse de Cromhorne
	2e Duo		Duo
	Basse de Cromhorne		Cornet
	Fugue légère		Voix humaine entière
	Récit de Cornet		Trio
	2e Cornet		Récit de Cromhorne
	Trio		Dialogue
	Récit de Cromhorne		Plein Jeu
	Trio à 3 Claviers		Allemande
	Plein Jeu au Positif		2e Allemande
	Allemande		

ORGAN

There is no information about the organ played by Chaumont. Assuming that the registrations described in his table *Du Melange des Jeux* refer to a precise instrument, the essential traits of this organ were: three manuals and pedal, with a rather large *Grand Orgue* based on *Montre 8* and *Bourdon 16* (including a *Quarte de Nasard* and *Grosse tierce*) and an *Echo* division (*Écho Cornet*). From the registrations it is not clear whether the organ had a *Récit*-division.

ANDRÉ RAISON
c. 1640 - 1719

Raison was born around 1640, perhaps in Nanterre. Nothing is known about his musical education. Around 1666 he was appointed organist of the Royal Abbey of *Sainte-Geneviève du Mont* in Paris, and, a few years later, also of the Jesuit church in *Rue Saint-Jacques*. In the *Rôle de la capitation* (tax book) of 1695, his name appears among the *Maîtres de 1ʳᵉ classe*, together with Marchand, François Couperin and de Grigny. Around 1699 he became organist of the *Grand Couvent et Collège des Jacobins*. Among his pupils was Louis-Nicolas Clérambault, who would later dedicate his *Livre d'Orgue* to him. Raison published two *Livres d'Orgue* in 1688 and 1714. He died in Paris in 1719.

WORKS

Livre d'Orgue Contenant Cinq Messes Suffisantes Pour Tous les Tons de l'Eglise ou Quinze Magnificats pour ceux qui n'ont pas besoin de Messe avec des Elevations toutes particulieres. Ensuite des Benedictus: Et une Offerte en action de Grace pour l'heureuse Convalescence du Roy. [...] Composé par André Raison Organiste de La Royalle Abbaye de Saincte Geneviesne du mont de Paris.

– 1688 –

The first *Livre d'Orgue* contains sufficient versets for the *Ordinarium* of five masses or, as Raison explained, for fifteen *Magnificats*, as the *couplets* were not related to a specific *cantus firmus*. None of the five masses contained an *Offertoire*, but at the end of the book there is a commemorative piece entitled *Offers du 5.ᵉ Ton, Le Vive le Roy des Parisiens* (see page 131). As the use of the pedal in some pieces is quite demanding (for example in the *Kyrie* that opens the book, see page 113), Raison suggested, for organists whose pedal technique was not sufficiently refined, to allow a second person to play the pedal part, or even to leave it out completely:

L'intention de L'Auteur est de Joüer aussi le plein jeu sans la Pedalle.	The author's intention is that the Plein jeu can also be played without the pedal.

Messe du premier ton

Kyrie
    Plein jeu gravement
    Autre Premier Kyrie pour un plein jeu accompagné d'une Pedalle de Trompette EnTaille
    Basse et dessus de Tromp. (ou Cornet separé)
    Trio
    Duo
    Dialogue

Gloria
    Plein Jeu
    Fugue sur toute sorte de jeux
    Cornet
    Recit de Cromorne
    Trio
    [Echo] Cromorne lentement / Cornet Separé guayment / Eco
    Basse de Trompette
    [Echo] Cornet separé ou Eco / Cromorne
    Dialogue grand Jeu

Sanctus	*Plein jeu*
	Recit de 2 dessus de tierce
	Benedictus. Basse et dessus de voix humaine
Elevation	*Trio a 3 Claviers*
Agnus Dei	*[Plein Jeu] Petit plein jeu guayment / Grand plein jeu lentement*
	Duo
Deo gratias	*Plein Jeu*

Messe du deuziesme ton

Kyrie	*Plein jeu gravement*
	Fugue grave sur la Tromp. ou Cromorne
	Trio En passacaille
	Fugue pour une basse et dessus de trompette
	Dialogue
Gloria	*[Plein Jeu] Petit plein jeu legerement / Grand plein jeu lentement*
	Cornet
	Recit de Cromorne
	[Dialogue à 2 dessus] La Trompette separé ou le Cromorne / La tierce ou le bourdon et la flutte
	Trio
	Duo gayment
	[Récit à 2 dessus] Cromorne / Cornet
	Fugue pour une basse de Trompette ou de Tierce
	Dialogue
Sanctus	*Plein jeu gravement*
	Recit de 2 dessus de tierce
	Benedictus. Fugue pour un Cromorne ou Voix humaine En Taille
Elevation	*Basse et Dessus de Voix humaine*
Agnus Dei	*Plein jeu gravement*
	Dialogue
Deo gratias	*Plein Jeu*

Messe du troisiesme ton

Kyrie	*Grand plein Jeu [gravement / Petit plein jeu viste]*
	Fugue grave sur La Trompette
	Duo
	Basse et dessus de trompette
	Dialogue
Gloria	*Plein jeu gravement*
	Recit de Tierce
	Duo
	Trio
	Cornet
	Basse et dessus de trompette (ou de tierce et Cornet separé)
	Recit de Cromorne
	Dessus et basse de voix humaine
	Dialogue

Sanctus	Plein jeu gravement Trio de Cromorne, et de Cornet separé ou d'Eco Benedictus. Trio a Trois Claviers ou a deux a L'ordinaire
Elevation	[Fond d'orgue] Le petit et gros bourdon avec le prestant
Agnus Dei	[Plein Jeu] Petit plein jeu viste / Grand plein jeu lentement Basse de trompette ou de Tierce Autre Second Agnus: Dialogue
Deo gratias	Petit plein Jeu

Messe du sixiesme ton

Kyrie	Plein Jeu Gravement Basse et Dessus de Trompette Trio En Chaconne Duo Dialogue
Gloria	[Plein Jeu] Petit plein jeu viste / Grand plein jeu lentement Cornet Trio en Dialogue Basse et Dessus de Trompette Recit de Cromorne ou de Tierce Trio Dessus et Basse de Voix humaine Recit [à 2 dessus] Cromorne / Cornet Dialogue
Sanctus	Plein jeu gravement Recit de Tierce Benedictus. Trio
Elevation	Cromorne ou Tierce en Taille
Agnus Dei	[Plein Jeu] Grand plein Jeu Lentement / Petit plein Jeu viste Duo
Deo gratias	Petit plein jeu

Messe du huictiesme ton

Kyrie	Plein Jeu gravement Imitation En Trio Sur Les petits et grands jeux Duo Basse et dessus de Trompette ou Cornet Separé Dialogue
Gloria	Plein Jeu Gravement Petit plein jeu Cornet & Eco Trio en Gigue [Récit à 2 dessus] Cornet / Cromorne

	Dialogue
	Recit de Cromorne
	Duo
	Dialogue
Sanctus	*Plein Jeu gravement*
	Recit de 2. dessus de Tierce
	Benedictus. Dessus et Baße de Voix humaine
Elevation	*Recit Sur le Nazard bourdon & montre*
Agnus Dei	*[Plein Jeu] Grand plein jeu Lentement / Petit plein Jeu Viste*
	Trio avec Reprise
Deo gratias	*Tierce en taille*
ou autre piece	
Varia	*Offerte du 5.e Ton, Le Vive le Roy des Parisiens A Son Entrée a*
	l'hotel de Ville Le Trentiéme de Januier 1687

Second Livre d'Orgue. Sur les Acclamations de la Paix tant Desirée.
Qui commence par l'Antienne Da Pacem Domine, avec une Fugue sur le même sujet
en d, la, re, b, mol. Ensuite un Prelude, et une Offerte en d, la, re, b, carre;
une Ouverture du septième ton, en d, la, re, avec les désirs d'une longue vie au Roy; et une
Allemande du sixième en g, re, sol. L'auteur adjoûte plusieurs Noëls Propres pour les Récits,
et Offertes au naturel, et transposé, avec plusieurs variations dans le goût du temps,
tant pour l'Orgue que pour le Clavecin.
Le tout composé par M.ʳ Raison organiste de l'Abaye Royalle de S.ᵗᵉ Gennevieve, Et du grand
Convent et College general des R.R. Peres Jacobins de Saint Jaques.

– 1714 –

The second *Livre d'Orgue* by Raison, published 26 years after the first, shows a clear change both in the choice of repertoire and musical style. Among the first four pieces – large compositions using the sonority of *Grands Jeux* – there is an *Ouverture du Septième ton* which is (as in the first *Livre d'Orgue*) a homage to the King with the text *Vive le Roi*. In the second part of the collection there are various *Noëls* of considerably different length, ranging from 9 to over 150 bars, and which – as specified in the title – can be performed either with organ or harpsichord.

Varia	*La Paix tant desireé - Petit plein jeu [c.f. al basso su Da pacem Domine]*
	Fugue sur Da pacem Domine. Sur les grands jeux
	Offerte en d, la, re b carre:
	Prelude en becarre Sur les grands jeux / Fugue / Fugue Sur les grands jeux
	Ouverture du Septième en d, la, re. Les grands jeux
	Allemande grave du 6.ᵉ en g, re, sol

Noëls	A la venüe de Noel
	Le même Noel en triple
	Voicy le jour solemnel De Noel
	Joseph est bien marié
	Or nous dites Marie
	Une jeune pucelle
	Noel poitevin
	Ou s'en vont ces gais Bergers
	Laissez paitre vos Bêtes
	O Dieu! que n'etois-je en vie! Ou bien que n'etois-je icy!
	O Createur
	Les Bourgeois de Châtres
	Noel des Sts Innosens
	Puer nobis nascitur. Elevation.
	Quoy! ma voisine
	A minuit fut fait un reveil
	Vous qui desirez sans fin
	Noel cette journée

JACQUES BOYVIN
c. 1649/55 – 1706

Boyvin was born in Paris. The date is unknown but estimated by musicologists as being somewhere between 1649 and 1655. At a very young age, in 1663, he was appointed organist at the church of *Quinze-Vingts*. He maintained this position until 1674, when he became *titulaire* of the Cathedral of Rouen, as indirect successor to Titelouze. In addition, he worked as an advisor and organ expert.

In Rouen, Boyvin had the opportunity to play the organ of the *Jacobins*; the first organ in the town to be equipped with a *tirasse* and a fourth manual (*Récit*), and an instrument that Boyvin described as *"un des plus grands ouvrages qu'il y ait aprés Nostre Dame et St Ouen"* [one of the largest organs that exists after Notre Dame and St Ouen]. This instrument was to inspire Boyvin for the reconstruction of the organ of the cathedral after the damage of the storm of 1683.[479]

In 1697 he also took on the position of organist at *Saint-Herbland*. He maintained this position for only a few years, before handling it over to Gaspard Corrette, at whose wedding he was a witness in 1700. In addition to the two *Livres d'Orgue*, Boyvin published a *Traité d'Accompagnament* in 1700 which was republished four times over the course of the following ten years. He died in Rouen in 1706.

WORKS

Premier Livre d'Orgue Contenant les huit Tons
A L'Usage Ordinaire de l'Eglise Composé par J. Boyvin
Organiste de l'Eglise Cathedralle Nostre Dame de Roüen.

– 1690 –

Boyvin's *Premier Livre d'Orgue* contains eight cycles related to the traditional *huit tons de l'église*, with the number of versets ranging from six to eleven. In addition to the traditional *mélanges* – it should be remembered that the volume contains an important table of registrations – Boyvin also mentioned *"les quels jusqu'icy n'avoient pas esté en usage"* [those which until now have never been used], perhaps referring to different combinations such as the *Trompette du Récit*, a stop which was fairly uncommon at the time, but present on Boyvin's organ in the Cathedral of Rouen.

1ᵉʳ ton
    Premier ton grand plein Jeu Continu
    Fugue Grave
    Recit de Cromhorne ou de petitte tierce
    Concert pour les fluttes
    Trio
    Fond D'orgue
    Duo
    Tierce en taille
    Trio a deux dessus
    Basse de trompette [recte: Dialogue de Basse de Trompette et Cornet separé ou
        dessus de la mesme trompette]
    Grand Dialogue

2ᵉ ton
    Second ton prelude
    Duo
    Recit de petit tierce, ou de nazarde, ou de cromhorne
    Trio a deux dessus
    Dialogue de recits de cromhorne et de cornet, ou bien de petite Trompette, et de
        petite tierce [recte: Dialogue de Récits et de Trios]
    Diminution de Cornet
    A 2 Choeurs
    Grand Dialogue
    Dialogue de voix humaine
    Dernier recit du second

3ᵉ ton
    Troisiesme ton plein jeu a 2 choeurs
    Fugue lic [lié ?]
    Duo
    Dessus de tierce en vitesses, et accords
    Trio
    Recit de cromhorne
    Cromhorne en taille
    Basse de Trompette
    Grand Dialogue

4ᵉ ton	Grand prelude a 5 parties A 2 Choeurs 4ᵐᵉ ton [Grand plein jeu]
	Trio
	Cornet ou Tierce
	Dialogue de recits, et de Trios
	Duo
	Tierce en taille
	Dialogue en fugue
	Prelude facile du 4 ton
5ᵉ ton	5ᵐᵉ ton plein jeu a 2 Choeurs
	Grand prelude avec les pedalles de trompette meslées
	Recit [de dessus]
	Petit cornet ou petite tierce
	Duo
	Tierce en taille
	[Dialogue de] voix humaine
	Trio pour la pedalle ou tire-clavier
	Dialogue [sur les grands jeux]
6ᵉ ton	Sixiesme ton plein jeu
	Fugue-quatuor
	Trio pour la pedalle
	Recit [de dessus]
	Trio a 3 Claviers
	Basse de Trompette
	Dialogue de cromhorne en taille et de cornet separé, ou sur tout le cromhorne
	Petit dialogue en fugue sans tremblant
	Grand Dialogue [recte: Dialogue sur les grands jeux et de Trios]
7ᵉ ton	7ᵉ ton Plein jeu continu
	Duo
	Basse de trompette
	Dialogue de recits meslé de trios
	Trio a deux dessus
	[Dialogue de] Voix humaine
	Dialogue [sur les grands jeux]
8ᵉ ton	8ᵉ ton Grand plein jeu a 3 Choeurs
	Fugue grave
	Duo
	Trio
	Dessus de tierce [alla fine: Tierce des deux mains et pedalle douce]
	Grand Dialogue

Second Livre d'Orgue, Contenant les Huit Tons,
a l'usage ordinaire de l'Eglise. Composé par J. Boyvin,
Organiste de l'Eglise Cathedrale de Roüen.

– 1700 –

The *Second Livre d'Orgue* follows the structure of the previous one, with eight cycles in the eight ecclesiastical modes, but a significantly smaller number of versets per cycle (ranging from five to eight). The volume is completed by a *Traité abregé de l'Accompagnement pour l'Orgue & le Clavessin*, which in fact has no connection with the organ pieces.

1er ton	Prelude grave	2e ton	Prelude
	Prelude a deux chœurs		Dessus de petite Trompette
	Duo		Duo
	Fugue grave		Trio a deux dessus
	Recit tendre		Grand Dialogue a quatre Chœurs
	Grand Dialogue		
		4e ton	Prelude
3e ton	Prelude		Fugue cromhatique
	Fugue		Recit grave
	Dessus de Cornet separé ou de petite Tierce		Dialogue de Recits et de Trios
	Basse de Cromorne		Duo
	Concert de Flûtes ou Fon d'orgue		Cromhorne en taille
	Grand Dialogue a quatre chœurs		Dialogue a deux choeurs
5e ton	Prelude		
	Duo	6e ton	Prelude
	Fugue		Recit grave
	Quatuor		Duo
	Basse de Cromhorne		Fugue
	Recit		Trio
	Tierce en taille		Grand Dialogue
	Grand Dialogue a quatre Chœurs		
		8e ton	Prelude
7e ton	Prelude		Trio a deux dessus
	Pour la Voix humaine		Basse de Trompette ou de Cromhorne avec le Cornet separé
	Duo		
	Fond d'orgue ou Concert de Flûtes		Fugue
	Recit grave		Recit grave
	Basse de Trompette		Dialogue en fugue sans tremblant
	Petit dialogue meslé de trios		

ORGAN

The organ of the Cathedral of Rouen, where Boyvin served from 1674, had been rebuilt a few years earlier, from 1658-63, by Pierre Thierry and Pierre Désenclos. Following a violent storm, it was again rebuilt and expanded by Robert Clicquot in 1689 under the directives of Boyvin:[480]

Grand Orgue	*Positif*	*Récit* (from c')
Montre 16	Montre 8	Cornet
Bourdon 16	Bourdon 8	Trompette
Montre 8	Prestant	
Bourdon 8	Flûte 4	*Écho* (from c°)
Prestant	Nasard	Bourdon ⎫
Flûte 4	Doublette	Prestant ⎭ always inserted
Double Tierce 3 1/5	Grosse Tierce [1 3/5]	Nazard + Tierce
Nasard	Larigot	Doublette
Doublette	Fourniture IV	Fourniture Cymbale III
Flûte 2	Cymbale III	Voix humaine
Grosse Tierce [1 3/5]	Cromorne	
Quarte	Vox humaine	
Flageolet		
Fourniture V		*Pédale* (30 notes)
Cymbale IV		Flûte 8
Cornet		Flûte 4
Trompette		Trompette
Clairon		Clairon
Cromorne	2 tremblants	
Vox humaine	Tirasse	

GILLES JULLIEN
1650/53 – 1703

The approximate date of Jullien's birth is deduced from his burial certificate, drawn up on 14 September 1703, where Jullien is described as *"50 ans ou environ"*. Little is known of his life or of his musical training. According to some sources, in 1667 (i.e. presumably between the ages of 14 and 17) he was appointed organist of the Cathedral of Chartres. Although the date of 1667 cannot be confirmed with certainty, it is clear that he managed to obtain this prestigious position at a young age. He remained in this position until his death in 1703. He was succeeded by his son Jean-François for six years, but the latter was dismissed in 1709.

Jullien left only one *Livre d'Orgue*, published in 1690, i.e. the same year as the *Premier Livre* by Boyvin and Couperin's two masses. At the end of the volume there is also a *Motet de Sainte Cæcille* for vocal and instrumental ensemble. A pre-announced second *Livre d'Orgue* never saw the light of day.

WORKS

Premier Livre d'Orgue Composé par G. Jullien
Organiste de L'Église Cathedralle nostre dame de chartes,
Contenant les huit tons de l'Église pour les festes Solemnels
Avec Un Motet de Ste Cæcille a trois Voix et Simphonie.

– 1690 –

Jullien's *Livre d'Orgue* follows the canonical structure of eight cycles built on the eight ecclesiastical modes. Each cycle contains between eight to thirteen versets, and the same forms are often repeated within the same cycle (e.g. 2 *Duos*, 2 *Dialogues*, etc.).

Each cycle presents at least two, but sometimes three, *Préludes*, i.e. *Pleins Jeux* structured in different ways: entirely on one manual, or on two manuals (*Positif: gayement – Grand Jeu: gravement*), or *à cinq partie[s]* with *pedalle de trompette en taille* but not linked to the *cantus firmus*.

1er ton	Prelude du premier ton	*2e ton*	Prelude (Grand Jeu gravement a cinq partie)
	Duo		Duo
	Trio		Recit de voix humaine
	Fugue		Basse de trompette
	Basse de Trompette		Trio
	Cromhorne en taille		Fugue Renversée a cinq parties
	Prelude		Dessus de Cromhorne ou de trompette
	Duo		Dialogue
	Fantesie Cromatique		Prelude [I]
	Fugue Sur ave maris Stella		Prelude [II]
	Dialogue		
	Prelude		
	Trio		
3e ton	Prelude a 5 partie	*4e ton*	Prelude
	Fugue		Dessus de voix humaine
	Duo		Duo
	Trio pour une Elevation		Basse de trompette [et Dessus de Cornet]
	[Basse et dessus de] Voix humaine		Trio pour une Elevation
	Trio a 2 dessus		Dessus de tierce ou cornet
	Basse de trompette		Trio
	Dialogue		Dialogue
	Prelude		Prelude
			Dessus de cromhorne ou trompette

5ᵉ ton	*Prelude a cinq partie*	6ᵉ ton	*Prelude*
	Duo		*Trio*
	Trio a 3 Claviers		*Fugue Grave*
	Dessus de tierce ou Cromhorne		*Dessus de voix humaine*
	Trio a 2 dessus		*Trio a 2 Dessus*
	Duo		*Dessus De cromhorne*
	Basse de Trompette		*Duo*
	Dessus de cornet [recte: Echo]		*Dialogue [I]*
	Tiarce En taille		*Dialogue [II]*
	Dialogue		*Prelude*
	Prelude		
7ᵉ ton	*Prelude Du 7ᵉ ton*	8ᵉ ton	*8ᵉ Ton Prelude a cinq partie*
	Duo		*Duo*
	Voix humaine		*Dessus De Cromhorne [ou de trompette]*
	Duo		*Fugue*
	Fugue		*Trio a 2 dessus*
	Dessus de tierce ou cornet		*Basse De trompette [et Dessus de Cornet]*
	Dialogue		*Fugue renversée*
	Prelude		*Dialogue*
			Prelude

FRANÇOIS COUPERIN
1668 - 1733

François Couperin – the most important member of the Couperin dynasty, thus earning the nickname *le Grand* – was born in Paris in 1668. His earliest musical impulses were most likely received from his father Charles, organist at *Saint-Gervais*. Upon the latter's death in 1679, the succession to *Saint-Gervais* was granted to François with effect from 1685, since at the time of his father's death François was only a little more than ten years of age. Meanwhile, Michel-Richard de Lalande (also, de La Lande), *Maître de musique* of the *Chapelle Royale* of Versailles, held the position *ad interim*.

In 1685, at the age of 18, François officially became organist of *Saint-Gervais*. The two, well-known *Messes pour les Paroisses* and *pour les Couvents* appeared in 1690, and are the only known organ compositions by François Couperin. De Lalande considered the two masses of the 22-year-old composer *"fort belles, et dignes d'Estre données au Public"* as stated in the *Extrait du Privilège*. A few years later, in 1693, Couperin was in addition appointed organist of the *Chapelle du Roy*, considerably improving his social status as well as his income.

From the last years of the seventeenth century onwards, Couperin's activity as a court musician, *Maître de musique* and composer rapidly intensified: it was during this period that he wrote many vocal, ensemble and instrumental works. Most notably, he composed for harpsichord four *Livres de Pièces de Clavecin*, published between 1713 and 1730, as well as writing the important treatise *L'Art de Toucher le Clavecin* (1716). Although after 1690 he would compose no other organ works, Couperin retained the position of organist at *Saint-Gervais* almost until his death in 1733.

WORKS

Pieces d'Orgue Consistantes en deux Messes
l'Une à l'usage ordinaire des Paroisses, Pour les Festes Solemnelles.
L'Autre propre pour les Convents de Religieux, et Religieuses.
Composées par F. Couperin,
S.ʳ de Crouilly Organiste de S.ᵗ Gervais

– 1690 –

The publication of the two masses of Couperin – as was also the case with several of Lully's works as well as the *Ballet de la Paix* by François Rebel and François Francœur – followed a special procedure that involved printing only the two initial pages: the title page and the required authorization (*Extrait du Privilège Royal*), while the entire musical section remained in manuscript form. In order to guarantee the authenticity of the content, a seal was placed on some of the pages which consisted of two interlaced "C"s (see opposite), signifying *Couperin de Crouilly*. In fact, in the *Privilège Royal* Couperin took the name of *Sieur de Crouilly*, as his father Charles had done before him.[481]

The choice to disseminate the works in manuscript form rather than in print was made for economic reasons: in 1690 the 22 year old Couperin's financial resources were limited; his appointment as *Organiste du Roy* – and consequent improvement of his economic status – would ensue only three years later. However, the aforementioned process of diffusion came at a price: circulation was limited in scope and there was a high risk of incidental errors by the copyists, as can be observed in the copy of the masses kept at the *Bibliothèque Nationale* in Paris. The two most reliable manuscripts – preserved in the *Bibliothèque Inguimbertine* of Carpentras (the only copy of the original version) and the *Bibliothèque Municipale* of Versailles – display some differences in the musical text, as well as accidentals, slurring as ornamentation.

The indications of registration of the various *couplets* in the two masses refer here to the manuscript Ms 1038 kept in the *Bibliothèque Inguimbertine* de Carpentras.

Messe pour les Paroisses

Kyrie	Plein chant du premier Kyrie, en Taille
	Fugue sur les jeux d'anches
	Recit de Chromhorne
	Dialogue sur la Trompette et le Chromhorne
	Plein chant
Gloria	Plein jeu
	Petitte Fugue sur le Chromhorne
	Duo sur les Tierces
	Dialogue sur les Trompettes, Clairon et Tierces du G.C. et le Bourdon avec le larigot du positif
	3° a 2 Dessus de Chromhorne et la basse de Tierce
	Tierce en Taille
	Dialogue sur la Voix humaine
	Dialogue en 3. Du Cornet et de la tierce
	Dialogue sur les Grands jeux
Offertoire	Offertoire sur les Grands Jeux
Sanctus	Plein chant du premier Sanctus en Canon
	Recit de Cornet
	Benedictus. Cromhorne en Taille
Agnus Dei	Plein chant de L'Agnus dei en basse et en Taille alternativement
	Dialogue Sur Les Grands Jeux
Deo gratias	Petit plein jeu

Messe pour les Couvents

Kyrie	Plein jeu
	Fugue sur la Trompette
	Recit de Chromhorne
	Trio a 2 Dessus de Chromhorne et la basse de Tierce
	Dialogue sur la Trompette du grand Clavier, et sur la montre le bourdon et le nazard du Positif
Gloria	Plein Jeu
	Petitte fugue sur le Chromhorne
	Duo sur les tierces
	Basse de Trompette
	Chromhorne sur la Taille
	Dialogue sur la voix humaine
	Trio en Dessus sur la Tierce et la basse sur la trompette
	Recit de tierce
	Dialogue sur les grands Jeux

Offertoire	Offertoire sur les Grands Jeux
Sanctus	Plein jeu
	Recit de Cornet
Élévation	Elevation. Tierce en Taille
Agnus Dei	Plein jeu
	Dialogue sur les grands jeux
Deo gratias	Petit plein jeu

ORGAN

The specification of the organ of *Saint-Gervais* at the time of François Couperin can be found on page 57.

LOUIS MARCHAND
1669 - 1732

Marchand was born in Lyon in 1669 into a family of organists and presumably received his first musical education from his father. At the age of 15 he became organist in Nevers, where his father was *titulaire* at the church of *Saint-Martin*. Perhaps the following year he moved to Paris, first as organist at the Jesuit college *Louis-le-Grand* and later at the *Maison Professe* of the same order.

Owing to his extraordinary talent, in the following years he became organist of several important churches in Paris and also (from 1708 to 1713) at the *Chapelle Royale* of Versailles, as successor to Nivers. The sources of the time describe him as an unparalleled keyboard virtuoso, with accounts of crowds of admirers who followed him from one church to another in Paris. He was also a regular guest in Parisian high society, where noble families competed to employ him as a private harpsichord teacher.

At the same time, the portrait of the personality of Marchand that emerges from the chronicles is certainly not the most flattering: in 1690 he defamed without grounds the organist Pierre Dandrieu of *Saint-Barthélemy* in order to take his place (without success – he had to pay the court costs); in 1701 his wife accused him of *"mauvaise conduite, dissipation, excès, violence, voyes de fait et mauvais traitements"*[482] [*misconduct, dissipation, excess, violence, assault and abuse*]; in 1702 upon Lebègue's death – and against the previous wishes of the deceased – he tried, without success, to take up Lebègue's position in a fraudulent manner. Episodes such as his challenging his colleague at the *Chapelle Royale*, François Couperin, over the authorship of *Les Bergeries*, or his alleged "escape from Dresden" in order to avoid a musical confrontation with Johann Sebastian Bach can hardly be said to depict the portrait of a gentleman. Marchand died in Paris in 1732.

WORKS

Pieces choisies pour l'Orgue de feu Le Grand Marchand Chevallier de l'Ordre de Jerusalem, Organiste du Roi, De la paroisse S.ᵗ Benoît, de S.ᵗ Honoré, Des R.R.P.P. Jesuites de la rue S.ᵗ Antoine, des R.R.P.P. Jesuites de la rue S.ᵗ Jacques, Et du Grand Convent des R.R.P.P. Cordeliers. Né à Lion. Mort à Paris le 17 fevrier 1732, agé de 61 an. Livre Premier.

– 1700/1740 –

According to the January 1700 issue of *Le Mercure Galant*, Marchand published a *Première suite de pièces d'orgue du premier ton* in that very year; a volume that was subsequently lost, but may well constitute (in whole or in part) the following posthumous publication of the *Pièces choises pour l'Orgue*. The *Plein jeu* that opens the book is worth noting: it is a 6-voice composition with double pedal (see p. 115).

[1.ᵉʳ ton]   *Plein Jeu*
              Fugue
              Trio
              Baße de trompette
              Quatuor
              Tierce en taille
              Duo
              Recit [de dessus]
              Tierce en taille
              Baße de trompette ou de cromorne
              Fond d'Orgue
              Dialogue

Manuscrit de Versailles

The *Manuscrit de Versailles* is not easy to read: some passages are hardly legible while others are crossed out completely, perhaps by Marchand himself; despite this they are still legible. It is likely that they are autographs, with the exception of the *Grand Dialogue* contained in the 3.ᵐᵉ *livre*.[483]

2ᵉ *livre*   Grand Jeu
             Basse de trompette
             Recit
             Grand Jeu
             Trio
             [Récit de dessus]
             [Fond d'Orgue?]
             [Fugue]
             [Duo]
             [Trio?]
             [Récit de Basse]
             [Duo]
             Te Deum premier coupler ou bien sur le plein jeu

                Jeux doux 2ᵉ Couplet
                3ᵉ Couplet Sanctus
                Recit sur le Cornet 4ᵉ Couplet
                5ᵉ Couplet basse de Tierce
                6ᵉ Couplet Duo
                7ᵉ Couplet Basse de trompette
                8ᵉ Couplet Trio
                Plain Jeu 9ᵉ Couplet
                Jeu doux
                Recit de Cromhorne
                Basse de Cromhorne
                Duo
                R.[écit]
                G.[rand] Jeu
                P.[lein] J.[eu]

[3.ᵐᵉ *livre*]   *Grand Dialogue composé par Mʳ Marchand à Paris. j696*
                Dialogue [fragment]
                [fragment without title]

    4ᵉ *livre*   *[Duo]*
                Fugue
                Trio
                Recit [de dessus]
                [Duo]
                Basse de trompette
                [Récit en taille]

    5.ᵉ *livre*   *Basse de cromhorne ou de trompette*
                Duo
                Recit [de dessus]
                Plain Jeu
                Fugue
                Basse de trompette ou de Cromorne
                [Récit en taille]

ORGAN

From 1708 to 1713, Marchand was one of the four organists at the *Chapelle Royale* of Versailles. This church as well as its organ had a rather troubled history. Between 1679 and 1681 Étienne Énocq and Robert Clicquot built an organ for the *troisième chapelle* of the palace; an instrument that was completed but never installed in the place for which it was planned, owing to new plans to build a new (but temporary) *quatrième chapelle*. Not until 30 years later, in 1710, did Robert Clicquot and Julien Tribuot finally install an organ for the (definitive) *cinquième chapelle*; an instrument that incorporated some of the elements built for the previous organ, but which was adapted to the larger acoustics of the new chapel. The precise specification of circa 1710 – i.e. relative to the period of Marchand's tenure in Versailles – is not known. Based on the project of the organ Énocq/Clicquot (*Memoire pour faire une orgue de huit pieds a quatre Claviers en la chapelle du Roy in Versailles,* dated 1679) and referring to *Le Marché ancien de l'Orgue de la Chapelle Du Chasteau De Versaille* (dated 1710) and other documents, the specification of the organ at the time of Marchand has been hypothesized as follows:[484]

Grand Orgue	*Positif*	*Récit*
Montre 16	Montre 8	Cornet
Bourdon 16	Bourdon 8	Trompette 8
Montre 8	Prestant	
Bourdon 8	Flûte 4	*Echo*
Prestant	Nasard 2 2/3	Cornet
Flûte 4	Doublette 2	
Grosse Tierce 3 1/5	Tierce 1 3/5	*Pédale*
Nasard 2 2/3	Larigot 1 1/3	
Doublette 2	Forniture	Flûte 8
Quarte de Nasard 2	Cymbale	Flûte 4
Tierce 1 3/5	Cromorne 8	Trompette 8
Fourniture		Clairon 4
Cymbale		
Grand Cornet	Tremblant fort	
Trompette 8	Tremblant doux	
Clairon 4	Accouplement Pos./G.O.	
Vox humaine 8	Tirasse G.O.	

GASPARD CORRETTE
1671 - ante 29 December 1732

Corrette was born in 1671 in Rouen, where Jacques Boyvin was *titulaire* of the Cathedral from 1674. The role of Boyvin as a musician, mentor, friend and even marriage witness was of fundamental importance to Corrette's life: in fact, the professional path of the two musicians was continuously intertwined. It is probably thanks to Boyvin that in around 1703 Corrette became organist in *Saint-Herbland*, and, when Boyvin was taken ill and could no longer perform the duties of organist in the Cathedral, he asked Corrette to deputise for him. Upon Boyvin's death, Corrette offered his services as organist to the cathedral chapter in the *interim* wthout payment, clearly in the hope of being chosen as successor, but to no avail as D'Agincourt was chosen in the end. Corrette also served as organist in *Saint-Pierre le Portier, Saint-Denis* and *Saint-Jean*.

In 1720 he settled in Paris and became apprentice to a dance teacher, who taught him *"son art de maître à danser et joueur d'instrument"* [his art of teaching dance and *instrumental playing]*. Thereafter, any trace of Corrette vanishes. In the marriage deed of his son, Michel, drawn up on December 29, 1732, Gaspard is referred to as a *défunt*. Neither the precise date nor the place of his death is known.[485]

WORKS

*Messe du 8.ᵉ Ton pour l'Orgue a L'Usage des Dames Religieuses,
et Utile a ceux qui touchent l'orgue.
Composée Par Gaspard Corrette
Organiste de l'Eglise Saint Herbland de Rouen.*

– 1703 –

The only publication for organ by Gaspard Corrette is the *Messe du 8.ᵉ Ton*, printed in Paris in 1703. It is composed – as the title states – *a L'Usage des Dames Religieuses* and is not linked to a *cantus firmus*. The presence of two versets for the *Gradual* is unusual: one is a *Trio* and the other (as an *alio modo*) a *Basse de Trompette ou de Cromhorne*.

Kyrie	*Premier Kyrie - Grand Plein Jeu*
	Fugue
	Cromhorne en Taille
	Trio a deux dessus
	Dialogue a deux Chœurs
Gloria	*Gloria Jn Excelsis - Prelude a deux Chœurs*
	Concert pour les Flûtes
	Duo
	Recit tendre Pour le Nazard
	Dialogue de Voix humaine
	Basse de Trompette ou de Cromhorne
	Dessus de Tierce par Accords
	Tierce en Taille
	Dialogue a deux Chœurs
Graduel	*Trio*
Offertorio	*Offerte - Grand Dialogue a trois Chœurs*
Sanctus	*Premier Sanctus - Plein Jeu*
	Second Sanctus - Duo
Elevation	*Elevation - Cromhorne en Taille*
Agnus Dei	*Plein Jeu a deux chœurs pour le premier Agnus Dei*
	Dialogue en Fugue, Pour le second Agnus dej
Deo gratias	*Grand Plein Jeu - Fin de la Messe*
Varia	*Graduel - Basse de Trompette ou de Cromhorne*
	Elevation - Fond d'Orgue

ORGAN

In the frontispiece of the *Messe du 8.ᵉ Ton* Corrette presented himself as *Organiste de l'Eglise Saint Herbland de Rouen*. It is not clear, however, whether he was already *titulaire* or only assistant. The organ of *Saint-Herbland* was built between 1685 and 1688 by Germaine Lefebvre:[486]

Grand Orgue	*Positif*	*Récit* (from c')	*Echo* (from f°)
Bourdon 16	Bordun 8	Cornet V	Bourdon
Montre 8	Montre 4	Trompette	Prestant
Bourdon 8	Flûte 4		Nazard
Prestant	Nasard		Doublette
Nasard	Doublette		Tierce
Doublette	Tierce		Fourn. Cimb. III
Quarte	Larigot		Voix humaine
Tierce	Forniture III		
Fourniture IV	Cymbale II		
Cymbale III	Cromorne		
Cornet			*Pédale* (29 notes)
Trompette			Bourdon 8 [Flûte?]
Clairon			Flûte 4
Vox humaine			Trompette

NICOLAS DE GRIGNY
1672 – 1703

Nicolas de Grigny was born in 1672 in Reims to a family of musicians: his father Louis, his grandfather and an uncle were active as organists in different churches. From 1693, Nicolas became organist of the abbey of *Saint-Denis* (at the time near Paris) where his brother André was sub-prior. According to a periodical of the time, *Le Mercure Galant*, it was in those years that de Grigny would have been a pupil of Lebègue. In 1695 he is registered in the tax book (*Capitation*) as *Maître de Première classe*, along with colleagues such as Dandrieu, Gigault and d'Anglebert. Around 1697 he was appointed organist of the Cathedral of Reims. The improvements to the organ made in 1696 would have been carried out under his direction.

In 1699, at the age of 27, he published his *Premier* (and only) *Livre d'Orgue*, which would later be copied by Johann Sebastian Bach and Johann Gottfried Walther; both of which have come down to us. From 1702, de Grigny was also organist at *Saint-Symphorien "gratuitement et par charité"*. He died in Reims on November 30, 1703 at the age of 31. His father succeeded him as a Cathedral organist.

WORKS

Premier Livre d'Orgue contenant une Messe et les Hymnes des principalles Festes de l'année Composé Par N. De Grigny Organiste de l'Eglise Cathedralle de Reims dédié a Messieurs les Vénérables Prevost, Doyen, Chantre, Chanoines, et Chapitre de l'Eglise Métropolitaine de Reims.

– 1699 –

The *Livre d'Orgue* of de Grigny, a milestone of the French organ repertoire, was reprinted for the first time by Christophe Ballard in 1711. In 1751, almost 50 years after the author's death, it was still in the catalogue of the publisher Jean-Pantaléon Leclerc. The volume contains a complete mass – for the *Fêtes doubles* and therefore based on the *cantus firmus* of the *Missa Cunctipotens genitor* – and *couplets* for the five most common hymns. For a tentative reconstruction of the *alternatim* structure of the *Hymnes*, see pages 49-50.

De Grigny's *Livre d'Orgue* contains numerous typographical errors and inconsistencies that require a careful critical reading by the performer (see page 18).

Messe

Kyrie	Kyrie en taille à 5
	Fugue à 5 qui renferme le chant du Kyrie
	Cromorne en taille à 2 Parties
	Trio en dialogue
	Dialogue sur les Grands Jeux
Gloria	Et in terra pax à 5
	Fugue
	Duo
	Recit de tierce en taille
	Baße de Trompette oû de Cromorne
	Dialogue
	Fugue à 5
	Trio
	Dialogue
Offertoire	Offertoire sur les grands Jeux
Sanctus	Premier Sanctus en taille à 5
	Fugue
	Recit de tierce pour le Benedictus
Elévation	Dialogue de Flûtes pour l'Elévation
Agnus Dei	Premier Agnus
	Dialogue
Communion	Dialogue à 2 Tailles de Cromorne et 2 deßus de Cornet p.r la Cõmunion
[Ita Missa est]	Plain Jeu

Hymnes

Veni creator	*Veni creator en taille à 5*
	Fugue à 5
	Duo
	Récit de Cromorne
	Dialogue sur les grands Jeux
Pange lingua	*Pange lingua en taille à 4*
	Fugue à 5
	Récit du Chant de l'Hymne précédent
Verbum supernum	*[Plein Jeu]*
	Fugue à 5
	Recit en dialogue
	Recit de Basse de trompette oû de Cromorne
Ave maris stella	*[Plein Jeu]*
	Fugue à 5
	Duo
	Dialogue sur les grands Jeux
A solis ortus	*[Plein Jeu]*
	Fugue à 5
	Trio
	Point d'Orgue sur les Grands Jeux

ORGAN

The precise specification of the organ of Reims Cathedral – where de Grigny served from 1696-97 until his death, and where he was active in the year of publication of his *Livre d'Orgue* – is not known. It was a large instrument based on a *Montre 16* and modified or rebuilt in 1647 by Étienne Énocq and enlarged to include three manuals (*Positif, Grand Orgue, Écho*) and pedal. In 1696, perhaps under de Grigny's direction, J. Wisbeck (or Vuisbeck) – a pupil of Clicquot – made some changes, including the addition of a *Récit* with *Cornet* and *Trompette*, a *Larigot* on the *Positif* and a *tirasse* to the *Grand Orgue*. The pedal included a *petit ravalement* to AA, with the contra-A activated by the as C♯ pedal key; it is not clear whether the *ravalement* is the work of Énocq or Wisbeck.[487]

PIERRE DU MAGE
1674 - 1751

Pierre du Mage was born in 1674 in Beauvais, where his father, from whom he received his first musical education, was organist of *Saint-Pierre* Cathedral. Around 1694 he moved to Paris to study with Louis Marchand and in 1703 was appointed *titulaire* of the new organ by Robert Clicquot in *Saint-Quentin*. Seven years later, in

1710, he became organist of the Cathedral of Laon. His duties there included rehearsing the choir and teaching organ to two choirboys, an activity that Du Mage neglected, causing friction with his superiors. After several admonitions, the chapter withheld part of his salary.

In 1719, Du Mage decided to leave the position of organist in order to became *"Conseiller du Roy, contrôleur au grenier à sel et directeur des Economats et Séquestres"* of the diocese of Laon. In 1733 his name appears again in a commission – jointly with Clérambault, Daquin and Antoine Calvière – in charge of evaluating the new organ built by François Thierry at Notre-Dame in Paris, thus proving that he had not completely abandoned his activity as an organist. He died in Laon in 1751.

WORKS

Du Mage apparently wrote two *Livres d'Orgue*. Four years after the publication of his first book, he obtained permission from the Laon Cathedral chapter to publish a *Second Livre d'Orgue*, but no traces of this work are to be found.

Ier Livre d'Orgue, contenant une Suite du Premier Ton,
Dédié a Messieurs les Vénérables Doyen Chanoines et Chapitre de l'Église Roïale de S.^{t}
Quentin. Composé Par le S.^{r} Du Mage Organiste de ladite Eglise.

– 1708 –

The *Ier Livre d'Orgue* was published in 1708 while du Mage was organist in Saint-Quentin and is dedicated to the Canons and the Chapter of that church, as can be read in the frontispiece of the book. In the preface, du Mage explains that he composed it *"selon la sçavant école et dans le goût de l'Jllustre Monsieur Marchand mon Maître"* [*according to the expert teaching and taste of my teacher, the illustrious Monsieur Marchand*].

[1.er ton]   *Plain Ieu*
Fugue
Trio
Tierce en taille
Baße de Trompette
Récit
Duo
Grand Jeu

ORGAN

The organ of *Saint-Quentin*, where du Mage was organist at the time of the publication of his *I.er Livre d'Orgue*, was entirely rebuilt between 1695 and 1703 under the direction of Lebègue, Nivers and François Couperin. The specification at the time would appear to be as follows:[488]

Grand Orgue	*Positif*	*Récit* (from f°)
Montre 16'	Montre 8'	Flûte 8'
Bourdon 16'	Bordun 8'	Bordun 4'
Jeu ouvert 8'	Prestant 4'	Doublette
Bourdon 8'	Flûte 4'	Trompette 8'
Prestant 4'	Nasard	
Flûte 4'	Doublette	**Echo** (from f°)
Grosse Tierce 3 1/5'	Quarte de nasard	Bourdon 8' + Prestant 4' (1 stop)
Nasard 2 2/3'	Tierce	Nazard + Quart + Tierce (1 stop)
Doublette	Larigot	Fourniture III
Quarte de nasard	Forniture IV	Cymbale II
Petite Tierce 1 3/5'	Cymbale III	Cromhorne 8'
Grosse Fourniture III	Trompette 8'	Voix humaine 8'
Petite Fourniture II	Cromorne 8'	
Cymbale IV	Clairon 4'	*Pédale*
Grand Cornet V		Flûte 8'
Trompette 8'		Flûte 4'
Cromorne 8'		Trompette 12'
Vox humaine 8'		Clairon 6'
Clairon 4'		

JEAN-ADAM GUILAIN
c. 1680 – post 1739

Very little is known about the life of Jean-Adam Guilain; not even the dates of his birth and death. His name appears for the first time in 1702 on the occasion of the publication of *"un Air nouveau de la composition de Mr Guilain, fameux organiste"* in *Le Mercure Galant*. In the *Privilège générale* for the print, granted in November 1739, his full name is mentioned – Jean Adam Guillame Freinsberg – suggesting possible German origins.

The collection of *Pieces d'Orgue pour le Magnificat*, the only known organ work of Guilain, is dated 1706 and dedicated to *Monsieur Marchand*, which has led to the hypothesis that Guilain was a pupil of Marchand. In addition to the four *Magnificats* for organ, there are also *Pièces de clavecin d'un goût nouveau*, published in Paris in 1739 and for which he had obtained the aforementioned *Privilège générale*.

WORKS

*Pieces d'Orgue pour le Magnificat sur les huit tons differens de l'Eglise.
Dediées a Monsieur Marchand Organiste de S.ᵗ Honoré,
des RR.PP. Jesuites, et du grand Convent des RR.PP. Cordeliers.
Par M.ʳ Guilain Organiste et Maitre de Clavecin. A Paris. L'An MDCCVI.*

– 1706 –

The *Pieces d'Orgue pour le Magnificat* have come down to us in two manuscripts, both kept at the *Staatsbibliothek* in Berlin. According to musicologists, one of the manuscripts may actually be from the indicated date (1706), whereas the second one would appear to have been written some decades later. The manuscript was probably intended for publication, but never saw the light of day. The title refers to *Les huit tons differens de l'Eglise*, from which one can infer that the author's intention was to compose four other *Magnificats* for the modes V, VI, VII and VIII.

The titles of the *couplets* refer to the Mus ms 30189 held in the *Staatsbibliothek* in Berlin.

Suite du I. Ton	Plein Jeu	Suite du II. Ton	Prelude
	Trio		Tierce en Taille
	Duo		Duo
	Basse de Trompette		Basse de Trompette
	Recit		Trio de Flutes
	Dialogue		Dialogue
	Petit plein Jeu		Petit plein Jeu
Suite du III. Ton	Plein Jeu	Suite du IV. Ton	Plein Jeu
	Quatuor		Cromorne en Taille
	Dialogue de Voix humaine		Duo
	Basse de Trompette		Basse de Cromhorne
	Duo		Trio
	Grand jeu		Dialogue
	Petit plein Jeu		Petit plein Jeu

LOUIS-NICOLAS CLÉRAMBAULT
1676 - 1749

Clérambault was born in Paris in 1676 into a family of musicians. He began his musical studies with his father Dominique – one of the famous *Vingt-Quatre Violons du Roy* – and then continued organ tuition with André Raison, to whom he later dedicated his *Livre d'Orgue*. In 1714 he was the successor to Nivers at the *Maison Royale de Saint-Cyr* as well as at *Saint-Sulpice*. From this time until his death, Clérambault would enjoy great prestige as organist, and even more so as a composer of vocal music. His first publication, printed in 1704, was the *Ier Livre de Pieces de Clavecin*, which includes two pieces in the style of the *prélude non mesuré*. Most of Clérambault's compositional output consists of vocal music, both sacred and secular; including six books of motets, hymns, *Airs spirituels et moraux*, and more than twenty-five secular cantatas and other pieces. He died in Paris in 1749.

WORKS

Premier Livre d'Orgue Contenant Deux Suites du I.^r et du IIe Ton. Dedié a Monsieur Raison Organiste de l'Abbaye Royale de Sainte Genevieve du Mont, Et des R.R. P.P. Jacobins de la rüe St Jacques. Par Mr Clerambault Organiste et Maître de Clavecin.

– 1710 ? –

Clérambault composed a *Premier Livre d'Orgue* (in fact, the only extant organ volume) which was perhaps printed in 1710, or 1714 according to other sources. It contained two cycles, each of seven *couplets* in the first and second mode; their most logical– but not necessarily exclusive – use was as *alternatim* for the *Magnificat*. The collection did not contain a preface but almost all the fourteen pieces gave indications concerning tempo and registrations.

Suite du Premier Ton	Suite du Deuxieme Ton
Grand plein jeu	Plein jeu
Fugue	Duo
Duo	Trio
Trio	Basse de Cromorne
Basse et Dessus de Trompette, ou de Cornet separé, en Dialogue	Flûtes
Récits de Cromorne, et de Cornet separé, en Dialogue	Recit de Nazard
Dialogue sur les grands jeux	Caprice sur les grands jeux

ORGAN

Although Clérambault was *titulaire* of important organs, including *Saint-Sulpice*, in the *Avertissement* contained at the end of the *Livre d'Orgue* he mentioned the possibility of playing his pieces on small instruments with *Jeux coupés*, i.e. stops divided between bass and treble:

J'ai composé ces pieces de maniere qu'on peut les joüer aussi facilement sur un cabinet d'orgue a jeux coupes que sur un grand Orgue, cest pourquoy dans la Basse de trompette, et dans les recits, les accompagnements des jeux doux ne passent pas le milieu du Clavier, non plus que les sujets du Dessus et de la Basse.[489]	I composed these pieces so that they could be easily performed both on a positive organ [cabinet d'orgue] with divided stops as well as on a large instrument; for this reason, in the Basse de Trompette and in the Récits the accompaniment of the Jeux doux does not cross the middle of the keyboard, nor do the subjects in the soprano or the bass.

It may, therefore, be relevant to present the following specification of an 18th century *Cabinet d'orgue* with divided stops:[490]

Positif	*Grand Orgue*	
Bourdon (B et D)	Bourdon	B = Basse
Flûte (B et D)	Prestant	D = dessus
Nasard (D)	Dessus de Flûte allemande	division c'-c#'
Doublette (B et D)	Nasard	
Tierce (D)	Doublette	
Cromorne (B)	Tierce	Tirasse Positif
Trompette de récit (B et D)	Plein-jeu IV	2 tremblants

JEAN-FRANÇOIS DANDRIEU
c. 1682 - 1738

Dandrieu was born into a family of "artist-artisans" and musicians, originally from Angers. His early talent is testified to by the fact that, at the age of five he played before the Duchess of Orléans at the court of *Louis XIV*. In 1704 he was appointed organist at *Saint-Merry* in Paris (formalized as *titulaire* a year later), and later at the church of *Saint-Barthélemy*, where his uncle, Pierre Dandrieu, was already organist. From 1721, he was also one of the four organists at the *Chapelle Royale*.

In addition to various *Livres de Clavecin* and different instrumental collections, Dandrieu published a treatise entitled *Principes de l'Acompagnement du Clavecin*. Several of his pieces, especially for harpsichord, could possibly be attributed to his uncle Pierre. He died in Paris in 1738. He dedicated only one volume to the organ, which was prepared for print shortly before his death and published posthumously in 1739.

WORKS

Premier Livre de Pièces d'Orgue Par Monsieur Dandrieu Organiste de la Chapèle du Roi et des Eglises Paroissiales de S.ᵗ Merri et de S.ᵗ Barthélemi.

– 1739 (posthumous) –

In the *Avertissement* Dandrieu explained that the entire work was divided into two books; in reality the *Second Livre* never saw the light of day. In the present collection the author published six *Suites*, three in a minor and three in a major key. Each *Suite* opens with an *Offertoire*, followed by some versets and then by a *Magnificat* in the same mode. Each of the six *Magnificats* presents an equal number of *couplets* (six). Each *couplet* is also accompanied by information concerning registration and tempo or character. It should be noted that rather than of using traditional ecclesiastical modes, Dandrieu used the modern terminology of major and minor tonalities here.

Pièces en D. La Ré [Mineur]

Ofertoire pour le Jour de Pâques	*Magnificat:* Plein Jeu
Ofertoire	Duo
Fugue sur l'Hymne Ave maris Stella	Trio
Fugue sur l'Hymne des Apôtres	Basse de Trompete
Basse de Cromorne	Flutes
Duo sur la Trompète	Dialogue

Pièces en D. La Ré Majeur

Ofertoire	*Magnificat:* Plein Jeu
Suitte de l'Ofertoire	Duo
Duo en cors de hasse sur la Trompète	Trio
Trio avec la Pedale	Basse et Dessus de Trompète
Duo sur la Trompète	Flutes
	Dialogue

Pièces en G. Ré Sol Mineur

Ofertoire - Suitte de l'Ofertoire	*Magnificat:* Plein jeu
Fugue [I]	Duo
Fugue [II]	Trio
Trio	Basse de Cromorne
Cromorne en Taille	Recit de Nazard
Duo sur la Trompète	Dialogue

Pièces en G. Ré Sol Majeur

Ofertoire	*Magnificat:* Plein Jeu
Tierce en Taille	Duo
Muzète	Trio
	Basse de Trompète
	Flutes
	Dialogue

Pièces en A. Mi La [Mineur]

Ofertoire	*Magnificat:* Plein Jeu
Fugue [I]	Duo
Fugue [II]	Trio
Trio avec la Pedale	Basse et Dessus de Trompete
	Recit de Trompete separée ou de Cromorne
	Dialogue

Pièces en A. Mi La Majeur

Ofertoire	*Magnificat:* Plein Jeu
Suite de l'Ofertoire	Duo
Muzete	Trio
Tierce en Taille	Basse et Dessus de Trompete
Duo sur la Trompète	Flûtes
	Dialogue

FRANÇOIS D'AGINCOURT
1684 - 1758

D'Agincourt was born in Rouen in 1684. He completed his musical studies with Boyvin in Rouen and later with Lebègue in Paris. In 1701 he became organist of the church of *Madeleine-en-la-Cité* in Paris, and, five years later, *titulaire* of the Cathedral of Rouen, his hometown, as successor to Boyvin. He was also appointed organist at the abbey of *Saint-Ouen*, and, in 1714 he was one of the four organists of the *Chapelle Royale*, taking Marchand's place.

Despite his intense activity as an organist, only his *Pièces de Clavecin* (published in 1733) and the *Airs à voix seule et basse continuo* (published in anthological collections in 1713 and 1716) are printed, while his organ works have survived only in manuscript form (although not in autograph).

WORKS

Pieces d'Orgue de M.ʳ D'Agincourt

The only known organ compositions by François d'Agincourt were copied by Père Alexandre Guy Pingré (1711-1796) in a collection preserved in the *Bibliothèque S.ᵗᵉ Geneviève* in Paris. These are 46 small pieces grouped into six *Suites*, ordered by modes. In some of the *Suites* – particularly the *1.ᵉʳ ton* – some *couplets* are presented in two variants.

1.ᵉʳ ton	Plain Jeu	*2.ᵉ Ton*	[Prélude]
	[Plain Jeu]		Recit de Nazard
	Fugue		Duo
	Duo		Basse de Cromorne
	Duo		Concert de Flûtes
	Recit		Dialogue
	Recit		Trio
	Trio		
	Trio		
	Basse de Cromorne	*5.ᵉ Ton*	Plain Jeu
	[Grand jeu]		Plain Jeu
			Fugue
4.ᵉ Ton	Plain Jeu		Duo
	Duo		Cornet
	Trio		Récit de Nazard
	Recit de Nazard		Concert de Flûtes
	Basse de Cromorne		Trio
	Concert de Flûtes		Dialogue
	Dialogue		[Plain Jeu]

6.ᵉ Ton	Plain Jeu	C sol ut mineur	Duo
	Duo		Trio
	Récit de Nazard		Recit de Nazard
	Basse de Cromorne		Concert de Flûtes
	Trio		Dialogue
	Dialogue		

LOUIS-CLAUDE DAQUIN
1694 – 1772

Louis-Claude Daquin (also d'Aquin, Dacquin, d'Acquin) was born in Paris in 1694. An *enfant prodige*, at the age of six he played before *Louis XIV*, and, at eight years of age he directed his motet *Beatus vir* at the *Sainte-Chapelle*. Later he studied under Louis Marchand. At the age of 12 he was appointed organist of the convent of *Petit Saint-Antoine*; in 1727 he secured the position of organist at *Saint-Paul* (competing with Jean-Philippe Rameau); in 1732 he succeeded his teacher Marchand at the *Eglise des Cordeliers*, and in 1739 he took Dandrieu's position at the *Chapelle Royale*.

From 1775, he was one of the organists of *Notre-Dame*. In 1735 he published his *1ᵉʳ livre de pièces de clavecin*. The only organ work that has survived is the *Nouveau Livre de Noëls (Œuvre II)*, published in Paris in 1757. He was also a prolific composer of vocal and instrumental music, both sacred and secular, much of which is now lost. The March 1773 issue of the *Journal encyclopédique* (i.e. a year after Daquin's death) refers to *deux livres d'orgue* by the composer; these too are now lost. In the description one can read:

On avertit que ce sont des fugues à deux ou trois dessus, des pleins jeux à deux pédales, des quatuor, des trio, des duo où les dessus et les basses travaillent tour à tour, des grands chœurs à quatre et cinq, remplis d'imitations ingénieuses, et des transitions inattendues, des chromornes à deux tailles etc.[491]	*Of note, there are fugues with two or three dessus [treble voices], pleins jeux with double pedal, quatuors, trios, duos where the treble and bass take turns playing fast passagges, grands chœurs of four and five voices, full of ingenious imitations and unexpected transitions, chromornes à deux tailles etc.*

WORKS

Nouveau livre de noëls pour l'orgue et le clavecin
Œuvre II

– 1757 –

Despite the fact that the twelve *Noëls* were primarily conceived *pour l'orgue et le clavecin*, Daquin specified that

[...] la plûpart peuvent s'éxécuter sur les Violons, Flutes, Hautbois, &c.[492]	*[...] most can be played with violins, flutes, oboes, etc.*

In the *Affiches* [*announcements*] of November 14, 1757 one can read:

*Ces Noëls sont les mêmes que M. Daquin exécute chaque année sur l'orgue de S. Paul, le dernier dimanche de l'Avent.*⁴⁹³	These Noëls are the same ones that M. Daquin plays every year on the organ of S. Paul on the last Sunday of Advent.

I Noel sur les jeux d'Anches sans tremblant
II Noel en dialogue, Duo, Trio, sur le cornet de récit, les tierces du positif et la pédalle de Flûte
III Noel en Musette, en Dialogue, et en Duo. Très tendrement
IV Noel en Duo, sur les jeux d'Anches, sans tremblant
V Noel en Duo
VI Noel sur les jeux d'Anches, sans tremblant, et en Duo
VII Noel en Trio et en Dialogue, le Cornet de récit de la main droitte, la Tierce du Positif de la main gauche
VIII Noel Etranger, sur les jeux d'anches sans tremblant et en Duo
IX Noel sur les Flûtes
X Noel Grand jeu et Duo
XI Noel en Récit en Taille, sur la Tierce du Positif, avec la Pédalle de Flûte, et en Duo, Lentement et tendrement
XII Noel Suisse, Grand Jeu, et Duo

MICHEL CORRETTE
1707 - 1795

Son of Gaspard Corrette, Michel was born in Rouen in 1707 and was first taught to play by his father. Around 1720 he moved to Paris where he continued his musical studies, probably under either Louis Marchand or Jean-François Dandrieu. From 1726 he occupied the position of organist in several churches, but, for the most part. he dedicated his time to composing vocal and instrumental works, both sacred and secular. He was also director of a music school for which he wrote as many as 17 music *Méthodes*.

He was a prolific composer of organ music. Of note are the three *Livres d'Orgue* (1737, 1750, 1756), two collections of *Noëls* (1741/1753, c. 1783), *VI Concerti a Sei Strumenti Cimbalo ò Organo obligati, tre Violini, Flauto, Alto Viola e Violoncello* (1756) and *XII Offertoires* (1766). In his later works, particularly in the *Pièces pour orgue dans un genre nouveau* (1787), he definitively broke with the classical compositional style. Michel Corrette died in Paris in 1795.

WORKS

Of Michel Corrette's organ works, only the three *Livres d'Orgue*, published between 1737 and 1756, are considered here.

Premier Livre d'Orgue Contenant Quatre Magnificat A l'usage des Dames Religieuses Et utile a ceux qui touchent de cet jnstrument Composé par Monsieur Corrette Organiste de Monseigneur le Grand Prieur de France. Oeuvre XVI.

– 1737 –

The first *Livre d'Orgue* contains *Magnificats* for the first four modes, each consisting of six *couplets*. The pieces that close the third and fourth cycle (the *Fuga doppia* and *Grand jeu* respectively) bear the title *"Cette piece se peut toucher sur le Clavecin"* [This piece can be played on the harpsichord]. In the preface to the volume, Corrette also signals eight pieces from his *Livre de Clavecin* that *"se peuvent toucher sur l'Orgue"* [can be played on the organ].

Magnificat du 1ʳ ton
  Plein jeu
  Duo
  Tierce en Taille
  Basse de Cromhorne
  Trio
  G(rand) jeu

Magnificat du 2ᵉ ton
  Plein jeu
  Duo
  Trio a trois Claviers
  Basse de trompette
  1ʳᵉ Musette [et 2ᵉ Musette]
  Grand jeu

Magnificat du 3ᵉ et 4ᵉ ton
  Plein jeu avec la Pedalle de Trompette pour toucher avec les deux pieds
  Recit de Nazar
  Duo à deux Basses
  Concert de flûtes
  Cromhorne en Taille
  Fuga doppia. Cette piece se peut toucher sur le Clavecin

Magnificat en a Mi la 3♯
très utile aux Dames Religieuses
  Plein jeu
  Duo
  Trio
  Recit de Trompette
  Musette
  Grand jeu que l'on peut jouer à l'Offertoire. Cette piece se peut toucher sur le Clavecin

IIe Livre de Pieces d'Orgue, Contenant le Ve VIe VII et VIII ton, Ce qui Composé avec le I.^r Livre les Huits tons de l'Eglise; A l'Usage des Dames Religieuses Et Utile à ceux qui touchent l'Orgue. On trouve dans le I.^r Livre la Maniere de Mêlanger les Jeux. Par Mr Corrette Chevalier de l'Ordre de Christ. Œuvre XXVI.

– 1750 –

Published 13 years after the *Premier Livre d'Orgue*, this volume is a natural continuation of the first, presenting *Magnificats* for the fifth to the eighth mode.

    5^e Ton   Plein jeu
                  Duo
                  Basse de Trompette [recte: Dialogue de basse et dessus]
                  Musette
                  Tambourin
                  Grand jeu

    VI Ton   Plein Jeu
                  Duo
                  Basse de Trompette [recte: Dialogue de basse et dessus]
                  Recit de Tierce
                  Trio [à deux dessus]
                  Grand jeu - Fuga

    VIIe Ton Plein Jeu
                  Duo
                  Recit de Trompette
                  Trio [à trois claviers]
                  Concert de Flûtes
                  Grand jeu

    VIII. Ton Plein jeu
                  Duo
                  Tierce en Taille
                  Recit de Trompette
                  Musette
                  Fuga [recte: Dialogue]

IIIe Livre d'Orgue de Mr Corrette, Organiste des G.^{ds} Jesuites. Contenant les Messes et les Hymnes de l'Eglise, Pour toucher en Trio sur la Trompette du G.^d Orgue avec le Fleurti sur le plein jeu du positif, et plusieurs des mêmes Plein-chants accomodés en Quatuor pour toucher sur le grand plein jeu avec les Pedalles. Plus des Fugues faciles pour chaqu'hymne de l'année, une suitte du 1.er ton, une Offertoire, les Antiennes de la Vierge avec des petites pieces et le Te Deum en plein-chants.

– 1756 –

The third *Livre d'Orgue* contains four masses, numerous hymns, a short *Suite du 1.^r ton* as well as an *Offertoire* and a *Te Deum*. In the masses, the number of *couplets* is often insufficient to cover the requirements; in the *Kyrie* of the first Mass

(*Solemnel majeur*) Corrette composed only one *couplet* followed by the words *"encore 4 Couplets"*, implying that the others were intended to be improvised. Most of the hymns, in fact, contain not more than one or two *couplets*.

Messe

Messe Solemnel majeur	1.*er* Kyrie (1 couplet, followed by the words *encore 4 Couplets*)
à l'usage Romain et Parisien	Gloria (8 couplets + *un petit plein jeu pour l'Amen*)
	Sanctus (1 couplet)
	Agnus dei (1 couplet)
Messe Solemnel Mineur	Kyrie (1 couplet)
	Le Gloria comme aux Festes Solemnels (no couplet)
	Sanctus (1 couplet)
	Agnus dei (1 couplet)
Messe double	Kyrie (1 couplet, followed by the words *4 Couplets*)
	Gloria (9 couplets)
	Sanctus (1 couplet)
	Agnus dei (1 couplet)
Messe double mineur	Kyrie (1 couplet)
	Gloria (9 couplets)
	Sanctus (2 couplets)
	Agnus dei (1 couplet)
	Grand jeu

Hymnes

Conditor	2 Couplets (*Cantus firmus* in the bass + *Fuga*)
Christe redemptor omnium	2 Couplets (*Cantus firmus* in the bass + *Fuga Grave*)
A solis ortus	2 Couplets (*Cantus firmus* in the bass + *Fuga*)
Ad cœnam	2 Couplets (*Cantus firmus* in the bass + *Fuga Allegro*)
Jesu nostra redemptio	2 Couplets (*Cantus firmus* in the bass + *Fuga Andante*)
Veni Creator	2 Couplets (*Cantus firmus* in the bass + *Fuga Moderato*)
O lux beata trinitas	2 Couplets (*Cantus firmus* in the bass + *Fuga Allegro*)
Pange lingua	2 Couplets (*Cantus firmus* in the bass + *Fuga Trio*)
Sacris solemnis	2 Couplets (*Cantus firmus* in the bass + *Fuga*)
Ave maris stella	2 Couplets (*Cantus firmus* in the bass + *Fuga ad libitum*)
Christe redemptor omnium	2 Couplets (*Cantus firmus* in the bass + *Fuga Largo*)
Exultet	1 Couplet + indication to play the *Fugue* of *Ave Maris Stella*
Urbs jerusalem beata	1 Couplet + indication to play the *Fugue* of *Ad cœnam*
Deus tuorum	1 Couplet + indication to play the *Fugue* of *Ad cœnam*
Iste Confessor	2 Couplets (*Cantus firmus* on the bass voice + *Fuga Allegro*)
Ave verum	4 Couplets
Alma	5 Couplets
Ave Regina	3 Couplets
Regina Cæli	3 Couplets
Salve Regina	5 Couplets
Christe redemptor	1 Couplet (*c.f.* in the bass: *Pedalles de Trompettes*)

A solis ortus	1 *Couplet* (c.f. in the bass: *Pedalles*)
Ad cœnam	1 *Couplet* (c.f. in the bass: *Pedalles*)
Jesu nostra redemptio	1 *Couplet* (c.f. in the bass: *Pedalles*)
Veni Creator	1 *Couplet* (c.f. in the bass: *Pedalles*)
Pange lingua	1 *Couplet* (c.f. in the bass: *Pedalles*)
Ave maris stella	1 *Couplet* (c.f. in the bass: *Pedalles*)
Deus tuorum	1 *Couplet* (c.f. in the bass: *Pedalles*)
Urbs jerusalem beata	2 *Couplets* (c.f. in the bass: *Pedalles* + *Quatuor à deux Claviers*)
Le G.ᵈ Kyrie	2 *Couplets* (c.f. in the bass: *Pedalles* + *Fuga*) related to the 1st *Kyrie*

Varia

Suite du 1.ʳ ton	Plein jeu
	Duo
	Trio [à deux dessus]
	Basse de Trompette [recte: et dessus de Cornet]
	Musette
	Grand Jeu
Offertoire - L'eclatante	[*Grand Jeu*]
Te Deum	16 *Couplets*

CLAUDE-BÉNIGNE BALBASTRE
1724 - 1799

According to the musicologist Érik Kocevar, Claude Balbastre was born in Dijon on December 8, 1724, and not in 1727 as is often reported. He began his musical studies with his father, Bénigne (organist at *Saint-Médard* and then *Saint-Étienne*). In the same town, Claude Rameau (brother of the much more famous Jean-Philippe Rameau) was also organist, and it is likely that he had a great influence on the musical education of the young Balbastre. From 1743 he was organist of Dijon Cathedral; a position he left in 1750 in order to move to Paris. In the French capital, Balbastre had an intense activity as an organist (at *Saint-Roch* and also later at *Notre-Dame* for three months per year), harpsichordist, court musician and composer of diverse musical genres.

Balbastre was known above all for his improvisations on *Noëls*. These improvisations – which attracted a large audience to *St. Roch* – were evidently often too lewd or considered unworthy for a sacred place, which caused the Archbishop to forbid them in 1762. With the French revolution and the fall of the monarchy, Balbastre's musical activity and social status came to an abrupt halt. Balbastre lived out his remaining years in poverty, dying in Paris in 1799.

WORKS

Livre Contenant des Pieces de different Genre d'Orgue Et de Clavecin Par Le S.ʳ Balbastre Organiste de la Cathedralle de Dijon.

– 1749 –

Balbastre published a collection of pieces specifically for organ in 1749, i.e. in his last year in Dijon. The collection is divided into five parts. The first part contains pieces for organ; the second part pieces for harpsichord; the third part pieces for violin and harpsichord; the fourth part three *Noëls* (without titles), while the fifth and last part contains some *Airs Parodies*. As far as the first part is concerned, its 40 pieces are not organized according to any harmonic or formal scheme. Although not specified, in most cases the style is such that the works could certainly be played on either organ or harpsichord. Only the pieces from the first part of the collection, i.e. the organ works, are listed below.

Prelude	*Duo*
Allegro	*Recit*
Gavotte	*Petite Chasse*
Allegro	*Fugue*
Fugue	*Fugue [recte: Basse de Trompette]*
Duo	*Dialogue*
Prelude	*Sonate en Duo*
Fugue	*Trio*
Duo	*Air*
Trio	*Concert de flute avec la voix humaine*
Dialogue	*Grand Jeux*
Duo	*Ariette lante*
Concert de flute et de voix humaine	*Trio*
Fugue	*Duo*
Ariette lante	*Trio*
Prelude	*Duo*
Trio	*Trio*
Fugue	*Trio a trois mains*
Trio	*Trio de flute et de voix humaine*
Duo	*Tapage*

Magnificat des huit Tonts De La composition du Sieur Balbastre.

This is the manuscript of the private collection of Beaudesson-Noël published in 2016 in facsimile by *Fuzeau* and containing two complete collections of *Magnificats* on the eight modes (i.e. 16 cycles in total), plus an additional *Magnificat du 1ᵉʳ Ton*. With the exception of this last piece, all other *Magnificats* start with a simple harmonization of the *plainchant* rather than the traditional, opening *Plein Jeu*. The second part of the manuscript is dated 1750.

Magnificat des huit Tonts De La composition du Sieur Balbastre

Magnificat du 1er ton	[harmonized plainchant] Duo Récit de flute Fugue Récit [de flute, basse de voix humaine] Basse de trompette Grand jeu	Magnificat du 2e ton	[harmonized plainchant] Duo Recit Trio Duo Prelude Fugue
Magnificat du 3e ton	[harmonized plainchant] Duo Recit Dialogue [de Grand Jeu et p.j.] Duo Prelude Rondot & Grands Jeux	Magnificat du 4e ton	[harmonized plainchant] Duo Recit Fugue [Récit de] Cornet Flute [et] Voix humaine [Dialogue de] petit jeu [et] G.J.
Magnificat du 5e ton	[harmonized plainchant] Duo Basse de trompette Recit Dialogue grand jeu Prelude [grand jeu - pe.j.]	Magnificat du 6e ton	[harmonized plainchant] Duo Recit [de] flute [et] V. h. Basse de trompette [Récit de] Cromorne Grand Jeu
[Magnificat du 7e ton]	[harmonized plainchant] Duo Recit Basse de trompette Jeux doux Fugue	Magnificat du 8e ton	Prélude / harmonized plainchant Duo Tierce en Taille Grand Jeu Eco Recit Fugue

Huit Magnificat De la Composition du Sr Balbastre en Lannee 1750

[Magnificat du 1er ton]	[harmonized plainchant] Duo Recit de flute Basse de Trompette Recit Grands Jeux en Dialogue	Magnificat du 2e ton	[harmonized plainchant] Duo sur le Cornet Basse de Trompette [Récit de] Cornet Grand Jeu
Magnificat du 3e ton	[harmonized plainchant] Duo Muzette Basse de Trompette Recit de Cornet Fugue	Magnificat du 4e ton	[harmonized plainchant] R[écit] Duo Basse de Trompette Trio Basse de Trompette
Magnificat du 5e ton	[harmonized plainchant] Duo Trio Basse de Trompette Trio [à 3 claviers] Fugue	Magnificat du 6e ton	[harmonized plainchant] Duo Recit Basse de cromorne Trio Grands Jeux en Dialogue

[Magnificat du 7ᵉ ton]	[harmonized plainchant] Récit [de] flute [et] Basse de violle Fugue Basse de Trompette Trio Dialogue	Magnificat du 8ᵉ ton	[harmonized plainchant] Duo Trio Basse de trompette Recit Fugue
Magnificat du 1ᵉʳ ton	Tierce en Taille [recte: Récit] Duo Fugue Trio Grand Jeu		

---

[470] Leguy 1997, ii.
[471] Degrutère 1992, 8.
[472] Guillet 1610, 4.
[473] Roberday 1660, a ij.
[474] Roberday 1660, a iij.
[475] Gigault 1682, 21.
[476] http://organ-au-logis.pagesperso-orange.fr/Pages/Abecedaire/StNicolas.html (accessed 7.12.2018).
[477] Lescat 1995, 10-11.
[478] Saint-Arroman 1994, 16.
[479] Degrutère 2004, VIII.
[480] Degrutère 2004, XI.
[481] Lescat 1999, 6.
[482] Lescat 1990, VIII-XI.
[483] Saint-Arroman 1990, XXXIII.
[484] Tschebourkina 2010, 173.
[485] Lescat 1991, 7-9.
[486] Degrutère 1991, 10-11.
[487] Saint-Arroman 2001, XII.
[488] Saint-Arroman 1995, 9.
[489] Clérambault c. 1710, 139.
[490] Lescat 1989, 6.
[491] Daquin 1757, 5.
[492] Daquin 1757, frontispiece, without page number.
[493] Daquin 1757, 4.

ILLUSTRATIONS

p. 5	Guillaume Louis Pécour: *Nouveau Recüeil de Dance de Bal et celle de Ballet* (Paris, c. 1713), p. 86.
p. 18	Nicolas De Grigny: *Et in terra pax à 5* (fragment) and *Dialogue sur les Grands Jeux* (fragment), taken from the facsimile edition *"Nicolas De Grigny: Premier Livre d'Orgue"*, p. XXI. Anne Fuzeau Productions (Courlay 2001), www.annefuzeau.com
p. 39	Henri du Mont: *Kyrie, Messa du Sixiesme Ton*, da *Cinq Messes en Plain-Chant* (Paris, c. 1669), p. 27.
p. 59-61 and 64	Photographs taken by the author
p. 71	Marin Mersenne: *Harmonie Universelle*, taken from the facsimile Fuzeau in: *Méthodes & Traités, Série I, France 1600-1800*, Volume I, p. 68, Anne Fuzeau Productions (Courlay 2005), www.annefuzeau.com
p. 72	Marin Mersenne: *Harmonie Universelle*, taken from the facsimile Fuzeau in: *Méthodes & Traités, Série I, France 1600-1800*, Volume I, p. 80, Anne Fuzeau Productions (Courlay 2005), www.annefuzeau.com
p. 73	Lambert Chaumont: *Methode d'accorder le Clavessin*, taken from the facsimile Fuzeau in: *Méthodes & Traités, Série I, France 1600-1800*, Volume II, p. 66, Anne Fuzeau Productions (Courlay 2005), www.annefuzeau.com
p. 216	Gilles Jullien: *Premier Livre d'Orgue*, taken from the facsimile Fuzeau in: *Méthodes & Traités, Série I, France 1600-1800*, Volume II, p. 52, Anne Fuzeau Productions (Courlay 2005), www.annefuzeau.com
p. 220	Étienne Loulié: *Elements ou Principes de Musique* (Christophe Ballard, Paris 1696), pp. 82-83.
p. 225	Louis Couperin: *Prelude de Mr Couperin, Manuscrit Bauyn*, p. 6.
p. 225	Nicolas Lebègue: *Prelude en d la re sol, Pieces de Clavessin* (Paris 1677), p. 1.
p. 230	Jean Henry D'Anglebert: *Pieces de clavecin* (Paris 1689), taken from the facsimile Fuzeau in: *Méthodes & Traités, Série I, France 1600-1800*, Volume II, p. 47, Anne Fuzeau Productions (Courlay 2005), www.annefuzeau.com
p. 240	François Couperin: *L'Art de Toucher le Clavecin* (Paris 1716), p. 74.
p. 263	Jean-Philippe Rameau: *Pièces de Clavessin avec une Méthode pour la Mechanique des Doigts* (Louise Roussel, Paris 1724), table, without page number.

BIBLIOGRAPHY

Anonymous from Nancy	Anonymous: *Estat des jeuz que contient l'orgue de Sainct-Epvre* (document without date). Archives de la ville de Nancy, cote GG2. In: http://hydraule.org/bureau/biblio/lopes/tables.pdf (accessed 7.12.2018)
Bacilly 1668	Bacilly, Bénigny de: *Remarques curieuses sur l'art de bien Chanter*. Paris: 1668.
Bourgeois 1550	Bougeois, Loys: *Le droict chemin de la musique*. Genève: 1550
Boyvin 1690	Boyvin, Jacques: *Premier Livre d'Orgue Contenant les huit Tons A l'Usage Ordinaire de l'Eglise* (Paris 1690). Facsimile edition in: Méthodes & Traités, Série I, France 1600-1800, Volume II. Courlay: Fuzeau 2005.
Boyvin 1700	Boyvin, Jacques: *Second Livre d'Orgue contenant les huit tons a l'usage de l'Eglise* (Paris 1700). Facsimile edition in: Méthodes & Traités, Série I, France 1600-1800, Volume II. Courlay: Fuzeau 2005.
Brossard 1703	Brossard, Sébastien de: *Dictionaire de Musique, contenant une explication des Termes Grecs, Latins, Italiens, & François les plus usitez dans la Musique*. Paris: Christophe Ballard 1703.
Caeremoniale FF. Minorum 1669	Cæremoniale ecclesiasticum ad usum FF. Minorum (Paris 1669). Facsimile edition in: Méthodes & Traités, Série I, France 1600-1800, Volume I. Courlay: Fuzeau 2005.
Caeremoniale Monasticum 1680	Cæremoniale Monasticum, jussu et auctoritate capituli généralis congregationis Sancti Mauri ordinis S. Benedicti editum (Paris 1680). Facsimile edition in: Méthodes & Traités, Série I, France 1600-1800, Volume II. Courlay: Fuzeau 2005.
Caeremoniale Monasticum Romano 1634	Cæremoniale Monasticum Romano (Paris 1634). Facsimile edition in: Méthodes & Traités, Série I, France 1600-1800, Volume I. Courlay: Fuzeau 2005.
Cérémonial de Bourges 1708	Cérémonial de Bourges (Bourges 1708). Facsimile edition in: Méthodes & Traités, Série I, France 1600-1800, Volume II. Courlay: Fuzeau 2005.
Cérémonial de Toul 1700	Cérémonial de Toul (Toul 1700). Facsimile edition in: Méthodes & Traités, Série I, France 1600-1800, Volume II. Courlay: Fuzeau 2005.
Chaumont 1695	Chaumont, Lambert: *Pieces D'orgue sur les 8 Tons* (Liège 1695). Facsimile edition in: Méthodes & Traités, Série I, France 1600-1800, Volume II. Courlay: Fuzeau 2005.
Clérambault c. 1710	Clérambault, Louis-Nicolas : *Premier Livre d'Orgue Contenant deux Suites du I.r et du II.e Ton* (Paris c. 1714). Facsimile edition in: Méthodes & Traités, Série I, France 1600-1800, Volume II. Courlay: Fuzeau 2005.
Corrette 1703	Corrette, Gaspard: *Messe du 8.ᵉ Ton pour l'Orgue* (Paris 1703). Facsimile edition in: Méthodes & Traités, Série I, France 1600-1800, Volume II. Courlay: Fuzeau 2005.
Corrette 1737	Corrette, Michel: *Premier Livre d'Orgue* (Paris 1737). Facsimile edition in: Méthodes & Traités, Série I, France 1600-1800, Volume II. Courlay: Fuzeau 2005.
Corrette 1753	Corrette, Michel: *Le Maitre de Clavecin pour l'Accompagnement, Methode Theorique et Pratique*. Paris: 1753.

Couperin 1713	Couperin, François: *Pieces De Clavecin composées par Monsieur Couperin Organiste de la Chapelle du Roy, etc. Et Gravées par Du Plessy. Premier Livre.* Paris: 1713.
Couperin 1716	Couperin, François: *L'Art de Toucher le Clavecin par Monsieur Couperin Organiste du Roy, etc.* Paris: 1716.
Couperin 1722	Couperin, François: *Troisième Livre de pièces de Clavecin composé par Monsieur Couperin.* Paris: 1722.
Daquin 1757	Daquin, Louis-Claude: *Nouveau Livre de Noëls pour l'orgue et le clavecin* (Paris 1757). Fac-similé Jean-Marc Fuzeau. La Musique Classique Française de 1650 à 1800. Collection publiée sous la direction de Jean Saint-Arroman. Courlay: Fuzeau 1993.
D'Alembert 1752	D'Alembert, Jean-Le Rond: *Élémens de musique, theorique et pratique, suivant les principes de Monsieur Rameau* (Paris: David, 1752); reprint ed., New York: Broude Brothers, 1966.
D'Anglebert 1689	D'Anglebert, Jean Henry: *Pieces de clavecin* (Paris 1689). Facsimile edition in: Méthodes & Traités, Série I, France 1600-1800, Volume II. Courlay: Fuzeau 2005.
Degrutère 1991	Degrutère, Marcel: *L'orgue de Gaspard Corrette*. In: *Gaspard Corrette, Messe du 8ᵉ Ton pour l'Orgue.* Fac-similé Jean-Marc Fuzeau. La Musique Française Classique de 1650 à 1800. Collection publiée sous la direction de Jean Saint-Arroman. Courlay: Fuzeau 1991.
Degrutère 1992	Degrutère, Marcel: *Présentation*. In: *Jehan Titelouze, Hymnes de l'Eglise pour toucher sur l'Orgue.* Fac-similé Jean-Marc Fuzeau. La Musique Française Classique de 1650 à 1800. Collection publiée sous la direction de Jean Saint-Arroman. Courlay: Fuzeau 1992.
Degrutère 2004	Degrutère, Marcel: *Présentation*. In: *Jacques Boyvin, Premier Livre d'Orgue 1690.* Fac-similé Jean-Marc Fuzeau. La Musique Française Classique de 1650 à 1800. Collection publiée sous la direction de Jean Saint-Arroman. Courlay: Fuzeau 2004.
Delair 1690	Delair, Denis: *Traité d'accompagnement pour le Théorbe et le Clavecin.* Paris 1690. Facsimile reprint. Genève: Minkoff 1972.
Denis 1643	Denis, Jean: *Traité de l'accord de l'espinette.* Paris: 1643.
Dom Bédos 1766-1778	Dom Bédos de Celles, François: *L'Art du Facteur d'Orgues* (Paris, 1ᵃ parte 1766; 2ᵃ e 3ᵃ parte 1770; 4ᵃ parte 1778). Facsimile edition in: Méthodes & Traités, Série I, France 1600-1800, Volume III. Courlay: Fuzeau 2005.
Dom Pierre 1669	Dom Pierre de Sainte Catherine: *Ceremonial Monastique des Religieuses de l'Abbaye Royale de Montmartre lez Paris* (Paris 1669). Facsimile edition in: Méthodes & Traités, Série I, France 1600-1800, Volume I. Courlay: Fuzeau 2005.
Douglass 1995	Douglass, Fenner: *The language of the Classical French Organ,* New and Expanded Edition. New Haven and London: Yale University Press 1995.
Dufourcq 1978	Dufourcq, Norbert: *Le Livre de l'Orgue Français 1589-1789, Tome III, La facture du Préclassicisme au Préromantisme.* Paris: A. & J. Picard 1978.
Du Mont 1669	Du Mont, Henry: *Cinq Messes en Plain-Chant.* 1ˢᵗ edition. Paris: Robert Ballard 1669.

Engramelle 1775	Engramelle, Marie-Dominique-Joseph: *La Tonotechnie ou l'art de noter les Cylindres* (Paris 1775). Facsimile edition in: Méthodes & Traités, Série I, France 1600-1800, Volume II. Courlay: Fuzeau 2005.
Frescobaldi 1635	Frescobaldi, Girolamo: *Fiori Musicali* (Venezia 1635). Edizione moderna a cura di Christopher Stembridge. Padova, Armelin Musica, 1997.
Gallat-Morin 1988	Gallat-Morin, Elisabeth: *Le livre d'orgue de Montréal. Un manuscrit de musique française classique.* Paris: Aux Amateurs de Livres 1988.
Gigault 1682	Gigault, Nicolas: *Livre de Musique dedié a la tres S$^{te.}$ Vierge* (Paris 1682). Facsimile edition in: Méthodes & Traités, Série I, France 1600-1800, Volume IV. Courlay: Fuzeau 2005.
Gigault 1685	Gigault, Nicolas: *Livre de Musique pour l'Orgue* (Paris 1685). Facsimile edition in: Méthodes & Traités, Série I, France 1600-1800, Volume II. Courlay: Fuzeau 2005.
Gilbert-Moroney 1989	Gilbert, Kenneth e Moroney, Davitt: *Preface to the revised edition.* In: *Œuvres complètes de François Couperin, III, Pièces d'Orgue.* Monaco: Édition de l'Oiseau-Lyre 1989 (second printing).
Gorenstein-Boyvin	Gorenstein, Nicolas: *Jacques Boyvin: Une Introduction à ses deux Livres d'Orgue.* Paris: Chanvrelin (without date but post 1997).
Gorenstein-Grigny	Gorenstein, Nicolas: *Nicolas de Grigny, Livre d'orgue.* (Prefazione). Organa Gallica. Fleurier: Editions du Triton 1994.
Guillet 1610	Guillet, Charles: *Vingt-Quatre Fantasies, a Quatre Parties, disposees selon l'ordre des douze Modes* (Paris 1610). Modern edition by Maurizio Gavioli (January 2012) in: imslp.com (accessed 7.12.2018)
Gravet 1996	Gravet, Nicole: *L'orgue et l'art de la registration en France du XVIe siècle au début du XIXe siècle.* Chatenay Malabry: Ars Musicae 1996.
Hardouin 1973	Hardouin, Pierre: *Le grand orgue de Notre-Dame de Paris.* Kassel: Bärenreiter, 1973
Hardouin 1996	Hardouin, Pierre: *Le Grand Orgue de l'Église Saint-Gervais a Paris,* Instruments Historiques, Série Les Orgues dirigée par Jean-Christophe Tosi. Courlay: Éditions Fuzeau Classique 1996.
Hotteterre 1719	Hotteterre-le-Romain, Jacques: *L'art de preluder sur la Flûte Traversier.* Paris: 1719.
Jullien 1690	Jullien, Gilles: *Premier Livre d'Orgue* (Chartres 1690). Facsimile edition in: Méthodes & Traités, Série I, France 1600-1800, Volume II. Courlay: Fuzeau 2005.
Kocevar 2016	Kocevar, Érik: *Claude Balbastre (1724-1799).* In: *Magnificat des huit Tonts De La composition du Sieur Balbastre. Manuscrit inédit Beaudesson-Noël.* Collection privée. Fac-similé Jean-Marc Fuzeau. La musique Française Classique de 1650 à 1800. Collection publiée sous la direction de Jean Saint-Arroman. Bressuire: Fuzeau 2016.
L'Affilard 1717	L'Affilard, Michel: *Principes tres-faciles pour bien apprendre la musique.* Paris: J.-B.-Christophe Ballard 1717.
Latry 2016	Latry, Olivier: *Caractéristiques des danses en France aux XVIIe et XVIIIe siècles.* 2016. In: https://www.orgue-en-france.org/wp-content/uploads/2016/08/caracteristiques-danses-france.pdf (accessed 7.12.2018)

Lebègue 1676	Lebègue, Nicolas-Antoine: *Les Pieces d'Orgue* (Paris 1676). Facsimile edition in: Méthodes & Traités, Série I, France 1600-1800, Volume II. Courlay: Fuzeau 2005.
Leguy 1997	Leguy, Jacques: *Préface*. In: *Eustache du Caurroy, Fantaisies a 5. Transcription pour Orgue, Présentation et Commentaire de Jacques Leguy*. Chatenay Malabry: Ars Musicae 1997.
Lescat 1989	Lescat, Philippe: *Les orgues de Clérambault*. In: *Louis-Nicolas Clérambault, Premier livre d'orgue*. Fac-similé Jean-Marc Fuzeau. La musique française de 1650 à 1800. Collection publiée sous la direction de Jean Saint-Arroman. Courlay: Fuzeau 1989.
Lescat 1990	Lescat, Philippe: *Biographie de Louis Marchand*. In: *Louis Marchand, Pièces d'ordue manuscrites (manuscrit de Versailles)*. Fac-similé Jean-Marc Fuzeau. La musique Française classique de 1650 à 1800. Collection publiée sous la direction de Jean Saint-Arroman. Courlay: Fuzeau 1990.
Lescat 1991	Lescat, Philippe: *Vie et œuvre de Gaspard Corrette*. In: *Gaspard Corrette, Messe du 8ᵉ Ton pour l'Orgue*. Fac-similé Jean-Marc Fuzeau. La Musique Française Classique de 1650 à 1800. Collection publiée sous la direction de Jean Saint-Arroman. Courlay: Fuzeau 1991.
Lescat 1995	Lescat, Philippe: *Les orgues de Lebègue*. In: *Nicolas-Antoine Lebègue, Second Livre d'Orgue*. Fac-similé Jean-Marc Fuzeau. La musique française classique de 1650 à 1800. Collection publiée sous la direction de Jean Saint-Arroman. Courlay: Fuzeau 1995.
Lescat 1999	Lescat, Philippe: *Notice bibliographique*. In: *François Couperin, Pièces d'Orgue*. Fac-similé Jean-Marc Fuzeau. La musique française de 1650 à 1800. Collection publiée sous la direction de Jean Saint-Arroman. Courlay: Fuzeau 1999.
Lescat 2000	Lescat, Philippe: *Les orgues de Dandrieu*. In: *Jean-François Dandrieu, Premier Livre de Pièces d'Orgue*. Fac-similé Jean-Marc Fuzeau. La Musique Classique Française de 1650 à 1800. Collection publiée sous la direction de Jean Saint-Arroman. Courlay: Fuzeau 1994/2000.
Loulié 1696	Loulié, Étienne: *Elements ou Principes de Musique, mis dans un nouvel Ordre*. Paris: Christophe Ballard 1696.
Manuscrit de Bourges	Anonymous: *Meslange Des Jeux de lorgue de Leglize de Bourges* (undated manuscript, estimated late 17th-early 18th century). Facsimile edition in: Méthodes & Traités, Série I, France 1600-1800, Volume II. Courlay: Fuzeau 2005.
Marais 1701	Marais, Marin: *Deuxième livre de pièces de viole*. Paris: 1701.
Marissal 1996	Marissal, Guy: *Présentation*. In: *Livre d'Orgue de Limoges*. Fac-similé Jean-Marc Fuzeau. La Musique Classique Française de 1650 à 1800. Collection publiée sous la direction de Jean Saint-Arroman. Courlay: Fuzeau 1996.
Mersenne 1636	Mersenne, Marin: *Harmonie Universelle* (Paris 1636). Facsimile edition in: Méthodes & Traités, Série I, France 1600-1800, Volume I. Courlay: Fuzeau 2005.
Mielke 1996	Mielke, Andreas: *Untersuchungen zur Alternatim-Orgelmesse*. 2 Bände. Kassel: Bärenreiter 1996.

Montéclair 1736	Montéclair, Michel Pignolet de: *Principes de Musique. Divisez en quatre partie.* Paris: 1736.
Moucherel 1734	Moucherel, Christophe: *Memoire Instructif pour faire les Devis, Desseins, Plans, Marchez & Receptions des Orgues* (Rodez 1734). Facsimile edition in: Méthodes & Traités, Série I, France 1600-1800, Volume II. Courlay: Fuzeau 2005.
Muffat 1698	Muffat, Georg: *Florilegium Secundum* (Passau 1698). In: Kolneder, Walter: *Georg Muffat zur Aufführungspraxis.* Sammlung Musikwissenschaftlicher Abhandlungen. Band 50. Baden-Baden: Verlag Valentin Koerner 1990.
Neumann 1993	Neumann, Frederick: *Performance Practices of the Seventeenth and Eighteenth Centuries.* New York: Schirmer Books 1993.
Nivers 1665	Nivers, Guillaume-Gabriel: *Livre d'Orgue Contenant Cent Pieces de tous les Tons de l'Eglise* (Paris 1665). Facsimile edition in: Méthodes & Traités, Série I, France 1600-1800, Volume I. Courlay: Fuzeau 2005.
Nivers 1687	Nivers, Guillaume-Gabriel: *Graduale Romano [...] Operâ & Studio Guillelmi Gabrielis Nivers.* Parigi: 1687.
Nivers 1689	Nivers, Guillaume-Gabriel: *Motets à voix seule, accompagnée de la basse continue, et quelques autres motets à deux voix, propres pour les religieuses. Avec l'art d'accompagner sur la basse continue, pour l'orgue et le clavecin. Par le sieur Nivers, organiste de la Chapelle du roy et de l'église Saint-Sulpice.* Paris: 1689.
Olier 1657	Olier, Jean-Jacques: *L'esprit des cérémonies de la messe* (1657). Reprint as ebook. ISBN epub: 9791033605195. Éditions Tempora, 2009.
Panetta 1987	Panetta, Vincent J. Jr: *Treatise on harpsichord tuning by Jean Denis.* Translated and edited by Vincent J. Panetta, Jr.. Cambridge: Cambridge University Press 1987.
Piroye 1712	Piroye, Charles: *Pieces Choisies de la Composition de Mr Piroye.* Paris: Guilleaume Cavelier 1712.
Ponsford 2011	Ponsford, David: *French Organ Music in the Reign of Louis XIV.* Cambridge University Press 2011.
Pruitt 1986	Pruitt, William: *A 17th-Century French Manuscript on Organ Performance.* Early Music, vol. 14, no. 2, 1986, pp. 237–251.
Raison 1688	Raison, André: *Livre d'Orgue* (Paris 1688). Facsimile edition in: Méthodes & Traités, Série I, France 1600-1800, Volume II. Courlay: Fuzeau 2005.
Rameau 1724	Rameau, Jean-Philippe: *Pièces de Clavessin avec une Méthode pour la Mechanique des Doigts.* Paris: 1724.
Rameau 1726	Rameau, Jean-Philippe: *Nouveau Système de Musique Theorique, Où l'on découvre le Principe de toutes les Regles necessaires à la Pratique, Pour servir d'Introduction au Traité de l'Harmonie.* Paris: J.-B.-Christophe Ballard 1726. Reprint ed. in: Jean-Philippe Rameau, Complete Theoretical Writings, Miscellanea, vol. 2, n.p.: American Institute of Musicology, 1967.
Rameau 1725	Rameau, Pierre: *Le Maître a Danser.* Paris: 1725.
Roberday 1660	Roberday, François: *Fugues, et Caprices, a Quatre Parties.* Paris: 1660.
Rousseau 1768	Rousseau, Jean-Jacques: *Dictionnaire de Musique.* Paris: 1768.

Saint-Arroman 1988/I	Saint-Arroman, Jean: *L'interprétation de la musique français 1661-1789. Volume I. Dictionnaire d'interprétation (Initiation).* Paris 1983-1988. Reprint Genève: Slatkine 2016.
Saint-Arroman 1988/II	Saint-Arroman, Jean: *L'interprétation de la musique français 1661-1789. Volume II. L'interprétation de la musique pour orgue.* Paris 1983-1988. Reprint Genève: Slatkine 2016.
Saint-Arroman 1990	Saint-Arroman, Jean: *L'écriture des manuscrits.* In: *Louis Marchand, Pièces d'orgue manuscrites (manuscrit de Versailles).* Fac-similé Jean-Marc Fuzeau. La musique française classique de 1650 à 1800. Collection publiée sous la direction de Jean Saint-Arroman. Courlay: Fuzeau 1990.
Saint-Arroman 1994	Saint-Arroman, Jean: *Les registrations de Nivers.* In: *Guillaume-Gabriel Nivers, 3. Livre d'Orgue des huit tons de l'église.* Fac-similé Jean-Marc Fuzeau. La musique française de 1650 à 1800. Collection publiée sous la direction de Jean Saint-Arroman. Courlay: Fuzeau 1994.
Saint-Arroman 1995	Saint-Arroman, Jean: *Pierre Du Mage, Premier Livre d'Orgue.* Fac-similé Jean-Marc Fuzeau. La musique française de 1650 à 1800. Collection publiée sous la direction de Jean Saint-Arroman. Courlay: Fuzeau 1995.
Saint-Arroman 2001	Saint-Arroman, Jean: *Nicolas de Grigny, Premier Livre d'Orgue.* Fac-similé Jean-Marc Fuzeau. La musique française de 1650 à 1800. Collection publiée sous la direction de Jean Saint-Arroman. Courlay: Fuzeau 2001.
Saint-Lambert 1702	Saint-Lambert, Monsieur de: *Les Principes du Clavecin.* Amsterdam: 1702.
Schünemann 1922	Schünemann, Georg: *Matthaeus Hertel's theoretische Schriften.* In: *Archiv für Musikwissenschaft.* 4. Jahrgang 1922, pp. 336–358.
Sonnet 1662	Sonnet, Martin: Cæremoniale Parisiense (Paris 1662). Facsimile edition in: Méthodes & Traités, Série I, France 1600-1800, Volume I. Courlay: Fuzeau 2005.
Tchebourkina 2010	Tschebourkina, Marina: *L'Orgue de la Chapelle royale de Versailles, Trois siècles d'histoire.* Coutances/Paris: Natives 2010.
Titelouze 1623	Titelouze, Jehan: *Hymnes de l'Eglise pour toucher sur l'Orgue* (Paris 1623). Facsimile edition in: Méthodes & Traités, Série I, France 1600-1800, Volume I. Courlay: Fuzeau 2005.
Titelouze 1626	Titelouze, Jehan: *Le Magnificat, ou Cantique de la Vierge pour toucher sur l'Orgue* (Paris 1626). Facsimile edition in: Méthodes & Traités, Série I, France 1600-1800, Volume I. Courlay: Fuzeau 2005.
Vanmackelberg 1967	Vanmackelberg, Maurice: *Les Orgues de Saint-Martin à Saint-Valéry-sur-Somme.* Recherches sur la Musique Française Classique 7 (1967). In: http://www.walcker-stiftung.de/Downloads/ Registrierungs-anweisungen/Registrierung_Saint-Valery-sur-Somme_1602.pdf (accessed 7.12.2018)

MUSICAL WORKS AND EDITIONS

Balbastre, Cl.-Bénigne	*Livre ... different Genre* (1749)	Facsimile c/o IMSLP Petrucci Music Library
Balbastre, Cl.-Bénigne	*Magnificat des huit Tonts*	Anne Fuzeau Productions, 2016
Boyvin, Jacques	*Premier Livre d'Orgue* (1690)	Éditions J.M. Fuzeau, 2004
Boyvin, Jacques	*Second Livre d'Orgue* (1700)	Les Éditions Outremontaises, 2012
Chaumont, Lambert	*Pieces D'Orgue* (1695)	Anne Fuzeau Productions, 2005
Clérambault, L.-Nicolas	*Premier Livre d'Orgue* (1710?)	Éditions J.M. Fuzeau, 1989
Corrette, Gaspard	*Messe du 8.ᵉ Ton* (1703)	Éditions J.M. Fuzeau, 1991
Corrette, Michel	*Premier Livre d'Orgue* (1737)	Facsimile c/o IMSLP Petrucci Music Library
Corrette, Michel	*Nouveau Livre de Noëls* (1740)	Les Éditions Outremontaises, 2008
Corrette, Michel	*II.ᵉ Livre* (1750)	Facsimile c/o IMSLP Petrucci Music Library
Corrette, Michel	*Nouveau Livre de Noëls* (1753)	Anne Fuzeau Productions, 2014
Corrette, Michel	*III.ᵉ Livre d'Orgue* (1756)	Facsimile c/o IMSLP Petrucci Music Library
Couperin, François	*Pieces d'Orgue - Paroisses* (1690)	Éditions J.M. Fuzeau, 1986
Couperin, François	*Pieces d'Orgue - Couvents* (1690)	Éditions J.M. Fuzeau, 1986
Couperin, Louis	*Pièces d'Orgue*	Éditions de l'Oiseau-Lyre, 2003
Dandrieu, J.-François	*Premier Livre* (1739)	Éditions J.M. Fuzeau, 1994/2000
D'Anglebert, J.-Henry	*Pieces de Clavecin* (1689)	Anne Fuzeau Productions, 2005
De Grigny, Nicolas	*Premier Livre d'Orgue* (1699)	Éditions J.M. Fuzeau, 2001
Du Caurroy, Eustache	*Fantasies a 3, 4, 5 et 6 parties* (1610)	Facsimile c/o IMSLP Petrucci Music Library
Du Mage, Pierre	*I.ᵉʳ Livre d'Orgue* (1708)	Éditions J.M. Fuzeau, 1989
Geoffroy, J.-N. (attrib.)	*Livre d'Orgue*	Éditions Heugel, 1974
Gigault, Nicolas	*Livre ... Sᵗᵉ Vierge* (1682)	Les Éditions Outremontaises, 2012
Gigault, Nicolas	*Livre ... pour l'Orgue* (1685)	Facsimile c/o IMSLP Petrucci Music Library
Guilain, Jean-Adam	*Suites pour le Magnificat*	Éditions J.M. Fuzeau, 2002
Guillet, Charles	*Vingt-quatre fantasies* (1610)	Maurizio M. Gavioli 2012
Jullien, Gilles	*Premier Livre d'Orgue* (1690)	Facsimile c/o IMSLP Petrucci Music Library
Lebègue, Nicolas	*Les Pieces d'Orgue* (1676)	Facsimile c/o IMSLP Petrucci Music Library
Lebègue, Nicolas	*Second Livre d'Orgue* (c. 1678)	Éditions J.M. Fuzeau, 1995
Lebègue, Nicolas	*Troisieme Livre d'Orgue* (1685)	Facsimile c/o IMSLP Petrucci Music Library
Marchand, Louis	*Pieces choisies pour l'Orgue*	Éditions J.M. Fuzeau, 1989
Marchand, Louis	*Manuscrit de Versailles*	Éditions J.M. Fuzeau, 1990
Nivers, G.-Gabriel	*Livre d'Orgue* (1665)	Facsimile c/o IMSLP Petrucci Music Library
Nivers, G.-Gabriel	*2. Livre d'Orgue* (1667)	Éditions J.M. Fuzeau, 1992
Nivers, G.-Gabriel	*3. Livre d'Orgue* (1675)	Éditions J.M. Fuzeau, 1994
Raison, André	*Livre d'Orgue* (1688)	Éditions J.M. Fuzeau, 1993
Raison, André	*Second Livre d'Orgue* (1714)	Facsimile c/o IMSLP Petrucci Music Library
Roberday, François	*Fugues, et Caprices* (1660)	Facsimile c/o IMSLP Petrucci Music Library
Titelouze, Jehan	*Hymnes de l'Eglise* (1623)	Éditions J.M. Fuzeau, 1992
Titelouze, Jehan	*Le Magnificat* (1626)	Éditions J.M. Fuzeau, 1992
Various composers	*Livre d'Orgue de Limoges*	Éditions J.M. Fuzeau, 1996
Various composers	*Livre d'Orgue de Montreal*	Éditions Jacques Ostiguy, 1985-88.

INDEX

Aguilera de Heredia, Sebastián 193
Albi 64
Alençon 53, 54
Angers 331
Archimbaud, Louis 15
Attaignant, Pierre 2
Auch 63
Bach, Johann Sebastian 18, 22, 162, 230, 321, 326
Bach, Wilhelm Friedemann 230
Baigneux 53
Balbastre, Claude 9, 11, 13, 45, 341-344
Ballard (famiglia) 24-25, 277, 281, 327,
Barbier, Nicolas 55, 279
Beauvais 328
Berlin 13, 331
Béziers 15, 82
Bibliothèque Inguimbertine 15, 319-320
Bibliothèque Nationale de France 12-14, 319
Boizard, Jean 59
Bollioud de Mermet, Louis 16
Bonfils, Jean 13
Bordeaux 53, 108
Bourgeois, Loys 201
Bourges 16, 47, 51, 80, 93, 110, 124, 133, 145, 151, 161, 177-178, 180, 188, 195, 295
Boyvin, Jacques 8, 11, 14, 25, 67-68, 76, 79, 81, 85, 89-91, 94, 108-109, 115, 120, 124, 127, 133, 135, 137-138, 145, 147, 151, 153-154, 158, 160, 165, 169, 171, 174, 176, 178, 181-182, 186, 191, 195, 197, 200, 203, 236-238, 242, 244, 247-248, 250-251, 253, 262, 312-316, 324, 335
Bruxelles 14
Caën 16
Calvière, Antoine 329
Carissimi, Giacomo 7
Carlier, Crespin 71, 279-280, 294
Carpentras 15, 45, 235, 319-320
Champion de Chambonnières, Jacques 17, 286
Chapelle Royale 39, 277, 299, 305, 318, 321, 323, 333
Charpentier, Marc-Antoine 7
Chartres 53, 64, 108, 295, 316
Chaumont, Lambert 11, 72-73, 75, 85, 119, 124, 136, 142, 145, 151, 153, 158, 160, 180, 182, 186, 188, 191, 195, 198, 200, 217, 242, 246, 253, 305-307
Choquel, Henri-Louis 220
Clérambault, Louis-Nicolas 6-7, 11, 14, 58, 114, 128-129, 138, 144, 242, 253, 308, 329, 331-333
Clermont 24
Clicquot, François-Henry 61
Clicquot, Louis-Alexandre 59, 71
Clicquot, Robert 66, 315, 323, 329
Corelli, Arcangelo 7
Corrette, Gaspard 11, 14, 28, 39, 42, 110, 120, 125, 133, 137-138, 145, 147, 152-153, 158-159, 163, 177, 181, 188, 191, 198, 200, 242, 247, 312, 324-326
Corrette, Michel 4, 11, 17, 24, 45, 49, 74-75, 85, 93, 110, 113, 125, 137-138, 152, 158, 161, 177, 188, 190, 198, 221, 337-341
Couperin, Charles 286, 318-319
Couperin, François 7, 11, 15, 17, 26, 37-39, 42, 57, 66, 68, 76, 84, 92, 118, 135, 143, 199, 205, 210, 224, 234-235, 239-240, 248, 262, 265, 267-268, 272-273, 318-321
Couperin, Louis 3, 7, 11-12, 23, 57, 68, 76, 79, 111, 140-141, 143, 145, 156, 167, 193, 224, 286-288
d'Agincourt, François 13, 15, 295, 324, 335-336
d'Alembert, Jean le Rond 16-17, 71, 74
d'Anglebert, Jean-Henry 12, 17, 80, 166, 230, 235, 239, 241-243, 247-250, 252, 284, 288, 326
Dalla Casa, Girolamo 227
Dandrieu, Jean-François 11, 45, 86, 93, 239, 241, 243, 248, 326, 333-334, 337
Dandrieu, Pierre 11, 321
Daquin, Louis-Claude 4, 329, 336-337
de Bacilly, Bénigny 17, 205
de Brossard, Sébastien 7, 17, 118, 163, 221
de Cabezón, Antonio 149
de Cailly, Gratien 54
de Grigny, Nicolas 6, 8, 11, 18-22, 26, 32-34, 36-38, 41-42, 49-51, 67-68, 76, 88-89, 95, 120-121, 130-131, 135, 138, 146-147, 162, 189, 223, 229, 295, 326-328

de Joyeuse, Jean 65, 82-83
de la Barre, Mr 228, 231
de La Chapelle, Jacques-Alexandre 220
de Lalande, Michel-Richard 318
de' Cavalieri, Emilio 9
Delair, Denis 214-215
Denis, Jean 72, 214
Désenclos, Pierre 315
Diderot, Denis 16
Dijon 341
Diruta, Girolamo 265
Dom Bédos de Celles ix, 16, 69, 84, 93, 112, 126, 168, 171, 192, 196
Domine Salvum fac regem 38, 43-44
Dornel, Louis-Antoine 13, 17
du Caurroy, Eustache 2, 12, 277-278, 281
Du Mage, Pierre 11, 23, 67, 76, 116, 152, 200, 328-330
du Mont, Henri 39, 299
Ducastel, François 305
Engramelle, Marie-Dominique-Joseph 16, 206-207
Énocq, Étienne 80, 323-324, 328
Francœur, François 319
Frescobaldi, Girolamo 8, 27, 131
Froberger, Johann Jacob 8, 285-286
Ganassi, Silvestro 227
Geoffroy, Jean-Nicolas 13, 295
Gigault, Nicolas 3, 11, 26-27, 37-38, 41-42, 66-67, 71, 81, 85, 111, 117, 129, 145, 157, 167, 194, 203, 207-210, 232-233, 288-294
Gisors 55
Gorenstein, Nicolas 21-22
Gravet, Nicolas 85
Guilain, Jean-Adam 13, 27, 45, 47, 75, 85-86, 138, 166, 330-331
Guillet, Charles 2, 11-12, 96, 281-283
Hardouin, Pierre 57
Herluyson, Claude 14
Hertel, Matthaeus 125
Hocquet, Nicolas 99
Hotteterre, Jacques-Martin 17, 204, 208, 247-248
Houdan 59
Huguet, Isaac 58, 97
Huy 305-306
Isnard, Jean-Esprit 60
Jeux coupés 58
Jullien, Gilles 11, 14, 67, 81, 94, 113, 117, 146-147, 161, 164, 169-171, 182, 189, 202-203, 210, 216, 244, 253, 295, 316-318
L'Affilard, Michel 6, 7, 17, 220
Lanes, Mathieu 15
Langhedul, Mathis 55
Laon 295, 329
Latry, Olivier 6, 220
le Vasseur, Symon 54
Lebègue, Nicolas-Antoine 4, 11, 14-15, 24-28, 38, 42, 45, 47, 56, 79, 85-86, 90, 118, 123, 133, 142, 144, 149-150, 153, 156-157, 159-161, 167, 175, 180-182, 184-185, 187, 190, 195-196, 199, 225, 237, 242, 248-249, 253, 295-299, 316, 321, 326, 330, 335
Leclerc, Jean-Pantaléon 327
Lefebvre, Germaine 326
Lépine, Jean-François 60, 66, 84
Liège 305
Limoges 14
Loulié, Étienne 17, 204, 207, 215-216, 219, 232, 243, 246-249
Lully, Jean-Baptiste 5-6, 13, 219, 236, 284, 298
Lyon 321
Marais, Marin 211
Marchand, Louis 8, 11, 13, 67, 113, 115, 128, 130, 133, 166, 208, 223, 251, 321-324, 328-331, 335-337
Mercure galant 322, 326, 330
Mersenne, Marin 1, 3, 12, 16, 56, 69, 70-72, 75, 80, 101-107, 110-111, 195, 228-229, 231, 279, 283-284, 306
Montréal (Livre d'orgue de) 14, 38, 45, 85, 185
Moucherel, Christophe 16, 64,
Mouzon 64
Muffat, Georg 6, 17, 236, 253-260
Nancy 97, 99-101
Nevers 321
Nivers, Guillaume-Gabriel 3, 11, 14-17, 32, 37, 42-43, 48-49, 51, 76, 79, 82-83, 85, 92-93, 101, 109, 111-112, 114, 118, 123, 127, 129, 136, 141-142, 144, 148, 150, 152, 173-175, 178-180, 193-196, 199, 202-203, 205, 213-214, 229, 237, 240-241, 244-246, 249, 262, 264-269, 299-305, 321, 330-331
Olier, Jean-Jacques 35
Pajot-D'Ozembray, Louis-Léon 220
Paris *Eglise des Cordeliers* 68, 322, 331, 336
Paris *Hôtel Royal des Invalides* 56

Paris *Jacobins* 81, 308, 311-312, 332
Paris *Madeleine-en-la-Cité* 335
Paris *Maison Royale Saint-Louis de Saint-Cyr* 299, 305, 331
Paris *Notre-Dame* 57, 101, 283-284, 329, 336, 341
Paris *Notre-Dame-des-Victoires* 284
Paris *Petit Saint-Antoine* 336
Paris *Quinze-Vingts* 312
Paris *Saint-Barthélemy* 321, 333
Paris *Sainte-Geneviève du Mont* 13, 15, 307, 335
Paris *Saint-Germain-des-Prés* 68
Paris *Saint-Gervais* 24, 55, 57, 63, 66, 68, 111, 286, 318-319
Paris *Saint-Merry (Saint-Médéric)* 24, 69, 175, 295, 299, 333
Paris *Saint-Nicolas-des-Champs* 71, 111, 288-290, 294
Paris *Saint-Paul* 336-337
Paris *Saint-Quentin* 66, 329-330
Paris *Saint-Roch* 4, 68, 341
Paris *Saint-Séverin* 68
Paris *Saint-Sulpice* 24, 299-301, 304-305, 331-332
Pécour, Guillaume Louis 4-5
Perpignan 84
Pescheur, Pierre 56-57, 111
Pignolet de Montéclair, Michel 17, 205, 221, 235-236
Pingré, Alexandre Guy 13, 15, 335
Piroye, Charles 1, 4, 11
Pitard, André 277
Poitiers 61
Ponsford, David 8, 23, 209, 235
Prélude non mesuré 8, 224-225, 332
Racquet, Charles 2, 12, 57, 96, 101, 283-284, 288
Raison, André 4-6, 11, 14, 24, 27-29, 39, 42-43, 65, 79, 82, 90-92, 109, 112-113, 116-118, 123, 131, 133, 136, 139, 142-143, 151, 153, 155-158, 160, 162-163, 167-168, 176, 180, 182, 185-187, 191, 194-195, 199, 205-206, 214, 223, 240-242, 246, 250, 252-253, 262, 269-272, 307-312, 331-332
Rameau, Jean-Philippe 17, 24, 73-74, 225, 241, 262-263, 271, 336, 341

Rameau, Pierre 4
Ravalement 65-66, 294, 299, 328
Rebel, François 319
Reims 18, 68, 326-328
Richard, Étienne 12
Roberday, François 2, 11, 76, 96, 284-285
Rognoni, Francesco 227
Rouen 25, 68, 75, 89, 115, 279-280, 312-313, 315, 324-326, 335, 337
Rousseau, Jean-Jacques 17, 71, 74, 209, 273
Saint-Arroman, Jean 18, 22,
Saint-Lambert, Mr de 17, 217-218, 220-221, 234, 237-238, 244, 249, 262, 264-269
Saint-Omer 279
Saint-Valéry-sur-Somme 58, 97-98
Sancta Maria, Tomás de 140
Sarlat 60, 66, 84
Sauveur, Joseph 16
Scheidt, Samuel 140, 149
Soissons 295
Sonnet, Martin 35, 222
Souvigny 61, 66
St Michel en Thiérache 59
St. Maximin 60
Stenay sur la Meuze 64
Sweelinck, Jan Pieterszoon 140, 149, 281, 284
Tempérament Ordinaire 74
Thierry, Alexandre 56
Thierry, François 58, 329
Thierry, Pierre 57, 283, 315
Thiéry, Marguerite 14, 38, 45
Titelouze, Jehan 2, 11-12, 24-25, 27-31, 45-49, 54-55, 62, 66, 76, 96, 113-114, 141, 156, 212-213, 231, 279-281
Toul 26, 40-41, 43, 46
Toulouse 15
Tours 14, 16, 38, 45, 110, 125, 138, 145, 152, 177-178, 198
Trichet, Pierre 16
Troyes 14, 85, 295
Versailles 8, 13, 128, 130, 235, 295, 318-319, 321-324
Vincent, Antoine 75, 294
Vitré 15
Walther, Johann Gottfried 18, 22, 326
Weckmann, Matthias 8
Wisbeck, J. 328

Printed in Poland
by Amazon Fulfillment
Poland Sp. z o.o., Wrocław